Comments from teachers who have participated in professional development workshops based on *Science Projects for Holidays throughout the Year* and other Terrific Science Press materials:

"Have you ever noticed how kids seem to turn into energy toys during the holidays?

They bounce off the walls with enthusiasm and excitement in the air. And why not? There are gifts to be made, cards to be sent, traditions to be celebrated, and fun to be had. For the teacher, going against this energy flow can be disastrous. What is needed is a way to harness all that enthusiasm so that learning can still take place. TOYS activities for the holidays do just that and much, much more. They capture the imagination and attention while delivering sound science content for both the teacher and students. TOYS are the best allies a teacher ever had in the battle against the holiday crazies."

Rose White, Leo Politi School, Los Angeles, CA

"Teachers can capture the excitement in holidays and celebrations to engage students in meaningful hands-on science to learn more about their world. They become an integral part of the celebration. The cycle of learning continues throughout the year."

Mary Jo Gardner, Fairmont Egan Elementary School, Kalispell, MT

"These activities not only bring about enthusiasm but help redirect the energy sparked by the holidays into the fascinating world of science. What a great way to keep students actively engaged in learning."

Veronica Newman, Oakdale Elementary School, Cincinnati, OH

"My students love learning science through TOYS. The Holiday book is an excellent way to tie science, social studies, and language arts together."

Peggy Kulczewski, Harding Elementary School, Monmouth, IL

"I received so many new ideas to try out in my classroom that my students will be enjoying learning science without even realizing it."

Regina Bonamico, Chauncy Rose Middle School, Terre Haute, IN

"The toys, experiments, and activities are classroom-friendly to students of all ages."

Mary Hurst, McKinley Elementary School, Middletown, OH

Other McGraw-Hill Books by Terrific Science Press

•••

Exploring Energy with TOYS

Investigating Solids, Liquids, and Gases with TOYS

Exploring Matter with TOYS

Teaching Physical Science through Children's Literature

Teaching Chemistry with TOYS

Teaching Physics with TOYS

About the Author

Terrific Science Press is a nonprofit publisher housed in the federally and state-funded Center for Chemical Education (Miami University Middletown in Ohio). At the Center, educators and scientists have worked together since the mid-1980s to provide professional developement for teachers through innovative approaches to teaching hands-on, minds-on science.

Science Projects for Holidays throughout the Year

••••••••••••••••••••••••••••••••••••••

Complete Lessons for the Elementary Grades

Mickey Sarquis
Linda Woodward
Miami University Middletown

Terrific Science Press
Miami University Middletown
Middletown, Ohio

**LEARNING
TRIANGLE
PRESS**
▲
*Connecting kids, parents, and teachers
through learning*

An imprint of McGraw-Hill

New York   San Francisco   Washington, D.C.   Auckland   Bogotá
Caracas   Lisbon   London   Madrid   Mexico City   Milan
Montreal   New Delhi   San Juan   Singapore
Sydney   Tokyo   Toronto

Terrific Science Press
Miami University Middletown
4200 East University Blvd.
Middletown, Ohio 45042
513/727-3318
cce@muohio.edu

Published by McGraw-Hill.

McGraw-Hill

A Division of The **McGraw·Hill** *Companies*

Photographs by Jeff Sabo, Applied Technologies, Miami University, Oxford, Ohio.

1 2 3 4 5 6 7 8 9   MAL/MAL   9 0 3 2 1 0 9 8

ISBN 0-07-064758-5

Product or brand names used in this book may be trade names or trademarks. Where we believe that there may be proprietary claims to such trade names or trademarks, the name has been used with an initial capital or it has been capitalized in the style used by the name claimant. Where our research has indicated a trademark symbol should be used, the symbol is used on the first mention within the body of the text (not in activity titles or captions). Regardless of the capitalization used, all such names have been used in an editorial manner without any intent to convey endorsement of or other affiliation with the name claimant. Neither the authors nor the publisher intends to express any judgment as to the validity or legal status of any such proprietary claims.

Support for *Science Projects for Holidays throughout the Year* was provided by a grant under the federally funded Dwight D. Eisenhower Mathematics and Science Education Act, administered by the Ohio Board of Regents.

This material is based upon work supported by the National Science Foundation under grant number ESI-9355523. This project was supported, in part, by the National Science Foundation. Any opinions, findings, and conclusions or recommendations expressed in this material are those of the authors and do not necessarily reflect the views of the National Science Foundation.

Library of Congress Cataloging-in-Publication Data

Sarquis, Mickey.
    Science projects for holidays throughout the year : complete
lessons for the elementary grades / Mickey Sarquis, Linda Woodward.
        p.   cm.
    Includes index.
    ISBN 0-07-064758-5 (pbk.)
    1. Science—Study and teaching—Activity programs—Juvenile
literature.   2. Holidays—Study and teaching—Activity programs
—Juvenile literature.   3. Scientific recreations—Juvenile
literature.   I. Woodward, Linda.   II. Title.
Q164.S26   1998
    507.8—dc21   98-36743
                                                          CIP

● Contents

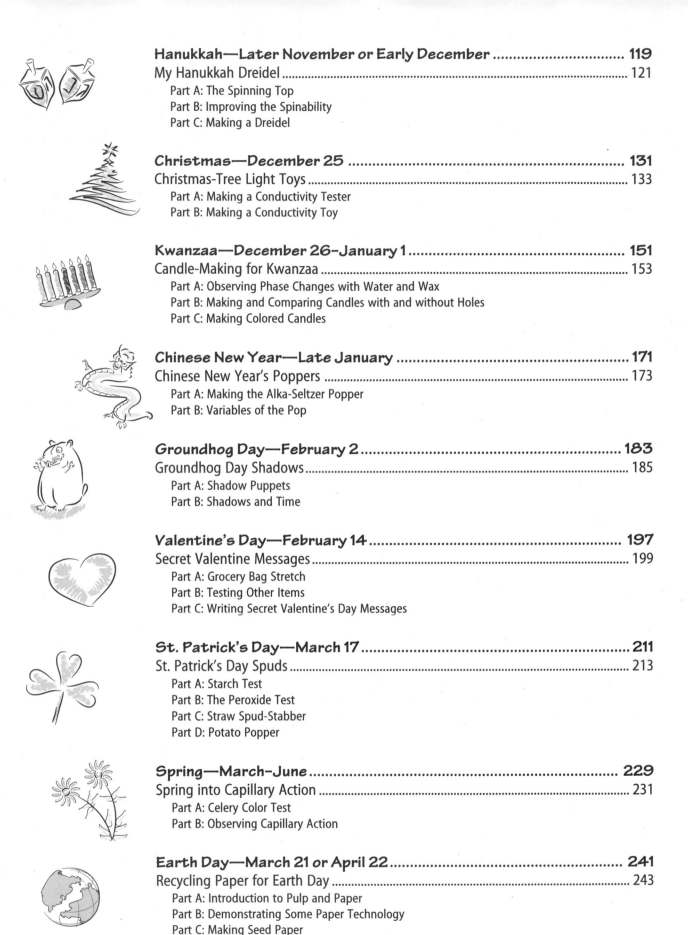

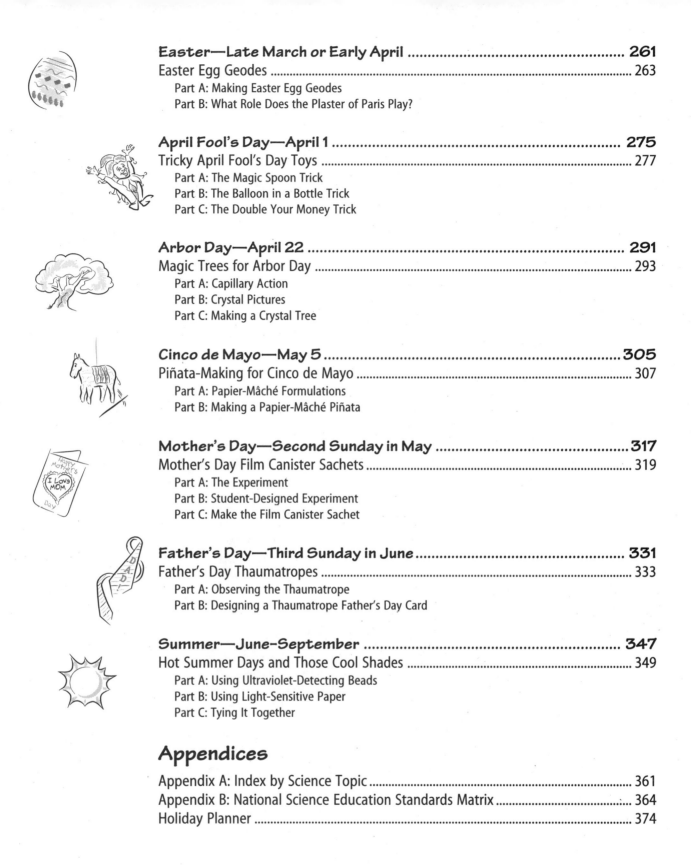

Acknowledgments

The authors wish to thank the following individuals who have contributed to the development of this book.

Terrific Science Press Design and Production Team

Document Production Manager: Susan Gertz
Technical Coordinator: Lisa Taylor
Technical Writing: Christine Cowdrey, Lisa Taylor
Technical Editing: Lisa Taylor
Illustration: Stephen Gentle, Jenny Stencil
Design/Layout: Susan Gertz, Stephen Gentle
Production: Christine Cowdrey, Stephen Gentle, Tracy Scobba, Jenny Stencil, Lisa Taylor
Laboratory Testing: Susan Gertz, Lisa Taylor, Linda Woodward

Reviewers

Brenda Dales, Miami University, Oxford, OH
Mary Jo Gardner, Fairmont Egan Elementary School, Kalispell, MT
Jerry Sarquis, Miami University, Oxford, OH
Sally Watkins, University of Southern Colorado (retired), Pueblo, CO
Linda Woodward, Miami University Middletown, Middletown, OH

Teachers

The activities in this book have been contributed and tested by more than 1,500 teachers in the Teaching Science with TOYS program and the Science-Literature Integration program. We wish to acknowledge their efforts in making these activities effective and relevant teaching tools.

Contributors

Judith Aiken, Ida Weller Elementary School, Centerville, OH
Shelley Arnold, Maple Dale, Cincinnati, OH
Teresa Applegate, Lincoln Heights Elementary School, Cincinnati, OH
Susan Baker, Walter Shade Elementary School, Dayton, OH
Bonnie Barkemeyer, Ronan Middle School, Ronan, MT
Elizabeth Barnes, Miami University Middletown student, Middletown, OH
Linda Blatt, Mt. Airy Elementary School, Cincinnati, OH
Angie Brinson, Coleman Academy of International Studies, Indianapolis, IN
Vicki Bumann, Samuel Taylor School, Louisville, KY
Laura Cannon, Comal Elementary School, New Braufels, TX
Doris Chicchon, Heinold Foreign Language Academy, Cincinnati, OH
Bill Colborn, Trinity North Elementary School, Washington, PA
Carole Colegate, Morgan Elementary School, Ross, OH
Christina Cornelssen, Cameron Park Elementary School, Cincinnati, OH
Judy Cramer, Kamehameha Elementary School, Honolulu, HI
Cyndy Curran, Iditarod Elementary School, Wisilla, AK
Brenda Dales, Miami University, Oxford, OH
Sharon Dautermann, Williams Avenue Elementary School, Norwood, OH
Elizabeth Dickinson, Finger Lake Elementary School, Palmer, AK
Arlene L. Doan, Bethany Grade School, Bethany, IL
Kelley Dunn, Edison Elementary School, Dayton, OH
Mary Kay Eckhart, Kinder Elementary School, Miamisburg, OH
Elaine Evans, St. Therese Lisieux, Munhall, PA
Maureen Everhart, Summit Country Day School, Cincinnati, OH
Andrew Flannery, Miami University Middletown student, Middletown, OH

Misty Gawith, Towanda Grade School, Towanda, KS
Diana Garver, Ada Elementary School, Ada, OH
Gail Gilchrist, Cherry Valley Elementary School, Polson, MT
Patricia Goodnight, John Eaton Elementary School, Washington, DC
Laura Gower, Richmond Heights Middle School and Elementary School, Richmond Heights, OH
Chris Gregory, Bethany High School, Bethany, IL
Sherry Gries, Heinold Foreign Language Academy, Cincinnati, OH
Julie Hall, Towanda Grade School, Towanda, KS
Paula Halm, Heritage Hill Elementary School, Cincinnati, OH; TOYS District Leader
Tina Hansbauer, St. Margaret of York Elementary School, Loveland, OH
Sharla Hayes, Towanda Grade School, Towanda, KS
Rosa Hernandez, Rosemont Avenue School, Los Angeles, CA
Shelley Hilderbrand, Franklin High School, Franklin, OH
Mary Hurst, McKinley Elementary School, Middletown, OH
David Hogan, Woodrow Wilson Elementary School, Middletown, OH
Debbie Hogerson, Cherry Valley Elementary School, Polson, MT
Debbie Hollingshead, Edison Elementary School, Dayton, OH
Jeanne Hotle, Parkway School District, Chesterfield, MO
Andrea Johnson, Pablo Elementary School, Ronan, MT
Susan Jones, Barnette Elementary School, Fairbanks, AK
Sherry Kembre, St. James Elementary School, Cincinnati, OH
Diedri Kennedy, Roosevelt Elementary School, Middletown, OH
Karen Kinyon, Benjamin Franklin Elementary School, Manitowoc, WI
Jennifer Kreeft, Staten Island Children's Museum, Staten Island, NY
Susan Krueckeberg, Weller Elementary School, Centerville, OH
Val Krugh, Tri-County Christian High School, Fairfield, OH
Peggy Kulczewski, Lincoln Elementary School, Monmouth, IL
Paulette Larson, Edison Elementary School, Dayton, OH
Moana Leong, Kamehameha Elementary School, Honolulu, HI
Tom Lerch, Tenneco Packaging (retired), Middletown, OH
Bob Lux, Evendale Elementary School, Cincinnati, OH
Phil McBride, graduate student, Center for Chemical Education, Miami University, Middletown, OH
Sue McCabe, Forest View Elementary School, Cincinnati, OH
James McCarthy, Norris School, Staten Island, NY
Cathleen McStroul, Alice Smith Elementary School, Reno, NV
Judy Mack, Normandy Elementary School, Dayton, OH
Luann Martin, John Tyler School, Staten Island, NY
Chris Mellish, Cincinnati Christian School, Cincinnati, OH
Jennifer Muia, Lockland Elementary School, Cincinnati, OH
Mary Neises, Bauer Elementary School, Dayton, OH
Veronica Newman, Oakdale Elementary School, Cincinnati, OH
Linda Newton, Lockland Elementary School, Cincinnati, OH
Kenneth Nielsen, Miami University Middletown student, Middletown, OH
Nancy O'Hair, Alice Smith Elementary School, Reno, NV
Karen Perkins, Cos Cob Elementary School, Greenwich, CT
Tom Pierson, Edgewood Middle School, Hamilton, OH
Maria Richter, Heinold Foreign Language Academy, Cincinnati, OH
Barb Sanders, Valley View, Menomonee Falls, WI
Maria Sarcona, I.S. 27, Staten Island, NY
Kathleen Sommer, Miami University Middletown student, Middletown, OH
Cynthia Stanford, Williams Avenue Elementary School, Cincinnati, OH
Joy Tanigawa, El Rancho High School, Pico Rivera, CA
Winnie Tracy, Harrison Elementary School, Harrison, OH
Darlene Tucker, Thomas Jefferson, Menomenee Falls, WI
Terri Turner, Towanda Elementary School, Towanda, KS
Linda Wagner, Benjamin Franklin Elementary, Menomenee Falls, WI
Rose White, Leo Politi Elementary School, Los Angeles, CA
Dick Wiegand, Ryan Middle School, Fairbanks, AK
Patricia Wilkinson, Clifton Elementary School, Cincinnati, OH
Bryan Wilson, Miami University Middletown student, Middletown, OH
Erich Zeller, Los Angeles Elementary School, Los Angeles, CA
Sonya Zumbiel, Allison Street Elementary School, Norwood, OH

• Foreword

Holidays and special events are times of excitement and energy. Children are quick to pick up on this excitement. One of our teachers has dubbed it the "holiday crazies." If the "crazies" are viewed to be an obstacle, productive learning can be difficult, but if dealt with as a positive thing, this youthful enthusiasm can provide the motivation for otherwise untapped learning opportunities.

Science Projects for Holidays throughout the Year was developed to help teachers turn the "holiday crazies" into a fun and exciting time to learn about science. Holiday celebrations and science make a great team—because the crafts often associated with holidays are typically rooted in science, tying them to productive hands-on science lessons makes for good learning experiences.

This book unites holidays with fun crafts or experiments that teach important science skills and concepts. The 23 physical science lessons in this book are firmly grounded in the National Science Education Standards and are structured as meaningful investigations that help students make sense of science by drawing connections between scientific phenomena and their own world. Additionally, each lesson also includes ideas for writing, art and music, mathematics, and social studies extensions related to the holiday, the culture in which the holiday is celebrated, or the concept studied in the science activity.

Science Projects for Holidays throughout the Year is one of several books to result from the National Science Foundation-funded Teaching Science with TOYS program and the Ohio Board of Regents-funded Science-Literature Integration program, located at Miami University in Ohio. The goal of the TOYS program is to enhance teachers' knowledge of chemistry and physics and to encourage the use of activity-based, discovery-oriented science instruction. The goal of the Science-Literature Integration project is to encourage the integration of science with language arts, a discipline that shares many of the process skills used in science.

I hope you and your students find that these activities make both holidays and science more interesting, relevant, and fun—both to learn and to teach.

Mickey Sarquis, Principal Investigator
Teaching Science with TOYS

● Introduction

Holidays and other special days are times of excitement and energy. Wouldn't it be wonderful if your students approached science with the same excitement? *Science for the Holidays* was developed to help you tap into the energy of such special celebrations and use it to teach science.

Science for the Holidays offers 23 complete lessons for teaching hands-on, discovery-oriented physical science in the elementary classroom. Each lesson is a tightly integrated learning episode with clearly defined objectives supported and enriched by all facets of the lesson, including historical and cultural backgrounds; reading of both fiction and nonfiction; writing; and, where appropriate, social studies, art, music, mathematics, and other subjects. Along with the science content objectives, many process objectives are woven into every lesson.

These lessons are intended to help you make the most of all of your classroom time. By converting class periods around holidays and other celebrations into rich educational opportunities, these lessons will complement and enrich your curriculum while providing fun for you and your students. We encourage you to use these lessons to meet the needs of your students and your district's science objectives. See Getting the Most Out of This Book, page 6, for suggestions on doing so.

Why Use Holiday-Based Integrated Science and Language Arts Lessons?

Many holidays and other special days are celebrated during the school year. Time close to these celebrations often includes a number of craft projects appropriate to the occasion. Certainly these activities are fun for students and help raise their awareness of the holidays being observed, but science and other subjects are often pushed aside to make room for these efforts. Elementary teachers feel the pressure of including more high-quality science instruction while being responsible for students' achievement in many subjects. Teachers face a frustrating dilemma: to choose between taking time for special activities and addressing instructional goals. However, incorporating holiday activities need not involve sacrifice. This multidisciplinary collection can help you resolve the "either/or" dilemma by blending science, social studies, history, arts and crafts, and children's literature into a fun yet educational experience.

Holiday-based integrated science lessons provide venues for students to actively investigate their world using process skills that span subject areas: observing, communicating, classifying, predicting outcomes, and drawing conclusions. "When we are confronted with a problem or puzzling situation in real life, we hardly stop to think, 'Which part is mathematics, which physical education, which science,…and so on?' Rather we…bring to bear whatever we need to know or do without regard for the source….Understood this way, knowledge and skills are organically integrated in real life." (Beane, 1995) Integrated learning enables children to build on this natural relationship between subjects.

The fun element in holiday science projects provides an extra boost to the learning process: "Increased motivation and conceptual understanding will occur if both the fun and mental aspects of scientific play are reunited." (O'Brien, 1993)

References

O'Brien, T. "Teaching Fundamental Aspects of Science with Toys." *School Science and Mathematics, 93*(4), April 1993, 203–207.

Toward a Coherent Curriculum; Beane, J.A., Ed.; Association for Supervision and Curriculum Development: Alexandria, VA, 1995; pp 6–10.

Support for the Development of This Book

The lessons in this book were developed through the support of two professional development programs for teachers offered through Miami University's Center for Chemical Education: the Ohio Board of Regents-funded Science Integration in Today's Elementary Schools (SITES) project and the National Science Foundation-funded Teaching Science with TOYS program. These programs promote the creative integration of activity-based, discovery-oriented science instruction into the elementary school curriculum by addressing state and national standards for science education without overburdening the already busy elementary school teacher. Both programs share a common emphasis of preparing teachers to provide carefully constructed learning opportunities that are motivating, engaging, and intimately linked to the children's world.

The interdisciplinary lessons in this set have grown out of the SITES and TOYS programs with classroom teachers having contributed to the development, review, and classroom testing of these materials. These lessons are designed to engage children in multisensory experiences that sharpen both their process skills and content knowledge.

Through SITES, TOYS, and their affiliated programs, more than 1,500 teachers have brought literature- and toy-based science into their classrooms. Through written materials such as this book, it is our hope that even more teachers and students can share in the fun of doing and learning science.

To learn more about these and other professional development opportunities for teachers at Miami University, check out our World Wide Web site (*http://www.muohio.edu/~ccecwis/*) or write to

Center for Chemical Education
Miami University Middletown
4200 East University Blvd.
Middletown, OH 45042
cce@muohio.edu

● Organization of the Lessons

Each lesson in this book provides complete instructions for using the lesson in your classroom. These lessons have been classroom-tested by teachers like yourself and have been demonstrated to be effective, safe, and practical in elementary classrooms. Each lesson is organized into two main sections: an introduction to the holiday or season, and a guide for conducting the lesson. The guides are divided into five parts: Building Bridges, Science Activity, Integrating with Language Arts, Other Lesson Extensions, and National Science Education Standards. Each of these parts has several sections, which are described below.

Introduction to the Holiday

- This section contains the date and culture/religion (if appropriate) of the holiday or season and, if appropriate, descriptions of similar holidays and customs in other cultures. This information is written for the teacher and is intended to be adapted for presentation to students; it is not intended as a student handout.

First Page of the Lesson

- This page contains the name of the lesson and a brief description of the link between the holiday and the science activity.
- Key Science Topics—This list includes the specific science topics covered by the science activity.
- Time Required—This section lists the estimated time required for setup, performance, and cleanup for the science activity. (The setup time does not include the time necessary to assemble materials, since such times will vary widely. It also does not include time required for extensions.)
- Photograph—A photograph of the toy, key materials, or activity setup appears beside Key Science Topics and Time Required.

Part 1: Building Bridges

- Building Student Knowledge and Motivation—This section includes an idea for a science center activity that serves as an opening strategy for the lesson. These activities help students develop common background knowledge prior to studying the holiday and doing the science activity.
- Bridging to the Science Activity—This section includes ideas for activities and/or discussions. These activities and discussions draw upon the student experiences from Building Student Knowledge and Motivation and set the stage for doing the activity.

Part 2: Science Activity

- Materials—Materials are listed for Bridging to the Science Activity, Getting Ready, the Procedure, and the Extension(s) for Further Science Inquiry. Materials are divided into amounts per class, per group, and per student for each part. Most materials can be purchased from grocery, discount department, or hardware stores. Quantities or sizes may be listed in English measure, metric measure, or both, depending on what is clear and appropriate in each case. Sources are listed for unusual items.
- Safety and Disposal—Special safety and/or disposal procedures are listed if required.
- Getting Ready—Information is provided in Getting Ready when preparation is needed before beginning the activity with students.
- Procedure—The steps in the Procedure are directed toward you, the teacher, and include cautions and suggestions where appropriate. Each Procedure is divided into two or more parts. In most cases, parts should be done in the order indicated, but for some activities, parts are independent of each other and can be done in any order or combination.
- Extension(s) for Further Science Inquiry—Extensions are methods for furthering student understanding of the science topic. Each activity contains at least one Extension for Further Science Inquiry.
- Science Explanation—The Science Explanation explains the science covered in the activity and, where appropriate, contains historical information about how related technology was developed. This explanation is written to you, the teacher, and is intended to be modified for students.
- References for the Science Activity—This section cites reference materials used to develop the science activity and explanation.

Part 3: Integrating with Language Arts

This section contains ideas for integrating the rest of the lesson with children's literature and writing.

- Featured Fiction and/or Nonfiction Book—The Featured Fiction or Nonfiction Book is a children's book that links well with the science concept, the holiday or season, or the culture in which the holiday is celebrated. We have included books that represent as wide a variety of cultures as possible. In some cases, both fiction and nonfiction books are featured. A brief paragraph after each featured book provides ideas for reading and discussing the book.
- Writing Extensions—The suggested writing extensions are intended to give students different types of opportunities to communicate what they have learned about the holiday, the culture in which the holiday is celebrated, the science objective, or one of the books listed under Featured Books or Additional Books. As such, these extensions can serve as assessment tools. The writing extensions in these lessons span a range of levels, from emergent to fluent.
- Additional Books—This section lists fiction and nonfiction books related to the science activity, the holiday or season, or the culture in which the holiday is celebrated.

Part 4: Other Lesson Extensions

This section lists extensions for art and music, mathematics, and social studies, as well as activities to do just for fun. These extensions cover a range of grade levels; teachers can choose ones appropriate for their level and adapt others as necessary.

Part 5: National Science Education Standards

This section lists the National Science Education Standards addressed throughout the entire lesson, including the holiday introduction, the science activity, and all of the extensions. The standards are grouped in four categories used in the National Science Education Standards for grades K–3 and 4–6: Science as Inquiry, Physical Science, Science and Technology, and History and Nature of Science.

Notes and Icons

Icons appear throughout the book in the left-hand margins and are described below.

 Notes are preceded by an arrow and appear in italics.

 Cautions are preceded by an exclamation point and appear in italics.

● Getting the Most Out of This Book

We hope that you find this book helpful in preparing fun, exciting, and informative holiday-related scientific investigations for your classroom. However, each of the lessons in this book contains much more than just the instructions for a holiday craft or an isolated science activity—they are multidisciplinary, inquiry-based learning opportunities that will enhance an elementary school curriculum. This section reviews the pedagogical concepts behind the lessons as well as tips and suggestions to help you make the most out of instructional time. The seven topics covered in this section are as follows:

- Meeting the Needs of Your Students presents suggestions for adapting the lessons in this book for students of different grade levels and abilities.
- Integrating the Holidays, Science Activities, and Books describes the book's strategy for weaving these elements into a cohesive lesson.
- Standards for Science Education discusses published standards for science education and how this book relates to them.
- Assessment describes different approaches to assessing student performance throughout each lesson.
- Teaching with Classroom Centers explains the concept of centers as used in this book and presents suggestions for setting up and using centers in your classroom.
- Using Science Journals presents suggestions for integrating journal writing into your students' science investigations.

Meeting the Needs of Your Students

This book was written and classroom-tested with a focus on the needs and abilities of elementary school children. However, the science content is rich enough to enable you to easily adapt the lessons for upper grades as well. Additionally, whether you teach in a traditional or multi-age classroom, we understand that the individual needs of your students may span a wide range, mandating some modification or adaptation of even the best of lessons. To assist you in such efforts, the lessons in this book include an array of science, reading, writing, social studies, and art elements that span a variety of challenge levels and learning experiences. In our testing, teachers have reported that the format and information provided with these lessons made for fun, successful, and rewarding learning experiences for their classes.

Integrating Celebrations, Science, and Language Arts

The activities and books used in this module have been chosen to coordinate with holidays and special celebrations from a range of cultural traditions. Each science activity relates in some way to the celebration, and each accompanying book tells a story or provides information that relates to the celebration and/or the science activity. While many of the activities involve making a holiday craft, the procedures do so within a scientific context, with instructions for presenting the central science concept.

At the beginning of each lesson is a brief description of the holiday to which it is related. This information, intended for the teacher, can be adapted as necessary for the students.

Each lesson sets the stage for the science activity with a discussion, learning center, or other method for stimulating student interest in the science concept to be covered. Then the class conducts the science activity. Afterward, students listen to a featured fiction and/or nonfiction book that is related to the holiday/celebration, the science activity, or both.

Most of the lessons include suggestions for further reading on topics related to the holiday, the culture in which the holiday is celebrated, or the science concept. Appendix B contains an alphabetical listing of all featured books used in the lessons as well as all books listed as suggestions for further reading. Older students may also conduct independent research to find related reading materials.

Standards for Science Education

The science activities in this book have been designed to help elementary teachers meet standards for science education, most notably the National Science Education Standards compiled under the direction of the National Research Council. This book is organized around the National Science Education Standards for grades K–4 and 5–8. A list of the standards addressed by each lesson is included at the end of the lesson, in Part 5. The standards are grouped in four of the major categories set forth in the National Standards: Science As Inquiry, Physical Science, History and Nature of Science, and Science and Technology. Each of these categories contains one or more subcategories, which also correspond to the National Standards. A table of all lessons and the standards they address is included in Appendix B.

Understanding the Nature of Science
The National Science Education Standards states that as a result of activities in grades K–4, students should develop the abilities necessary to do scientific inquiry and to understand the process of scientific inquiry.

Science shares many of the same information-processing procedures and skills used in other subjects, including reading, mathematics, and social studies. This is why we believe that interdisciplinary lessons engage children in using process skills that are complemented and reinforced in multiple ways. Such lessons serve to provide rich learning experiences. For example, as students do science investigations, follow scientific procedures, analyze data, and think as scientists, they also develop effective reading skills by observing, communicating, classifying, predicting and verifying outcomes, and drawing conclusions. This provides for simultaneous improvement of science and reading skills.

Physical Science Content Standards
An understanding of the physical world is an essential component of scientific literacy. To help you teach physical science concepts, the lessons in this book are grouped into three sections based on the Physical Science Content Standard for Grades K–4 from the National Science Education Standards: Properties of Objects

and Materials; Position and Motion of Objects; and Light, Heat, Electricity, and Magnetism. An important idea to remember is that students are expected to develop an understanding of these concepts as a result of observation and manipulation of objects and materials in their environment. Every lesson in this book gives students the opportunity to develop their understanding through such experiences.

Science and Technology Standards

Most of the lessons in this book involve making holiday-related crafts. An integral part of many of these lessons is the process of design. Students are often required to propose modifications to a process, implement those modifications, evaluate the results, and communicate their results. Such projects help students to develop an understanding of the relationship between science and technology. Indeed, as the National Science Education Standards states, design is the technological parallel to inquiry in science.

History and Nature of Science

Understanding how people in the past approached science and technology can help motivate students and provide examples of scientific inquiry and technological design in action. It can also help them understand that science is something that people—people just like them—do. Many of the lessons involve technologies that have been developed gradually over hundreds, or even thousands, of years, with contributions by people of many cultures. These technologies include candle-making, paper-making, agriculture, and fragrance chemistry. In addition, the Birthday lesson includes a list of scientists, their birthdays, and their notable achievements, providing a jumping-off point for studying the history of science, a 5–8 content standard under History and Nature of Science.

The Particle Nature of Matter

An important issue that arises when teaching physical science content in the elementary grades is how to approach teaching about the particle nature of matter. To be able to explain the nature and interactions of matter, it is necessary to know about the nature of the particles that make it up. As adults, you have probably heard and used the terms atoms, molecules, and ions. Remember, however, that young children do not have the conceptual background to distinguish correctly between these three terms. In the primary grades, we strongly recommend that you use the general term "particles" with students to prevent creating misconceptions that will later be difficult to correct. Additionally, with elementary students, limit your discussion to the general idea that all matter is made up of particles that are too small to be seen by the human eye and that, in spite of our inability to see these particles, their existence accounts for matter as we know it. The discussion of the various types of particles (atoms, molecules, ions) should be held to later years in the curriculum when the students are conceptually ready for this level of detail. Our recommendations are consistent with those of the American Association for the Advancement of Science Benchmarks for Science Literacy and the National Science Foundation-funded S_2C_2 (School Science Curriculum Conference) report, a joint report of the American Chemical Society and the American Association of Physics Teachers.

Reference

National Research Council. *National Science Education Standards;* National Academy: Washington DC, 1996.

Assessment

Assessment and learning are two sides of the same coin. Assessments enable students to let teachers know what they are learning, and when students engage in an assessment exercise, they should learn from it. Paper-and-pencil tests are a familiar and ubiquitous form of assessment. But in light of what we are hoping to teach students about both the process and content of science, traditional tests requiring students to choose one of a few given answers or fill in the blank measure only a fraction of what we need to know about their science learning. The National Science Education Standards advocates using diverse assessment methods, including performances and portfolios as well as paper-and-pencil tests.

Emerging from among a host of terms describing current assessment options (for example, authentic, alternative, portfolio, and performance), the term active assessment has been proposed by George Hein and Sabra Price in their book *Active Assessment for Active Science.* They define "active assessment" as a whole family of assessment methods that actively engage the learner and can also be interpreted meaningfully by the teacher. Almost any of the experiences that make up the lessons in this book can also serve as active assessments. For example, brainstorming sessions, science journal entries, data and observations from science investigations, and writing extensions can all be part of developing a picture of what students are learning. For this reason, we have not identified any particular portion of the lessons in this book as assessments. We hope that as you use the lessons in this book, you will engage in many different forms of active assessment, thus maximizing the opportunity for all students to demonstrate their accomplishments and understanding.

References

American Association for the Advancement of Science. *Benchmarks for Science Literacy;* Oxford University: New York, 1993.

Hein, G.E.; Price, S. *Active Assessment for Active Science;* Heinemann: Portsmouth, NH, 1994.

National Research Council. *National Science Education Standards;* National Academy: Washington DC, 1996.

Padilla, M.; Muth, D.; Padilla, R.L. "Science and Reading: Many Process Skills in Common," *Science Learning: Processes and Applications.* 1991; 14–19.

Teaching with Classroom Learning Centers

Most of the lessons in this book involve using classroom learning centers in Part 1, Building Bridges. Centers are small areas of a classroom set aside for independent learning. You also might call them stations or learning areas. Typically, they include a variety of materials for students to manipulate, read, and look at. Learning centers can be an integral part of everyday classroom instruction, or they can be used as temporary learning stations for a specific activity. A center is not just a physical space to work on tasks such as ditto sheets or workbooks. Rather, centers should provide opportunities for creativity, problem solving, critical thinking, and learning by doing. Science centers can provide motivation to take on difficult challenges while helping younger children develop the concentration skills necessary to complete multiple-step activities.

Reference

Ingraham, P. *Creating and Managing Learning Centers: A Theme-Based Approach;* Crystal Springs: Peterborough, NY, 1996.

Using Science Journals

Almost all of the lessons in this book require students to record systematic observations, experimental procedures, data, results, and conclusions. Keeping a regular science journal including all science investigations throughout the year is an excellent way for students to organize information. Also, regular use of science journals throughout the lessons in this book will give students many opportunities to practice writing skills in the context of doing science. Writing is an integral part of the process of scientific inquiry. When working as scientists, students must record observations and data, organize and summarize results, and draw conclusions. Often they must communicate both the process of the investigation and its results to others through words and/or pictures.

Writing can be viewed as hands-on thinking: It gives students opportunities for reflection and active processing of learning experiences. As a result of regular writing experiences, students gain a better understanding of what they know.

References

Saul, W. *Science Workshop: A Whole Language Approach;* Heinemann: Portsmouth, NH, 1993.
Zikes, D. *Reading & Writing Across the Curriculum; Dinah-Might Activities:* San Antonio, TX, 1994.

● Safety

The hands-on science investigations in this book will add fun and excitement to science education in your classroom. However, even the simplest activity can become dangerous when the proper safety precautions are ignored, when the activity is done incorrectly, or when the activity is performed by students without proper supervision. The science investigations in this book have been extensively reviewed by classroom teachers of elementary grades and by university scientists. We have done all we can to assure the safety of the activities. It is up to you to assure their safe execution!

Be Careful—and Have Fun!

- Always practice activities yourself before performing them with your class. This is the only way to become thoroughly familiar with the procedures and materials required for an activity, and familiarity will help prevent potentially hazardous (or merely embarrassing) mishaps. In addition, you may find variations that will make the activity more meaningful to your students.

- Activities should be undertaken only at the recommended grade levels and only with adult supervision.

- Read each activity carefully and observe all safety precautions and disposal procedures.

- You, your assistants, and any students observing at close range must wear safety goggles if indicated in the activity and at any other time you deem necessary.

- Special safety instructions are not given for everyday classroom materials being used in a typical manner. Use common sense when working with hot, sharp, or breakable objects, such as flames, scissors, or glassware. Keep tables or desks covered to avoid stains. Keep spills cleaned up to prevent falls.

- Recycling/reuse instructions are not given for everyday materials. We encourage you to reuse and recycle the materials according to local recycling procedures.

- In some activities, potentially hazardous items such as hot-melt glue guns or ovens are to be used by the teacher only.

Birthday

Any Date
Cultures: Various

Birthday celebrations (as well as other holidays celebrated on specific dates) were made possible by the invention of the calendar. Before 4,000 B.C., people relied on the phases of the moon and the changing of the seasons to determine the day, and records of important events were inaccurate. When the first calendars were invented in 4,000 B.C., people could keep track of important days from year to year, such as birthdays, weddings, and anniversaries of special events. With a calendar, individual days could be tracked and the anniversaries of important events observed.

At first, only kings and royalty had birthday celebrations. The entire kingdom or nation would pay homage to royalty on their birthdays, which were marked by feasting and dancing. In ancient Greece, the heads of important families celebrated their birthdays, but these celebrations were smaller and limited to the family. Gradually, customs changed and other people besides leaders began to observe their own birthdays. After the tradition of sending birthday cards began in England in 1850, birthday celebrations became more common.

Many customs and symbols have been associated with birthdays for centuries. Birthday parties were held at first for protection. People thought that evil spirits would visit them on their birthdays, as these days marked a change in their lives. Times of change were seen as opportunities for evil spirits to come and influence people. Family and friends gathered around the birthday person, played games, and had fun to ward off the evil spirits. Gifts were given as a token of good luck for the coming year.

Another popular custom at birthdays is lighting candles on a birthday cake. Ancient Greeks took round cakes topped with lit candles to the temple of Artemis, goddess of the moon, on her feast day. The round, glowing cakes, which symbolized the moon, began to be used for birthday celebrations to symbolize Artemis's blessings for the celebrant. The Germans also made cakes with candles for birthdays. The candles represented the light of life, and the smoke was said to take wishes up to heaven. This belief led to the present-day custom of making a wish and blowing out the candles on the cake.

Birthday

Any Date
Cultures: Various

Although everyone has a birthday, not all people celebrate their birthdays in the same way. Many cultures have customs that are different from those common in America:

- In Japan, children used to celebrate their birthdays on January 1 no matter what day of the year they were born. These celebrations tied in with the New Year festivities. Today, however, many Japanese children celebrate their birthday on the day they were born.

- A Korean child's first birthday is the most important. A feast is held, and family and friends set gifts before the child. The items the child picks up are said to tell his or her future.

- Birthdays of Hindu children are very religious. The child is taken to the temple, where a special service is held, and the child receives a blessing from the priest. The birthday child also does not have to attend school that day. When Hindu children turn 16, they no longer celebrate their birthdays.

- In Mexico, the focal point of the birthday celebration is the piñata, a custom that was started more than 300 years ago. A piñata is a large clay or papier-mâché form covered with decorative tissue paper and filled with candy and small gifts. (To learn more about piñatas, see the activity "Piñata-Making for Cinco de Mayo.") Blindfolded children take turns trying to hit the piñata with a stick. When it breaks, the treats fall to the ground and the children scramble to gather them up.

- Many children in Christian communities are named after saints, and instead of celebrating on their own birthdays, some celebrate on the feast days of their saints. A small religious service is held in honor of the saint, followed by a meal of the child's favorite foods. In some communities, children celebrate both their birthdays and the feast days of their patron saints.

References

Canfield, A. "Birthday Facts from Hallmark," Hallmark: Kansas City, MO, February, 1992.

Gibbons, G. *Happy Birthday;* Scholastic: New York, 1986.

Motomora, M. *Happy Birthday!;* Raintree: Milwaukee, WI, 1989.

Birthday Water Globes

● ●

Although birthdays have been around as long as humans, it wasn't until the 1800s that birthday celebrations

became common. Gift-giving is an important part of birthday celebrations in many cultures. In this activity,

students make water globes that are perfect to give as birthday presents.

● ●

Key Science Topics

- density
- physical properties
- viscosity

Time Required

Setup	30	minutes
Performance	45–60	minutes
Cleanup	10–15	minutes

A homemade water globe and a commercial water globe

15

Part 1: Building Bridges

Building Student Knowledge and Motivation

Prior to the lesson, create a learning center containing several birthday symbols, such as candles, a wrapped box, and birthday cards. Let students bring in old birthday cards they may have to add to the collection. Tell the students when they visit the center to look for symbols associated with birthdays. Let them add symbols of birthdays they think should be included but may be missing. Discuss their "treasure" or "golden" birthday year (for example, turning 10 on the 10th).

Ask students if they know of any famous people who were born on their birthdays. Share with the students the table of Birthdays of Famous Scientists (provided at the end of this lesson). Assign each student the scientist born on or closest to his or her birthday. As the birthdays occur, have students give a short report on their famous scientists and on themselves.

Bridging to the Science Activity

Set out clear bottles containing matter in various states. For solids, use a birthday candle, glitter, sequins, and artificial snow. For liquids, use corn syrup, vegetable oil, rubbing alcohol, and water, each in a different bottle. At least one bottle should be "empty"—containing only air. Some bottles could contain more than one state of matter. Ask students to identify the materials as solid, liquid, and/or gas.

Discuss where each material is in the bottles and how it relates to the other materials. What would happen if some materials were mixed together? Would one material sink to the bottom or float on top?

Part 2: Science Activity

Materials

For Bridging to the Science Activity
- several clear bottles with tight-fitting lids
- several different solids, such as the following:
    - birthday candle
    - glitter
    - sequins
    - artificial snow
- corn syrup
- vegetable oil
- rubbing alcohol
- water

For Getting Ready

Part A, per class

- masking tape and pen for labels
- the following 4 clear liquids
  - water
  - vegetable oil
  - rubbing alcohol
  - light corn syrup

  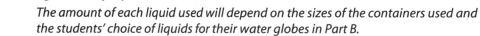

  The amount of each liquid used will depend on the sizes of the containers used and the students' choice of liquids for their water globes in Part B.

Part A, per group

- 4 small, clear bottles with tight-fitting lids

Part B, per class

- hot-melt glue gun and glue

Part B, per student

- small, clear bottle or jar with tight-fitting lid

  Wyler's® bouillon jars work extremely well in terms of both sealing ability and attractiveness of the final product. Baby-food jars tend to be difficult to re-seal, but Teflon® plumber's tape may solve the leaking problem. If possible, test different types of jars in advance.

- small birthday candle
- (optional) penny or small stone

  Use this item only with jars that are too tall and narrow for you to glue a candle in easily.

For the Procedure

Part A, per class

- commercial water globe or one you have made in advance

Part A, per group

- set of 4 bottles with liquids prepared in Getting Ready
- empty small clear bottle
- ½-teaspoon measures
- glitter, sequins, and/or artificial snow

  Artificial snow is a seasonal item that is available from craft or decorating stores in fall and winter.

- additional volumes of the liquids used in Getting Ready

Part B, per class

- additional volumes of the "best" liquid or mixture, chosen in Part A
- ½-teaspoon measure
- (optional) Teflon® plumber's tape

Part B, per student
- small, clear bottle or jar with candle prepared in Getting Ready
- ½ teaspoon glitter, sequins, artificial snow, and/or tiny confetti in fun shapes

For the Extension for Further Science Inquiry
- sample water globe containing artificial snow
- small, clear bottles or jars with tight-fitting lids
- water or the 50/50 water-corn syrup mixture
- a variety of water-insoluble, fine white solids, such as sand, crushed vermiculite, crumbled Styrofoam™, and rice

 You can provide these or have the students bring them in. Be sure that any used are safe to handle. Salt and sugar are not suitable, because they will quickly dissolve and disappear in water.

Safety and Disposal

Only the teacher or another adult should use the hot-melt glue gun. Use caution when applying glue. Use caution when using glass jars with young students. No special disposal procedures are required.

Getting Ready

For Part A

For each group, fill and label four clear bottles, each containing one of the following liquids: water, vegetable oil, rubbing alcohol, and light corn syrup.

For Part B

Secure one birthday candle inside each of the small jars using a hot-melt glue gun. (See Figure 1.)

 If the jars are short, the candles may need to be cut off at the bottom so they will fit. If the jars are too tall and thin for you to glue the candle to the bottom, glue the candle to a penny or small rock; it can move freely as part of the glitter-sequin display. If you are sure the jars will seal tightly, you may want to try gluing the candle to the inside of the lid and setting the finished water globe upside down.

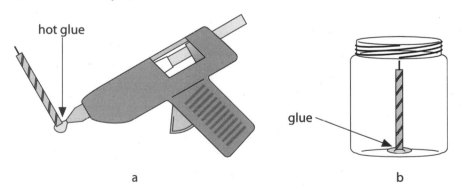

hot glue

glue

a

b

Figure 1: Secure a candle to the bottom of a jar by
(a) applying hot glue to the base of the candle and
(b) placing the candle in the jar.

Procedure

Part A: Finding the Best System

1. Show the students a commercial water globe or one that you have made in advance. Tell them their challenge will be to build something similar, given the liquids and solids you provide.

2. Give each group four different bottles, each containing a different clear liquid: corn syrup, vegetable oil, rubbing alcohol, and water. Tell them they should place no more than ½ teaspoon each of glitter, sequins, and/or artificial snow in each bottle, seal the bottle, and shake it. Let the students observe the four bottles and compare the similarities and differences of the solids and liquids. Discuss how these bottles are different from and similar to the water globe.

3. Let each group select a different mix by combining two of the four liquids in a 50/50 ratio in the fifth jar and repeating step 2. They should share their results with the class.

   In preparing the 50/50 mixtures, students will discover that oil and water and oil and corn syrup don't mix. Some mixing will occur between the oil and alcohol. In the other combinations (water-corn syrup, water-alcohol, alcohol-corn syrup), the liquids will mix, but it may take some time for mixing to be complete.

4. Let the class decide which mixture best matches the commercial toy. Have students record their reasons for their choice in their science journals. Students will use this mixture in Part B.

   Normally, classes find that the 50/50 water-corn syrup mixture best matches the liquid in the commercial toy.

Part B: Making the Birthday Water Globe

1. Give each student a small jar with a birthday candle already glued to the bottom or to a penny or rock.

2. Have students fill the jars to about 1 cm below the rim of the jar with water or with the mixture the class found to produce the best results in Part A.

3. Have students add no more than ½ teaspoon of snow and glitter to the jar.

4. (optional) If students are using baby-food jars or other jars that don't seal tightly, wrap Teflon tape around the threads on the rim of the jar two or three times.

   Be sure to wind the Teflon tape in the same direction as the lid will turn to seal the jar.

5. Have students put the lids on and close the jars tightly.

6. Have students evaluate their water globes in comparison to the commercial one, including cost, time to prepare, artistic value, etc. Have them write a brief analysis of these issues.

Extension for Further Science Inquiry

Show students a commercial water globe containing artificial snow. Have them try building a water globe containing a water-insoluble white solid that simulates artificial snow. Possibilities include sand, crushed vermiculite, crumbled Styrofoam, or rice. Challenge students to try different solids until they find the one they believe to be the best. The class should evaluate the tested solids by discussing factors that give each its own characteristics.

Science Explanation

The following explanation is intended for the teacher's information. Modify the explanation for students as required.

Density and Viscosity

In these activities, two factors simultaneously affect the behavior of the sequins, glitter, and craft snow in the liquids in the jars; the relative densities of the solids and liquids used, and the viscosity of the liquid.

The density of a solid determines whether it sinks or floats in water. All things in the universe are made of tiny particles. The heavier these particles are and the more closely they are packed together, the more dense the object is. All materials have characteristic densities. An object that is more dense than water sinks in water, except when surface tension interferes. An object that is less dense than water floats on water.

When a solid is placed in various liquids, the solid will either sink or float, depending on how its density compares to that of the liquid. The densities of the liquids suggested for use in Part A are as follows: rubbing alcohol—0.78 g/mL, vegetable oil—0.9 g/mL, water—1.0 g/mL, light corn syrup—1.22 g/mL, 50/50 light corn syrup/water—1.1 g/mL, and 50/50 rubbing alcohol/water— .90 g/mL.

Notice that you cannot entirely predict the rate of movement of the solid based on the density of the liquids. For example, vegetable oil is less dense than water but the glitter sinks more slowly in vegetable oil. This brings us to the second factor: viscosity of the liquid. Viscosity is a liquid's resistance to flow. We commonly describe liquids with high viscosities as thick or syrupy. Oil, corn syrup, and 50/50 light corn syrup/water are all more viscous than plain water, alcohol, or the alcohol/water mixture.

In preparing the 50/50 mixtures of oil and water, students will discover that oil will not mix with either water or corn syrup. Some mixing will occur between the oil and alcohol. In the other combinations (water-corn syrup, water-alcohol, alcohol-corn syrup), the liquids will mix, but it may take some time for mixing to be complete.

Although both density and viscosity affect the behavior of the solids in the globes, they are not directly related. For example, oil is more viscous than water, but it is also less dense than water.

The History of Water Globes

Water globes (also called snowdomes, snowglobes, and other names) were invented in France in the 1800s and were originally used as paperweights. They appeared at the Paris Universal Exposition in 1878 and quickly spread throughout Europe. Since then snowglobes have become popular gifts and collector's items. They may be made of glass or plastic and come in a wide variety of shapes, sizes, and themes. The liquid inside may be water or a mixture of water and polyethylene glycol (an antifreeze and thickener). Finding a recipe for attractive "snow" continues to be something of a challenge. Early domes contained bone chips; fragments of porcelain, china, and pottery; sand; sawdust; bits of minerals such as meerschaum; and even ground rice. Plastic domes often contain plastic snow. The two remaining German manufacturers keep their snow recipes secret.

References for the Science Activity

Bernstein, L. *Concepts and Challenges in Physical Science,* 3rd ed.; Globe: Englewood Cliffs, NJ, 1991.
McMichael, N. *Snowdomes;* Abbeville: New York, 1990.
"Household Density Column"; *Fun with Chemistry: A Guidebook of K–12 Activities,* 2nd ed.;
     Sarquis, M., Sarquis, J., Eds.; Institute for Chemical Education: Madison, WI, 1991; Vol. 1,
     pp 115–118.
Sarquis, J.L.; Sarquis, M.; Williams, J.P. "Density Batons," *Teaching Chemistry with TOYS: Activities
     for Grades K–9;* McGraw-Hill: New York, 1995; pp 53–57.

Part 3: Integrating with Language Arts

Featured Fiction Book: *Birthday Blizzard*

Author: Bonnie Pryor   Illustrator: Molly Delaney
Publisher: Morrow   ISBN: 0-688-09423-6
Summary: A blizzard hits and Jamie's birthday plans change.

Show students the cover of *Birthday Blizzard* and identify items that relate to celebrating a birthday. Does the character on the cover look happy or sad? Why? Ask the students if they would rather celebrate a birthday alone or with other people. Ask the students to predict what will happen in the story. Read the story aloud to the students.

Writing Extensions

- Pretend that you are at home on your birthday watching a blizzard outside. What would you do to have fun?
- Describe what the five liquids you used in the snowglobe activity feel like. What do they smell like?

Additional Books

Fiction

Title: *Birthday*
Author and Illustrator: John Steptoe
Publisher: Owlet   ISBN: 0805053417
Summary: A child celebrates his eighth birthday with all the people of a fantasied African community.

Title: *A Birthday Basket for Tía*
Author: Pat Mora   Illustrator: Cecily Lang
Publisher: Aladdin   ISBN: 0689813287
Summary: With the help of her cat, Chica, Cecilia prepares a special gift for the ninetieth birthday of her great-aunt (her Tía). She prepares a celebration basket filled with things to remind Tía of the wonderful moments that she and Cecilia have shared.

Title: *The Birthday Swap*
Author and Illustrator: Loretta Lopez
Publisher: Lee & Low   ISBN: 1880000474
Summary: A five-year-old Mexican-American girl who will not be six until December has a great deal to celebrate when her sister swaps birthdays with her in the summer.

Part 4: Other Lesson Extensions

Art and Music

- Decorate the outside of the jar (leaving lots of space empty to see inside) with an appropriate background scene for the water globe.
- Have the students write one or more additional verses for the song "Happy Birthday."

Mathematics

- Have students determine how many minutes and seconds it takes for all the solids in the water globe to sink to the bottom. Is the sinking rate different with three shakes compared to 10 shakes of the globe? How do the times for the four bottles in Part A differ?

Social Studies

- Have students investigate birthday customs of other cultures. Discuss differences as a class.

Part 5: National Science Education Standards

Science as Inquiry Standards:

Abilities Necessary to Do Scientific Inquiry
Students question which liquid would work best in a water globe.

Students compare and contrast different liquids.

Students share the results of using various combinations of liquids.

Physical Science Standards:

Properties of Objects and Materials
The liquids and solids used in the investigation have observable properties.

The liquids and solids tested have properties that depend on the properties of their components.

The materials used in the water globes include solids, liquids, and gases (air).

Science and Technology Standards:

Abilities of Technological Design
Students question how to make the best water globes.

Students use their observations of different liquids to design their water globes.

Students construct individual water globes.

Students evaluate their water globes by comparing them with a commercial globe in terms of issues such as cost, artistic value, etc.

Students write brief analyses of their design processes and products.

History and Nature of Science Standards:

Science as a Human Endeavor
Water globes were invented in the 1800s, and people are still searching for better ways to make artificial snow for water globes.

Students learn about the lives and accomplishments of scientists from various social and ethnic backgrounds who work in diverse scientific fields.

History of Science
Students study individuals who have contributed to the traditions of science.

Birthdays of Famous Scientists

Birthdate	Scientist	Birth Country	Interesting Facts
January 8, 1942	Stephen Hawking	England	Pioneered the study of black holes and has developed most of the theories concerning them; proponent of the "Big Bang" theory.
January 10, 1877	Frederick Cottrell	America	Created electrostatic precipitators, which help remove pollution from steam and industrial dust; separated helium from natural gas.
January 14, 1943	Shannon Lucid	America	First American woman to live in space, she boarded the MIR space station on March 22, 1996; her first flight as an astronaut was aboard the space shuttle Discovery in June, 1985.
January 15, 1850	Sonia Kovalevsky	Russia	Studied physics and mathematics privately at a time when public university lectures were not open to women; best known for her work with partial differential equations.
January 16, 1932	Dian Fossey	America	Leading authority on mountain gorillas; spent years living in the African jungles to study gorillas; the movie *Gorillas in the Mist* was based on her life.
January 17, 1706	Benjamin Franklin	America	Discovered electricity in lightning; invented the lightning rod, the rocking chair, bifocal eyeglasses, and daylight savings time.
January 19, 1736	James Watt	Scotland	Invented a newer, more efficient steam engine; perfected the rotary engine; coined the term "horsepower." The "watt" was named for him.
January 22, 1775	André Ampère	France	Founded and developed electrodynamics; wrote the laws of electric currents. The energy unit "amp" is named for him.
January 23, 1918	Gertrude Elion	America	Helped develop chemotherapy treatment for cancer; won the 1988 Nobel Prize in Medicine.
February 8, 1700	Daniel Bernoulli	Netherlands	Studied many branches of science; pioneered the study of hydrodynamics, the name of which he created; developed the Bernoulli Principle and Bernoulli's equation used in aerodynamics.
February 8, 1834	Dmitri Mendeleev	Russia	Developed the periodic table of elements for chemistry; also formulated the periodic law of chemistry.
February 9, 1809	Charles Darwin	England	Developed the theories of evolution and natural selection; categorized species of animals; also studied geology.
February 15, 1564	Galileo Galilei	Italy	Developed laws of acceleration; discovered the moon was mountainous; found four moons of Jupiter; first to see Saturn's rings, although due to the poor power of his telescope he believed they were satellites.
February 18, 1745	Alessandro Volta	Italy	Developed the first electric battery; invented the precursor to the capacitor; invented tools to detect atmospheric current. The electric unit "volt" was named for him.
February 18, 1838	Ernst Mach	Austria	Studied ballistics; created the Mach number, the ratio between the speed of an object and the speed of sound.

 Reproduced from *Science Projects for Holidays throughout the Year*, published by McGraw-Hill.

Birthdays of Famous Scientists, cont'd.

Birthdate	Scientist	Birth Country	Interesting Facts
February 19, 1473	Nicholas Copernicus	Poland	Founder of modern astronomy, he proved that the sun is the center of the solar system, and not the Earth as was previously thought; developed the modern view of our solar system.
February 28, 1901	Linus Pauling	America	Molecular biologist who won two Nobel Prizes, one in Chemisty in 1954 and the Peace Prize in 1962; he advocated vitamin C as a treatment for colds and chemotherapy for mental diseases.
March 3, 1847	Alexander Graham Bell	Scotland	Invented the telephone and the multiple telegraph; was one of the original founders of the National Geographic Society; experimented with flight.
March 7, 1792	John Herschel	England	Son of William and friend of Charles Babbage; developed process to measure solar energy; catalogued the stars of the southern sky; discovered and explained the Herschel Effect on photosensitive surfaces.
March 8, 1788	Antoine Becquerel	France	Grandfather of electrochemistry; developed the constant current cell; was the first of four generations of scientists spanning two centuries.
March 12, 1790	John Daniell	England	Studied electrochemistry; created constant current cells used to power telegraphs; experimented with the fusion of metals.
March 14, 1879	Albert Einstein	Germany	Developed the theory of relativity and its related equation $e=mc^2$, which states that the mass of a body is a measurement of its energy content; also proved that light is bent by gravitational fields; won the 1921 Nobel Prize in Physics.
March 16, 1750	Caroline Herschel	Germany	Discovered three nebulae, including the Andromeda nebula's companion; discovered eight comets; assisted her brother, William, with his observations that led to the discovery of Uranus.
March 23, 1912	Wernher von Braun	Germany	Pioneered rocketry and advocated the exploration of space; headed the development of the Saturn V rocket that launched the Apollo moon missions.
March 24, 1820	Alexandre-Edmond Becquerel	France	Worked with electricity, magnetism, and optics; invented the phosphoroscope used to identify phosphorescent materials.
March 27, 1845	William Röntgen	Germany	Discovered the X-ray, which has a shorter wavelength than visible light; won the first Nobel Prize in Physics in 1901.
April 14, 1629	Christiaan Huygens	Netherlands	Discovered Titan, one of Saturn's satellites, and accurately described the rings of Saturn; explained the refraction and reflection of light; studied centrifugal force and collisions.
April 15, 1452	Leonardo da Vinci	Italy	Best known for his artwork, da Vinci also studied optics, gears, hydraulics, and the eye; among some of his sketches include renderings of the modern parachute and helicopter.

Reproduced from *Science Projects for Holidays throughout the Year*, published by McGraw-Hill.

25

Birthdays of Famous Scientists, cont'd.

Birthdate	Scientist	Birth Country	Interesting Facts
April 15, 1707	Leonhard Euler	Switzerland	A mathematician who collaborated with Daniel Bernoulli in his work with hydrodynamics; developed the theory of lunar motion.
April 16, 1867	Wilbur Wright	America	With his brother, Orville, he developed and built the first airplane, successfully flying it on December 17, 1903.
April 22, 1904	J. Robert Oppenheimer	America	Director of the laboratory that designed and built the first atomic bomb; opposed the development of the hydrogen bomb and advocated the use of atomic power as an energy source, not a weapon.
April 22, 1909	Rita Levi-Montalcini	Italy	Experimented with the epidermal growth factor of skin; won the Nobel Prize in Medicine in 1986.
April 23, 1858	Max Planck	Germany	Developed quantum theory and quantum mechanics; studied absorption and radiation of black bodies; won the Nobel Prize in Physics in 1918.
April 25, 1874	Guglielmo Marconi	Italy	Invented the wireless telegraph, or radio; received the first transatlantic wireless communication; won the 1909 Nobel Prize in Physics.
April 27, 1791	Samuel Morse	America	Perfected the electric telegraph; considered to be inventer of telegraph although the original idea was not his; developed Morse code for telegraph communication.
April 28, 1900	Jan Hendrick Oort	Holland	Confirmed theory of the Milky Way's rotation; said that comets originate in a cloud that orbits the sun at a great distance (the Oort Cloud) and are deflected into the inner solar system by gravitational disturbances.
May 11, 1918	Richard Feynman	America	Assisted with the development of the nuclear bomb; created the Feynman diagram, a set of notation used to describe and calculate subatomic reactions; won the 1965 Nobel Prize in Physics.
May 12, 1910	Dorothy Crowfoot Hodgkin	England	Determined the structure of vitamin B12; took the first X-ray diffraction polargraph of pepsin; performed structural analyses of penicillin and insulin; won the Nobel Prize in Chemistry in 1964.
May 15, 1859	Pierre Curie	France	With his wife Marie and friend Antoine-Henri Becquerel, pioneered the field of radioactivity; won the 1903 Nobel Prize in Physics.
May 26, 1865	Max LeBlanc	Poland	Showed that hydrogen and oxygen were discharged at electrodes during electrolysis; laid the groundwork for understanding electrode processes.
May 26, 1951	Sally Ride	America	First American woman in space, she flew on two missions aboard the space shuttle Challenger: on June 18, 1983, and in October 1984.
May 27, 1907	Rachel Carson	America	Marine biologist who studied the effects of insecticides on the environment; wrote *Silent Spring* to warn people of the effects of insecticides and pollution on the environment.

Birthdays of Famous Scientists, cont'd.

Birthdate	Scientist	Birth Country	Interesting Facts
June 13, 1831	James Maxwell	Scotland	Studied electricty and magnetism; developed the theory of electromagnetic fields; showed that light is only one type of electromagnetic radiation.
June 14, 1736	Charles de Coulomb	France	Worked with electricity and magnetism; proved the inverse-square law of electricity and magnetism; the energy unit "coulomb" is named for him.
June 16, 1902	Barbara McClintock	America	Contributor to the study of DNA; showed genes could shift from generation to generation; won the 1983 Nobel Prize in Medicine.
June 23, 1912	Alan Turing	England	Helped design computers; did groundwork in the development of artificial intelligence; instrumental in breaking the "German Enigma" code cipher during WWII.
June 25, 1864	Walther Hermann Nernst	Prussia	Bridged Planck's quantum theory with the dynamics of chemical processes; wrote the third law of thermodynamics; won the Nobel Prize in Chemistry in 1920.
June 26, 1824	William Thomson Kelvin	Ireland	Established the law of conservation of energy; discovered the Thomson Effect of thermoelectricity; introduced the Kelvin temperature scale, which sets 0° as the absolute lowest limit of temperature (theoretically).
July 11, 1811	William Grove	Scotland	Electrochemist who developed two constant current batteries, one of which was the forerunner of the modern fuel cell; showed electrolysis could occur through glass.
July 19, 1921	Rosalyn Sussman Yalow	America	Researches the medical use of radiation; studies the effect of hormones on body chemistry; won the Nobel Prize in Medicine in 1977.
July 22, 1822	Johann Gregor Mendel	Austria	Father of genetics; produced the first accurate and scientific explanation for hybridization; his conclusions formed the basic tenets of genetics.
July 24, 1897	Amelia Earhart	America	First female pilot to cross the Atlantic Ocean alone and the first pilot to cross the Atlantic twice; on one of the final legs of her around-the-world trip, her plane disappeared without a trace in the Pacific Ocean.
August 1, 1818	Maria Mitchell	America	First professional American female astronomer; first woman elected to the Academy of Arts and Sciences; pioneered the study of sunspots; discovered and studied comets, nebulae, and planetary satellites.
August 5, 1946	Shirley Jackson	America	First African-American woman to receive a Ph.D. in Theoretical Solid State physics from MIT; was appointed the chairperson of the Nuclear Regulatory Commission in 1995.
August 9, 1776	Amedo Avogadro	Italy	Distinguished between atoms and molecules; determined molecular weights of known elements; the Avogadro number, the number of atoms or molecules in a mole of any substance, was named for him.
August 13, 1814	Anders Ängstrom	Sweden	Showed that each gas emits a single, characteristic spectrum, which allows astronomers to identify gases present in stars; the angstrom, .0000001 millimeter, was named for him.

Reproduced from *Science Projects for Holidays throughout the Year*, published by McGraw-Hill.

27

Birthdays of Famous Scientists, cont'd.

Birthdate	Scientist	Birth Country	Interesting Facts
August 19, 1871	Orville Wright	America	With his brother, Wilbur, he developed and built the first airplane, successfully flying it on December 17, 1903.
August 30, 1871	Ernest Rutherford	New Zealand	Discovered and named alpha and beta radiation waves; proposed theory of the radioactive transformation of atoms; won the 1908 Nobel Prize in Chemistry.
September 9, 1737	Luigi Galvani	Italy	First to discover the phenomenon of deceased muscle tissue reacting to electric charges; the term galvanic, meaning "producing a direct current" is named for him.
September 15, 1852	Edward Bouchet	America	First African-American to graduate from Yale; first African-American to earn a Ph.D. from an American university; taught physics and science and held various administrative postions in high schools and universities.
September 15, 1930	Patsy Sherman	America	Discovered the chemical that led to the development of Scotchgard® when she spilled the chemical on her shoe; she observed later that the area on which the chemical landed stayed clean while the rest of her shoe was dirty.
September 19, 1819	Jean Foucault	France	Made the first accurate determination of the speed of light in a laboratory; demonstrated the Earth's rotation mechanically using a pendulum; showed that light travels faster in air than in water.
September 22, 1791	Michael Faraday	England	Wrote the 1st and 2nd laws of electrochemistry; coined the terms "electrode," "electrolyte," and "ion"; developed the first transformer, electric generator, and electric motor.
September 29, 1901	Enrico Fermi	Italy	Created artificial radioactivity; his early work with fission led to the development of the nuclear bomb; founded the Argonne National Laboratory; won the Nobel Prize in Physics in 1938.
October 5, 1882	Robert Goddard	America	Pioneer of rocket science; developed the theory of rocket propulsion; designed, built, and tested the first liquid-fuel rocket in 1926.
October 7, 1885	Niels Bohr	Denmark	Developed the modern theory of atomic structure; coined the term "isotope"; helped develop atomic power and felt it should be used as a source of energy, not as a weapon; won the Nobel Prize in Physics in 1922.
October 21, 1833	Alfred Nobel	Sweden	Invented dynamite; set up the Nobel Foundation to award prizes in physics, chemistry, medicine, literature, and world peace, awarding the first prizes in 1901; the Nobel Prize for Economics was added in 1969.
October 28, 1914	Jonas Salk	America	Studied microbiology and immunology; developed the vaccine for polio and worked on the development of a vaccine for influenza (the "flu").
November 7, 1867	Marie Curie	Poland	Discovered radium; coined the term "radioactivity" and worked with her husband Pierre and friend Antoine-Henri Becquerel to pioneer the field; first scientist to receive two Nobel Prizes, one in Physics in 1903, the second in Chemistry in 1911.

Birthdays of Famous Scientists, cont'd.

Birthdate	Scientist	Birth Country	Interesting Facts
November 9, 1934	Carl Sagan	America	Determined that Venus was hotter than previously thought due to the greenhouse effect; found that Titan, one of Saturn's moons, has organic molecules similiar to the building blocks of life; pioneered exobiology.
November 12, 1842	John Strutt Rayleigh	England	Discovered the element argon; developed the theory of Rayleigh scattering which explains why the sky is blue and the sunset is red; won the Nobel Prize in Physics in 1904.
November 15, 1738	William Herschel	Germany	Made the first recorded discovery of a planet when he found Uranus; also discovered the sixth moon of Saturn; observed and described binary stars; made detailed observations of our solar system.
November 20, 1889	Edwin Hubble	America	Father of modern extragalactic astronomy; first to provide evidence for the expansion of the galaxy; NASA named the telescope they launched into space on April 25, 1990, after him.
November 22, 1905	Karl Jansky	America	While trying to determine the source of radio static, he discovered that the interference was coming from extraterrestrial sources; this led him to develop radio astronomy, the use of radio waves to study the universe.
November 27, 1701	Anders Celsius	Sweden	Proved Newton's theory that the Earth was flattened at the poles; created the Celsius temperature scale.
November 28, 1926	Darleane Hoffman	America	Studies the chemical and nuclear properties of the heaviest elements to produce new radioactive isotopes; received the 1997 National Medal of Science.
November 29, 1656	Edmund Halley	England	Computed the motion of comets, established the periodicity of their elliptical orbits, then predicted when one would return—it did, and this comet is known as Halley's comet; pioneered the field of geophysics.
November 29, 1803	Johann Doppler	Austria	Discovered that the frequency of a wave in motion is relative to the source or observer also in motion, which is known as the Doppler Effect and is used in meteorologic and radar systems.
December 9, 1906	Grace Murray Hopper	America	Rear admiral in the Navy; pioneer of computer technology; helped devise the first commercial electronic computer; invented COBOL (common business-oriented language) for computer programming.
December 14, 1546	Tycho Brahe	Denmark	Discovered and developed the laws of planetary motion; his observations helped disprove the notion of celestial spheres and helped prove Copernicus' heliocentric view of the solar system.
December 15, 1852	Antoine-Henri Becquerel	France	Worked with the Curies on radioactivity and shared with them the 1903 Nobel Prize in Physics; studied the infrared spectra and x-rays; represented the third generation of Becquerel physicists.

Reproduced from *Science Projects for Holidays throughout the Year*, published by McGraw-Hill.

29

Birthdays of Famous Scientists, cont'd.

Birthdate	Scientist	Birth Country	Interesting Facts
December 16, 1776	Johann Ritter	Poland	Discovered the ultraviolet end of the spectrum; created the first dry-cell battery and the first storage battery; experimented with the electrical stimulation of muscles and sensory organs.
December 17, 1778	Humphry Davy	England	Had a hand in discovering 10% of the elements of the periodic table, including chlorine, iodine, potassium, sodium, calcium, magnesium, and silicon; studied the effects of nitrous oxide (laughing gas).
December 20, 1890	Jaroslav Heyrovsky	Czechoslovakia	Created the polargraph used for the study of electrode processes; won the Nobel Prize in Chemistry in 1959.
December 24, 1818	James Joule	England	Developed the general law of energy conservation and the quantitative law of heat production; the joule, the international unit of electrical, mechanical, and thermal energy, was named for him.
December 25, 1642	Isaac Newton	England	Developed the law of universal gravitation; discovered that white light is made up of the colors of the spectrum; wrote the three laws of motion; built the first reflecting telescope.
December 26, 1791	Charles Babbage	England	His theoretical work on computers paved the way for modern computers; invented the cow catcher and speedometer, and determined postal rates for long-distance packages.
December 27, 1571	Johannes Kepler	Germany	Wrote the three laws of planetary motion; refined the heliocentric theory of the solar system; said the sun provided the driving force to keep the planets of our solar system in orbit; proved planets had elliptical orbits.
December 27, 1654	Jakob Bernoulli	Switzerland	Daniel Bernoulli's father and a mathematician, worked mostly with the theory and equations of gravity of uniformly moving bodies.
December 27, 1822	Louis Pasteur	France	Studied fermentation and bacteria; advanced the germ theory of infections; developed the process of pasteurization, in which food is heated to kill bacteria; developed the rabies vaccine.

Grandparent's Day

First Sunday after Labor Day
Culture: United States (similar holiday in Japan)

Created in 1978, Grandparent's Day is one of the United States' newest holidays. Michael Goldgar, a grandfather from Atlanta, Georgia, began the campaign for legislation to declare the first Sunday after Labor Day as a day for honoring grandparents. A resolution was signed by both houses of Congress and then-President Jimmy Carter to establish the annual holiday.

Although the manner in which Grandparent's Day is celebrated may differ, the holiday is set aside to honor and show love and appreciation for grandparents and elderly citizens. Special meals for grandparents are planned, and cards and gifts are given or sent, depending on the distance between families. Hallmark Cards, Inc. estimated that approximately 4 million greeting cards were sent to grandparents for Grandparent's Day in 1996.

In 1966, Japan established a national holiday called Respect-for-the-Aged Day, which honors elderly citizens. This day commemorates the building of the first Hidenin (home for the aged) by Prince Shotuku in the 7th century. Mayors visit the aged citizens in their towns, and gifts and congratulations are given. Elderly friends and relatives are taken on picnics, or special dinners are held in their honor. And although older citizens of many age groups are honored, the oldest are given special accolades. According to Ministry of Health and Welfare reports, there were more than 5,500 Japanese citizens over the age of 100 in September, 1994.

Although not every culture sets aside a day specifically to honor the elderly, many cultures respect and honor their aged throughout the year by giving them a special place in society and in the family, especially in traditional Asian cultures. In China, the elderly often live with their children and/or grandchildren and contribute substantially to the family, caring for young children, assisting with housework, or ensuring that traditions and legends are passed on to the next generations. The elderly are the "pillars" of the clan in Indochinese families and are given great respect. Their knowledge of cultural history and traditions links generations, helping to bring the family as a whole closer together.

Grandparent's Day
First Sunday after Labor Day
Culture: United States (similar holiday in Japan)

Even in today's "high-tech" world, in which access to information around the world is almost instantaneous, some cultures still rely on the spoken rather than written word to pass along traditions, values, and legends to the next generation. The elderly in these oral-tradition-based societies are especially revered because they are the keepers of cultural history and knowledge, the only link between the past and the present. Knowledge of herbal or plant medicines, legends about natural phenomena, and the history of the people and customs are just some of the many pieces of cultural information passed on orally from the old to the young. In some cultures, these stories are shared around a campfire at night or during long, cold winters. Elderly healers and shamans train their successors over several years, showing them the plants that can be used for healing as they appear throughout the seasons. In some tribes in the Central African Republic, older men pass on their knowledge to the younger men in a building called a "male house." The elders of the Penan tribe, who live on the island of Borneo, share the significance of natural signs as they happen each season, such as pointing out the specific butterflies that seem to herald the arrival of herds of wild boar in the area.

As technology continues to spread, oral history and knowledge are in jeopardy of being lost. As young people move to cities to attend school and find jobs, few are left behind to hear the stories of the elderly. Secrets of traditional remedies, tribal legends, and sacred customs are not being passed on, or they are being misinterpreted by the younger generations who are not as close to the culture as they have been in the past. Recognizing this problem, people in many cultures are working to prevent the loss of these cultural treasures.

References

"As America's grandparents change, Hallmark Grandparents Day cards keep pace," Hallmark Cards press release, August, 1995.

Gozdziak, E. "New Branches...Distant Roots: Older Refugees in the United States," *Aging;* 1989, (359), 2–7.

Japan Window; http://www.jwindow.net/search/CALENDAR/EVENTS/Event815352882.html; 1997.

Klugman, C.M. "The Honored Aged," *CWRU, The Magazine of Case Western Reserve University;* 1997, 9(2), 20–24.

Linden, E. "Lost Tribes, Lost Knowledge," *Time;* 1991, 138(12), 46–56.

Suminagashi Greeting Cards
for Grandparent's Day

To honor grandparents and senior citizens, people in the United States celebrate Grandparent's Day in

September on the first Sunday after Labor Day. Across the Pacific Ocean in Japan, September 15,

Respect-for-the-Aged Day, is set aside as a national holiday to honor the elderly. This activity uses a

traditional Japanese art form to create greeting cards for Grandparent's Day.

Key Science Topics

- hydrophobic and hydrophilic
- solutions

Time Required

Setup	10	minutes
Performance	45	minutes
Cleanup	10	minutes

A piece of suminagashi

Part 1: Building Bridges

Building Student Knowledge and Motivation

Set up a learning center where students can draw and display pictures of grandparents or other senior citizens who have greatly influenced their lives. Have students discuss feelings they have about grandparents. Discuss where grandparents are in the family tree. Have students interview their grandparents (if they are alive) or ask other family members about grandparents. Talk about the history of the holiday and how it is celebrated in different parts of the world. Invite grandparents or senior friends to the classroom to tell students about their lives or to share a talent. The greeting cards students make in the Science Activity can also be used as thank-you notes for visitors.

Bridging to the Science Activity

If an overhead projector is available, use it to do the demonstration in step 1. If one is not available, move directly to the student-conducted version described in step 2.

1. Fill a shallow, clear pan or petri dish about half full with water and place it on an overhead projector. Sprinkle a little ground pepper or cinnamon on top of the water and ask students to describe what they see. Dip one end of a cotton swab into some liquid soap and lower the soapy end into the water. Quickly remove it and ask the students to report what they observe. Try touching the soapy tip to other places in the water to create swirl patterns at various sites. Then gently place a piece of paper on the water and remove it. The paper will pick up the pepper or cinnamon in the pattern seen on the water.

2. Let the students repeat this experiment using small bowls or shallow pans and small pieces of paper. Tell students that artists have used this phenomenon for centuries to create works of art. This process is a variation of a traditional Japanese art form called suminagashi, which involves ground ink and water.

Tell students that Japan has a national holiday called Respect-for-the-Aged Day, when the elderly are given gifts by their families, community, and friends. Americans celebrate a similar holiday called Grandparent's Day. Tell students that they will be using suminagashi to create greeting cards to send to their grandparents or other loved ones.

Part 2: Science Activity

Materials

For Bridging to the Science Activity
Per class
- shallow pan such as a transparent, colorless pie pan or petri dish
- water
- ground pepper or cinnamon
- cotton swab
- liquid soap
- paper
- small bowls or shallow pans
- small pieces of paper
- newspaper or paper towels
- (optional) overhead projector

For Getting Ready
- cotton swabs
- art-quality drawing paper
- scissors

For the Procedure
Part A, per class
- (optional) overhead projector
- shallow pan such as a transparent, colorless pie pan
- water
- cotton swabs (prepared in Getting Ready)
- permanent-type India ink
- small amount of oil from forehead or nose, or vegetable oil
- stirring stick or toothpick
- art-quality drawing paper cut to a size that will fit in the shallow pan
- sink or tub to receive discarded water

Part B, per group
- all materials listed for Part A except the overhead projector
- additional paper for greeting cards
- 1 of the following
  - sewing needles and thread in various bright colors, in addition to black and white
  - needlepoint needles and raffia

For the Extension for Further Science Inquiry
Per class
- all materials listed for the Procedure
- assortment of papers, such as oaktag, construction, newsprint, and tissue
- assortment of fabric scraps
- variety of oils, such as olive, peanut, baby, and corn

Safety and Disposal

Spilled ink will cause permanent or difficult-to-remove stains on clothing; wearing aprons or smocks is advisable. No special disposal procedures are required.

Getting Ready

1. To prevent disappointment, test the activity in advance with your drawing paper and ink to make sure that the ink transfers with a minimum of smearing. If too much smearing occurs, try different paper.

2. Cut double-ended swabs in half with scissors.

3. Cut the paper to be used to fit inside the shallow pans. Be sure to cut sufficient sheets to allow groups to do their testing and individuals to produce their own suminagashi.

Procedure

Part A: The Basics of Suminagashi: A Teacher Demonstration

Demonstrate to the class how to carry out the procedure called suminagashi as described in steps 1–9. The demonstration is most effectively done using an overhead projector and a transparent, colorless pie pan. Be sure to ask students to report what they see and speculate on what causes the phenomenon to occur.

1. Pour enough water into the pie pan to cover the bottom.

India ink will stain clothing and skin.

2. Dip the tip of one of the cotton swab halves into the India ink. (Very little ink is needed—too much ink makes the pattern very difficult to observe.) To apply the ink to the water, use a quick "touch-remove" action, barely touching the inky swab tip to the center of the water's surface and immediately withdrawing the tip. Keep the inky swab to use again in step 5.

3. Discuss observations. (The ink will form a thin layer on the surface of the water.) For younger students, you can chart these observations; for older students, have them record their own.

4. Put a very small amount of oil on the tip of a second, clean cotton swab half. Do this either by lightly rubbing it on your forehead or nose, or by barely dipping it into a oil container. Touch the oily swab tip to the center of the spreading ink. Discuss and record observations.

5. Again, barely touch the inky swab tip to the center of the water and quickly remove; then touch the center of the ink with the oily swab tip.

6. Repeat step 5 several times. Record the observations.

7. VERY GENTLY swirl the surface with a stirring stick or toothpick to make a complex pattern of the ink. Record the observations.

Stirring too vigorously will spoil the effect.

8. Place a piece of art-quality drawing paper on the water, press down any corners that curl up, then lift the paper off the surface. Let the paper drip for a moment, and lay the resulting suminagashi artwork flat (ink side up) on newspaper or paper towels. Pass the suminagashi around the classroom for the students to observe. (If ink still appears on the surface of the water, you may try to collect it on another piece of paper. However, this second printing is typically very washed out and not as intense as the first. Generally, to prepare another design, you must begin again with fresh water, as the oil coats the water surface.)

9. Discard inky, oily water into a sink or tub.

10. Have students review and discuss their observations. Encourage them to formulate possible explanations of how suminagashi works and to prepare to defend and support their opinions with their recorded observations. Through a class discussion, lead students to an understanding of the scientific concepts behind suminagashi. (See the Science Explanation.)

Part B: The Suminagashi Experiments

1. Divide the class into groups and challenge the students to repeat the procedure you demonstrated in Part A.

2. Ask the students if it is possible to
   • add too much ink,
   • add not enough ink,
   • add too much oil,
   • add not enough oil,
   • add too much water, or
   • add not enough water.

3. After they have discussed this as a class, give each group a different question and have them design an experiment to answer that question. Tell them their overall task as a class is to make the sharpest pattern possible changing only their assigned variable. Tell students to decide exactly the procedure they will follow and record it in their science journals.

4. Allow the groups to test their procedures after you have reviewed them for safety, messiness, and general logic.

5. Have groups evaluate the results of their procedures and repeat them as necessary to determine a definitive answer to their assigned question.

6. Have the groups share results with the class as a whole and allow the class to decide on a method that produces the optimal result.

7. Allow students to apply what they have learned and make their own pieces of suminagashi artwork.

8. Once the artwork has dried, have students turn their best piece of suminagashi into a greeting card as follows: Write and edit the message the card will contain. Using another sheet of paper that is the same size as the

paper the suminagashi is on, fold both sheets in half and write the final, edited copy of the message on the blank sheet. Align the message sheet with the cover sheet (the message sheet on top) and attach them with a double length of sewing thread, passing through the folds of the two sheets twice so that the loose ends of the threads are on the front of the card where they can be tied in a bow. Raffia threaded on a needlepoint needle could also be used to secure the two parts of the card together.

Extension for Further Science Inquiry

Have students investigate the results of using different paper, fabrics, or oils to make suminagashi artwork.

Science Explanation

The following explanation is intended for the teacher's information. Modify the explanation for students as required.

The Science of Suminagashi

India ink (similar to the sumi, or black ink, used in Japanese art) is a special mixture of very, very fine particles of a black pigment suspended in water. The black pigment is either carbon black or lampblack, which are both chiefly forms of carbon. When a small amount of India ink is placed on the surface of the water, the finely divided particles of black pigment spread out, forming a very thin carbon layer on the water's surface. This is because of two important factors: 1) carbon and water do not mix under normal conditions, and 2) the very fine pieces of carbon float on top of the water because of water's high surface tension. Carbon black and lampblack are actually more dense than water. However, the surface tension of water makes it act like it has a tight plastic skin and allows it to support some materials that are more dense than it is, especially if these materials are fine particles.

Oil will similarly spread out over the surface of water. This spreading again is because of two important factors: 1) oil does not mix with water (oil and water are said to be immiscible, which means they don't mix), and 2) oil is less dense than water (thus the oil floats on top of the water).

The fact that mixing does not occur when either oil and water are combined or the carbon black/lampblack pigment and water are combined is because no attractive forces exist between oil and water or between carbon and water. In fact, both the black pigment and the oil are said to be hydrophobic ("hydro" meaning "water" and "phobic" meaning "fearing"). Hydrophobic substances are not attracted to and do not mix with water. Conversely, a substance that is attracted to water is hydrophilic ("philic" meaning "loving").

In this activity, the presence of both ink and oil prevents either material from completely spreading out. Thus, as drops of ink and oil are placed alternately on the water, they form a series of concentric circles. Gentle swirling of the water surface disturbs the symmetrical pattern of the circles but does not allow the separated oil and ink to join up. Thus, a swirled pattern results. The pattern can be transferred to paper because the black pigment is attracted to the paper. When the paper is laid on the water's surface, the ink adheres to the paper, maintaining its swirled pattern. Another familiar form of carbon, the graphite used in "lead" pencils, has a similar affinity for paper.

The History of Suminagashi

Suminagashi, meaning "spilled ink," is a process of floating ink patterns on the surface of water and transferring the patterns to paper. Sumi, or Chinese ink made from pine soot, is a traditional material but not necessarily the only ink used. Because one property of water is that it is always moving, no two suminagashi designs can ever be exactly alike.

No one knows exactly when the process of suminagashi was invented, but elegant specimens exist dating from the 12th century in Japan. Knowledge of the history of this art form comes mostly from surviving specimens, scattered notes, and legends. Records indicate that one family, the Hiroba family of Echizen, had almost exclusive rights to the secret of this art up until the 19th century. According to legend, an ancestor of the Hiroba family, Jiyemon, received the secret of suminagashi as a divine gift on February 1, 1151, as a reward for his faithful worship at Kasuga Shrine. He then moved from his home at Nara to Takefu, which contained abundant supplies of clear water suitable for making suminagashi. For more than 400 years, the family produced suminagashi exclusively for the Imperial household. During the years from 1680 to 1709, another family by the name of Uchida produced suminagashi acknowledged as equal to that produced by the Hiroba family, but during the Edo Era (1603–1867), the shogun passed laws to prevent suminagashi from being copied by others and supported the Hiroba family with a generous pension. In the last half of the 19th century, when the shogunate fell, suminagashi techniques were at last able to be copied by others. As a result, other styles were developed. After World War II, demand for quality artistic papers declined sharply. The art still survives, but the quality of today's work does not equal that of the past.

References for the Science Activity

Chambers, A. *Suminagashi;* Thames and Hudson: London, 1991; pp 6–16.

Sarquis, J.L.; Sarquis, M.; Williams, J.P. "Sumi Nagashi"; *Teaching Chemistry with TOYS: Activities for Grades K–9;* McGraw-Hill: New York, 1995; pp 189–194.

Shakhashiri, B.Z. *Chemical Demonstrations, A Handbook for Teachers of Chemistry,* University of Wisconsin, Madison, WI: 1989, Vol. 3; pp 301–304, 358–359.

Suzuki, C. Dept of Education, Shiga University, Hiratsu, Ohtsu, Shiga Japan. Abstract P3.35, 11th International Conference on Chemical Education: York, England, August 1991.

Part 3: Integrating with Language Arts

Featured Fiction Book: *Grandfather's Journey*

Author and Illustrator: Allen Say
Publisher: Houghton Mifflin ISBN: 0-395-57035-2
Summary: A Japanese-American man recounts his grandfather's journey to America, which he later also undertakes, and the feelings of being torn by a love for two different countries.

Show the cover of *Grandfather's Journey* and discuss the illustration. Ask, "What do you see? Where is this happening? If this is taking place on the ocean, let's consider ocean water for a moment—what kind of water do we find in the ocean? Is ocean water a mixture?" *Yes, because it is composed of water, salt, and other minerals. It has many properties like those of water but also properties from its other components.*

Tell the students that you are going to read a story about a man who is a blending or mixture of two cultural experiences. Ask them to listen to see if they can identify what the two cultures are and how this occurred.

After reading the story, ask: "Where did the story end? Where did it begin? What were the two cultures? What did the characters like about America? What did they like about Japan? Who is the person speaking in the story?" *The author.*

Writing Extensions

- Have students use their science journals to write a summary of the experiment they designed and the results they found.
- Have students write explanations of how they think suminagashi works.
- Reread *Grandfather's Journey* aloud to students and have them pay very careful attention to the words chosen by the author. Have each of them jot down favorite words or phrases from the story, then share the listed vocabulary with peers in cooperative groups. Each group can select four words or phrases which represent to them the best of all their individual offerings in the group. To create a "Found Poem" composed by the entire class, have a read-around from group to group, with each group reading aloud one word or phrase at a time without interruption until all groups have shared all their selections. If the class Found Poem is audiotaped, students can transcribe it onto a wall chart or poster for all students to reread and continue to enjoy at their leisure. Alternatively, students can make Found Poems individually or in pairs if they have access to copies of text, recording their poems on paper. Students can also put their chosen words and phrases on individual sentence strips and rearrange them over and over again until they capture the essence of the literature piece or until they express what the students want to communicate. Poems like these serve to focus readers on the power of the author's syntax and word choice. They also serve as great illustrations of the many different ways of interpreting text.

- Use a Venn Diagram to help students recall and organize the reasons the author and his family liked both America and Japan. Were there any reasons that fit both places? If so, where would they be placed in the diagram?
- Have each student use a Venn Diagram to explain about two places or two things they like equally. Have them use the middle section of the diagram to list any features the two places or things might have in common.
- Have students create a double-entry journal page labeled "What I Like Best about My Home State (or City)" and "What I Like Best about (another place of choice)." Have them list and illustrate the merits of each locale. Have them use these lists to create their own books about an imaginary journey to those two places. Students can also do a "creative imitation" of *Grandfather's Journey* by experiencing a careful rereading of the text, leading to an analysis of the ways in which the author tells his story, expresses his ideas, and chooses words. After identifying these patterns, students can pattern their own "journey books" in the same style as the author.
- Have students interview grandparents or elderly family members. Ask them to use a Venn diagram to illustrate how grandparent's schools compare to schools today.
- Introduce Japanese Haiku poetry, poems that are only 17 syllables long.

Additional Books

Fiction

Title: *Wilfrid Gordon McDonald Partridge*
Author: Mem Fox   Illustrator: Julie Vivas
Publisher: Kane/Miller   ISBN: 0-916291-26-X
Summary: A young boy helps elderly Miss Nancy find her memory.

Title: *Abuela*
Author: Arthur Dorros   Illustrator: Elisa Kleven
Publisher: Puffin   ISBN: 0-14-056225-7
Summary: Rosalba and her grandmother share an adventure of an imaginary flight across the Manhattan skyline.

Title: *Knots on a Counting Rope*
Authors: Bill Martin, Jr., & John Archambault   Illustrator: Ted Rand
Publisher: Henry Holt   ISBN: 0-8050-0571-4
Summary: A Native American grandfather retells his grandson's life story and after each retelling, he ties another knot in the boy's counting rope. When the rope is full of knots, the child will know his life history by heart.

Title: *Fathers, Mothers, Sisters, Brothers: A Collection of Family Poems*
Author: Mary Ann Hoberman   Illustrator: Marylin Hafner
Publisher: Little, Brown   ISBN: 0-316-36736-2
Summary: A collection of humorous and serious poems to celebrate every kind of family member, including mothers and fathers, aunts and uncles, stepbrothers, stepsisters, and cousins.

Title: *Our Granny*
Author: Margaret Wild
Illustrator: Julie Vivas
Publisher: Ticknor & Fields
ISBN: 0395670233
Summary: Two children compare their granny with others. Some grannies have thin legs, fat knees, crinkly eyes, or big soft laps. Their granny has a wobbly bottom and wears an old red sweater that was grandpa's. She has a style all her own—and to the children who love her, this granny is perfect. Full of warmth and good humor.

Title: *The Patchwork Quilt*
Author: Valerie Flournoy
Illustrator: Jerry Pinkney
Publisher: Dial
ISBN: 0-8037-0097-0
Summary: Using scraps cut from the family's old clothing, Tanya helps her grandmother make a beautiful quilt that tells the story of her family's life.

Title: *Treasure Nap*
Author: Juanita Havill
Illustrator: Elivia Savadier
Publisher: Houghton Mifflin
ISBN: 0-395-57817-5
Summary: On an afternoon when it is too hot to sleep, a young girl asks to hear the story of how her great-great-grandmother came to the United States from Mexico, bringing a special treasure.

Title: *When I Go Camping with Grandma*
Author: Marion Dane Bauer
Illustrator: Allen Garns
Publisher: BridgeWater
ISBN: 0-8167-3448-8
Summary: A child enjoys a camping trip with Grandma that includes hiking, canoeing, fishing, and cooking out.

Title: *Homeplace*
Author: Anne Shelby
Illustrator: Wendy Anderson Halperin
Publisher: Orchard
ISBN: 053106882X
Summary: As a grandmother and grandchild trace their family history, they learn the story of one house that for 200 years has grown and changed and gathered in one family. They also learn about the love, caring, and support that has been passed down from one generation to the next. Beautiful pencil and watercolor illustrations enhance this delightful book of family.

Part 4: Other Lesson Extensions

Art and Music

- Have students use larger pieces of paper and larger pans to create gift wrapping paper.
- Study a sample of washi (Japanese handmade paper) and try to imitate this handmade paper process. See the "Recycling Paper for Earth Day" activity for instructions for making handmade paper. To better imitate washi, add grass

clippings and scraps of construction paper to the blender before creating the pulp. Once the paper has been removed from the mold and deckle and laid out to dry, strategically place clover and other delicate wild plants on the pulp to add design elements similar to the ones found on Japanese papers. Traditional washi is translucent, but the paper made for the Earth Day activity will not be translucent. Try using shredded white tissue paper instead of newspaper or office paper to create translucent paper.

- Have students write Japanese or Chinese calligraphy numbers with black paint and watercolor brushes.
- Have students create origami items to decorate gifts.

Mathematics

- Have students brainstorm names that they call their grandparents. List names for grandmother and grandfather on two separate sheets. Create graphs from the two lists by having each student draw a heart next to the name he or she uses for each grandparent. The resulting graphs will show which grandparent names are the most popular among students.

Social Studies

- Find out how long a generation is and count the number of generations represented in *Grandfather's Journey*.
- Have students interview their parents, grandparents, and older relatives to explore their heritage. When did their ancestors come to America? From which countries did they come? On a piece of posterboard, students can organize the information in a chart or family tree. Hang the posters around the room and allow the students to look at them to learn more about each other.
- Read the book *Homeplace* (see Additional Books). Through this book, students learn that relatives who have lived before us are part of our past.

Part 5: National Science Education Standards

Science as Inquiry Standards:

Abilities Necessary to Do Scientific Inquiry

Students question how variables will affect the results of suminagashi.

Students design and conduct a simple investigation to study how changing certain conditions (such as the amount of oil used) will affect the results of suminagashi.

Students evaluate their results and those of other groups to determine how to produce the optimal result. Each group shares what it has learned with the class.

Physical Science Standards:

Properties of Objects and Materials
Objects are made from one or more materials and can be described by the properties of these materials. Using different paper will produce different results when making suminagashi.

Science and Technology Standards:

Abilities of Technological Design
Students propose ways to produce the sharpest suminagashi pattern.

Students implement their proposals by making one or more test suminagashi patterns.

Students evaluate their suminagashi and those of other groups and use their observations to modify their design for producing the sharpest suminagashi.

Students share their results and conclusions with the class.

History and Nature of Science Standards:

Science as a Human Endeavor
The art and science of suminagashi has been practiced in Japan for many centuries.

Autumn

Autumn, or fall, is a season of change and preparation. Students return to school after a summer of playing. Crops are harvested and stored for the long winter. In the middle and high latitudes, trees burst into color and then the leaves fall. The days grow shorter as winter approaches, and temperate regions prepare for the cold season ahead.

The oscillations and "wobbles" in the Earth's rotation about its axis and its revolution around the sun cause the exact start of autumn to vary each year. Astronomically, autumn begins when the sun reaches the intersection of the celestial equator (the projection of the Earth's equator in space) and the ecliptic (the plane the Earth travels in around the sun), midway between the summer and winter solstices. This event is called the autumnal equinox.

At the equinox, the periods of day and night are of the same length. From then on, the daylight hours grow progressively shorter until the winter solstice, when the day is the shortest it will be that year. As the hemisphere entering autumn begins tilting away from the sun, less sunlight is absorbed by this hemisphere, and the temperatures there become cooler. Autumn in the northern hemisphere begins on September 22 or 23 and ends on December 22 or 23 (the winter solstice). In the southern hemisphere, the seasons are reversed, and autumn is between March 20 or 21 and June 21 or 22.

Autumn is a very important season for agricultural societies. Everyone helps gather the harvest, as this food will feed them for the coming winter. The full moon nearest the autumnal equinox, the "harvest moon," appears above the horizon at sunset for a number of days each autumn, giving enough light to allow farmers to continue harvesting for a few more hours. Once the harvest has been gathered, the community celebrates with a large feast. The American holidays of Thanksgiving and Halloween were once harvest festivals (see "Give Thanks for Corn!" and "Spooky Spiders and Webs" in this book for more information). After the celebrations, people continue preserving food, transferring wine to casks, and preparing for the long winter ahead.

During the Industrial Revolution, a worldwide transition which began about 1750, the world economy shifted from one fueled by agriculture and handicrafts to one fueled largely by manufacturing and industry. Many people in more and more cultures abandoned agriculture as a livelihood, leaving this job to an ever-decreasing minority. As a result, these cultures no longer marked the turning of the seasons by the planting and harvesting of crops. Instead, they turned to other signals to alert them to the changing of the seasons.

One of nature's most visible signs that autumn is approaching in temperate climates is the changing colors of leaves on certain trees, called deciduous trees. As the hemisphere experiencing autumn begins to tilt away from the sun, the rays of the sun are less direct, and therefore leaves of deciduous trees produce less of the chlorophyll that gives them their green color. This decreased production of chlorophyll allows other pigments in the leaves to become visible, causing the leaves to change from green to red, yellow, or orange, depending upon the type of tree. Because the leaves can't produce the food they need due to the decreased amount and concentration of sunlight, they die and fall off the tree. The trees stay alive through the winter, though, because their trunks contain stored food that helps them survive until spring, when the leaves bud and grow again.

Not all trees undergo color change. Evergreen trees, such as pine trees, stay green all year. On an evergreen, a particular leaf or set of leaves may live from two to five years. The tree continually loses some leaves but maintains full foliage all year. On the other hand, the leaves of winter-deciduous trees, like oaks and maples, live for only one growing season and die in the autumn and early winter. Most deciduous trees drop their dead leaves, but some, such as the American beech and some oaks, retain their dead leaves until spring, when new leaves appear. Not all trees fit neatly into one category; for example, some hardwoods, such as the bayberry, retain green leaves through the winter and then drop them in the spring when new leaves appear.

References

"autumn" *Britannica Online.* http://www.eb.com:180/cgi-bin/g?DocF=micro/42/35.html (accessed 28 January 1998).

Elias, T.E. *The Complete Trees of North America: Field Guide and Natural History;* Van Nostrand Reinhold: New York, 1980, p 12.

Hatch, J.M. *The American Book of Days,* 3rd ed.; H.W. Wilson: New York, 1978.

Chromatography of Autumn Colors

In temperate North America, one of the most obvious signs of autumn is the dramatic change in the colors of many leaves. The colored pigments are always present in the leaves; the decline in the production of green chlorophyll simply enables the other colors to become visible. In this activity, students use chromatography to separate the colored pigments in leaves.

Key Science Topics

- capillary action
- chromatography
- solutions

Time Required

Setup   10 minutes
Performance   30 minutes
Cleanup   5 minutes

Leaf chromatography apparatus

Part 1: Building Bridges

Building Student Knowledge and Motivation

Create a center containing several symbols of autumn, including colorful leaves and gourds. Ask students to think about what relationship these symbols have to autumn. Encourage the students to add other symbols that they feel should be included in the collection. Alternatively, have a "Fall Show-and-Tell" in which students bring in items indicating the approach of fall to share with the class.

Have students press leaves in books or make leaf rubbings with crayons. Press a leaf by first placing it between two layers of paper towel and then carefully placing this "sandwich" between the pages of a hardcover book and closing the book. Allow the leaf to dry between the pages for about a week. Make a leaf rubbing by placing a sheet of paper over the leaf and gently rubbing a crayon on its side over the sheet. The pattern of the leaf should appear on the paper.

Have the students look at all the colors in the fall leaves. Ask what color leaves are in the summer. *Usually green.* Do they think the fall colors are there in the summer as well? Tell them they will be doing an investigation to find out.

Bridging to the Science Activity

Before working with leaves, introduce paper chromatography. Tell students that chromatography is a method scientists use to separate substances such as colored pigments.

1. Have students do paper chromatography using the following steps:

    a. Cut a rectangular strip of coffee-filter paper about 6 inches long and 1 inch wide. Use a pencil to draw a horizontal line about 1 inch above the bottom of the strips and write your name in pencil at the top of the strips (as shown in Figure 1). Use a black, water-soluble marker to trace along the pencil line.

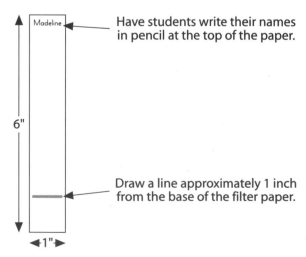

Figure 1: Have students set up their chromatography filter strips.

b. Hold the strip next to a tall, narrow cup or glass so that the bottom edge of the strip almost reaches the bottom of the cup. Push a pencil through the top of the coffee-filter strip exactly even with the rim of the cup. (See Figure 2.)

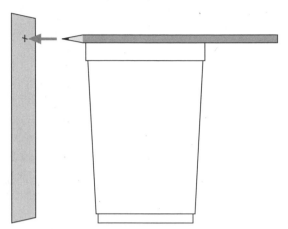

Figure 2: Push a pencil through the piece of filter paper. Make sure the bottom of the paper almost reaches the bottom of the cup.

c. Fold down the upper end of the coffee filter (above the pencil or pen) so that it lies as flat as possible. (See Figure 3.)

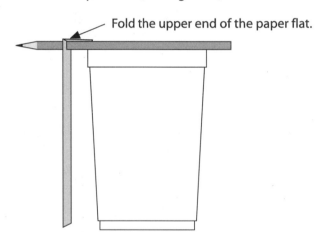

Fold the upper end of the paper flat.

Figure 3: Fold the coffee-filter strip so the upper end is as flat as possible over the top of the pencil.

d. Set the impaled strip in the cup so that the pencil rests across the rim, holding the strip in place. (See Figure 4.)

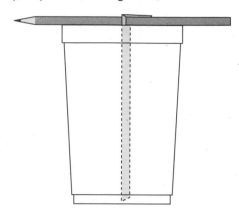

Figure 4: Set the impaled strip in the cup with the pencil resting across the top of the rim.

e. Pour about ½ inch of water into the cup. Predict what will happen when you put the paper in the water. Then carefully lower the paper into the cup, black line down, so that the marker line is ¼ to ½ inch above the water. If the marker line accidentally dips below the water level, discard the paper, rinse out the cup, and start over.

f. Observe the paper, the black line, and the water level. (As the water moves up the paper, the black line begins to separate, and the colors move up the paper.)

g. When the water has moved up the paper almost to the top, remove the strip from the cup and lay it on a paper towel to dry.

2. Ask students to describe the paper now. Ask students where they think the colors on the paper came from. Show students a few leaves. Ask them whether they think different colors could be separated from green leaves, and if so, what colors they would be.

Part 2: Science Activity

Materials

For Bridging to the Science Activity
Per group
- scissors
- ruler
- water
- black, water-soluble marker

Water-soluble Mr. Sketch® pens by Sanford® or Vis-a-Vis® overhead projector pens work well. Try markers in advance to be sure they provide the desired separation. Do not use water-soluble markers sold as "washable." They give poor results.

Per student
- coffee filter at least 6 inches in diameter
- pencil
- tall, narrow cup or glass

For the Procedure

Part A, per student or group
- coffee filter at least 6 inches in diameter
- scissors
- tall, narrow cup or glass
- pencil
- piece of aluminum foil large enough to cover the mouth of the cup or glass
- penny or nickel
- green leaf, preferably from a tree or bush that turns an attractive color in autumn, such as a maple, red oak, dogwood, or sweetgum

If possible, include leaves from a variety of species. Do this activity as early as possible in the season to ensure an ample supply of green leaves. Leaves that have already changed color or dried up will not yield good results.

Part B, per student or group
- coffee filter/cup setup prepared in the Procedure, Part A
- rubbing alcohol

For the Extension for Further Science Inquiry
- all materials listed for the Procedure, Parts A and B
- different types of plant materials

Safety and Disposal

Do not allow students to ingest the rubbing alcohol. Isopropyl alcohol is flammable and intended for external use only. Avoid contact with the eyes, since damage can result. If contact does occur, rinse eyes with water for 15 minutes and seek medical attention. Wash your hands after handling this liquid. No special disposal procedures are required.

Getting Ready

Before doing the activity with the class, do the Procedure yourself with each kind of leaf you plan to use to be sure they all yield the separation desired.

Procedure

Part A: Preparing the Filter Paper

Have students prepare the coffee filter as follows:

1. Cut a rectangular strip of coffee filter about 6 inches long and 1 inch wide.

2. Impale the filter-paper strip as in Bridging to the Science Activity, steps 1b–1d.

3. Lay a piece of foil over the mouth of the cup and gently press it down over the pencil to make a close-fitting lid. (See Figure 5.) Carefully remove the foil lid without disturbing its shape, take the impaled coffee-filter strip out of the cup, and remove the pencil from the strip.

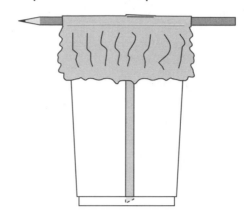

Figure 5: Make a "lid" from a piece of aluminum foil by gently pressing it down over the pencil and coffee-filter strip.

4. Use the pencil to draw a rectangular box about ½ inch up from the bottom of the rectangular strip. (See Figure 6.)

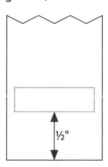

½"

Figure 6: Draw a box with a pencil about ½ inch above the end of the coffee-filter strip.

5. Transfer leaf pigment to the filter paper as shown in Figure 7. Lay a leaf across the coffee-filter strip, with the bottom edge of the leaf even with the bottom edge of the strip. Place the penny or nickel on its edge on the leaf at about the point where the pencil box was drawn. Pressing down firmly, roll the coin across the leaf. Lift the coin and repeat the rolling procedure several more times.

For very large leaves, such as sycamore leaves, you may want to cut the leaves into smaller pieces.

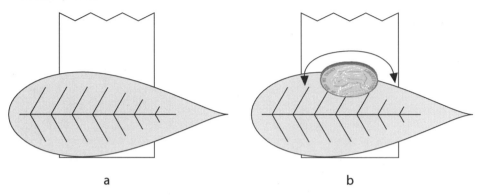

a   b

Figure 7: (a) Cover the rectangle with a leaf and then (b) roll the edge of a coin firmly over the leaf. Lift the coin and repeat at another location.

6. Move the leaf slightly so that a fresh patch of leaf is directly over the pencil line or box. Roll the coin a few more times over the leaf to deposit more leaf pigment. Pick up the leaf and look at the filter paper. A green bar should appear about ½ inch up from the bottom of the strip, at about the place where the pencil box was drawn. (See Figure 8.)

Figure 8: A green bar of leaf pigment should appear in the pencil box.

Part B: Doing the Chromatography

Have students perform the chromatography as follows:

1. Pour rubbing alcohol into the cup to a depth of about ⅛ to ¼ inch.

2. Push the pencil back through the strip. Carefully lower the impaled strip into the cup. The end of the strip should extend into the alcohol, but all of the green bar must be above the alcohol. (See Figure 9.)

It is essential that the green bar be above the level of the alcohol. Otherwise, the pigments will simply dissolve in the liquid rather than be carried up the paper as the alcohol rises by capillary action. If the green bar will dip into the alcohol, pour out some of the alcohol or crease the coffee-filter strip near the pencil to make sure the green bar does not come in direct contact with the alcohol.

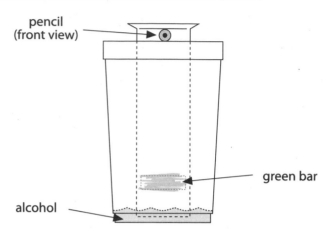

pencil
(front view)

green bar

alcohol

Figure 9: Lower the strip so that the end is in the alcohol. Make sure the green bar is above the level of the alcohol.

3. Have students carefully set the foil lid on top of the cup.

The lid is important because it traps the alcohol vapor and limits evaporation.

4. Observe the coffee-filter strip as the colors move up. The chromatography effect is apt to be easiest to detect in the first 5 minutes.

5. When the moving alcohol solvent rises to within 1½ inches of the top of the cup, remove the coffee-filter strip from the alcohol. Take out the pencil and lay the strip on a clean surface. Immediately use the pencil to mark the highest point reached by the colors, outline each region of color, and label each area of color with the name or initial of the color. (See Figure 10.)

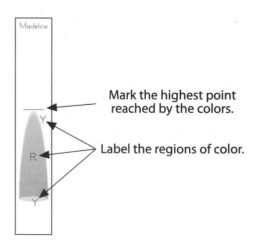

Madeline

Mark the highest point reached by the colors.

Label the regions of color.

Figure 10: Mark the chromatograms to show color separations.

Part C: Analyzing the Results

Have the class compare and discuss their chromatograms. Prepare a table of results for each type of leaf, listing the name of the species, the colors found in the chromatogram, and the order of the colors. Compare chromatograms for different species to determine similarities. For example, did all leaves produce yellow? Was yellow always the fastest-traveling color? Tell the students that the reds they see in the fall are also found in the green leaves but that the red pigments don't separate out as well in alcohol as the yellow pigments do.

Extension for Further Science Inquiry

Substitute different types of plant materials for the leaves used in the Procedure. For example, try dark-colored flowers such as chrysanthemums. Encourage students to bring in plant materials they would like to try. Have students predict what colors will be separated. After students perform the chromatography, have them compare the resulting pigment patterns with the patterns produced from leaves.

Science Explanation

The following explanation is intended for the teacher's information. Modify the explanation for students as required.

Chlorophyll is responsible for the green color in most leaves. The green color masks other pigments present in the leaves. These other pigments include carotenoids (orange-red), anthocyanins (purple-red), xanthophyll (yellow), and tannin (browns). The color change of leaves in autumn occurs because, as the hemisphere experiencing autumn begins to tilt away from the sun, the rays of the sun are less direct, and therefore leaves of deciduous trees produce less of the chlorophyll that gives them their green color. This decreased production of chlorophyll allows other pigments in the leaves to become visible, causing the leaves to change from green to red, yellow, or orange, depending upon the type of tree. While reds and purples are not easily observable with the solvent system used in this activity, the yellow can be separated from the chlorophyll.

The pigments in the leaves dissolve in the solvent and move up the paper. The rate of travel depends on two factors: the magnitude of the attraction between the pigments and the solvent and between the pigments and the paper. Because the attractions for each of the component substances are different, the pigments separate from one another as the solvent moves. Those substances with greatest attraction for the solvent move up the paper the farthest; those with greatest attraction for the paper move the least.

References for the Science Activity

VanCleave, J. *Biology for Every Kid;* John Wiley & Sons: New York, 1990.

Sarquis, J.L.; Sarquis, A.M.; Williams, J.P. "Chromatography Color Burst"; *Teaching Chemistry with TOYS: Activities for Grades K–9;* McGraw-Hill: New York, 1995; pp 195–200.

Part 3: Integrating with Language Arts

Featured Nonfiction Book: *Why Do Leaves Change Color?*

Author: Betsy Maestro

Publisher: HarperCollins

Illustrator: Loretta Krupinski

ISBN: 0-06-445126-7

Summary: Describes the various fall changes that occur to numerous types of leaves, using colorful illustrations. It uses simple text geared to the primary level and includes hands-on activities using leaves.

Before reading the book, have students brainstorm reasons why leaves change. After reading the book have students make a book about trees and the leaf changes that occur each season. They should write descriptions of their pictures.

Have students make a flip book containing the various color changes of leaves on a tree as the seasons progress.

Writing Extensions

- Before reading the book, have the students use this prompt to write: "When I saw the big pile of fall leaves, I…" Make a class book using their final work. Following this activity, read *Fresh Fall Leaves* (see Additional Books).
- Take a piece of construction paper and glue various types of leaves to create a human figure. Have students write a story called "The Fall Adventures of Leaf Man" or "The Fall Adventures of Leaf Woman."

Additional Books

Fiction

Title: *The Big Tree*

Author: Bruce Hiscock

Publisher: Macmillan

ISBN: 0-689-71803-9

Summary: Follows the development of a large old maple tree from its growth from a seed during the American Revolution to its maturity in the late twentieth century.

Title: *Fresh Fall Leaves*
Author: Betsy Franco   Illustrator: Shari Halpern
Publisher: Scholastic   ISBN: 0590273639
Summary: Tells of various things you can do with fall leaves.

Title: *Max and Maggie in Autumn*
Author: Janet Craig   Illustrator: Paul Meisel
Publisher: Troll   ISBN: 081673349X
Summary: Maggie goes to visit her friend Max to help him rake leaves. Together they notice various autumn signs. They have an enjoyable time raking leaves, but when they go in search of the "perfect pumpkin," their friendship is tested.

Title: *Red Leaf, Yellow Leaf*
Author: Lois Ehlert
Publisher: Harcourt Brace Jovanovich   ISBN: 0-15-266197-2
Summary: A child describes the growth of a maple tree from seed to sapling. This book contains colorful illustrations and an informative section regarding tree parts and care.

Title: *A Tree is Nice*
Author: Janice Mary Udry   Illustrator: Marc Simont
Publisher: Harper & Row   ISBN: 0-06-443147-9
Summary: This book tells, in a story style, various ways to appreciate trees.

Nonfiction

Title: *It Could Still Be a Leaf*
Author: Allan Fowler
Publisher: Children's Press   ISBN: 051646017X
Summary: Using photographs, this book describes various leaf concepts such as the color changes, season changes, and leaf types.

Title: *When Autumn Comes*
Author: Robert Maass
Publisher: Henry Holt   ISBN: 0805023496
Summary: Using photographs, this book describes colors and activities of the fall season.

Part 4: Other Lesson Extensions

Art and Music

- Have students make leaf rubbings or prints and study the patterns produced.
- Have students make collages of leaf rubbings or actual leaves.

Mathematics

- After removing the paper from the solvent, have the students use a pencil to mark how far the solvent has moved up the paper. When the paper is dry, they should measure how far the solvent traveled. Also have them measure how far each of the pigments has traveled (from the beginning line to the area with the most dense pigment). Then have them calculate the retardation (or retention) factor, called the R_f value, for each pigment.

$$R_f = \frac{distance\ traveled\ by\ pigment}{distance\ traveled\ by\ solvent}$$

  Students should compare their R_f values with the others in their class. Under the same conditions (same solvent, paper, temperature, etc.), the R_f should be the same for the same pigment. Do the students think some of their different leaves contain the same pigment(s)? Did having R_f values help in the comparison?

- Take your class on a leaf walk and have students collect various types of leaves that have already fallen. In the classroom, students should sort and classify their leaf collection by size, color, shape, and other categories. Students may use the various classifications to create simple math sentences, or they may make a class graph of the various categories. Students can also use measurement skills to record the area of numerous leaves via a simple grid.

Part 5: National Science Education Standards

Science as Inquiry Standards:

Abilities Necessary to Do Scientific Inquiry

Students question whether leaf colors can be separated by paper chromatography and what colors might separate out.

Students use their experience with ink chromatography to guide them in investigating leaf chromatography.

Students set up a paper chromatogram apparatus.

Students observe the separation of the leaf pigments on their chromatograms and compare their results with others. This information is used to develop an explanation of what colors are contained in leaves.

Students share their work with the class and participate in a discussion of results and explanations.

Physical Science Standards:

Properties of Objects and Materials

Ink and leaf pigments can be dissolved in appropriate solvents and separated by chromatography.

Science and Technology Standards:

Abilities of Technological Design

Students question whether other plant materials will separate as well as or better than the leaves.

Students perform chromatography on other plant materials and evaluate the results.

Columbus Day

Second Monday in October
Culture: United States

At 2:00 a.m. on October 12, 1492, a crewman aboard the *Pinta*, one of three ships led by Christopher Columbus on his quest to find a shorter route to the Orient and India, spotted an island after more than a month of sailing without seeing land. Columbus went ashore later that morning and was met by a tribe of aboriginal people. Believing he had indeed landed in the East Indies, islands off the coast of India, Columbus called the inhabitants "Indians." However, he actually landed on the island known as San Salvador, off the coast of Florida, and the inhabitants were part of the Arawak tribe. Columbus returned to the "New World" three times after the first visit, but he never found the gold, spices, and other riches he had expected to find in the Indies. Despite this, he died believing he had found a new route to the Orient.

Columbus' arrival in the "New World" is commemorated by countries all over the world. His native country, Italy, holds special religious services, festivals, and reenactments of the October 12 events every year. Spain, the country that funded and sponsored the original voyage, also holds festivals and services in honor of Columbus' discovery. The first observance of Columbus Day did not take place in the United States until 1792, the 300th anniversary of the original voyage. Few, if any, celebrations followed until 1892, the 400th anniversary, when President Benjamin Harrison issued a proclamation encouraging all citizens to participate in commemorative activities.

In the early 1900s, the Knights of Columbus, a Roman Catholic society for men, led a campaign urging legislators to declare October 12 a legal holiday. New York became the first state to do so in 1909, and soon more than 30 states were following New York's lead. President Lyndon Johnson in 1968 signed a law designating the second Monday in October as the official observance of Columbus Day. Today, cities, states, and countries around the world continue to commemorate Columbus' voyage with parades, ceremonies, and services.

Columbus Day

Second Monday in October
Culture: United States

Other countries around the world also celebrate their own days of discovery, founding, and establishment of settlements:

- Festivities on January 1 in Taiwan celebrate the establishment of the Republic of China by Chang Kai Shek in 1949.
- The first Monday in January is a holiday in Australia commemorating the establishment of the first British settlement in 1788.
- The Japanese honor their country's first emperor on February 11, the day he rose to power in 660 B.C. and unified the island as an empire.
- In Switzerland, the people celebrate the establishment of the Swiss Confederation on August 1, an event that occurred in 1291.
- August 2 on the islands of Trinidad and Tobago is a day to commemorate the landing of Christopher Columbus. He reached those islands in 1498, six years after his first voyage to the "New World."
- North Koreans celebrate the founding of their Democratic Republic in 1948 on September 9.

Columbus Day is not without controversy, especially in countries that are part of the "New World." Some groups of people object to the use of the term "discover" to describe an arrival in a land already occupied by long-established civilizations. Another cause for objection is the fact that Columbus and his men treated the indigenous peoples of the "New World" very harshly, taking slaves who were then subjected to horrible conditions, and demanding gold on pain of imprisonment, mutilation, and death. However, these facts are largely omitted from most retellings of the Columbus story.

References

Hatch, J.M. *The American Book of Days,* 3rd ed.; H.W. Wilson: New York, 1978; pp 918–920.

Spicer, D.G. *The Book of Festival Holidays;* Women's Press: New York, 1937; pp 18–19.

A Columbus Day Challenge

Christopher Columbus set out from Spain in 1492 to find a shorter route to India, the spice capital of the world at that time. Instead, he landed on an island off the coast of Florida in the Caribbean Sea. Boats have changed since Columbus' day, but the principles of buoyancy haven't, and students use these principles to test the load-carrying capacity of plastic-cup "boats."

Key Science Topics

- buoyancy
- density
- solutions

Time Required

Setup	10 minutes
Performance	30–45 minutes
Cleanup	10 minutes

A plastic "boat" floating in a salt-water solution

Part 1: Building Bridges

Building Student Knowledge and Motivation

Discuss the history of Columbus' trip to America and show the students pictures of Columbus' ships. Compare these ships to ones used today. Set up a center that includes pictures and models of boats of different shapes and sizes (ocean vessels, lake vessels, barges, yachts, speedboats, freighters, rowboats, canoes, aircraft carriers, etc.) and encourage students to bring in or draw pictures of their own. Construct and paint a big cardboard refrigerator box to represent the *Santa Maria*. Three or four students should be able to sit in this "boat" and read about Christopher Columbus. A sail can be fashioned from an old sheet or paper-roll paper and attached to a broomstick mast.

Bridging to the Science Activity

Set up a table with a variety of objects, some that sink in water and others that float, such as wooden blocks, plastic toys, fruits or vegetables, rocks, household items, and several toy boats. Near or above the display, place a sign that reads "Do these items sink or float?" Place a large tub full of water near the display to permit students to test their hypotheses. Allow students to examine the objects and determine whether they sink or float. When they have had a chance to form and test their hypotheses, lead a discussion about why the objects either sink or float in water.

Part 2: Science Activity

Materials

For Bridging to the Science Activity
- various small waterproof objects, some of which sink in water and some of which float
- large tub of water

For Getting Ready
Per class
- 2 cups table salt
- 2-L bottle
- water

For the Procedure
Part A, per group
- saturated salt-water solution prepared in Getting Ready
- 2, 6- to 8-ounce clear plastic cups
- masking tape and pen for labels

- water
- 3-ounce disposable plastic bathroom cup or other cup of similar size
- clear tape
- 20–30 pennies or other small masses
- paper towels

Part B, per group
- all materials listed for Part A
- additional 6- to 8-ounce clear plastic cup
- additional 3-ounce plastic bathroom cup

For the Extension for Further Science Inquiry
Per student or group
- all materials listed for the Procedure
- 1 or more of the following:
  ◦ paper or plastic plate
  ◦ clay
  ◦ aluminum foil

Safety and Disposal

No special safety or disposal procedures are required.

Getting Ready

Make a saturated salt solution by pouring 2 cups of table salt into a 2–L bottle and filling the bottle almost to the top with tap water. Put the cap on the bottle and shake the bottle vigorously for 10 minutes. Some solid should remain at the bottom of the bottle. Alternatively, add the salt, shake, and let the mixture set for about 24 hours, shaking occasionally. Let it set without shaking for the last 30 minutes so the liquid in the bottle clears and a solid remains in the bottle.

Procedure

Part A: Sailing a Boat in Fresh Water and Salt Water

1. Discuss with students the types and shapes of boats that they have seen or ridden on. Ask about what kind and weight the cargo might be. Discuss the two different kinds of water boats sail on (fresh and salt).

2. Divide the class into groups. Show them the salt-water solution you prepared in Getting Ready and explain what it is. Have each group label a 6- to 8-ounce cup "saturated salt-water solution" using masking tape and a pencil. Have the groups fill the labeled cup to within about 1 inch of the rim with saturated salt-water solution and then label and fill another cup to within about 1 inch of the rim with tap water.

3. Have each group cut out a copy of the centimeter scale (provided at the end of this lesson) and tape it to the outside of a 3-ounce disposable plastic cup, with the bottom of the scale aligned with the bottom of the cup. (See Figure 1.) The scale should be completely covered with clear tape to protect it from the water.

Figure 1: Tape the scale to the outside of the 3-ounce cup.
Be sure the bottom of the scale is aligned with the bottom of the cup.

4. Have each group carefully load about 20 pennies into the 3-ounce disposable plastic cup and set this "boat" in the cup of fresh water. Have the group observe the scale on the side of their boat and note the mark that is closest to the water level. (See Figure 2.) Have students add or remove pennies as necessary to make the closest mark on the scale line up with the water level as exactly as possible. Have them record this mark and the number of pennies in the boat.

If the boats do not ride level in the water, students should shift the cargo as necessary.

Figure 2: Observe the scale on the side of the boat, and note the mark that is closest to the water level.

5. Have each group remove its boat from the fresh water and dry it off, leaving the pennies in the boat.

6. Have each group set its boat in the cup of saturated salt-water solution and observe which mark is closest to the water level. Have them record this mark.

7. Have students add pennies as necessary until the mark they recorded in step 4 lines up with the water level. Have them record the number of pennies they added.

8. Have all of the groups report the marks at which their boats floated in both fresh and salt water. Discuss why the boats floated at different heights. Discuss how the results students observed can be applied in the real world.

Part B: The 50/50 Challenge

1. Ask the students to predict at what level the boat would float in a 50/50 mixture of tap water and saturated salt-water solution.

2. Using a spare 3-ounce plastic cup as a measure, have them pour 3 ounces of tap water into a clean cup, pour in an equal amount of saturated salt-water solution, and mix the resulting solution thoroughly.

3. Have each group dry off their boat and remove pennies as necessary until the number of pennies equals the number they recorded in Part A, step 4. Have them set the boat in the salt-water solution they just made and observe which mark is closest to the water level. Have them record this mark.

4. Discuss results. Did the boats float at a level halfway between the levels for fresh water and saturated salt-water solution? *The level probably is not exactly halfway between, because it is difficult to measure the salt and water exactly with the materials used in this activity, but the level should be close to halfway between the two original levels.*

Extension for Further Science Inquiry

Determine effective cargo-loading strategies. Ask, "Does it matter where or how the cargo is placed?" Have groups design and conduct experiments to find out. Have groups report their results once the experiments are complete.

Science Explanation

 The following explanation is intended for the teacher's information. Modify the explanation for students as required.

Objects either sink or float in a liquid because of their density relative to the density of the liquid. All things in the universe are made of tiny particles. The density of an object depends on two factors: the mass of the individual particles and how closely packed the particles are. The heavier the particles are and the more closely they are packed together, the more dense the object. An object that is more dense than the liquid sinks in that liquid. An object that is less dense than the liquid floats. When salt is dissolved in water, the solution becomes more dense; the more salt dissolved, the greater the density of the solution. Thus, an object that sinks in tap water might float in a salt-water solution.

A floating object displaces a volume of solution that has a mass equal to that of the object. This is an application of Archimedes' principle. Because salt water is more dense than tap water, a given mass of salt water will occupy less volume than the same mass of tap water. (In other words, a given volume of salt water will have a greater mass than the same volume of tap water.) Therefore, the volume of salt water that is equal in mass to the boat is less than the volume of tap water that is equal in mass to the boat; this is graphically represented by Figure 3. The boat needs to displace a smaller volume of salt water to float, so less of the boat is submerged in the salt water than in the tap water. Thus, as students observe in the activity, the boat floats higher in the salt-water solution and lower in the tap water.

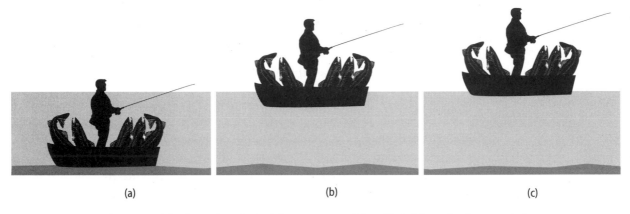

(a) (b) (c)

Figure 3: (a) A boat loaded with too many fish will sink in a freshwater lake.
(b) The same boat might float in ocean water, which is more dense.
(c) The boat would float even higher in the Great Salt Lake, which is even more dense than the ocean.

The lines on the boat in this activity are analogous to the "Plimsoll lines," or International Load Lines, found on all ships today. Plimsoll lines are determined by calculating freeboard, the distance from the waterline to the freeboard deck of a fully loaded ship, as measured amidships. (The freeboard deck is the deck below which all bulkheads are made watertight.) Safe amounts of freeboard vary with different conditions, such as the type of cargo, the waters to be navigated, and the season of the year. The outer hull of the ship is marked with a set of lines for tropical freshwater, fresh water, tropical zone, summer, winter, and winter North Atlantic. A ship bound for one of these waters must maintain at least the amount of freeboard indicated by the Plimsoll line—in other words, that particular line must not be underwater when the ship is fully loaded. The Plimsoll line was invented by Samuel Plimsoll in the 19th century as a way to prevent the overloading of ships, a practice responsible for many deaths among sailors due to shipwrecks.

References for the Science Activity

Evening Post Web Site. Best of Bristol. Samuel Plimsoll. http://www.epost.co.uk/standards/plimsoll.html (accessed 11 March 1998).

"freeboard" *Britannica Online.* http://www.eb.com:180/cgi-bin/g?DocF=micro/219/26.html (accessed 11 March 1998).

"Plimsoll line" *Britannica Online.* http://www.eb.com:180/cgi-bin/g?DocF=micro/471/77.html (accessed 11 March 1998).

Sarquis, J.L.; Sarquis, M.; Williams, J.P. "Pencil Hydrometers," *Teaching Chemistry with TOYS: Activities for Grades K–9;* McGraw-Hill: New York, 1995; pp 137–142.

Part 3: Integrating with Language Arts

Featured Fiction Book: *Encounter*

Author: Jane Yolen   Illustrator: David Shannon
Publisher: Voyager   ISBN: 0-15-201389-X
Summary: A Taino Indian boy on the island of San Salvador recounts the landing of Columbus and his men in 1492.

Featured Nonfiction Book: *In 1492*

Author: Jean Marzollo
Publisher: Scholastic   ISBN: 0-590-44414-X
Summary: Rhyming text describes Christopher Columbus' first voyage to the New World.

Read the Featured Fiction and Nonfiction books to the students. Discuss how the books are different in their points of view and the ways they portray the same events and people.

Writing Extensions

- Have students write to the animals in *Who Sank the Boat?* (see Additional Books) and explain to them why the boat sank and what they can do to prevent it from happening again.
- Have students make up a list of rules to follow when boating or canoeing.

Additional Books

Fiction

Title: *Paddle-to-the-Sea*
Author and Illustrator: Holling Clancy Holling
Publisher: Houghton Mifflin   ISBN: 0-395-29203-4
Summary: A small canoe carved by an Indian boy makes a journey from Lake Superior all the way to the Atlantic Ocean.

Title: *Who Sank the Boat?*
Author and Illustrator: Pamela Allen
Publisher: Coward-McCann   ISBN: 0-698-20576-6
Summary: A cow, donkey, sheep, pig, and mouse attempt to go for a boat ride, yet they all end up in the water instead. They try to solve the dilemma of who really sank the boat.

Nonfiction

Title: *Boats*
Author: Anne Rockwell
Publisher: E.P. Dutton   ISBN: 0-525-44219-7
Summary: Depicts boats and ships of varying sizes and uses.

Title: *A Book about Christopher Columbus*
Author: Ruth Belov Gross   Illustrator: Syd Hoff
Publisher: Scholastic   ISBN: 0-590-09891-8
Summary: Describes the life and voyage of Christopher Columbus.

Title: *A Picture Book of Christopher Columbus*
Author: David A. Adler   Illustrators: John & Alexandra Wallner
Publisher: Holiday House   ISBN: 0-440-84699-4
Summary: A brief account of the life and accomplishments of Christopher
      Columbus.

Part 4: Other Lesson Extensions

Art and Music

- Have students make a poster to go with one of the boating rules they
  developed as a Writing Extension.
- Have students work in groups to make up new verses to the tune of "Row,
  Row, Row Your Boat." Have each group sing its verse for the class.

Mathematics

- Have students compare the data they recorded during Parts A and B of the
  Procedure. How many pennies did they need to add to make the boats float
  at the fresh-water level in the salt-water solution and the 50/50 solution?
  Have students calculate the loads as percentages of each other.
- Present your students with the problem below, either after the lesson or on a
  bulletin board. Post some of their solutions and the original problem together
  on the board and allow them to see what their classmates have devised.
  - A father and his three children are on their way to the market. To get
    there, they must cross a river in a small boat that can hold only
    200 pounds. The father weighs 185 pounds. One child weighs 90 pounds,
    one weighs 75 pounds, and the third weighs 60 pounds. How can the
    entire family get across the river in the boat? *One possible solution: Two
    children (A and B) cross the river. A stays on the shore and B rows back.
    The father crosses alone. A takes the boat back and picks up C. After
    crossing the river, C returns alone to the other shore, picks up B, and the
    two children row to the other side to join the rest of the family.* What is
    the minimum number of trips the boat must make across the river to
    transport all four people? *It requires a minimum of seven trips.*

Social Studies

- Have students research different kinds of boats, who used them, when they were used, and why different types are suited for different uses. Alternatively, assign students to study different cultures and investigate their boats.
- Study the voyages of other famous explorers, such as Magellan, Balboa, and Hudson.
- Discuss the historical significance of Columbus' voyages. Ask students if they think the term "discovery" is an appropriate word to use for Columbus' arrival. Have students conduct research about Columbus' dealings with the indigenous peoples on his subsequent visits and compare their findings with descriptions in various children's books about Columbus. (See Additional Books.) You, the teacher, may want to read the following article about portrayals of Columbus in children's literature: Bigelow, W. "Once Upon a Genocide: Christopher Columbus in Children's Literature." *Language Arts,* Vol. 69, February, 1992, 112–120.
- Research the life and work of Samuel Plimsoll, inventor of Plimsoll lines, and the effect of his invention on conditions in the shipping industry.

Part 5: National Science Education Standards

Science as Inquiry Standards:

Abilities Necessary to Do Scientific Inquiry
Students question how boats float differently in fresh water versus salt water.

Students use "boats" with cargo to investigate how high they float in fresh water and in salt water.

Students read a scale to measure the level at which their boats float.

Students use their observations to construct an explanation of why the boats float at different heights.

Students discuss their observations and conclusions and how they can be applied to real-world situations.

Physical Science Standards:

Properties of Objects and Materials
Objects and substances, including the boat, fresh water, and salt water, have observable properties such as density and mass that can be measured.

Position and Motion of Objects
The position of the boat can be described by locating it relative to the water's surface.

Science and Technology Standards:

Abilities of Technological Design
Students question how best to load cargo into their boats.

Students propose how best to position the cargo.

Students test their proposals of where and how the cargo should be placed in their boats.

Students evaluate their cargo-packing techniques and those of other students and make modifications based on these evaluations.

Students report their results to the class.

History and Nature of Science Standards:

History of Science
Students learn about the effect of Samuel Plimsoll's invention on safety in the shipping industry.

Scale Template (in centimeters)

5.0	5.0	5.0	5.0	5.0
4.5	4.5	4.5	4.5	4.5
4.0	4.0	4.0	4.0	4.0
3.5	3.5	3.5	3.5	3.5
3.0	3.0	3.0	3.0	3.0
2.5	2.5	2.5	2.5	2.5
2.0	2.0	2.0	2.0	2.0
1.5	1.5	1.5	1.5	1.5
1.0	1.0	1.0	1.0	1.0
0.5	0.5	0.5	0.5	0.5

5.0	5.0	5.0	5.0	5.0
4.5	4.5	4.5	4.5	4.5
4.0	4.0	4.0	4.0	4.0
3.5	3.5	3.5	3.5	3.5
3.0	3.0	3.0	3.0	3.0
2.5	2.5	2.5	2.5	2.5
2.0	2.0	2.0	2.0	2.0
1.5	1.5	1.5	1.5	1.5
1.0	1.0	1.0	1.0	1.0
0.5	0.5	0.5	0.5	0.5

5.0	5.0	5.0	5.0	5.0
4.5	4.5	4.5	4.5	4.5
4.0	4.0	4.0	4.0	4.0
3.5	3.5	3.5	3.5	3.5
3.0	3.0	3.0	3.0	3.0
2.5	2.5	2.5	2.5	2.5
2.0	2.0	2.0	2.0	2.0
1.5	1.5	1.5	1.5	1.5
1.0	1.0	1.0	1.0	1.0
0.5	0.5	0.5	0.5	0.5

5.0	5.0	5.0	5.0	5.0
4.5	4.5	4.5	4.5	4.5
4.0	4.0	4.0	4.0	4.0
3.5	3.5	3.5	3.5	3.5
3.0	3.0	3.0	3.0	3.0
2.5	2.5	2.5	2.5	2.5
2.0	2.0	2.0	2.0	2.0
1.5	1.5	1.5	1.5	1.5
1.0	1.0	1.0	1.0	1.0
0.5	0.5	0.5	0.5	0.5

Reproduced from *Science Projects for Holidays throughout the Year*, published by McGraw-Hill.

73

Halloween

October 31
Culture: United States

The holiday we know as Halloween has its origins in an ancient Celtic festival called "Samhain" (pronounced "sow-in"), celebrated at the end of October. The Celts, a tribe of people who lived in Ireland, Great Britain, and parts of western Europe, were an agricultural people who depended on the land for their survival. Samhain marked the end of the growing season, and therefore the end of the year. After the harvest, the Celtic people held a festival to thank the sun and give it strength and support for its coming battle with the cold, dark winter.

The Celts also believed that all those who died during the previous year came back for a brief visit with their families on Samhain. These departed souls allegedly played tricks on the living, and the Celts appeased the dead by lighting fires and setting out food and drink. Groups of people walked from house to house seeking donations for a community feast. Good wishes were given to those who were generous, and tricks were played on the stingy. Because people were afraid to walk around out of doors while ghosts were abroad, they wore scary masks to fool the ghosts into thinking they were ghosts as well. The contemporary practice of "trick-or-treating" evolved from these customs.

The "jack-o'-lantern" was also a part of Samhain. A Celtic folk tale told of a man named "Stingy Jack" who made a deal with the devil. When Jack died, he was not allowed into heaven, but since the devil had promised not to take Jack's soul either, he was condemned to roam the dark, cold spirit world. To light Jack's way, the devil gave him a small piece of burning coal. Jack carved out a turnip and placed the coal inside, creating a lantern. The Celts made similar lanterns out of potatoes, turnips, and beets to light their way on Samhain. When the descendents of the Celts, the Irish and Scots, came to America, they discovered that pumpkins made excellent and easy-to-carve jack-o'-lanterns, and the tradition of pumpkin carving at Halloween was born.

As the Roman Empire and Christianity spread throughout Europe to Ireland and Great Britain, the festival of Samhain began to change. The Romans introduced apple bobbing, a custom of their own harvest festivals, and the Catholic Church moved its spring feasts that honored the dead, All Saints' and All Souls' Days, to November 1 and 2, hoping to remove the pagan connotations from Samhain. October 31, the day before All Saints' Day, was then called "All Hallow's Evening," "All Hallow's E'en," and eventually "Halloween."

Halloween came to the United States in the early 19th century with immigrants from Scotland and Ireland. By the late 1800s, Halloween was a national observance. The first city-wide, supervised Halloween party was held in the early 1920s in Anoka, Minnesota.

A number of other festivals similar to Halloween are celebrated by various cultures to honor and commemorate the dead:

- On April 5, the Chinese celebrate Ching Ming, a day to sweep tombs and honor the dead. Grave sites are cleaned and decorated with flowers and pictures.
- In parts of Germany, Walpurgis Eve, the spring counterpart of Samhain, is celebrated on April 30, six months after Samhain, and it marks the beginning of the growing season. As with Samhain, the spirit world is believed to be closer to the normal world on this day, and the dead are supposed to walk the Earth.
- The Day of the Dead, or Día de los Muertos, is a Mexican celebration honoring the dead. This holiday has origins in ancient Aztec rituals, but some observances today blend Aztec and Catholic traditions. Families create altars in their homes and place flowers, candles, loaves of special bread (pan de los muertos), food favored by the deceased, candy skulls, skeleton statues, toys, pottery, and pictures of the deceased on the altar. The souls of dead loved ones are believed to visit and absorb the essence of this offering, strengthening themselves for their journey to the realm of the dead.
- Buddhists celebrate the Bon Festival in mid-July to mid-August. Lanterns are lit, ancestors are remembered, and families gather together for feasts. The Buddhist calendar is based on phases of the moon, so the festival falls at different times in the Gregorian calendar (the calendar used in the United States) each year.
- The Autumn Equinox (September 23–24) is set aside in Japan as a day to remember and honor ancestors.

References

"Halloween" *Britannica Online.* <http://www.eb.com:180/cgi-bin/g?DocF=micro/255/99.html> (accessed 18 Dec 1997).

Harrowven, J. *Origins of Festivals and Feasts;* Kaye & Ward: London, 1980; pp 85–91.

Hatch, J.M. *The American Book of Days,* 3rd ed.; H.W. Wilson: New York, 1978; pp 968–971.

Ickis, M. *The Book of Festival Holidays;* Dodd, Mead: New York, 1964; p 125.

Kalman, B. *We Celebrate Halloween;* Crabtree: New York, 1985; pp 41–42.

Zia Holiday Pages. Halloween History. http://www.zia.com/holidays/halloween/history.htm (accessed Jan 1998).

Spooky Spiders and Webs

● ●

Spooky things are afoot on Halloween, and strange things can happen! In this activity, students make spooky rolling spider toys and race them on different surfaces to investigate forces and motion. Students also make glue "spiderwebs" for their spiders after testing different glues and "spinning" surfaces.

● ●

Key Science Topics

* friction
* motion
* physical properties

Time Required

Setup	10–20	minutes
Performance	15–20	minutes for Part A
	30–40	minutes for Part B
	30–40	minutes for Part C plus
		1–2 days for glue to dry
Cleanup	10	minutes

A Speedway Spider and a glue spiderweb

Part 1: Building Bridges

Building Student Knowledge and Motivation

Prior to the lesson, create a learning center containing different Halloween items. Be sure to include fake spiders and spiderwebs. Let students bring in Halloween items they may have to add to the collection. Tell the students when they visit the center to look for recurring symbols associated with Halloween. Let them add symbols of Halloween they think should be included but may be missing.

Bridging to the Science Activity

Read *Anansi the Spider,* by Gerald McDermott (Henry Holt, ISBN 0-8050-0311-8), to the class. This West African tale describes the troubles the spider folk hero has in the wild and how his six sons rescue him from danger. Discuss how spiders must move quickly to avoid being caught by a predator. Also discuss the fact that many spiders spin webs to catch food. Ask students where they think spider silk comes from and how spiders build webs. Tell the students that they will create spider toys that can move quickly, like real spiders. Then they will create webs for their spider toys.

Part 2: Science Activity

Materials

For Getting Ready only
Part A, per class
• (optional) spray paint

For the Procedure
Part A, per class
• tacky glue, another strong glue, or hot-melt glue gun and glue

Part A, per student
• zipper-type plastic bag, paper cup, or plastic cup
• 2 small wiggle-eyes (from a craft store)

Part A, Method 1, per student
• 1 of the following:
   ◦ cap from a plastic 2-L soft-drink bottle and either a ½-inch marble or a steel ball-bearing
   ◦ 1-inch marble and a film canister from a roll of 35-mm film
• 8, 3-inch pieces of black pipe cleaner

Part A, Method 2, per student
- hole punch (Students can share.)
- 2-tablespoon (30-mL) medicine or nut cup

  The wood bead must be able to fit into the cup.

- wood craft bead 34 mm in diameter
- 5 twist-ties about 6 inches long or 5, 6-inch lengths of plastic-coated wire twists for gardening (twist-tie-like material available in pre-cut lengths or reels at gardening stores)
- tape

Part B, per class
- different surfaces for the speedway, such as butcher paper, wood, sandpaper, linoleum, carpet
- rulers or centimeter tapes

Part C, per student or group
- sheets of the following materials
  - copier paper
  - piece of wax paper at least 6 inches x 6 inches
  - piece of plastic wrap at least 6 inches x 6 inches
  - piece of aluminum foil at least 6 inches x 6 inches
  - zipper-type plastic bag
  - disposable plastic dinner plate
- glue or glue gel

  Washable glue does not work well.

- (optional) other types of glue

For the Extensions for Further Science Inquiry
- all the materials listed for the Procedure
- extra ball bearings/beads
- extra canisters/cups
- different types of glue

Safety and Disposal

Spray painting and gluing with a hot-melt glue gun should be done only by an adult. No special disposal procedures are required.

Getting Ready

1. If desired, spray paint the bottle caps or the medicine or nut cups at least 24 hours before doing the activity.

2. Place the materials for each student in a zipper-type plastic bag or a paper cup.

3. If you are using hot-melt glue, you may wish to do some of the gluing described in Part A of the Procedure before class. You should not allow students to do their own gluing with a hot-melt glue gun.

Procedure

> *Parts A and B of the following procedure are independent of Part C; the two sets can be done in either order.*

Part A: Making the Speedway Spiders

> *Two different construction methods are described for your convenience. The basic investigation is the same for either construction method. You may wish to have the class make some of each and compare.*

> Have each student build a Speedway Spider according to Method 1 or 2:
> *Younger students may require help.*

Method 1

1. Glue wiggle-eyes to the top front of the bottle cap or canister as shown in Figure 1.

Figure 1: Glue wiggle-eyes to the top of the bottle cap or canister.

2. Glue four pieces of pipe cleaner to each side of the spider as in Figure 2. Legs should be glued flush with the opening of the bottle cap or canister and point straight up.

> *Depending on the type of glue being used, you may need to allow some time for the glue to dry before continuing with the activity.*

Figure 2: Glue four pieces of pipe cleaner to each side of the spider.

3. When the glue is completely dry, bend the pipe cleaner pieces over in the middle and at the ends to look like spider legs. (The legs should touch the table. See Figure 3.)

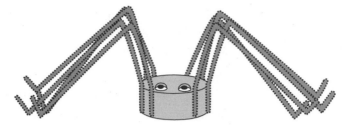

Figure 3: Bend the pipe cleaner legs in the middle and at the ends to make spider-like legs.

4. Place the marble or ball-bearing underneath the bottle cap or canister. (It does not need to be fastened to anything.) The spider is ready to roll!

Method 2

1. Use the hole punch to punch two holes directly opposite each other about ½ inch from the open end of the medicine or nut cup.

2. Tie one end of one twist-tie (called the axle) around the middles of two other twist-ties (to make legs). Push the other end of the axle through one hole in the cup, through the hole in the bead, and out the other hole in the cup. Tie the axle around the middles of the two other twist-ties. (See Figure 4a.)

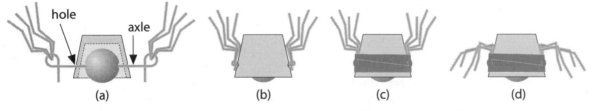

Figure 4: Assemble the Speedway Spider by Method 2.

3. Bend the legs away from the opening of the cup, hold them flat against the side of the cup, and tape around the cup and the legs where they exit the cup on each side. (See Figures 4b and 4c.) Bend the legs to look like spider legs. (See Figure 4d.)

4. Glue wiggle-eyes near the top of the cup.

5. Turn the now-assembled Speedway Spider so the bead is down. The spider is ready to roll!

Part B: Experimenting with Speedway Spiders

1. Ask students how they can make the spiders move. Try some of their suggestions.

2. Set a spider where students can see it and ask if it can move by itself. Point out that forces are always needed to make stationary objects move.

3. Ask students what factors affect how far the spider goes. *Possible answers include the type of surface and how hard you push the spider.*

4. Show students the various surfaces to be used, such as linoleum, paper, carpet, and wood. Ask students to predict how far the spiders will go on the different surfaces; for example, ask the students which would make the faster speedway: the carpet or the linoleum.

5. Have students test the accuracy of their predictions by rolling the Speedway Spiders over each surface. Have the students flick the spiders with their index fingers to give the spiders the initial push. (You may want to have them practice a few times to learn to give the same size push each time.) Mark the stopping places of the spiders with masking tape.
   Experiment with positioning the legs so that the spider does not tip over when pushed.

6. Have students measure the distances traveled by the spiders. We recommend the use of centimeter tapes or rulers.

7. Have students make a bar graph of the results. If possible, make the colors of the bars correspond to the colors of the surfaces.

8. Explain that the spiders slow down and eventually stop because of friction. Friction is caused by the spider's marble, ball-bearing, or bead and legs rubbing against the surface of the speedway. Rough surfaces like carpet produce more friction than smooth ones like linoleum.

9. (optional) Challenge students to find other surfaces on which their spiders could run more quickly or more slowly.

Part C: Glue Spiderwebs

1. Discuss the fact that many spiders make webs to catch prey. Ask if any students have ever watched a spider spin a web. Explain that spider silk is a liquid produced by glands in the spider's abdomen. Abdominal pressure forces the silk liquid though structures called spinnerets, which open to the outside through spigots. The silk becomes solid just before it emerges from the spider's body. Tell students that they will make their own "spiderwebs" from glue using a similar process.

2. Remind students that spiders spin their webs in the air but that this is not possible for students to do with glue because glue does not dry quickly enough. Therefore, they will need to "spin" their webs on a flat surface. Tell students, "Glue is sticky; to make a web, we must find a substance that will allow us to peel off the glue easily."

3. Give each group a sheet of copier paper, a piece of wax paper, a piece of plastic wrap, a piece of aluminum foil, a plastic bag, and a disposable plastic dinner plate. In terms of ease of peeling the web off the surface, ask the students to predict which material will make the best surface for their spiderwebs.

4. Have students test each surface by drawing a single line of glue a few inches long. After the glue dries (which may take several hours), have the students carefully peel off the glue. Ask, "Which surface allowed the glue to be peeled off most easily?" and "On which surface did the glue dry most quickly?" Also, the appearance of the glue lines may vary. On some surfaces, the glue line may separate into beads or spread out considerably. Have students consider the effect these properties may have on the finished web and propose possible explanations for why the glue behaved differently on different surfaces.

5. Have students make a spiderweb on the surface they determine to be best as follows:

   a. Squeeze glue onto the surface in the shape of a spiderweb (spiral with lines coming out from the center, as in Figure 5.) Make sure that each line intersects with at least one other line.

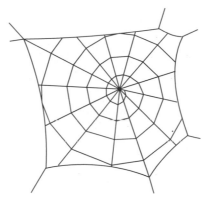

Figure 5: Squeeze glue in the shape of a spiderweb.

   b. Allow the glue to dry overnight. Record the appearance of the web on the material.

   c. Carefully peel the spiderweb off the surface, trying not to break the strands of the web. Record the ease with which the web peels off the surface.

   Some kinds of glue may need more than 24 hours to dry. If the web does not peel off easily, wait a few more hours and try again.

Extensions for Further Science Inquiry

- Use butcher paper for a speedway. Mark the paper with circles, lines, etc. Have students test their skills in aiming for these targets. Discuss the tactics they used in their attempts to get their spiders to stop at targets. For example, did students push harder (increase the force) to make the spiders reach targets far away but push less hard (decrease the force) to make the spiders stop at closer targets? Discuss how inertia and friction affect the spiders' movements.
- Have Speedway Spider races. Discuss how the push influences the distance the spider travels. (The greater the force, the greater the distance the spider travels.) Also, discuss how the amount of friction between the spider and the

surface of the speedway affects the distance traveled. (The greater the friction, the smaller the distance traveled by the spider.)

- Make a double Speedway Spider by gluing two bottle caps, one behind the other, and using two ball-bearings or marbles underneath the caps. (See Figure 6.) Race the one-cap spiders against the two-cap spiders. Observe and explain the results of the races.

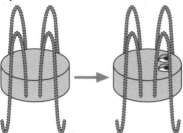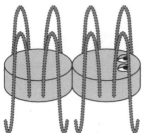

Figure 6: Make a double Speedway Spider.

- Use other types of glue, such as wood glue and special craft glues, to make spiderwebs.

Science Explanation

The following explanation is intended for the teacher's information. Modify the explanation for students as required.

Speedway Spiders

An object at rest tends to stay at rest; a force (a push or a pull) is needed to cause an object at rest to move. An object in motion has inertia of motion—with no other outside forces, it will remain in motion until friction between the object and outside surfaces slows down the motion and the object eventually stops.

In Part B of this activity, the students give the spiders a push to start them moving. Rolling friction between the marble/ball-bearing/bead and the speedway, and sliding friction between the legs and the speedway cause the spider to slow down and stop.

Glue Spiderwebs

In Part C, students discover that some glues and surfaces produce better glue spiderwebs than others. Differences in qualities such as peeling ability and web appearance are caused by differences in the properties of the glues and surfaces used. The chemical compositions of the glues and surfaces determine their affinity for each other. In this activity, the high affinity of all of the glues for paper makes it impossible to pull webs off the paper intact. The lower affinity of the glues for plastic makes it easier (to varying degrees) to pull the webs off plastic surfaces. The properties of the glues and surfaces also determine how well the glue lines hold their shape when squeezed onto the surfaces.

Reference for the Science Activity

"Arachnids: MAJOR ARACHNID ORDERS: Spiders: Form and Function: Specialized Features.:Silk." *Britannica Online.* http://www.eb.com:180/cgi-bin/g?DocF=macro/5000/25/63.html (accessed 9 March 1998).

Part 3: Integrating with Language Arts

Featured Fiction Book: *How Spider Saved Halloween*

Author: Robert Kraus
Publisher: Scholastic   ISBN: 0590421174
Summary: Halloween is almost spoiled by two pumpkin-smashing bullies until Spider, dressed as a walking, talking pumpkin, scares them away.

Writing Extensions

- Read the poem "Do Spiders Stick to Their Own Webs?" from *Where Fish Go in Winter and Answers to Other Great Mysteries* by Amy Goldman Koss (Price Stern Sloan, ISBN 0843122188) for fun and information. Have students create their own Halloween poems.
- Set up a learning center containing nonfiction books about spiders. Have each student look up an interesting spider and draw it on an index card. Students should also record their spiders' names and at least one fact about the spiders on the cards. Display the reports on a bulletin board.
- For younger students, read the nursery rhyme "Little Miss Muffett." (This rhyme can be found in Mother Goose books or other collections of nursery rhymes.) Ask students whether they are afraid of spiders or know people who are. Have them write about their feelings about spiders and why some people are afraid of spiders.
- After reading *The Itsy Bitsy Spider* (see Additional Books), have students add their own verse using the same pattern and beat as the book.
- Have students develop pre-writing "webs" relating to spiders, Halloween, or a subject of their choice. Use these webs to develop stories or essays.

Additional Books

Fiction

Title: *Anansi the Spider*
Author and Illustrator: Gerald McDermott
Publisher: Henry Holt   ISBN: 0-8050-0311-8
Summary: In this traditional Ashanti tale, Anansi the spider folk hero is saved from terrible fates by his six sons. But which of his sons should he reward? Anansi's predicament is resolved in a touching and highly resourceful fashion.

Title: *Creepy Crawly Critters*
Author: Nola Buck   Illustrator: Sue Truesdell
Publisher: HarperCollins   ISBN: 0064442225
Summary: Itchy witches, glowing goblins, and sly spiders are some of the
   characters in this hilarious collection of tongue twisters for beginning readers.

Title: *Dream Weaver*
Author: Jonathan London   Illustrator: Rocco Baviera
Publisher: Harcourt Brace   ISBN: 0152009442
Summary: While walking on a mountain path, a young boy discovers a yellow
   spider spinning her web, and as he quietly watches her he sees the world
   from a different perspective.

Title: *The Ghost-Eye Tree*
Authors: Bill Martin, Jr. & John Archambault Illustrator: Ted Rand
Publisher: Scholastic   ISBN: 0-590-43324-5
Summary: A young boy and his older sister walk from home to the end of town
   on a dark and scary night to get a bucket of milk for their mother. Their
   exciting trip is described through their conversation.

Title: *The Hallo-Wiener*
Author and Illustrator: Dav Pilkey
Publisher: Scholastic   ISBN: 0-590-41729-0
Summary: Oscar is a little dog with a big problem—the other dogs tease him all
   the time. Now it's up to Oscar to prove that a little wiener can be a real
   winner.

Title: *The Itsy Bitsy Spider*
Author and Illustrator: Iza Trapani
Publisher: Whispering Coyote   ISBN: 1-879085-77-1
Summary: The itsy bitsy spider encounters a fan, a mouse, a cat, and a rocking
   chair as she makes her way to the top of a tree to spin her web.

Title: *The Roly-Poly Spider*
Author: Jill Sardegna   Illustrator: Tedd Arnold
Publisher: Scholastic   ISBN: 0590471198
Summary: After eating a beetle, a caterpillar, a bumblebee, and other insects, a
   plump spider gets temporarily stuck in a waterspout.

Nonfiction

Title: *Extremely Weird Spiders*
Author: Sarah Lovett
Publisher: John Muir   ISBN: 1-56261-007-4
Summary: Text and photos introduce unusual spiders.

Title: *Read About Spiders*
Author: Dean Morris
Publisher: Raintree   ISBN: 0-8393-0004-2
Summary: An introduction to various species of spiders, their physical
    characteristics, and their behavior patterns.

Part 4: Other Lesson Extensions

Mathematics

- Study animals with different numbers of legs (two, four, six, eight, or none). If appropriate, discuss prefixes (bi- and quad-) that are sometimes used to describe the number of legs an animal has. Discuss centipedes and millipedes. Do they really have 100 or 1,000 legs as their names suggest? If possible, find photographs of these two animals and have students count their legs. Since the numbers are not likely to match the names, ask students how they think the animals got their names. Does having more legs necessarily make an animal a faster runner?

Social Studies

- Read aloud or have students read *Anansi the Spider* (see Additional Books). Anansi is a famous trickster. Have students find stories about Anansi and research trickster stories from other cultures. Make a chart of characteristics of tricksters and trickster stories.

Just for Fun

- "Cook up" a batch of Swamp-water Punch for the students using the following ingredients:
    - 2 large cans of concentrated orange juice
    - 2 L (about 2 quarts) white grape juice
    - 10 drops green food coloring
    - washed, assorted plastic spiders or flies in plastic ice cubes, rubber snakes, or other scary plastic crawlies
    - 2, 2-L bottles of carbonated lemon-lime soda pop
    - punch bowl and ladle
    - water

This recipe makes enough punch for a large class (30–35 students), at about 6 ounces per student. Adjust as needed for larger or smaller groups. Prepare the punch as follows:

1. Put everything except the plastic crawlies and soda into a large punch bowl and stir.
2. Dump two trays full of ice cubes into the bowl.

3. Float the washed plastic crawlies on top of the punch.
   Make sure none of the plastic crawlies are ladled into the drinking cups—students could choke on them.
4. When it is time to serve the punch, pour the soda into the bowl. The concoction will start to fizz and bubble, bouncing the flies, spiders, and snakes in and out of the ghastly brew!

Part 5: National Science Education Standards

Science as Inquiry Standards:

Abilities Necessary to Do Scientific Inquiry
Students question which surface makes the best speedway for the spider.

Students conduct tests to see how far the spiders will roll on each surface.

Students mark and measure the distances traveled by the spiders on the various surfaces.

Students use their measurements to determine which surface makes the best speedway and use their observations to propose an explanation.

Students make bar graphs to present their results and discuss their explanations as a class.

Physical Science Standards:

Properties of Objects and Materials
Materials, such as the surfaces used in the investigation, have many observable properties. In this case, the texture determines how good the surface is as a speedway or a spiderweb surface.

Position and Motion of Objects
The distance the spider travels is described by its final position relative to its initial position.

The position and motion of the spiders are changed by pushing them. To compare the effect of the surfaces, the strength of the initial push must be constant.

Motions and Forces
The motion of the spiders is affected by the friction between the spiders and the surfaces over which they move.

Science and Technology Standards:

Abilities of Technological Design

Students question how to make the best glue spiderweb.

Students recognize that for the web-spinning surface to be useful, the glue web must be able to be peeled easily off the surface on which it is made, and they test various surfaces to determine which one is best.

Students test a variety of surfaces to find which one the web peels off most easily.

Students consider how well the glue peels off each surface and use the best surface in their web construction.

Students share their results and conclusions and discuss why the glue behaves differently on different surfaces.

Thanksgiving

Fourth Thursday in November
Culture: United States

In a cave in Mexico's Tehuacan Valley, archaeologists discovered remains of the world's oldest known ear of corn, dating back to 5,000 B.C. Native Americans since then were instrumental in cultivating the many varieties and developing the uses of corn that we know today. Corn is unique among cereals in its dependence on humans for survival as a species. While corn's wild relatives have seeds encased in hard shells that protect them in the ground during winter, the seeds of today's corn lack this protection from rot and must be removed from the cob and protected until spring.

Corn fueled Mayan, Aztec, and Native American cultures for thousands of years, holding both nutritional and symbolic value. A Hopi Indian legend states that Yaapa, the Mockingbird, placed different types of corn before the Indian tribes. The Navajo took yellow, the Sioux white, the Havasupai red, the Ute flint, and the Apache the longest ears. The Hopi took the smallest ear that remained, blue corn, symbolizing that they would have a long but hard life. Blue corn is an important part of many Hopi ceremonies.

When Columbus arrived in the New World in 1492, he was presented with a gift of corn by the natives who greeted him. He hardly took notice of the cobs because he was more concerned with finding gold and riches, but he took the gift back to Europe with him. Within 100 years, cultivation of corn was sweeping the continent and moving into Asia.

Without corn, what we have come to call the first Thanksgiving would never have happened. The Pilgrims' first winter in America was a harsh one, and about half of the 101 passengers of the *Mayflower* died. In the spring of 1621, the survivors began building wooden houses and planting crops. Squanto, a Pawtuxet Indian, introduced corn to the Pilgrims and taught them how to plant and cultivate it. The October harvest was bountiful, and the Pilgrims gathered to give thanks. They invited the Indians who had helped them, and it was a joyous celebration.

They did not repeat the feast the next year, however. Since ancient times, people would have a day of "thanksgiving" for a variety of reasons, such as a bountiful harvest, survival of a harsh season, or a victory in battle. These were always one-time celebrations to commemorate a single event. The Romans were known for grand harvest festivals during which they would give thanks to their gods for the harvest. They carried this tradition with them to Europe as their empire spread. The Pilgrims, who came from the formerly Roman-controlled Britain, adopted the tradition and brought it to America. Native American tribes also celebrated the harvest by holding a powwow once the crops were gathered and stored for the winter. The "first Thanksgiving" was a combination of these two traditions.

In 1671, the people of Charlestown, Massachusetts, commemorated the "first Thanksgiving" on June 29 with a great feast. However, it was not until 1863 that the modern holiday of Thanksgiving was established. President Abraham Lincoln set aside the fourth Thursday in November of that year as a national holiday to commemorate the Thanksgiving of 1621 and to pray for a speedy end to the Civil War. U.S. citizens have observed this date annually ever since.

Other cultures around the world celebrate days of thanksgiving as well. Although these mostly celebrate harvests, some are to honor military victories or to commemorate other important cultural events.

- Koreans celebrate Chusongnal (meaning "autumn night") as their day of thanksgiving in September. This feast marks the very end of the rice harvest season and is the last day of Chusok, their harvest festival.
- In Canada, the second Monday in October is set aside for Thanksgiving, a day to celebrate the harvest and give thanks.
- Citizens of St. Vincent and the Grenadines, islands in the Caribbean Sea near Jamaica, celebrate Thanksgiving on October 27. This harvest holiday also commemorates the islands' independence from Britain.

References

Gaer, J. *Holidays Around the World;* Little, Brown: Boston, 1953; pp 159–160.

Hatch, J.M. *The American Book of Days,* 3rd ed.; H.W. Wilson: New York, 1978; pp 1053–1056.

Archiving Early America Web Site. Thanksgiving. http://earlyamerica.com/earlyamerica/firsts/thanksgiving/index.html (accessed 9 Feb 1998).

Raloff, J. "Corn's Slow Path to Stardom," *Science News.* 1993, *143*, 248–250.

Rhoades, R.E. "Corn, the Golden Grain," *National Geographic.* 1993, *183*(6), 98–117.

Give Thanks for Corn!

· ·

Corn was an important crop in America long before movie theaters were invented. Native Americans had been cultivating corn since at least 5,000 B.C., and they shared their knowledge with the Pilgrims. Thanks to the Indians, we know a variety of ways to prepare corn, including the most "pop"ular way: popping it. In this activity, students will learn what makes popcorn pop.

· ·

Key Science Topics

- chemical changes
- gases
- phase changes
- physical properties
- pressure-volume relationships in gases

Time Required

Setup	20–30	minutes
Performance	50–60	minutes
Cleanup	10–15	minutes

Popcorn

Part 1: Building Bridges

Building Student Knowledge and Motivation

Set up a "Corn Center." Display some, but not all, of the following items: a large jar filled with corn kernels, cornmeal, grits, hominy, cornstarch, Fritos, tortilla chips and salsa, blue corn chips, corn oil, fresh corn-on-the-cob, dried corn husks for making tamales, cans of creamed and kernel corn, decorative corn in various hues, corn cereals, and a bag or microwave container of popcorn. Encourage students to bring in more corn items from home to add to the display; these could include recipes as well. You may want to number the items in the display to make it easier to refer to them in journals and discussion. Have students observe, identify, and describe the items in their science journals. Also have them speculate about the use of each product.

 Decorative corn can usually be found in the produce section of the grocery store with gourds. This type of corn, which comes in all shades of yellow, orange, brown, and blue, is a visible reminder of the biological diversity in this plant family that the Indians shared with the immigrant Europeans.

Have students share the information in their journals. Challenge the students to name other products made from corn and other uses for corn.

Bridging to the Science Activity

After the students have discussed the products made from and uses for corn, ask, "Do you know what a corn plant looks like?" Share with students some of the history of corn and its importance to Native Americans and to the Pilgrims who arrived in the United States in the 1600s.

Refer to the jar full of corn kernels and say, "There are a lot of uses for these little kernels, including making popcorn. Have you ever wondered what makes them turn into popcorn? Would you like to find out?" Tell the students that they will be examining unpopped and popped kernels to try to solve this mystery.

Part 2: Science Activity

Materials

For the Procedure
Part A, per class
- ¼ cup popcorn
- hot-air popcorn popper (An oil popper can be substituted.)
- large measuring cup
- large bowl

 Be sure the bowl is large enough to hold the popped popcorn. If you do not have a bowl that is big enough, you will need extra bowls.

Science Projects for Holidays throughout the Year

Part B, per class
- pan
- water
- hot plate
- glass soda or vinegar bottle
- balloon
- (optional) oven mitt

Part C, per class
- ¼ cup popcorn
- zipper-type plastic bag
- hammer
- popcorn popper
- large measuring cup
- large bowl

Part D, per class
- all materials listed for Part B
- scissors

Part E, per group

- 20 kernels of popcorn
  Several different brands can be tested; use 20 kernels of each brand.
- 25-mL graduated cylinder
- piece of aluminum foil approximately 12 cm x 12 cm square
- 250-mL beaker
- balance
- 2–3 tablespoons of cooking oil
- sharpened pencil
- hot plate
- oven mitt
- large graduated cylinder or metric measuring cup

For the Extensions for Further Science Inquiry
❶ Per class (or group)
- ¼ cup popcorn
- water
- paper towels
- popcorn popper
- large bowl
- large measuring cup

❷ Per class
- ¼ cup popcorn
- cookie sheet or other oven-proof tray
- access to an oven

Safety and Disposal

Follow the standard safety precautions for working with hot plates and hot materials. An oven mitt is recommended for handling the pan and heated bottle in Part B. Be sure students stand back from the popper, because kernels are hot when thrown from a hot-air popcorn popper.

Getting Ready

You may want to pop some corn in advance for eating at the conclusion of the activity. This would be especially appropriate if you plan to do the first Mathematics Extension. (See Part 4, Other Lesson Extensions.)

Procedure

Part A: Comparing the Volumes of Popped Kernels

1. Measure ¼ cup fresh (not soaked or dried) corn kernels and pop them.

2. Measure the volume of the popped corn.

3. Discuss with the class how the volume of the popped corn compares to the starting volume of the unpopped corn. Have the students suggest possible factors that could account for the popping phenomenon.

Part B: The Popcorn Model—A Demonstration

Do the following demonstration to show the students what is occurring with the small amount of water inside each unpopped kernel as it is heated:

1. Fill the pan half full of water and start to heat it.

2. Place approximately ½ cup room-temperature water in a bottle. Stretch the neck of a balloon over the mouth of the bottle. Ask, "What's in the bottle?" *Water and air.*

   Be careful when you place the bottle in the hot water; hot water can cause severe burns.

3. Ask the students to predict what would happen if this bottle of water was placed in hot water. Place the bottle in the pan of very hot, almost boiling water. (See Figure 1.)

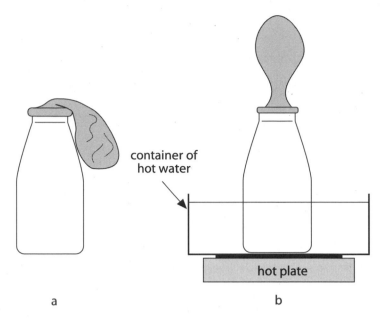

container of
hot water

hot plate

a   b

*Figure 1: Stretch a balloon over the opening of a bottle. Place the
bottle in the pan of very hot, almost boiling water.*

4. Have the students observe what happens. Chart and discuss their
   observations. Explain how the students' observations are related to the
   expansion and subsequent explosion that takes place inside an unpopped
   corn kernel. (See the Science Explanation.)

5. Have students write in their science journals about the science of the popping
   corn.

Part C: Kernels with Holes

1. Challenge the students to predict the effect hammering kernels of popcorn
   would have on their popping ability.

2. Place ¼ cup fresh popcorn kernels in a plastic bag and hammer them gently
   several times, just enough to crack all of the kernels without crushing them
   completely.

3. Pop this corn as in Part A.

4. Measure the volume of the popped corn and compare the results with those
   of Part A.

5. Chart student observations and discuss possible reasons for the differences in
   volume.

Part D: The Holey Kernel Model

1. Challenge students to describe how the Popcorn Model proposed in Part B
   can be modified so it is consistent with the experiments done in Part C.

2. Try several student suggestions, taking precautions to stay well within safety
   guidelines.

3. Be sure to try the following holey model by cutting a 1- to 2-cm hole in a balloon and repeating Part B with this balloon.

4. Lead the students in a discussion of the role the sealed, strong outer hull of the popcorn plays in its ability to pop.

Part E: The Percent Moisture in Popcorn (for older students)

1. Measure the volume of 20 kernels of regular popcorn using a 25-mL graduated cylinder.

2. Make a lid for the 250-mL beaker using the 12-cm x 12-cm piece of aluminum foil.

3. Determine the mass of the 20 kernels of popcorn as follows:

   a. Weigh an empty beaker and the foil lid.

   b. Put the 20 kernels of popcorn into the beaker, then weigh the beaker, popcorn, and foil lid.

   c. Find the mass of the unpopped corn by subtracting the first mass from the second.

4. Add oil to just cover the kernels and weigh the beaker and foil lid once again. Determine the mass of the popcorn plus oil.

5. Wrap the aluminum foil lid over the mouth of the beaker, then make several small holes in the center of the foil with a sharp pencil.

Watch carefully to make sure the oil doesn't start to burn or decompose. If it does, lower the heat or remove the beaker from the heat source.

6. Cautiously heat the beaker using a hot plate until the kernels have popped.

Use caution when poking the hole, as steam can cause severe burns.

7. Cautiously remove the hot beaker from the heat. Poke a sharp pencil through the foil lid to make a bigger hole through which steam can escape. Let the beaker stand for a minute or two to let all the steam escape. Ask the students where the steam comes from.

8. After the beaker has cooled, weigh it with the lid and the popped corn. The difference between this mass and the one from step 4 is the mass of water lost.

9. Determine the percent moisture in the sample using the following formula:

$$\% \ moisture = \frac{mass \ of \ H_2O \ lost}{mass \ of \ unpopped \ corn} \times 100\%$$

10. Measure the volume of the popped corn using the large graduated cylinder or measuring cup.

11. Calculate the change in volume as a percent:

$$\% \ increase \ in \ volume = \frac{volume \ of \ popped \ corn}{volume \ of \ unpopped \ corn} \times 100\%$$

12. Repeat this procedure using different brands of popcorn. Be sure to use the same number of kernels for each trial.

13. Discuss the results and relate them to the most desirable moisture level of popcorn.

Extensions for Further Science Inquiry

- Have students propose methods for adding water to unpopped corn kernels. Challenge the students to consider what might happen to popcorn kernels that have previously been soaked in water for 2–3 hours. Ask them to design an experiment to find this out. As a class, decide what procedure to use. For safety reasons, if an oil popper is used, pat the kernels dry with a paper towel before placing them in hot oil. It is recommended that the popping procedure used in Part A also be used for this extension.
- Dry ¼ cup popcorn kernels by placing them in a single layer on a tray in an oven at 90°C (190°F) overnight. Repeat Part C, steps 1, 3, and 4 with these oven-dried corn kernels. Explain to the students how you dried the corn so they understand the conditions. Compare the final volumes of the fresh, hammered, and dried kernels. Discuss possible reasons for the differences.
- Compare the results of these Extensions for Further Science Inquiry with previous results. As a class, use these observations to decide which moisture level produced the best results. Discuss whether adding or removing water from popcorn before popping would improve the quality of the product.

Science Explanation

 The following explanation is intended for the teacher's information. Modify the explanation for students as required.

Popcorn, a cereal grain, is primarily composed of starch and water. As the corn is heated, the water inside the kernel turns to steam. The pressure of the steam increases and pushes against the outer layer of the kernel. This outer layer, called the pericarp, holds in the steam until the pressure builds up to about 9 atmospheres (that is, nine times normal atmospheric pressure). Then the outer layer breaks open, and the kernel explodes, or pops. In the process, the starch expands. This is the white solid we eat. The water escapes as steam and can be seen after it condenses into liquid.

If the outer husk is cut or punctured, the water vapor escapes as it is heated, and pressure cannot build up inside the husk. Therefore, the kernels do not pop.

The amount of moisture in the kernel controls the quality of the "pop." Popcorn with a moisture content of 10–14% usually pops best. The oven-dried kernels may pop, but their final volume will be much less than the final volume of moistened kernels. Kernels soaked in water, as in the Extension for Further Science Inquiry, will pop, but their final volume will also be less than that of the control kernels because the hulls are softer and will pop at a lower internal pressure.

References for the Science Activity

Van Cleave, J. *Janice Van Cleave's 200 Gooey, Slippery, Slimy, Weird and Fun Experiments;* John Wiley and Sons: New York, 1993; p 107.

"The Popcorn Pop"; *Fun with Chemistry: A Guidebook of K–12 Activities;* Sarquis, M., Sarquis, J., Eds.; Institute for Chemical Education: Madison, WI, 1993; Vol. 1, pp 71–75.

"Popping Corn," *Science Resources for Schools.* 1986, *3*(3).

Sibley, L.K. "Popcorn," *Chem Matters.* 1984, *2*(3), 10–13.

Part 3: Integrating with Language Arts

Featured Fiction Book: *The Legend of Food Mountain*

Author: Harriet Rohmer   Illustrator: Graciela Carrillo
Publisher: Children's Press   ISBN: 0-89239-022-0
Summary: This Aztec legend recounts how a giant red ant helped the ancient god Quetzalcoatl bring corn to the first people of the Earth.

Before you begin reading, show students the last page of the book, which contains picture symbols for Food Mountain, speech or song, and raindrops. As you read, have students study each picture carefully to see if these symbols are used. Discuss the problem faced by the first people and how corn solved the problem. After finishing the story, discuss the meaning of the last sentence of the story, pages 22–23. What are the people in this picture doing?

Featured Nonfiction Book: *The Pilgrims' First Thanksgiving*

Author: Ann McGovern   Illustrator: Joe Lasker
Publisher: Scholastic   ISBN: 0-590-40617-5
Summary: This easy-to-understand historical account of the plight of the Pilgrims makes several references to corn and popcorn and gives the menu of the first Thanksgiving feast. This book is good for reading aloud and is suitable for middle/upper elementary.

After you finish the story, discuss the hardships of the Pilgrims and how the Indians helped them to survive. Discuss the importance of corn to the Pilgrims. Ask the students why the first harvest was such a cause for celebration. If you also read the Featured Fiction Book, *The Legend of Food Mountain*, discuss elements common to both stories (hungry people are fed with corn, rain is necessary to grow food).

Writing Extensions

- If you did the first Extension for Further Science Inquiry, have students use their science journals to write a summary of the experiment they designed and the results they found.
- Have students use the information from the Extension for Further Science Inquiry and the reading of the two books to create an acrostic poem for CORN, THANKSGIVING, or other related words such as POPCORN or MAIZE. See the two examples below:

Corn on the cob
Or popped,
Roasted, or boiled—
Nutritious and delicious.

Turkey and dressing
Heaped on plates,
All of the family
Near.
Kids and parents,
Sisters and brothers,
Grandparents, too,
Invited to dinner.
Voices lifted
In laughter and song.
Now harvest is over.
Give thanks.

Additional Books

Fiction

Title: *The Dragon Thanksgiving Feast: Things to Make and Do*
Author: Loreen Leedy
Publisher: Holiday House   ISBN: 0823408280
Summary: Dragons celebrate Thanksgiving by preparing and enjoying a great feast. This book includes instructions for activities and games related to the holiday.

Title: *How Many Days to America?*
Author: Eve Bunting   Illustrator: Beth Peck
Publisher: Clarion   ISBN: 0-395-54777-6
Summary: Refugees from a Caribbean island embark on a dangerous boat trip to America, where they have a special reason to celebrate Thanksgiving.

Title: *Oh, What a Thanksgiving!*
Author: Steven Kroll   Illustrator: S.D. Schindler
Publisher: Scholastic   ISBN: 0-590-44874-9
Summary: David is a young man with a very vivid imagination. As he learns about the origins of Thanksgiving in school, he constantly switches from the present to the past and imagines himself as one of the Pilgrims living the history he is learning.

Title: *People of Corn: A Mayan Story*
Author: Mary-Joan Gerson   Illustrator: Carla Golembe
Publisher: Little, Brown   ISBN: 0316308544
Summary: A Mayan version of the story of Creation describes how the Maya
    believed that corn, much more than a food, was the spirit of life itself and
    explains their belief that the first people on Earth were actually made from
    corn.

Title: *The Popcorn Dragon*
Author: Jane Thayer   Illustrator: Lisa McCue
Publisher: Morrow   ISBN: 0-688-0887-67
Summary: Though his hot breath is the envy of all the other animals, a young
    dragon learns that showing off does not make friends. When he discovers that
    his hot breath will pop corn, he adopts a new and better strategy for making
    friends.

Title: *Thanksgiving at the Tappletons'*
Author: Eileen Spinelli   Illustrator: Maryann Cocca-Leffler
Publisher: HarperCollins   ISBN: 0-06-443204-1
Summary: When calamity stalks every step of the preparations for the Tappletons'
    Thanksgiving dinner, they realize that there is more to Thanksgiving than
    turkey and trimmings.

Nonfiction

Title: *Cornzapoppin'!*
Author: Barbara Williams
Publisher: Holt, Rinehart, and Winston   ISBN: 0-030-1436-67
Summary: This book is a guide to the history, growing, buying, storing, popping,
    and flavoring of popcorn as well as special recipes, decorating ideas, and party
    ideas for occasions throughout the year.

Title: *...If You Sailed on the Mayflower in 1620*
Author: Ann McGovern
Publisher: Scholastic   ISBN: 0-590-45161-8
Summary: Questions and answers describe the voyage of the Mayflower and the
    Pilgrims' first year in the New World.

Title: *Popcorn*
Author: Millicent Selsam
Publisher: Morrow   ISBN: 0-688-2208-35
Summary: Describes the growth cycle of the type of corn used to make popcorn.

Title: *The Popcorn Book*
Author and Illustrator: Tomie de Paola
Publisher: Holiday House   ISBN: 0-823-4031-49
Summary: Presents a variety of facts about popcorn and includes two recipes.

Title: *The Story of the First Thanksgiving*
Author: Elaine Raphael and Don Bolognese
Publisher: Scholastic   ISBN: 0-590-44674-7
Summary: Presents the story of the first Thanksgiving as celebrated by the
         Pilgrims and the Wampanoag Indians. Includes a drawing activity section at
         the end of the book.

Part 4: Other Lesson Extensions

Art and Music

- Have students use a variety of seeds such as unpopped corn and different varieties of beans to create turkey mosaics by gluing the seeds to a flat surface. The shape should be sketched on the flat surface before students begin arranging and gluing the seeds in place.
- Have students make corn husk dolls.
- Using toothpicks, popcorn, and glue, have students create their own popcorn sculptures.
- Have students add food coloring to Karo® corn syrup and pour it over popped corn. Have them butter their hands and shape the coated popcorn into edible Thanksgiving sculptures.
- Have students use a dried gourd and a few corn kernels or other seeds to create maracas. Make a small hole in one end of the gourd to insert the seeds, seal with tape or hot glue, and allow students to decorate the maracas with brightly colored paint, markers, or crayons.

Mathematics

- Place a hot-air popcorn popper in the middle of a wide-open space covered with a clean sheet or lengths of butcher paper. The activity can also be done outside with chalk on the sidewalk if you have a long extension cord. Have the students estimate how far the individual kernels will travel. Mark these spots. Turn on the popper and pop the corn. After the popping has ceased, have students do the following:
  ○ measure the distance of the kernel farthest from the machine,
  ○ measure the distance of the closest kernel,
  ○ notice the pattern of the distribution (Circular? Random?), and
  ○ compare the results with the estimated distances.

  ➤ *We do not recommend the use of an oil popper for this extension, as hot oil may fly out of the popper and cause severe burns.*

- Have students estimate the number of popcorn kernels in a large jar and write their guesses with their signatures on a large chart posted by the jar. Whoever comes closest to the actual count is the winner. The winner, and possibly one or two runners-up, can choose prizes to take home from among the corn products.

- Challenge students to verify the number of kernels in the big jar. Although counting each kernel is one solution, it takes a lot of time and is not the easiest method. Encourage students to find other ways to count the kernels. For example, they could measure ¼ cup of kernels, count these, then measure how many ¼ cups are in the jar. Multiplying this number by the number of kernels in ¼ cup will give a fairly accurate count.
- Have students test different brands of popcorn to determine which has the best popping ratio (calculated as the number of kernels popped/total number of kernels). Have them graph the results. Discuss possible reasons for the differences.

Social Studies

- Read to the students from an encyclopedia or nonfiction resource about the origin of corn in the Americas, about its importance in the development of many indigenous cultures (such as Mayan and Aztec), and about the various types of corn cultivated by these peoples. The June, 1993, issue of *National Geographic* has an extensive article about corn, tracing the grain from its earliest days in Mexico until today. It also lists the many uses of the grain.

Just for Fun

- Make some of the projects mentioned in *The Dragon Thanksgiving Feast: Things to Make and Do* (see Additional Books). For example, make the Turkey Popcorn Holder, Pumpkin Cornbread, Pilgrim Punch, etc.
- Have students make popcorn balls.
- String popcorn for feeding birds or decorating Christmas trees.

Part 5: National Science Education Standards

Science as Inquiry Standards:

Abilities Necessary to Do Scientific Inquiry

Students question how popcorn pops and what happens if the shell is broken before heating.

Students pop regular popcorn and cracked popcorn and compare results.

Students use volume measuring devices to compare unpopped corn, regular popped corn, and corn popped after cracking.

Students use their observations from their investigations and from the modeling demonstrations to explain why popcorn pops.

Students share their observations and explanations through class discussion.

Older students use mathematics to determine the percentage of moisture in popcorn.

Physical Science Standards:

Properties of Objects and Materials

Samples of popcorn, both unpopped and popped, have volumes that can be measured.

Water, including water trapped in popcorn, will vaporize when heated.

Science and Technology Standards:

Abilities of Technological Design

Students question whether adding or removing some water from the popcorn before popping would improve the quality of the product.

Students propose methods for adding water to the unpopped corn.

Students compare the results of popping regular, soaked, and oven-dried popcorn. They use their observations to decide which moisture level produces the best result.

Students discuss their results and conclusions regarding the most desirable moisture level of popcorn.

History and Nature of Science Standards:

Science as a Human Endeavor

Agricultural technology has been practiced for millennia.

Winter

Before calendars were widely used, people relied on nature to tell time. They used the phases of the moon, the height of the sun in the sky, and the changes in weather to determine how much time passed between events. They also watched animals and plants for clues to when winter, spring, summer, and autumn were approaching. As leaves fell off trees and animals fattened up, people in temperate regions knew that the cold weather and short days of winter were coming. In response, they stored food and fuel to get them through the darkest season.

Ancient tribes held festivals during winter to encourage the sun to return and to give it strength for its battle with the darkness. Light was a central part of these winter festivals. In Persia, December 25 was the "dies solis invicti nati," or "Birthday of the Invincible Sun." The Persians believed that by feasting and celebrating they could support the sun and speed its return to their lands.

Most winter celebrations included lighting large bonfires to fight the cold and darkness. Yule logs were lit inside the home to encourage the sun to return. Gifts were exchanged and feasts were held to keep spirits up during the cold, dark season. Homes were filled with evergreens, mistletoe, and holly—plants that remain green all year long—as symbols of nature's power to defy the destructiveness of winter. As Christianity spread throughout the world, these and many other traditions of winter festivals were incorporated into the Christian holiday of Christmas, celebrated on December 25.

Unless you live on or very near the Equator, where temperatures do not change much and the days are always 12 hours long, you experience a winter season. When you experience winter and the harshness of the season depend on where you live. Astronomically, winter occurs in each hemisphere when that hemisphere is tilted away from the sun. Since the sun's rays are slanted when they hit the part of the Earth inclined away from the sun, that hemisphere is exposed to a lower amount of solar energy. Also, the sun is lower in the sky, which causes the days to be shorter and the nights longer. If you lived at or very near the north or south poles, nights during winter could be 24 hours long. When the Earth is at its perihelion (the point in its orbit when it is nearest the sun) on January 2, the northern hemisphere nevertheless is experiencing winter because it is tilted away from the sun and is not receiving as much direct solar radiation.

Seasons can be defined two ways: astronomically and meteorologically. The four astronomical seasons are all three months in length. Meteorological seasons, on the other hand, vary from place to place. Some places lying between the Tropic of Cancer (23½° north of the equator) and the Tropic of Capricorn (23½° south of the equator) experience only two meteorological seasons, which are characterized by different amounts of rainfall and are usually referred to as "wet" and "dry" seasons. In the northern hemisphere, astronomical winter starts around December 21–22 and ends around March 21–22. Above the Tropic of Cancer, the weather associated with "winter"—arctic winds and snow—can begin as early as November and continue until March or April for some regions of the northern hemisphere. In the southern hemisphere, astronomical winter starts around June 21–22 and ends around September 21–22.

Winter weather in the southern hemisphere is usually not as harsh and cold as winter weather in regions of the northern hemisphere. Because of the distribution of land in the southern hemisphere, the climates below the Tropic of Capricorn are very different from the climates above the Tropic of Cancer. The cold continental climates—those responsible for harsh, snowy winters—found in regions between the 30° and 60° latitudes do not occur in the southern hemisphere because large land masses are absent at these southern latitudes. Marine climates rather than continental climates have a greater effect on the southern parts of Africa and South America because the land masses of these continents get much narrower below the Tropic of Capricorn. In addition, the habitable land in the southern hemisphere is not as affected by polar climates as the land in the northern hemisphere because the world oceans buffer the southern tips of South America, Africa, and Australia from Antarctica's polar continental climate. The island group off South America known as Tierra del Fuego is the southernmost permanently-habitable land on Earth. It lies at 56°S, as far south of the equator as the southern panhandle of Alaska is north, and is approximately 750 miles from the Antarctic shores. North America, Europe, and Asia extend much farther north than 56° and are connected by ice shelves and glaciers to the Arctic.

References

Asimov, Isaac. "By Land and By Sea," *The Road to Infinity;* Avon Books: New York, 1979; pp 72–84.

"Climate and Weather: CLIMATIC CLASSIFICATION" *Britannica Online.* http://www.eb.com:180/cgi-bin/g?DocF=macro/5001/34/121.html; (accessed 3 Feb 1998).

Harrowven, J. *Origins of Festivals and Feasts;* Kaye & Ward: London, 1980; pp 133–134.

Hatch, J.M. *The American Book of Days,* 3rd ed.; H.W. Wilson: New York, 1978; pp 1128, 1143.

Brrr! Winter Can Be Freezing!

The days are growing shorter, the temperature is dropping, and the leaves are falling off the trees. Winter is coming! In ancient times, festivals were held to herald the coming of the coldest, shortest season of the year and to give strength to nature to help in the battle against winter. This activity shows students what effect the freezing temperatures associated with winter can have on living organisms.

Key Science Topics

- capillary action
- freezing
- phase changes

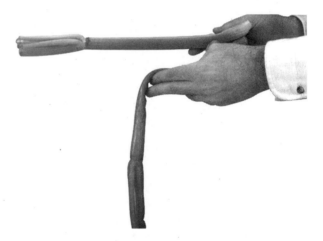

Firm celery and limp celery

Time Required

Setup   10 minutes plus freezing time
Performance   30–40 minutes and overnight
Cleanup   10–15 minutes

Part 1: Building Bridges

Building Student Knowledge and Motivation

A few days prior to doing this activity, display a collection of fiction and nonfiction books on snow, ice, and other seasonal subjects for free-choice reading and read-aloud sharing time. Students can use these and other books to investigate how plants and animals adapt to winter. Have the students generate a list of words relating to ice and winter for student writing. The students should have a clear concept of real and make-believe stories and be able to distinguish between the two. If desired, have the class begin decorating the room with snowflakes (see Part 4, Art and Music Extension) and snowmen. Set a stick of celery (with leaves) in the learning center a few days before doing the activity so students can observe as it becomes limp.

Bridging to the Science Activity

If students live in regions that experience freezing temperatures in winter, ask them what happens to flowers left outside unprotected after a hard freeze. Discuss how tender vegetation is killed by freezing temperatures. For students in mild climates that do not experience freezing temperatures, read a story about this. Or, you can bring in a live flower and one that has been frozen in a freezer. Explain that in some geographic regions, temperatures can be as cold as (or colder than) a freezer.

Part 2: Science Activity

Materials

For Getting Ready
Per group
- stick of celery

For the Procedure
Part A, per group
- limp stick of celery

 These could come from the stalk from the learning center.

- stick of fresh celery
- bowl of cool water

Part B, per group
- celery stick frozen in Getting Ready
- bowl of cool water

Part C, per class
- 2, 1-pint zipper-type plastic bags
- 2 bowls or zipper-type plastic bags larger than the 1-pint bags listed above
- access to a freezer

Safety and Disposal

No special safety or disposal procedures are required.

Getting Ready

Freeze one stick of celery for each group. Allow one stick of celery for each group to become limp.

Procedure

Part A: Limp and Firm Celery

1. Give each group of students one stick of limp celery and one fresh, firm stick. Ask students to compare the two and record differences between them. Discuss what could have caused the differences students observe.

2. Instruct half of the groups to place their limp celery sticks in a bowl of cool water. Have the remaining groups lay their limp sticks out on a table. Allow the sticks to sit overnight. (The fresh sticks can be discarded.)

3. Observe all of the sticks. Ask students what the difference is between them now. *The ones left out of water are still limp, while the ones placed in water are now firm.* Discuss reasons for the change.

Part B: What Happens When Celery Freezes?

1. Give each group a stick of frozen celery. Allow them to examine it and then allow it to thaw completely. Have them examine it once again and then record their observations.

2. Have the groups put the thawed celery in cool water overnight. Ask students to observe and offer explanations.

Part C: The Model

1. Completely fill one zipper-type plastic bag with water. Make sure that the bag is completely filled and feels firm when zipped shut.

2. Partly fill a second bag with water and zip it shut.

3. Put each bag in a bowl or larger bag and pass them both around, allowing students to observe and record differences.

4. Put both bags in the freezer until they are frozen solid.

5. Pass both frozen bags around and allow students to observe and record any differences. Ask students to describe what happened to the frozen bags. Discuss which of these bags best models what happened to the celery when it was frozen.

Extensions for Further Science Inquiry

- Students can apply their knowledge to new situations and the world around them by learning about the Cincinnati Zoo's Center for Reproduction of Endangered Wildlife (CREW) program. CREW scientists help preserve endangered species by freezing their sperm, eggs, and embryos and later thawing and implanting them into host mothers of related (but not endangered) species. Classroom materials related to the CREW project are available from CREW. Contact CREW at 513/961-CREW (2739) and ask to speak with an education specialist. Additionally, teachers within driving distance of Cincinnati, Ohio, can arrange a class visit to CREW.
- Have students read *Will We Miss Them?* (see Additional Books). Have students research the use of cryopreservation to protect endangered species.

Science Explanation

 The following explanation is intended for the teacher's information. Modify the explanation for students as required.

The fluid in plant and animal cells (called cytoplasm) is primarily water. Cytoplasm plays an important role in every aspect of a cell's life. The two bags of water represent cells of a plant or animal under two different conditions. The full bag represents a cell that contains a normal amount of water. The partly full bag represents a cell that contains a little less water than normal—in other words, a cell that is partially dehydrated.

When you put the bags in the freezer, the water in the bags freezes and expands. If it has no room to expand (as in a closed container), its container may break. That's why frozen cans of soda often burst and frozen car radiators often crack. In the same way, the full bag (normal cell) breaks open when frozen while the partially filled bag (dehydrated cell) does not. If a cell breaks open, it dies.

The difference between the fresh celery and the limp celery is the same as the difference between the two bags of water. One is normally hydrated, and one is slightly dehydrated. As you might guess, the limp celery is the dehydrated one. Typically, the cell fluid gives form and firmness to the cell, just as the water in the full bag makes the bag feel firm. Note the contrasting limpness of the partially filled bag. The form and firmness of the individual cells give form and firmness to the entire plant. The firm celery stick contains more water in its cells than the wilted stick. When you place the wilted celery in cold water, water moves back into the cells through a process called osmosis. The stalk becomes firm again.

So what happened to the frozen celery? To understand this, think about what happened to the water-filled bag. When normally hydrated celery freezes, the water in each cell expands, and many of the cells burst, just as the full bag of water did. As a result, the celery becomes limp when thawed. You cannot make it firm again by putting it in ice water, because the damaged cells can no longer hold any water. Animal cells are often damaged by freezing in the same way. Cells that survive the initial freezing intact are often damaged by tiny ice crystals moving about inside the cell as the cell fluid begins to thaw. Some plants and animals that live in freezing environments have special chemicals in their cells called cryoprotectants, which provide natural protection from freezing damage. The CREW scientists who freeze and then thaw live plant and animal cells use synthetic cryoprotectants to prevent damage from freezing. These chemicals slightly dehydrate the cells and also reduce damage from ice crystals. (For more about CREW, see the Extension for Further Science Inquiry.)

Part 3: Integrating with Language Arts

Featured Fiction Book: *50 Below Zero*

Author: Robert Munsch   Illustrator: Michael Martchenko
Publisher: Firefly   ISBN: 0-920236-91
Summary: In the middle of a winter night, when the temperature outside is -50°F, Jason's father sleepwalks all over the house. After each episode, Jason returns his father to bed. Finally, Jason's father sleepwalks outside and freezes solid. Jason brings his father back into the house and thaws him out.

Read *50 Below Zero* to the class. The students will probably enjoy repeated readings of this book. Ask students what parts of the story could happen in real life and what parts are make-believe. Discuss how animals and plants adapt to winter. If possible, have a representative from a nearby zoo bring specimens of plants and animals to class and teach a lesson on how these organisms survive in cold temperatures. Discuss appropriate clothing for people during cold weather.

Writing Extensions

- Have students read environmental science books related to CREW's work and write about how scientists can overcome the problems the students observed in this activity.
- Have students read science fiction stories involving cryopreservation of people. (Students may also have seen movies involving cryopreservation; *The Empire Strikes Back,* the second *Star Wars* film, is one example.) Have them write about whether they think cryopreservation of people will ever be a reality.
- Have students write poetry to describe ice through the senses. They should consider how ice feels and looks and whether it makes sounds.

- Have students write acrostic poems based on words related to winter and ice. Use a word or a phrase that begins with each letter in the word you choose to use. The following are two examples:

Icicles and snowflakes
Crystals of all sizes
Expanded water

Woolly clothes
Ice
Northern lights
Too cold
Entirely too cold
Really too cold

Additional Books

Fiction

Title: *The Mitten*
Adapter and Illustrator: Jan Brett
Publisher: G.P. Putnam's Sons   ISBN: 0-399-21920-X
Summary: A little boy loses a new mitten in the snow. Several animals decide to get out of the cold and squeeze into the mitten. The bear's sneeze shoots all the animals out of the mitten and the mitten into the air. The boy finds his stretched mitten and returns home.

Title: *Once Upon Ice and Other Frozen Poems*
Author: Various
Publisher: Wordsong/Boyds Mills   ISBN: 1563974088
Summary: Inspired by photographs of ice in primarily natural forms, writers Jane Yolen, X.J. Kennedy, Lee Bennett Hopkins, and others capture their thoughts in poetry.

Title: *The Snowman*
Author: Raymond Briggs
Publisher: Scholastic   ISBN: 0-590-97511-0
Summary: A picture book of a boy and his magical snowman.

Title: *Wintertime*
Author: Ann Schweninger
Publisher: Puffin   ISBN: 0-590-61744-3
Summary: A dog family explores the changes that happen in nature during the winter.

Nonfiction

Title: *Animals in Winter*
Author: Ron Fisher
Publisher: National Geographic Society   ISBN: 0-87044-453-0
Summary: This book contains information and pictures of animals in winter.

Title: *Plants in Winter*
Author: Joanna Cole   Illustrator: Kazue Mizumura
Publisher: Thomas Y. Crowell   ISBN: 0690628854
Summary: This book describes different ways by which plants of all kinds are protected through the cold weather.

Title: *The Science Book of Water*
Author: Neil Ardley
Publisher: Harcourt Brace Jovanovich   ISBN: 0-15-200575-7
Summary: This book contains 11 easy-to-do experiments that help primary students explore water's properties.

Title: *What Do Animals Do in Winter?*
Author: Melvin & Gilda Berger   Illustrator: Susan Harrison
Publisher: Ideals   ISBN: 1571020411
Summary: Describes how animals migrate, sleep, hide, and change color to adapt to winter conditions.

Title: *Will We Miss Them?*
Author: Alexandra Wright   Illustrator: Marshall Peck
Publisher: Charlesbridge   ISBN: 0-881-06489-0
Summary: This book tells why some animals are becoming endangered species, including bald eagles, African elephants, blue whales, Galapagos tortoises, mountain lions, whooping cranes, grizzly bears, manatees, muriqui monkeys, rhinoceroses, mountain gorillas, and crocodiles. (This book can be used with the Extension for Further Science Inquiry, which is about the use of cryopreservation techniques to save endangered species.)

Title: *Winter Across America*
Author: Seymour Simon
Publisher: HarperCollins   ISBN: 0786800194
Summary: Describes the natural history of winter in different parts of the United States.

Part 4: Other Lesson Extensions

Art and Music

- Use a lid from a 3-pound coffee can (or any can of that approximate size) to trace several circles on tagboard. Cut them out to use as circle templates. Have students trace and cut out a couple of circles on white construction paper and put their names on the back. Have students fold the paper in half three times to make a narrow wedge and cut it into intricate snowflake shapes. Have them brush on a mixture of 3 tablespoons salt and ¼ cup water to form crystals. Allow the snowflakes to dry overnight and hang them around the room.

Mathematics

- Plug one end of a clear, colorless drinking straw with a piece of oil-based clay. Pour enough water into the straw to fill it about halfway. Keeping the straw upright to prevent the water from spilling, tape the straw to a cardboard toilet-paper tube or paper-towel tube so the bottom edges line up. (See Figure 1.)

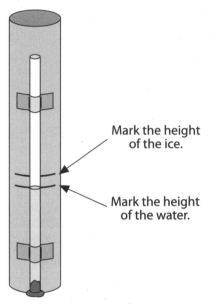

Mark the height of the ice.

Mark the height of the water.

Figure 1: Set up a water-freezing apparatus and mark the levels of water and ice.

Use a pen or marker to draw a line on the cardboard tube exactly even with the height of the water in the straw. Stand the straw-tube apparatus in a freezer and allow the water to freeze completely. Remove the apparatus from the freezer and mark the tube at the height of the ice. How did the markings compare? To make this activity more quantitative, have students mark the tube in centimeters starting from the bottom and calculate the percent change in height of the water column according to the following formula:

$$\% \ expansion = \frac{(height \ ice - height \ water)}{height \ water} \times 100\%$$

- Have students place containers of water outside on a day when the temperature is below freezing and monitor the temperature of the water. Place one container in the sun and one in the shade to compare any differences. They can predict how long it will take the water to freeze. They will need to check the containers every 15 minutes or so. Record temperatures, checking times, predictions, and the actual freezing time on a chart.

Social Studies

- Research how the Inuit people (Eskimos) survive at the very low temperatures of the far North.
- Identify cold regions on Earth and research the kinds of animals and plants that survive there. How do they adapt? What happens to animals in winter in these areas? What happens to plants?

Just for Fun

- Plan a winter wardrobe for an imaginary trip to a very cold climate.
- Draw a thermometer on the board and mark off degrees in Fahrenheit and Celsius. Show students the point on the thermometer at which water freezes and where it begins to melt. Point out that this is the same temperature. Tell students to pretend they are icicles. Use a pointer to indicate temperature. Move the temperature up and down and have students "melt" (by moving apart from each other) or "freeze" (by moving close to each other and not changing neighbors) according to the temperature.

Part 5: National Science Education Standards

Science as Inquiry Standards:

Abilities Necessary to Do Scientific Inquiry

Students question what happens to celery under three environmental conditions: in water, out of water, and in the freezer.

Students investigate the impact different environmental conditions have on celery.

Students use their observations of the celery along with the model of frozen cells to develop an explanation of the effects of freezing the celery.

Students discuss their observations and explanations.

Physical Science Standards:

Properties of Objects and Materials

Substances have many characteristic properties. The properties of celery change when its environment changes.

Substances can exist in different states—solid, liquid, and gas. The celery cells contain water, which ruptures the cells when it freezes and expands.

Hanukkah

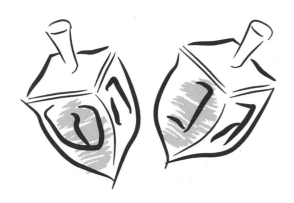

Eight Days in November or December
Culture: Jewish

Hanukkah is an eight-day Jewish holiday that occurs in November or December. Also known as "the Festival of Lights," Hanukkah commemorates a miracle said to have occurred after the defeat of the Greeks in 165 B.C. The Greek armies had overrun Jerusalem, the holiest of Jewish cities, and had used the Jewish temple to worship their own gods, outlawing the practice of Jewish rituals. Judah the Maccabee, the leader of the Jewish people at this time, rallied his people to defeat the Greeks and reclaim their temple.

The Jews rededicated the temple by purifying it, burning incense, and relighting the branched lamps called menorahs that stood in the courtyard. These lamps were to burn night and day using special oil consecrated for use in the temple. According to tradition, only one cruse (an earthenware container) of consecrated oil could be found—enough to keep the lamps burning for one day. The Hanukkah story states that the lamps burned for eight days, enough time to obtain more consecrated oil. Hanukkah (which means "dedication") commemorates the victory over the Greek armies and the miracle of the oil.

A central symbol of Hanukkah is the menorah, a branched lamp that holds nine candles (or sometimes nine wicks in oil). The family gathers around the menorah each night to light the candles. One candle, called the shamash, is used to light each of the others. On the first night, the shamash and one other candle are lit. Each night thereafter, an additional candle is lit until all are burning brightly on the last night of Hanukkah. Since no work can be done by the light of the menorah, the family tells stories, reads from the Torah (the Jewish scripture), and plays games. A popular Hanukkah game involves the dreidel, a four-sided top. A different letter is carved into each side of the top, and these letters are used to teach Jewish history and to play games. (See Figure 1.)

Nun   Gimmel   Heh   Shin

Figure 1: These four Hebrew letters are found on the four sides of a dreidel.

These letters represent the saying, "Nes Gadol Haya Sham," meaning "A great miracle happened there," reminding children of the Hanukkah miracle. In Israel, dreidels are made with the letter Peh instead of Shin, and the saying changes to "Nes Gadol Haya

Poh"—"A great miracle happened here." The letters also represent the four kingdoms that were prophesied to dominate the Jewish people. Nun represents Babylon, Gimmel is Persia, Shin is Greece, and Heh is Rome.

During the Greek occupation of Israel (332–167 B.C.), the Greeks outlawed the study of the Torah, so the Jewish people had to study in secret. If a Greek soldier passed by, the people would pretend to be playing the dreidel to disguise the fact that they were studying their history and the Torah. In the game, each letter on the dreidel represents a different action. At the beginning of the game, each player is given a certain number of coins or candies, which are called counters. Each player puts one counter into the kupah, or "kitty," before spinning the dreidel. Depending upon which side lands up, a certain action is taken:

If the dreidel lands on...	You...
Nun	take nothing from the kupah
Gimmel	take all the pieces from the kupah
Heh	take half the pieces from the kupah
Shin (or Peh)	add a piece to the kupah

Play continues until one player has won all the counters or until players decide to stop. Another version of the dreidel game assigns point values to the letters. The player who reaches a predetermined amount first is the winner.

Although the dates of Hanukkah change every year in the Gregorian calendar (the calendar using the months January–December), it occurs on the same days of the Hebrew calendar, beginning on the 25th day of Kislev. Unlike the solar Gregorian calendar, which is based on the Earth's movement around the sun, the Hebrew calendar is lunar, using the moon's movement around the Earth to determine the months.

References

The Arab World Web Pages. Jerusalem Through History. http://www.arabworld.com/jerusalem/htmls/history.htm (accessed Feb 1998).

Hatch, J.M. *The American Book of Days,* 3rd ed.; H.W. Wilson: New York, 1978.

Ickis, M. *The Book of Festival Holidays;* Dodd, Mead: New York, 1964.

Right to Left Software. About the Hebrew Calendar. http://www.rtlsoft.com/hebrew/calendar/about.html (accessed Jan 1998).

Sinclair, Y.A. "The Dreidel"; Ohr Somayach/Tanenbaum College: Jerusalem, Israel, 1995.

Strassfeld, M. "What's Hanukkah," *The Jewish Holidays: A Guide and Commentary;* Harper and Row: New York, 1985.

Subar, R., Ohr Somayach, Jerusalem, personal communication, 1997.

My Hanukkah Dreidel

For centuries, Jewish children have experienced the principles of rotational motion as they played with their "dreidels," traditional tops that are used as part of the Hanukkah celebration. In the game, the dreidel is spun. The character that lands face up when the dreidel stops dictates what the players do. In this activity, students will make their own dreidels and study what factors affect the spinning motion of the tops.

Key Science Topics

- friction
- motion
- rotational inertia

Time Required

Setup   30 minutes
Performance   30–45 minutes
Cleanup   5 minutes

A homemade dreidel

Part 1: Building Bridges

Building Student Knowledge and Motivation

Prior to the lesson, create a learning center containing several different dreidels. Let students bring in dreidels they may have to add to the collection. Tell the students when they visit the center to look for recurring symbols associated with Hanukkah. Let them add symbols of Hanukkah they think should be included but may be missing.

Bridging to the Science Activity

Bring out a variety of spinning tops for demonstration and student experimentation. Ask students to describe the various tops according to their size and shape. Find what is common about all of the tops. Most likely, they all have a wide middle and narrow to about a 1-millimeter point on the bottom. Ask students how they would design a top of their own.

Part 2: Science Activity

Materials

For Bridging to the Science Activity
Per class
* variety of tops

For Getting Ready only
Per class
* scissors
* wire cutters
* pencil sharpener with variable hole size

For the Procedure
Part A, per student
* 2½-inch-long piece of ¼-inch-diameter dowel rod (See Getting Ready.)
* commercial toy top
* 3-inch-diameter circle of oaktag or paperboard (See Getting Ready.)
  These circles could be cut out of cereal boxes.

* short rubber band

Part B, per class
* hot-melt glue gun and glue, or rubber cement

Part B, per student
- top made in Part A
- 6 small paper clips
- 6 pennies

Part C, per class
- hot-melt glue gun and glue, or rubber cement

Part C, per student
- Dreidel Template (provided at the end of this lesson)
- 3-inch x 3-inch piece of oaktag or paperboard (These could be cut out of cereal boxes.)
- top made in Part B
- other materials suggested by students

For the Extensions for Further Science Inquiry
Per student
- all materials listed for the Procedure, Part B
- 6 washers with center holes large enough to fit over the ¼-inch dowel rod

Safety and Disposal

For younger students, gluing with hot glue or rubber cement should be done only by an adult. No special disposal procedures are required.

Getting Ready

1. Cut an oaktag or paperboard circle 3 inches in diameter for each student. Younger students might find it easier to make a top with the oaktag circle 2½ inches in diameter, so that the pennies touch all the way around the circle in Part B. Poke a starter hole in the exact center of each oaktag circle.

2. Cut dowel rods to 2½-inch lengths. They cut easily with wire cutters. With a pencil sharpener, sharpen each dowel rod to nearly a point (about 1 mm wide) to reduce surface friction. The sharpening must be well centered on the dowel rod. This can be accomplished if you use a sharpener with the variable hole size set for ¼ inch.

Procedure

Part A: The Spinning Top

1. Give each student a dowel rod and challenge the class to make their dowel rods spin. After experimenting, let students demonstrate what they tried. (The dowel rod quickly falls over on its side.)

2. Give each student a commercial toy top and ask the class to repeat the spinning task using the same method they used with the dowel rods. Ask them to compare results with the previous spin. Ask them, "What does the

dowel rod need to work like the toy top?" *A wider middle or more mass around the middle.*

3. Give each student one oaktag or paperboard circle. Show the class how to poke the point of the dowel through the center of the shape without tearing the hole any bigger than necessary. Have each student wrap a short rubber band around the dowel rod so it fits tightly and slide it to fit just below the tagboard. (See Figure 2.) Tell the students to place the tagboard at different heights on the dowel rod and try spinning it. Have students experiment to find the optimal position of the tagboard circle. *The sharpened end of the dowel rod should protrude about ¾ inch.*

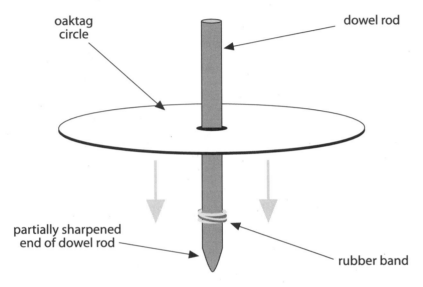

Figure 2: Make a top by sliding an oaktag circle down a dowel rod. Adjust the rubber band until it touches the circle.

4. Have the students compare the spinning ability of their homemade tops with that of the commercial top. Discuss reasons for the differences.

Part B: Improving the Spinability

1. Discuss methods that might be used to improve the spinning ability of the homemade tops.

2. Give each student six small paper clips and instruct them to clip the paper clips at approximately equal intervals around their oaktag circles. Tell them to test this new version for its spinning ability. Allow students to experiment. Ask these questions: "Is it now harder or easier to start the top spinning?" *It should be slightly harder to start to turn the top.* "Does the top have more or less spin time now when you release it?" *It will usually have a longer spin time with this extra mass.* Ask students what adding the paper clips did to the mass of the top. *Increased it.*

3. Have a student from each group remove the six paper clips and hold them in one hand. Have them hold six pennies in the other hand. Ask, "Which feels heavier?" *The pennies feel heavier.*

4. Have students predict what will happen if pennies are glued to the top instead of paper clips and record their predictions. Glue six pennies at equal intervals on each student's top. Have the students practice spinning this top and record their observations.

5. Discuss the observations of the different tops. Focus the discussion on the variable (mass) and how changes in this variable affected the spinning of the top.

Part C: Making a Dreidel

1. Show the students the Dreidel Template (if not used above) and give each student a template and a piece of oaktag or paperboard.

2. Challenge students to make their own dreidels, applying what they learned in Parts A and B. They can use the dowel rods and rubber bands from Parts A and B to make the dreidels. See Figure 3 for a sample design.

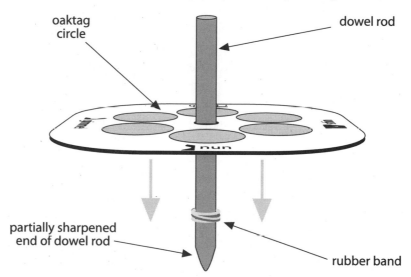

Figure 3: Make a dreidel by applying principles learned in Parts A and B.

3. Allow students to demonstrate their dreidels to the class.

Extension for Further Science Inquiry

Test a different variable (the position of the mass on the top) by using washers with a center hole large enough to fit over the dowel rod. Have students brainstorm about adding weights and then experiment with the mass of six washers stacked in the center and then with the six washers glued near the perimeter.

Science Explanation

The following explanation is intended for the teacher's information. Modify the explanation for students as required.

Tops are fun to play with because they keep spinning for some time after being set in motion. In this activity, students observe that the duration of the spin is affected by the amount of mass near the edge of the circle. Why? Once in motion, an object (such as a top) that rotates about an axis (in this case, the dowel rod) tends to keep rotating about its axis. The resistance of an object to a change in its rotational state of motion is called rotational inertia. When the top is spun it tends to keep spinning because of this inertia. When more mass is added near the edge of the circle, the rotational inertia is increased. The increased rotational inertia makes it harder to start the top turning, but once it has started turning it will continue to spin longer. Friction causes the top to slow down and eventually stop spinning.

Rotational inertia depends not only on the mass of the spinning top but also on the location of the mass. The farther the mass is located from the axis of rotation, the greater the rotational inertia. A top with six washers glued near the perimeter will have more rotational inertia than a top with the same six washers stacked near the center. Many real machines have the mass located far from the axis of rotation in order to increase the rotational inertia and rotational kinetic energy.

References for the Science Activity

Hewitt, P.G. *Conceptual Physics;* Addison-Wesley: Menlo Park, CA, 1987; pp 187–201.

Taylor, B.A.P.; Poth, J.; Portman, D.J. "The Six-Cent Top"; *Teaching Physics with TOYS: Activities for Grades K–9;* McGraw-Hill: New York, 1995; pp 57–63.

Part 3: Integrating with Language Arts

Featured Fiction Book: *The Magic Dreidels: A Hanukkah Story*

Author: Eric Kimmel
Publisher: Holiday House

Illustrator: Katya Krenina
ISBN: 0823412741

Summary: While attempting to retrieve his new dreidel from the well, Jacob meets a goblin who gives him two magic dreidels in its place, but when Jacob is tricked by Fruma Sarah and loses both of them to her, he decides to return to the goblin for help in getting them back.

After reading the story, have students work in cooperative groups with various materials to create and invent a device to help Jacob retrieve his dreidel from the well. This invention must not only retrieve the dreidel but also have some kind of spinning action when doing so. After they have finished, groups may demonstrate their invention to the class. You may want to decorate a large cardboard box, such as one from a washing machine or stove, as a well and place a small dreidel or top at the bottom for students to retrieve.

Writing Extensions

- Have students describe how to spin tops with their fingers, with a string, and with a rubber band.
- Have students write about a fictional spinning top, where it travels, and what it sees.

Additional Books

Fiction

Title: *Hanukkah!*
Author: Roni Schotter   Illustrator: Marylin Hafner
Publisher: Trumpet Club   ISBN: 0440845165
Summary: Using rhythmic style, this book visits a family during an evening of a Hanukkah celebration.

Title: *Hershel and the Hanukkah Goblins*
Author: Eric Kimmel   Illustrator: Tina Schart Hyman
Publisher: Holiday House   ISBN: 0-8234-0769-1
Summary: Traveler Hershel of Ostropol is tired and hungry, and is looking forward to celebrating Hanukkah in the next village. Yet he finds the villagers aren't celebrating because they are scared of goblins that are haunting the old synagogue. Determined to save Hanukkah, Hershel uses his wits to rid the village of the goblins.

Title: *In the Month of Kislev*
Author: Nina Jaffe   Illustrator: Louise August
Publisher: Puffin   ISBN: 0-14-055654-0
Summary: It is time for the whole village to celebrate Hanukkah in the month of Kislev. The peddler's family is so poor that they cannot even enjoy a single latke. Yet by standing under the rich merchant's window, the children enjoy the rich smells of the food and they go to bed happy. Yet the merchant wants to fine the children for stealing the smells of his latkes.

Title: *Jeremy's Dreidel*
Author: Ellie Gelman
Publisher: Demco Media   ISBN: 0606053840
Summary: Jeremy signs up for a Hanukkah workshop to make unusual dreidels and creates a clay dreidel with braille dots for his dad, who is blind.

Title: *Latkes and Applesauce*
Author: Fran Manushkin   Illustrator: Robin Spowart
Publisher: Scholastic   ISBN: 0590422650
Summary: A family is ready to celebrate Hanukkah, but a blizzard covers all the apples and potatoes. They fear there will be no latkes and applesauce this year.

Title: *One Yellow Daffodil*
Author: David A. Adler   Illustrator: Lloyd Bloom
Publisher: Harcourt Brace   ISBN: 0152005374
Summary: During Hanukkah two children help a Holocaust survivor to once again embrace his religious traditions.

Part 4: Other Lesson Extensions

Art and Music

- Teach students the song, "My Dreydel" from *Singable Songs for the Very Young,* sung by Raffi with Ken Whiteley (MCA Records, Universal City, CA, 1976; ISRN: 0881100371).
- Teach the students "The Hanukkah Song," from *Holiday Songs for All Occasions,* words and music by Jill Gallina (Kimbo Educational, Long Branch, NJ, 1978; Music #KIM 0805C). Have the students perform the song for other classes.

Mathematics

- Use a variety of tops and measure the length of time that they spin. Graph the results as a bar graph. Give each top three tries and take the highest number.
- Set up 10 each of two different-colored golf tees (inverted) on a paper plate. (Use five tees of each color for younger students). Spin the top and count how many of each color get knocked over. Write a number sentence to describe what happened, such as, "Three white tees fell down and six blue tees were knocked over." How many in all did the top hit? How many more blue tees were knocked over than white tees? (For older students): What percent of the blue tees were knocked over? What percent of all the tees were knocked over?

Social Studies

- Divide the class into small groups of four or five and allow them to play the dreidel game (see the description of Hanukkah at the beginning of this activity for an explanation of the rules). Use small, wrapped candies as counters; they can be eaten at the end of the activity.

Just for Fun

- Have available a variety of materials to make dreidels, such as clay and milk cartons, and sharpened pencils. Have contests between different dreidel designs to determine which one will spin longest.

Part 5: National Science Education Standards

Science as Inquiry Standards:

Abilities Necessary to Do Scientific Inquiry

Students question how a top should be designed so that it will spin well.

Students investigate the ability of a dowel, a commercial toy top, and a homemade dowel top to spin.

Students use their observations of the various tops to develop an explanation of what factors affect spinning ability.

Students discuss their observations and explanations as a class.

Physical Science Standards:

Position and Motion of Objects

The position and motion of a top can be changed by pushing and pulling (that is, spinning) it.

Science and Technology Standards:

Abilities of Technological Design

Students question how the basic design of their tops could be improved.

Students propose adding weight to their tops to make them spin better.

Students add paper clips and pennies to their tops.

Students evaluate the results of their design changes in terms of spinning ability.

As a class, students discuss the differences in mass of the various tops and dreidels and how this affects their ability to spin.

My Hanukkah Dreidel

Dreidel Template Sheet

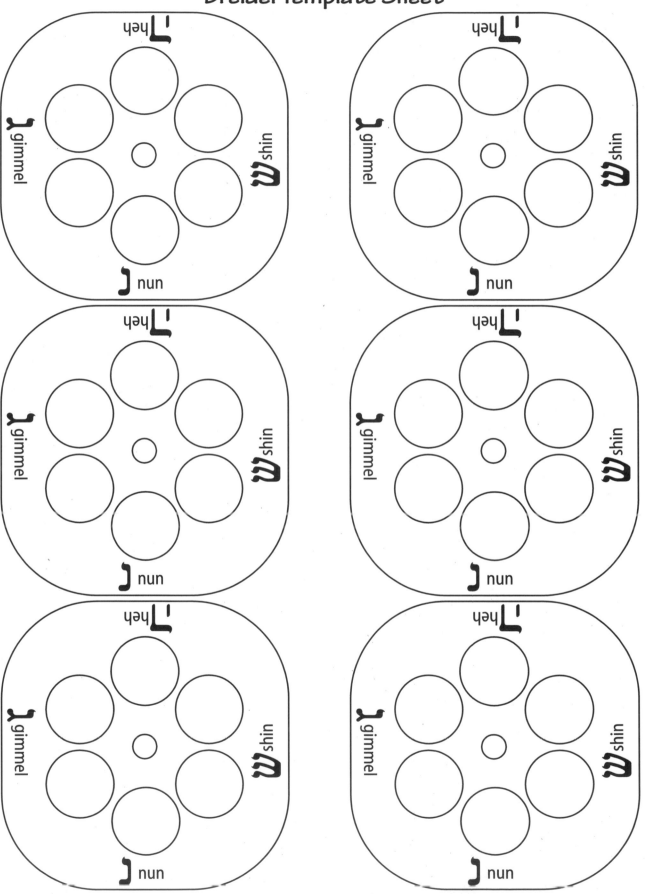

Reproduced from *Science Projects for Holidays throughout the Year*, published by McGraw-Hill.

Christmas

December 25
Culture: Christian

One of the most important Christian holidays is Christmas, the celebration of the birth of Jesus Christ. Although Jesus' exact birthdate is unknown, early Christian leaders chose December 25 for this celebration to give religious meaning to secular festivals celebrated by early Romans. One such festival was Saturnalia, an ancient Roman celebration of peace and gift-giving celebrated at the time of the winter solstice, around December 22 or 23. No wars could be fought during this time, and no one was sent to prison or punished. When Christianity became the official religion of the Roman empire, the people did not want to give up this holiday, so church leaders renamed the holiday and associated it with Jesus, himself a man of peace and giving.

The earliest recorded observance of Jesus' birth and early life was in 200 A.D. A group of Egyptian Christians celebrated Jesus' baptism on January 6. In 336 A.D., people in Rome began commemorating Jesus' birth. King Arthur is credited with the first recorded Christmas celebration in Britain in 521 A.D., and the first Christmas in America was celebrated in 1607 at Jamestown, Virginia. Although most of the Christian denominations observe Christmas, the method of observance varies from denomination to denomination. Because of Christmas' growing consumer popularity, many non-Christians also observe the holiday's secular traditions.

Many of the symbols and traditions of Christmas have their origins in ancient winter and winter solstice festivals:

- Christmas trees: Romans hung trinkets on pine trees during Saturnalia, and Egyptians brought green date palm trees indoors for their winter solstice rites. Martin Luther was the first to bring a pine tree inside at Christmas in the 16th century. He decorated it with lit candles to show his children how the stars looked in the forest, and the tradition of lighting trees began. When German mercenaries came to the United States to help fight during the War of Independence, they brought this tradition with them.
- Evergreens, mistletoe, and holly: Egyptians, Romans, and other Europeans decorated with these plants during the winter because they stay green all year long, symbolizing nature's strength and perseverance through the winter. Mistletoe was also a symbol of peace and hope. Whenever enemies met

underneath mistletoe, they would drop their weapons and embrace. The current tradition of kissing those you meet under mistletoe developed from this custom.

- Yule logs and fire: Persians and Europeans lighted huge bonfires during winter festivals to support the sun in its battle against darkness. In Germany, a special log called a Yule log was cut and would burn for days in the family fireplace.
- Gift giving: To brighten the dark winters, people in Rome and other parts of Europe exchanged gifts. The people believed that the merrymaking would dispel the darkness and encourage the sun to return. Today, different cultures have symbolic gift-giving characters central to their Christmas customs:
  - In America, Santa Claus is the gift giver. The modern-day image of Santa, with his red suit and white beard, was developed by artists in the 1860s. The artists derived this image from Clement Clarke Moore's 1822 poem "A Visit From St. Nicholas," more popularly known as "Twas the Night Before Christmas."
  - Sinterklaas is the Dutch gift giver, and he has a book in which he notes who has been good and who has been bad. This legend inspired Clement Clarke Moore to write his poem.
  - The Christkindl, or Christ Child, delivers presents to German children. On Christmas eve, children are not allowed in the room where the Christmas tree stands. When they are finally allowed in the next morning, they are too late to catch the Christkindl leaving the gifts.
  - A woman named Befana leaves gifts for Italian children on January 6. Legend states that Befana was a grandmother who lived in Bethlehem at the time of Jesus' birth and delayed going to see him. When she finally did, Mary and Joseph had already left the stable with Jesus. Since then, Befana has traveled around searching for baby Jesus, leaving gifts in every home in case he is there.
  - In other parts of Europe, St. Nicholas leaves candy and gifts for good children on December 6, which is his feast day, or on December 25. St. Nicholas was the Bishop of Myra, a town in Turkey during the 4th century, and he was very fond of children. "Santa Claus" is a contraction for "St. Nicholas."

References

Catholic Online December Saints Page. http://www.catholic.org/saints/decsts.html (accessed Feb 1998).

"Christmas" *Britannica Online.* http://www.eb.com:180/cgi-bin/g?DocF=micro/126/49.html (accessed 3 Feb 1998).

Eton Vintners. The Christmas Page. http://etonvintners.co.uk/xmas.html (accessed 3 Feb 1998).

Hatch, J.M. *The American Book of Days,* 3rd ed.; H.W. Wilson: New York, 1978; pp 1141–1146.

Harrowven, J. *Origins of Festivals and Feasts;* Kaye & Ward: London, 1980; pp 133–155.

Ickis, M. *The Book of Festival Holidays;* Dodd, Mead: New York, 1964, pp 150–153.

"Moore, Clement Clarke" *Britannica Online.* http://www.eb.com:180/cgi-bin/g?DocF=micro/403/35.html (accessed 3 Feb 1998).

Christmas-Tree Light Toys

Christmas (December 25) is one of the most important Christian holidays. Celebrating the birth of Jesus Christ, this holiday is one of peace and giving. At Christmas, evergreen trees are often decorated with ornaments and lights. In this activity, students will study electrical circuits as they make Christmas-tree light toys.

Key Science Topics

- electrical circuits
- conductivity

Time Required

Setup	5 minutes
Performance	30–40 minutes
Cleanup	5 minutes

A conductivity tester

Part 1: Building Bridges

Building Student Knowledge and Motivation

Prior to the lesson, create a learning center containing a variety of symbols or pictures of symbols commonly associated with Christmas, such as Christmas trees, wrapped gifts, stars, Santa Claus, and reindeer. Be sure to include Christmas-tree lights in the center. Tell the students when they visit the center to look for recurring symbols associated with Christmas. Let them add symbols of Christmas they think should be included but may be missing.

Bridging to the Science Activity

Take the string of Christmas lights from the learning center and ask students "What must be done to make these lights work?" *They must be plugged in.* Ask students if their families ever had to throw out Christmas light strings because the strings wouldn't light up anymore. Discuss reasons that lights might not work. Tell students you have discovered a way to use broken strands to make fun Christmas toys. Show students a section of Christmas-tree lights with one bulb and two wires intact. Tell them they should never put these wires into a wall socket. Discuss electrical safety. Bring out two AA batteries and ask students to suggest ways to use these batteries with a terminal strip attached as a source of energy to light the bulb. Discuss suggestions. Connect the bulb wires to the battery terminal strip wires and observe. Discuss observations.

Part 2: Science Activity

Materials

For Getting Ready
Per class
- wire stripper
- all materials listed for Part A of the Procedure
- all materials listed for Part B, Option 2, of the Procedure

For the Procedure
Part A, per class
- conductivity tester prepared in Getting Ready

Part A, per group
- aluminum foil
- piece of Christmas-tree light strand with 1 bulb and 2 wires (See Getting Ready.)

 The lead wires should be 3–4 inches long.

- 1 of the following sets of materials:
  - 2 AA batteries and a commercial AA battery holder
  - 2 AA batteries; aluminum foil; 2, 5- to 6-inch pieces of insulated wire; and electrical or masking tape (You will make your own holder.)
  - 9-volt battery and commercial battery clip

  We recommend using the two AA batteries with a battery holder. While 9-volt batteries with battery clips are easy to use, they will cause the bulbs to burn out quickly, and the battery itself will not last nearly as long as the AA batteries.

- rubber band
- paint stick
- tape
- large metal paper clip
- metal thumbtack
- paper or small piece of cardboard
- insulated wire about 6 inches long
- various materials to test for conductivity, such as paper, coin, plastic, tape, wood, or pencil lead

Part B, Option 1, per group
- conductivity tester made in Part A
- scissors
- 3-inch x 5-inch index card
- hole punch
- aluminum foil
- clear tape

Part B, Option 2, per class
- homemade conductivity toy prepared in Getting Ready

Part B, Option 2, per student
- conductivity tester made in Part A
- 4, 4- to 6-inch pieces of 22- to 24-gauge bare (unvarnished) copper wire (smaller in diameter than the wire listed above)

  Paper-covered twist-ties can be used instead; just be sure to strip off all of the paper.

- aluminum foil
- 6- to 8-inch-long piece of 18- to 22-gauge bare (unvarnished) copper wire
- 4 thumbtacks
- additional Christmas-tree light bulb (of a different color than the one in the conductivity tester) with lead wires
- drinking straw

For the Extensions for Further Science Inquiry
❶ Per group
- all materials listed for the Procedure
- additional sections of Christmas-tree lights

❷ Per group
- empty cartridges from Polaroid® film
- sections of Christmas-tree lights

Safety and Disposal

Warn students not to insert any of the wires into wall sockets. Dispose of batteries according to local ordinances.

Getting Ready

1. Strip about ¾–1 inch of both ends of all of the long, insulated wires. Also strip both ends of the Christmas-tree light segments.

2. Make two conductivity testers according to the instructions in the Procedure, Part A.

3. Use one of the conductivity testers to make a conductivity toy for Part B, Option 2, as follows:

   a. Remove the foil from the paint stick.

   b. Pull the thumbtack (inserted when making the conductivity tester) up slightly, unhook the light-bulb lead, and wrap the center of one of the thinner bare copper wires around the thumbtack twice. Then firmly push the tack into the wood and cover it as before. (See Figure 1.)

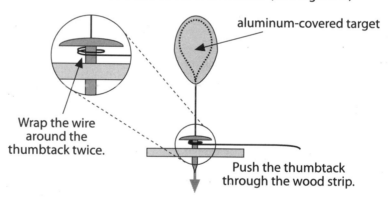

aluminum-covered target

Wrap the wire around the thumbtack twice.

Push the thumbtack through the wood strip.

Figure 1: To make the target, wrap the wire around the thumbtack twice. Push the thumbtack through the wood strip. Make one end of the wire into a loop, bend the wire up, and cover it with aluminum foil.

   c. Shape one end of this bare copper wire into a loop and bend the wire so it sticks straight up from the paint stick. Wrap the loop with aluminum foil. This will serve as a target. (See Figure 1.)

d. Hook the other end of this bare copper wire to the free end of the
conductivity tester's light bulb. (See Figure 2.)

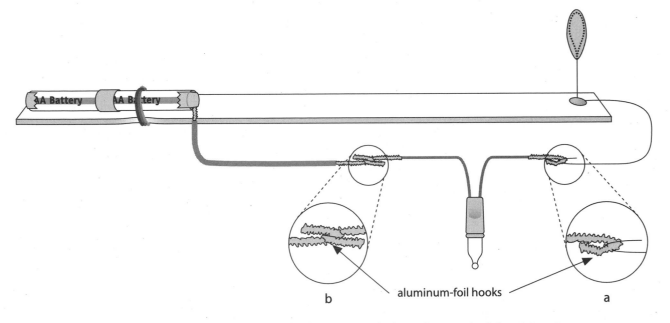

aluminum-foil hooks

b   a

*Figure 2: After you make the target, (a) Hook the other end of the thin wire
to one of the leads of the light holder. (b) Hook the other end of the light holder
to the thicker copper wire that connects back to the battery holder.*

e. Unhook the conductivity tester's pointer from the battery holder and
replace the pointer with the thicker copper wire. This thicker copper wire
will be the new pointer.

f. Test the circuit by touching the pointer to the aluminum-foil target. The
light should come on.

g. Push three thumbtacks loosely into the stick between the target and the
batteries as shown in Figure 3.

h. Wrap the center of a bare copper wire twice around one thumbtack and
push the thumbtack into the wood. Repeat with the other two
thumbtacks.

i. Form a loop in one end of each copper wire. Bend these ends so that the
three loops stand up straight, as shown in Figure 3.

j. Twist the straight ends of the three bare copper wires together. (See Figure 3.)

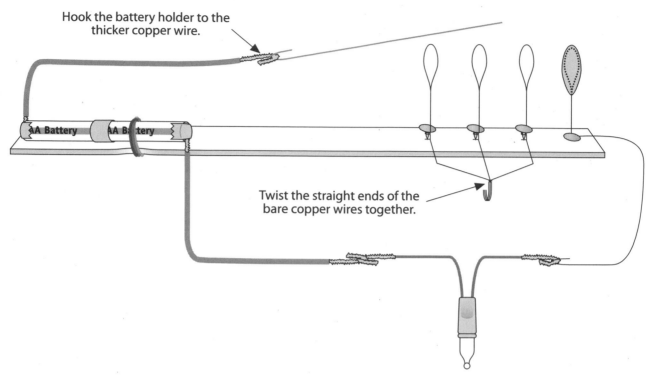

Hook the battery holder to the thicker copper wire.

Twist the straight ends of the bare copper wires together.

Figure 3: Begin assembling the Christmas-tree light toy.

k. Hook one side of a different-colored light to these twisted copper wires. Press the wires together firmly. (See Figure 4.)

l. Hook the other side of the second light to the battery holder. (See Figure 4.)

m. Push the end of the pointer through the three loops, trying to touch the target without touching the loops. If the pointer touches the target, one lamp lights. If the pointer touches any one of the other copper wires, the other lamp lights. (See Figure 4.)

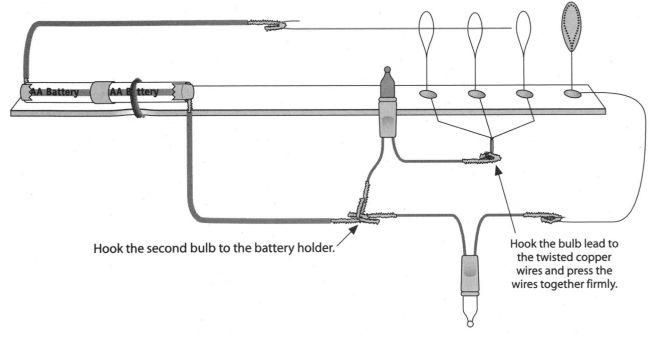

Hook the second bulb to the battery holder.

Hook the bulb lead to the twisted copper wires and press the wires together firmly.

Figure 4: Finish assembling the Christmas-tree light toy.

n. Cut a 2-inch section of drinking straw to use as a protective cover for the lead of the battery holder that is connected to both bulbs. When you are finished using the toy, unhook this lead from the bulb leads and slide the cover over it. This cover will prevent the circuit from being closed if the toy is jostled and thus will prevent the battery from being drained during storage.

Procedure

Part A: Making a Conductivity Tester

1. Show the students your conductivity tester. Tell them each group will make its own according to the following directions:

   a. Wrap a small piece of aluminum foil (approximately 1 inch x 2 inches) around the stripped ends of every insulated wire. Twist the foil tightly to secure it to the wire and make a long, thick, wirelike end. Then bend these foil extensions into hooks. (The purpose of the foil is to reinforce the thin wires in the lights and make it easier to connect and disconnect the components of the devices quickly.)

b. Put the two AA batteries in a battery holder. If you choose not to purchase battery holders, make your own according to the following instructions (see Figure 5):

(1.) Fold a small piece of aluminum foil (about 1 inch x 2 inches) into a square "pillow" about ½ inch x ½ inch.

(2.) Squash the foil pillow firmly between the negative terminal of one AA battery and the positive terminal of the other AA battery. Use electrical or masking tape to fasten the batteries together tightly at the point where they meet.

(3.) Tape one end of a long insulated wire to the exposed negative terminal of the two-battery unit. Tape the end of another long insulated wire to the exposed positive terminal. These two wires are the leads to your homemade battery holder.

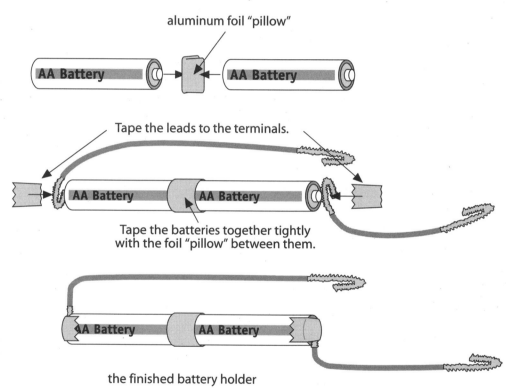

Figure 5: Make a homemade battery holder for two AA batteries.

c. Use a rubber band to attach the batteries to the paint stick near the handle end of the stick.

d. Attach a large metal paper clip to the top of the paint stick near the end with a thumbtack. Being careful not to stick yourself, push the thumbtack about halfway into the stick. (See Figure 6.)

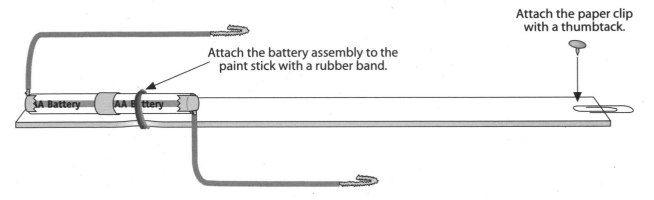

Attach the paper clip with a thumbtack.

Attach the battery assembly to the paint stick with a rubber band.

Figure 6: Begin assembling the conductivity tester.

e. Hook one end of one of the light bulb wires around the tack. (See Figure 7.) Then firmly push the tack as far as possible through the wood. The point of the tack will probably come through the underside of the stick. To prevent the tack from sticking anyone, cover the point of the tack with thickly folded paper or a piece of cardboard and secure by wrapping the paint stick and tack cover with tape.

f. Hook the other lead of the light bulb to one of the leads from the battery clip. (See Figure 7.)

g. Hook one end of the long, insulated wire to the other lead of the battery clip. (See Figure 7.) This long wire will be the pointer.

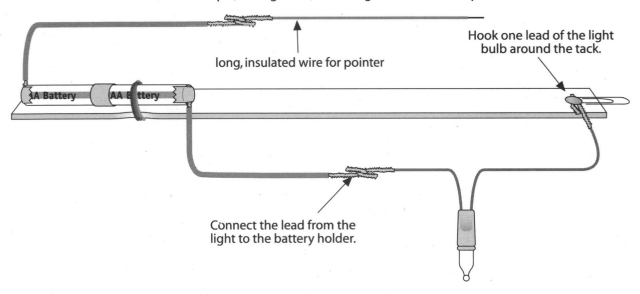

Hook one lead of the light bulb around the tack.

long, insulated wire for pointer

Connect the lead from the light to the battery holder.

Figure 7: Finish assembling the conductivity tester.

h. Touch the free end of the pointer to the metal paper clip or the aluminum foil. The bulb should light up, indicating that the circuit is complete. If the bulb does not light, check all of the connections, pressing hooks together more firmly if necessary. If you are using a homemade battery holder, make sure that the batteries are pressed together tightly.

If the pointer doesn't reach the paper clip, replace the pointer with a longer piece of wire or slide the batteries closer to the tack.

2. Have the groups use their conductivity testers to determine whether various solids are conductors or insulators. This can be done by placing the material to be tested, such as paper, coin, plastic, tape, wood, or pencil lead (which is actually graphite) in or against the paper clip and touching the bare wire to the object.

3. Have groups make a list of conductors and insulators and discuss their findings with the class.

Part B: Making a Conductivity Toy

Choose one of the following two conductivity toy designs for your students to make.

Option 1: Making a Conductivity Quiz Circuit Board

1. Show students how to make conductivity quiz circuit boards out of the conductivity testers they made in Part A, using the following instructions:

a. As shown in Figure 8, wrap a piece of aluminum foil approximately 7 inches x 3 inches over most of the end of the paint stick. About ½ inch at the very end of the stick (farthest from the batteries) should remain uncovered. Tape the aluminum foil together on the back of the stick.

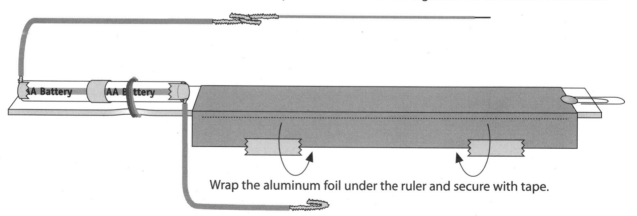

Wrap the aluminum foil under the ruler and secure with tape.

Figure 8: Wrap aluminum foil around the paint stick.

b. Cut a 1-inch x 5-inch strip from a 3-inch x 5-inch index card.

c. Punch holes in the card strip as shown in Figure 9. Print "yes/no" quiz questions on the card strip as shown. (Students may make up their own questions on any subject.)

d. Tape the back of the card strip with clear plastic tape (see Figure 9 for one example) to cover (insulate) all holes corresponding to incorrect answers. (Tape may be applied in a different pattern than the one shown in Figure 9, depending on how the questions are arranged. For example, students may want to make all questions "yes," or make three "no" and one "yes.")

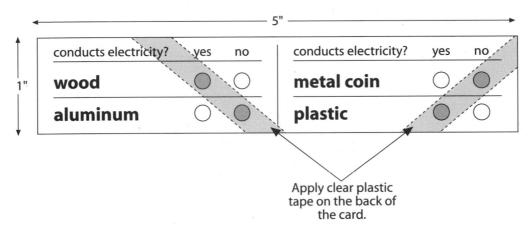

Apply clear plastic tape on the back of the card.

Figure 9: Print "yes/no" quiz questions on the card strip and cover the holes for incorrect answers with clear tape.

e. Position the quiz card on top of the aluminum foil and tape the quiz card to the paint stick. Tape only the ends of the card so that you do not cover up the holes. (See Figure 10.)

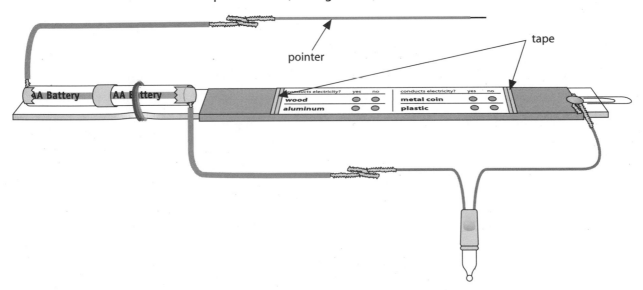

Figure 10: Attach the quiz card to the Conductivity Quiz Circuit Board.

2. Have each group test its conductivity quiz circuit board by touching the pointer to the answer circles.

Option 2: Designing a Christmas-Tree Light Toy

1. Show the students the conductivity toy you made in Getting Ready. Ask them to work in groups to draw, write, or discuss instructions for adapting their

conductivity testers into such toys. Allow the groups to modify their conductivity testers and test their designs.

2. Have students write a set of instructions for using and storing the toys. They will include these instructions with the gift.

Extensions for Further Science Inquiry

- Have students experiment with using several different light sections connected in series circuits to determine the number of sections that can be connected and still be lighted by the batteries. Students could connect lights in a parallel circuit, including one blinking light, and determine the results.

- Show students a fun and fascinating way to make simple and series circuits by using the empty cartridges from Polaroid film and sections of Christmas tree lights. Each used cartridge contains a 6-volt lithium battery, which is used to advance the film while it is in the camera but which maintains its electrical charge and usefulness once the film is used up. Individual light sections can be cut from a long strand of lights. Each bulb needs to have two 3- to 4-inch lengths of coated wire with the copper ends exposed. The two little silver "eyeholes" on the flat side of the cartridge are the electrical terminals of the battery. When one wire from the light bulb is placed in one terminal and the other wire in the other terminal, the circuit is completed and the bulb lights.

Science Explanation

The following explanation is intended for the teacher's information. Modify the explanation for students as required.

The conductivity tester, conductivity quiz, and toy use a simple electric circuit. Electric current in a wire, as in this activity, is the movement of electrons. Every electric circuit has two essential components: a source of electricity (electrical energy) and one or more objects through which the electricity may travel. A familiar energy source is the battery. The source could also be a generator, or it could be an AC outlet in the wall through which electricity comes from a generator that might be far away. To perform a function, a device such as a light bulb can be part of the circuit. When the circuit is completed, the device performs a useful function. The device could be a bell, buzzer, light bulb, toaster, curling iron, or alarm clock. The most common material used to conduct electricity is a covered copper wire, but electricity can also be conducted by a metal plate, water that contains ions to allow conduction, or a human being. An object through which electricity will travel is called a conductor. An object that will not conduct electricity is called a nonconductor, or insulator. The circuit may contain additional components, the most common of which is probably the switch. A switch is simply a device for opening or closing the circuit without disturbing any of the other connections.

In the conductivity tester in this activity, the circuit's basic components can be seen. The batteries act as the energy source; the metal materials provide the path through which the electricity flows. The light bulb is the electricity-using device, and the free end of the long, insulated wire acts as a switch, completing the circuit when it touches the aluminum foil. Figure 11 shows a diagram of this circuit.

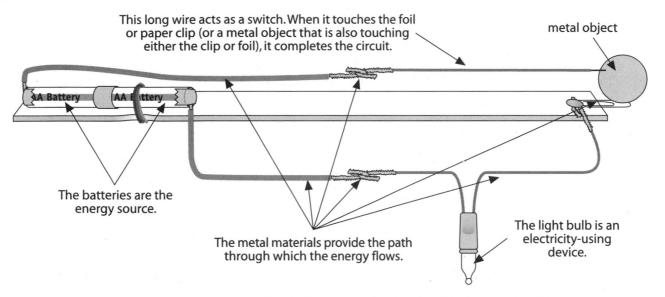

This long wire acts as a switch. When it touches the foil or paper clip (or a metal object that is also touching either the clip or foil), it completes the circuit.

metal object

The batteries are the energy source.

The metal materials provide the path through which the energy flows.

The light bulb is an electricity-using device.

Figure 11: Students can see the basic elements of a circuit with the conductivity tester.

A schematic diagram of this circuit would resemble the one shown in Figure 12.

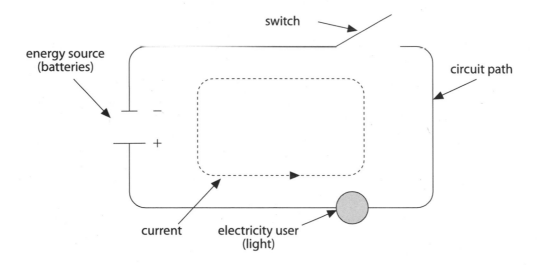

switch

energy source (batteries)

circuit path

current

electricity user (light)

Figure 12: A schematic diagram of the circuit represents how the conductivity tester works.

When the switch is closed (the free end of the wire touches the aluminum foil or a conductor that is touching the paper clip) the circuit is completed and the current flows. The current consists of electrons traveling through the circuit. In the conductivity quiz, the pieces of clear tape covering the aluminum foil under incorrect answers act as insulators, preventing the circuit from being completed when the incorrect answers are selected.

References for the Science Activity

Perkins, R. Institute for Chemical Education, 1991.

Taylor, B.A.P. "Doc Shock;" *Exploring Energy with TOYS: Complete Lessons for Grades 4–8;* McGraw-Hill: New York, 1998; p 207–213.

Part 3: Integrating with Language Arts

Featured Fiction Book: *The Amazing Christmas Extravaganza*

Author: David Shannon
Publisher: Scholastic   ISBN: 0590480901
Summary: Much to the dismay of his neighbors and family, Mr. Merriweather's Christmas display grows from a simple string of white lights into an outrageous spectacle.

Before reading the story, show students the cover of the book. Talk about what kinds of outdoor Christmas decorations students have seen or may have at home. As you read the story, draw students' attention to the strings of lights around many of the pages of text. Discuss how the lights change as the story progresses. Also, ask students why Mr. Merriweather suddenly becomes dissatisfied with his decorations after Mr. Clack's visit, despite the fact that originally he was very happy with them. Why does Mr. Merriweather continue to add to his decorations even after his display surpasses Mr. Clack's? At first the neighbors like the display, but then they become angry. Why? (If you did the first Extension for Further Science Inquiry, in which students determine how many lights can be lit with two AA batteries, ask students how their observations relate to the electrical problem in Mr. Merriweather's neighborhood. How could the neighbors have handled the problem differently? After the story is finished, ask students if they have ever become dissatisfied with a possession or achievement just because someone else owned or did more. What did they do about the situation?

Writing Extensions

- Have students use their science journals to describe and sketch their initial designs for their conductivity toys, record evaluations by other students, and describe and sketch design modifications.
- String white or colored lights in the classroom. Have students describe them.
- Have students draft a letter from the neighbors to Mr. Merriweather describing what his display is doing to the neighborhood and how the problem could be solved.

Additional Books

Fiction

Title: *Christmas Lights*
Author: Ann Fearrington
Publisher: Houghton Mifflin   ISBN: 0395710367
Summary: On Christmas night the Merriweather family drives into town to see all the displays of lights.

Title: *The Lonely Christmas Tree*
Author: Donald Cripe   Illustrator: Karen S. Gruntman
Publisher: Bud's   ISBN: 0964962500
Summary: A little Christmas tree living in a large Christmas tree forest dreams of having tinsel and lights but isn't chosen because of his crooked trunk and sparse branches.

Title: *O Christmas Tree*
Author: Vashanti Rahaman   Illustrator: Frane Lessac
Publisher: Boyds Mills   ISBN: 1563972379
Summary: Christmas is coming, and Anselm wants a Christmas tree more than anything. But there are no evergreens in the West Indies, and the ones that arrive on the boat from the north are in bad shape. Anselm believes that Christmas will not be Christmas without a tree, but Miss Mary, Anselm's neighbor, shows the boy that the islands have their own kinds of Christmas trees.

Nonfiction

Title: *Holly, Reindeer and Colored Lights*
Author: Edna Barth
Publisher: Houghton Mifflin   ISBN: 0899190375
Summary: Examines the origins of Christmas symbols—trees, ornaments, Yule logs, Santa Claus, cards, Christmas colors, and many other holiday observances.

Part 4: Other Lesson Extensions

Art and Music

- Have students create pictures or sculptures incorporating one or more battery-powered Christmas lights. For example, they could draw a reindeer and push a red light through the paper to create a light-up nose, or they could sculpt a person holding a lighted "candle."
- Have students sing Christmas carols, such as "O Christmas Tree."

Mathematics

- Have students decorate the classroom or a tree with strings of white lights. (The tree could be a ficus or other nonseasonal plant.) Have them calculate how many strands they will need for the project given strands with a certain number of bulbs (such as 50 or 100). How many strands would they need if the strands had a different number of bulbs?
- Divide students into groups and give each group a 50-light strand of colored lights. Have students count the number of bulbs of each color their group's strand has and have them report their findings to the class. Calculate a class average for each color. Have students use their calculated averages to estimate the number of bulbs of each color that would appear in a 100-light strand. Have them count an actual 100-light strand and determine whether their estimate was accurate. Discuss why or why not.

Social Studies

- Have students research how Christmas trees were lighted before electricity. Discuss the safety aspects of various ways of lighting trees.

Part 5: National Science Education Standards

Science as Inquiry Standards:

Abilities Necessary to Do Scientific Inquiry
Students question what types of solids are conductors and what types are insulators.

Students investigate the conductivity of a variety of solids.

Students use their conductivity testers as tools to learn more about the properties of various solids.

Students group conductors and insulators and use the groups to generalize what types of solids conduct and what types do not.

Students discuss their findings as a group.

Physical Science Standards:

Properties of Objects and Materials
The ability to conduct electricity or function as an insulator is a characteristic property of substances.

Objects are made of one or more materials and can be described by the properties of the materials from which they are made. Some materials that conduct electricity are made of metal.

Light, Heat, Electricity, and Magnetism
Electrical circuits can produce light if the circuit is complete.

Science and Technology Standards:

Abilities of Technological Design

Students question how to make their conductivity testers into conductivity toys.

Students design conductivity toys using their testers and other inexpensive, readily available materials.

Students evaluate their toys and those of other groups and modify their designs as desired before making their final toys.

Students write instructions for using and storing their toys.

Kwanzaa

December 26-January 1
Culture: African-American

Kwanzaa, from the Swahili word "kwanza" meaning "first fruits," is an African-American holiday developed in 1966 by Dr. Maulana Ron Karenga. Patterned after African harvest festivals, Kwanzaa is a celebration of family unity and the goodness of life. The seven days of Kwanzaa are dedicated to the seven principles of Nguzo Saba (the "Way of Life"): unity (umoja), self-determination (kujichagulia), collective responsibility (ujima), cooperative economics (ujamaa), purpose (nia), creativity (kuumba), and faith (imani). An extra "a" was added to the word "kwanza" to make the number of letters in the name match the number of principles.

One of the main symbols of Kwanzaa is the kinara, a candelabra that holds one mshumaa (candle) for each of the seven principles. One black candle stands in the middle, with three green candles on the left and three red candles on the right. Each evening, the family gathers to light the day's candle and discuss the principle it represents. On December 31, the second-to-last day of the holiday, the family joins the community for a feast called "karamu." The community members share their accomplishments during the year and together they give thanks to their Creator for what they have been given.

When Karenga was developing the Kwanzaa holiday, he looked to the harvest festivals of his people's African ancestors as well as to the rituals of African-American slaves from the early days of our country. By using the symbols of the past, Karenga hoped to unite and strengthen the African-American people toward a fuller, more productive future. The symbols of Kwanzaa are as follows:

- The mkeka, a straw mat, symbolizes tradition as the foundation on which all else rests. The kinara, corn, unity cup, and gifts are placed on the mkeka.
- The kinara, the candle holder, represents the original stalk from which all people sprang.
- The mshumaa, the seven candles, are for the seven principles on which early African societies were based.
- The muhindi, ears of corn, represent the children (kernels) and the parents (stalk) and their ability to produce offspring, symbolizing the immortality of the culture.

- The kikombe cha umoja, or unity cup, is a symbol of the first principle of Nguzo Saba. Each member of the family drinks from the unity cup, reinforcing the commitment to unity and collective work.
- The zawadi, or gifts, represent the rewards of labor of both the parents and children. Children especially are rewarded for good deeds performed and good grades earned throughout the year.

Other cultures celebrate the harvest and "first fruits" in different ways and at different times of the year because of varying climates around the world.

- In India in mid-January, the Hindu people celebrate Pongal Sankrandi, a three-day harvest festival marked by feasting and celebration.
- Seven weeks after Passover, Jewish people celebrate their festival of the first fruits, Shavuot, which usually takes place in May. This holiday commemorates Moses receiving the Ten Commandments and the first five books of the Bible (the Pentateuch) on Mount Sinai.
- Chusok, the Korean harvest festival, takes place in August or September. The Korean calendar is based on lunar months, and Chusok is scheduled for the full moon of the 8th lunar month.
- Halloween (October 31) was originally a Celtic harvest and new year festival celebrated in Ireland (see "Spooky Spiders and Webs" in this book for more information). Because the Celts were an agricultural society, they based their year on the growing seasons. When the harvest was brought in, the old year was considered to be ending and the new one beginning.
- The Day of the Dead (November 1-2) is celebrated in Mexico and by Mexican-Americans. It is a harvest festival as well as a time to remember those who have died.
- The fourth Thursday in November is Thanksgiving day in America (see "Give Thanks for Corn!" in this book for more information). This day commemorates the first harvest for the Pilgrims in the New World in 1621.

References

Banks, V.J.R. *The Kwanzaa Coloring Book;* Sala Enterprises: Los Angeles, 1985, pp 18–19.

"Celebrations of Light," *Totline.* November/December 1995, 4–5.

Earthlink Holiday Page, "Kwanzaa;" http://www.earthlink.net/holidays/kwanzaa

"Kwanzaa" *Britannica Online.* http://www.eb.com:180/cgi-bin/g?DocF=micro/332/39.html (accessed 10 Feb 1998).

Silverthorne, E. *Fiesta!;* Millbrook: Brookfield, CT, 1992, pp 32–34.

Candle-Making for Kwanzaa

Kwanzaa (December 26–January 1) is a seven-day African-American holiday celebrating unity and shared harvests. Among the main symbols of Kwanzaa are the mshumaa, colored candles that sit in a seven-branched candelabra called a kinara. In this activity, students will learn how to make the candles that are an important part of the Kwanzaa rituals.

Key Science Topics

- melting
- phase changes
- physical properties

Time Required

Setup	45	minutes
Performance	60	minutes
Cleanup	20	minutes

Red, black, and green ice candles

Part 1: Building Bridges

Building Student Knowledge and Motivation

Since students are typically on vacation from school during Kwanzaa, you may want to introduce this African-American celebration of goodwill and thanks before winter break or during the fall when other harvest festivals, such as Thanksgiving, are being celebrated.

Prior to beginning the lesson, create a learning center containing many types of candles. Try to include candles made in a variety of ways (molded, hand-dipped, and rolled from beeswax) as well as candles that are intended for specific celebrations (such as birthday candles and menorah candles). Be sure to include seven Kwanzaa candles (three red, three green, and one black), bundled together to indicate that they are used as a set. In the days prior to the lesson, give students an opportunity to visit the center and observe the candles. Tell students to think about how the different candles might have been made and what they might be used for.

Explain that the candles in the learning center are all made of a material called wax and that the students will be observing this material and using it to make their own candles.

Bridging to the Science Activity

Create a four-column chart and label the columns "name," "description," "how made," and "what for." Have students describe candles from the classroom center and contribute their ideas to the "how made" and "what for" columns. (The goal of this brainstorming exercise is to have students focus on their observations of the candles, not to produce correct answers.)

Point out that candles, including the bundle of red, green, and black candles from the classroom center, are an important part of many holiday rituals and celebrations. Review student ideas about these candles from the chart. If no one has mentioned Kwanzaa, briefly explain the meaning and symbolism of the holiday, especially the significance of the candles. Review student ideas from the "how made" column on the chart. Tell students that they will be making their own candles for a Kwanzaa celebration in the classroom.

Part 2: Science Activity

Materials

For Getting Ready

Per class

- old newspapers
- 3 clean, empty coffee cans (one for each color of wax) at least 13 ounces or larger
- hot plate, electric skillet, or similar heating device

  The heating device must be able to bring the wax to a temperature of about 175°–190°F. Most warming trays and slow cookers do not get hot enough.

- soup pot or saucepan large enough to hold all 3 coffee cans

  If you use an electric skillet (see item above), you do not need a separate pan.

- 7, ¾-pound boxes of paraffin

  Paraffin can be found in the canning goods section of grocery stores. It comes in boxes containing either three or four ¼-pound slabs. In some areas, paraffin is a seasonal item found only in late summer or fall.

- candy thermometer with clip
- 3 stirring sticks (one for each color of wax in Part C)
- oven mitts
- crushed ice
- 2, 3-ounce Solo® disposable plastic bathroom cups

  This activity has been tested with cups made by the Solo Cup Company. (Test other brands of cups in advance.) While larger Solo cups will work, the 3-ounce cups produce very attractive, votive-like candles, and your class will be able to make more candles with a given quantity of wax.

- 1 of the following items to transfer wax from the coffee cans to the molds
  - metal measuring cup
  - metal or heatproof plastic ladle
- 2 birthday candles

For the Procedure

Part A, per class

- ice cubes
- block of paraffin
- cooler
- 2 containers made of heat-resistant glass, such as Pyrex®
- wax-melting apparatus prepared in Getting Ready

Parts B and C, per class

- wax-melting apparatus prepared in Getting Ready
- cooking spray or vegetable oil
- 1 of the following items to transfer wax from the coffee cans to the molds
  - metal measuring cup
  - metal or heatproof plastic ladle

Parts B and C, per group
• scissors

Part B, per class
• 2 candles made in Getting Ready (one solid and one with holes)
• 2 birthday candles
• crushed ice
• 2–3, 3-ounce Solo disposable plastic bathroom cups

Part C, per class
• 4–5 black crayons, peeled
• 3-ounce Solo disposable plastic bathroom cup
• birthday candle
• (optional) matches
• (optional) Kwanzaa ceremonial objects described in the Introduction to Kwanzaa at the beginning of this activity
• object such as a shoebox lid or board to make a kinara

Part C, per group

Students should be divided into six groups. In a class of 30 students, each group will contain 5 students. According to this plan, each student in the group makes one candle, and the entire group makes an additional candle for the class kinara. If your class is smaller or bigger, adjust the group size and materials accordingly.

• 3-ounce Solo disposable plastic bathroom cups (1 per student plus 1 extra per group)
• 4–5 red or green crayons, peeled

Each group will be assigned one color of candles to make—red or green—and will need only that color of crayon. Three groups will use red, and three groups will use green. (You will make the black candle as a demonstration.) This is a perfect opportunity to use broken or misshapen crayons.

• birthday candles (1 per student plus 1 extra per group)
• crushed ice
• masking tape and pen for labels

For the Extension for Further Science Inquiry
Per class
• clean, empty coffee can (13 ounces or larger)
• hot plate, electric skillet, or similar heating device
• soup pot or saucepan

If you use an electric skillet (see item above), you do not need a separate pan.

• 3-4 boxes of paraffin
• crayon(s) of desired color
• candy thermometer with clip
• stirring stick
• oven mitt
• scissors

Per student

- 8-inch wick

  Thin cotton string works fine for wicks. You may use braided cotton wicking made for candles if you prefer. Wicking is available at craft stores that sell candle-making supplies and can also be ordered from the suppliers listed in Part 4, Resources.

- craft stick or pencil
- washer
- foam tray or pie pan

Safety and Disposal

Hot paraffin can cause severe burns. Only an adult should handle the coffee cans with melted paraffin. The use of oven mitts is highly recommended in moving or using hot paraffin.

Do not put coffee cans containing paraffin directly on a hot plate. If the paraffin gets too hot it smokes and can even ignite. To prevent overheating, always put the can of paraffin inside a larger pot with at least several inches of water and use the lowest heat setting that will melt the paraffin.

Any excess paraffin at project's end can be kept in the coffee can or poured into a carton or paper cup and saved for future use or discarded. The plastic-cup molds are also reusable if they have not been cracked. Do not pour melted paraffin into sinks or toilets. To keep the coffee cans for other use, pour off excess paraffin as explained above while the paraffin is still warm but not hot.

Getting Ready

1. Set up a wax-melting station and an area for setting out the candles to cool as follows:

   a. Cover a table with newspaper. The table should be large enough to set up the hot plate and pot and also to set out the students' candles to harden.

   b. Pour several inches of water into the soup pot or saucepan and set it on the hot plate or skillet. (If you are using an electric skillet, pour water directly into the skillet.)

   c. Put ¾ pound paraffin into each coffee can and clip a candy thermometer to the side of one can, with the thermometer on the inside of the can and extending down to the wax.

   At this point, you will have about 4 pounds of paraffin left. You will melt the additional paraffin after using the paraffin now in the cans.

   d. About 20–30 minutes before beginning the activity, set the cans in the water and turn the heating device to a medium-high setting. Stir the melting wax with the stirring sticks as needed.

   If the cans float, remove some of the water.

e. When the water begins just barely to simmer, turn the heating device down to a lower setting and allow the wax to finish melting. The wax should be between 175° and 190°F. If the wax is hotter than 190°F, turn the heating device down a little more to allow the wax to cool down.

By not heating the wax more than necessary, you reduce the risk of injury from spilled hot wax and also improve the quality of the finished candles.

2. Make two candles, one with ice and one without, according to the instructions in the Procedure, Part B, steps 3–6.

Procedure

Part A: Observing Phase Changes with Water and Wax

1. Create an observation chart with two columns labeled "water" and "wax" and with four rows labeled "cooler," "room temperature first," "hot plate," and "room temperature last."

2. Bring out a cooler containing ice cubes and wax. Take the ice cubes out of the container and ask the students to describe them (*solid, cold*). Let the students pass them around. Bring out the wax and pass it around. Ask the students to describe the wax (*solid, cold*). Chart student observations.

3. Ask students to predict what will happen to the ice and wax if they are allowed to warm to room temperature. Set the samples aside until they warm to about room temperature or take out samples already at room temperature. Pass them around for the students to observe. Have students measure the temperature of the water with a thermometer. It will be difficult to measure the temperature of the wax so instead ask students to speculate what the temperature of the wax is. Chart student observations.

4. Ask students to predict what will happen if the water and wax samples are warmed on a hot plate. Place each sample in its own heat-resistant glass container, set it in the water in the wax-melting apparatus prepared in Getting Ready, and heat it. Do not pass the warmed samples around, as they could cause burns. Instead, show students that you can pour each into another container. Ask students to describe what they see. Measure and record the temperature of the water and the wax. Chart student observations.

5. Ask students to predict what would happen if these two liquids were allowed to cool to room temperature. Discuss their predictions, asking them to explain their reasoning. Allow the samples to cool and observe that the water cools but stays a liquid, while the wax solidifies. Ask students what they would have to do to solidify the water.

6. Discuss the phase changes students observed in this part of the activity. Ask how the water phase change might be useful to them (making ice cubes). Ask students how this phenomenon might be useful to candle makers.

Part B: Making and Comparing Candles with and without Holes

1. Show the class the two candles you made in Getting Ready—one solid and the other with holes. Have them record their observations. Ask them to propose explanations for the differences. Do not tell them the answer, but ask them leading questions such as the following:
   - Do you think I cut out the holes?
   - Could I have added something that made the holes? If so, what could that be?
   - Could the observations you made in Part A help explain the differences?

2. Tell the students that you will demonstrate how to make these two types of molded candles and then they will have a chance to make their own. Tell them you want them to record or draw the steps involved with each so that later they can discuss how the procedures resulted in different products.

3. Demonstrate the candle-making procedures as follows:

   a. Coat the insides of two Solo cups, either by spraying them with cooking spray or rubbing the sides and bottom with cooking oil using fingers or a paper towel. Ask students what purpose the spray or oil serves. *It acts as a release agent, helping the candles to slide out of the molds without sticking.*

   b. Using the measuring cup or ladle, carefully pour melted wax into one of the oiled plastic-cup molds to fill it about three-fourths full. You may wish to wear an oven mitt to protect your hand from the hot can. Ask students what state of matter the melted wax is in. *Liquid.* Allow the wax to cool 10–15 minutes, and then place a small birthday candle upright in the center of the wax. Set the candle aside to cool for a few hours.

    It is important to wait 10–15 minutes before inserting the birthday candle, because if it is inserted too soon, the wax you just poured will be hot enough to melt the birthday candle, causing the wick to set crooked.

   c. Hold a small birthday candle upside down (wick toward the bottom) in the center of the other oiled plastic cup and pour crushed ice around the birthday candle to fill the cup about three-fourths full. Ask students what state of matter the ice (water) is in. *Solid.* Pour melted wax over the top of the ice to a level just higher than the ice. Allow the candle to harden (about 10–20 minutes).

4. Once the wax has hardened, allow students to observe both candles in their molds. Ask students what state the wax is in now. *Solid.* Discuss the differences and similarities between the two candles.

   You may need to wait until the following day to do this step because the candle you poured in step 3b will take 2–4 hours to cool completely.

5. Pour the water off the holey candle. Ask the students to explain why the water is now liquid. Ask them to explain what caused the holes.

6. Remove both candles from their molds and allow students to observe. The plain candle can stand right-side-up, but the ice candle will probably be uneven at the end that was at the bottom of the mold and should stand upside down. Use scissors to trim the birthday candle so that the ice candle can stand straight. (See Figure 1.) When the ice candle is set upside down, the wick end of the birthday candle will now be at the top. (You may need to scrape away some wax to expose the wick.)

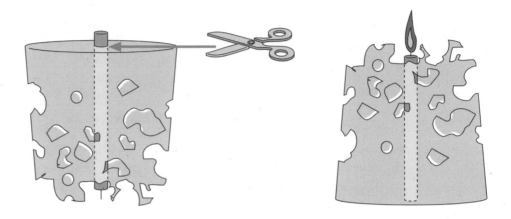

Figure 1: Trim the end of the birthday candle so the ice candle can stand straight when it is turned over.

Part C: Making Colored Candles

1. Tell the students that candles can be colored with crayons. Ask them to describe ways this might be done.

2. Demonstrate the method by dropping one peeled black crayon into the center of the hot wax. Allow the crayon to melt, and stir the wax thoroughly. Allow students to observe the wax, and ask them what could be done to make the color more intense. *Add more crayons.* Allow students to decide whether more crayons should be added to make the color more intense.

3. When the color of the wax has reached an intensity the students consider satisfactory, make one or more ice candles according to the instructions in Part B, steps 3a and 3c.

4. Divide the class into six groups. Assign three groups to make red candles and three to make green candles. Under close adult supervision, have the six groups make ice candles according to the procedure you demonstrated in Part B, steps 3a and 3c, but allow groups to decide how much ice they would like to add to make their candle. Use green and red crayons with fresh, uncolored paraffin wax and a different coffee can for each color.

   You may want to have an adult do all the pouring. Students could make both types of candles (with ice and without) or just one type.

5. Set up a classroom kinara with three red candles, three green candles, and one black candle. Set the candles on a board or in a shoebox lid to catch drips. If the intensity of any of the red or green candles differs, discuss reasons for the difference.

Extension for Further Science Inquiry

Through a facilitated discussion, help your students identify the important steps in the candle-making process they used. For example, your class might identify "melting wax," "coloring wax," "pouring wax," "inserting the wick," and "letting the candle harden" as the different steps. Help your students extend this reasoning to candle-making in general, no matter what the method. For example, the wax must be softened or melted, it is often colored, and it must somehow harden in the desired shape with the wick inside. Tell students they will use a different method of hardening the wax into another shape.

Making Dipped Candles

Using this procedure, students will make 4- to 6-inch candles. Set up a wax-melting station supervised by you or another adult. Color the wax as desired. Adjust the temperature of the heating device so the wax is between 155°F and 160°F.

 The temperature of the wax is extremely important when making dipped candles. You may need to add more paraffin to the cans during the candle-making process to keep the level high enough for dipping.

Have each student tie one end of his or her wick to a craft stick or pencil and tie a washer onto the free end of the wick to weight the wick. Divide students into small groups. Have the first group line up at the wax-melting station. Instruct the first student to put on an oven mitt, hold the craft stick or pencil, dip 4–6 inches of the wick into the wax, pull it out, hold a foam tray or pie pan under the wick to catch drips, give the oven mitt to the next student in line, and walk to the end of the line to wait for another turn. Have the next student dip his or her wick in the same fashion. Have students continue to take turns dipping until ¼-inch-diameter candles are formed; about 15–20 dips will accomplish this. After each group finishes the dipping, bring up a new group, and have students hang up their candles to cool for about an hour. Use scissors to trim the wicks to a height of about ½ inch above the wax.

Science Explanation

 The following explanation is intended for the teacher's information. Modify the explanation for students as required.

The Science of Candles

The candle-making process in this activity involves changes of state from solid to liquid and back to solid. Paraffin blocks and crayons are solid at room temperature. In the solid state, the particles that make up the paraffin and crayons are held in place by the attractive forces between the particles. While particles in the solid state are able to vibrate in place, they do not have enough energy to move from one place to another. Thus, solids have specific shapes.

The paraffin and crayons change to the liquid state when they are heated. This change from the solid state to the liquid state is called melting. The energy added to the particles allows them to overcome some of the attractive forces that were previously responsible for holding them in place. In the liquid state, the particles are still touching each other but are able to slip and slide past each other. Thus, the color of the crayon is able to spread throughout the wax. Also, because liquids take the shape of their containers, the wax can be poured into molds. Finally, wicks, which must be embedded in the candle from top to bottom, can be inserted easily into liquid wax.

As the liquid wax is allowed to cool, it gradually turns solid again. This liquid-to-solid transition is called freezing. (Many students have the misconception that freezing occurs only in freezers or at cold temperatures, as is the case with water. For wax, the freezing temperature is above room temperature.) The cooling wax hardens in the shape of the mold and firmly embeds the wick. The outside of the candle cools first, causing a solid "skin" to form on the top while the inside is still liquid.

When a candle is burned, wax is converted to another state of matter: gas. This liquid-to-gas transition is called vaporization. When the candle is lit, the wax in the wick melts due to the heat of the match. Additional wax in the candle itself melts from the heat of the burning wick. This liquid wax is drawn up the wick by capillary action and becomes a gas. This gas burns in oxygen present in the atmosphere.

Melting, freezing, and vaporization are examples of physical changes. The particles that make up the wax are the same composition regardless of the state they are in; the only difference is the amount of energy that the particles possess. The burning of the wax vapor, however, is a chemical change, and the wax particles and oxygen form carbon dioxide (a gas) and water vapor.

The History of Candle-Making

Fire has been used as a source of light for thousands of years. Evidence of sooty emissions near cave paintings suggests that torches or lamps were used during the Upper Paleolithic era (22,000 years before present). Beeswax candles have been found in Egyptian tombs dating from about 3,000 B.C. The earliest candles were probably rushlights, or torches, which were dried rushes soaked in molten tallow (animal fat). These lights did not have a wick like today's candles. Despite the fact that they smoked and had an unpleasant smell, they were cheap and thus were commonly used in England as late as 1800. Tallow was not the only material used for early candles: Chinese and Japanese candles were made of wax extracted from insects and seeds, and wax extracted from cinnamon was used in India, where the use of animal fat was forbidden. People in South America scraped wax from the leaves of the wax palm or used oil from jojoba nuts. Native Americans wedged oily fish (candlefish) into forked sticks and burned the fish.

The modern candle-making process began in the Middle Ages. From about the 13th century to the 15th century, candles were made by the dipping method. Tallow was the most common material, but beeswax, which burned cleaner and brighter and emitted a sweet smell, was also used. Beeswax candles were expensive, so only the wealthy and the church could afford them. The difference in quality (and price) between tallow and beeswax was so marked that beeswax chandlers formed a separate guild, the Guild of Wax Chandlers, to distinguish themselves from the Guild of Tallow Chandlers.

In the 15th century, a Parisian named de Brez invented the candle mold, which revolutionized the candle-making process. However, beeswax was not well suited for molding because it tended to stick to molds. It continued to be shaped by dipping until the 20th century, when silicon releasing agents were developed.

From the 15th century to the 18th century, the candle-making process remained relatively unchanged. In the late 18th century, a new source of wax became widely available. This material, called spermaceti, was made from oil obtained from the head cavities of sperm whales, or cachalots. Spermaceti wax was harder than either tallow or beeswax, and unlike tallow, it did not emit an unpleasant odor when burned. Spermaceti candles produced such bright light that their flames were used as a standard light measure for photometry. However, spermaceti candles were almost as expensive as beeswax and thus were not commonly used. Today they are no longer made at all because of whaling bans imposed in response to over-hunting of the sperm whale.

Most major advances in modern candle-making occurred during the 19th century. In the first half of the century, a Frenchman named Michel Eugene Chevreul discovered that tallow was actually composed of two different fatty acids and glycerine. By removing glycerine from tallow using alkali and sulfuric acid, Chevreul produced a new substance called stearine, or stearic acid. Stearine candles were harder and burned brighter and longer than tallow candles. The development of stearine made improvements in the wick possible. In 1825, another Frenchman named Cambaceres invented a braided wick pickled in mineral salt. This wick curled over as it burned and was completely consumed, making the task of continually trimming the wick unnecessary. In 1834, Joseph Morgan invented a candle-molding machine capable of making 1,500 candles in an hour. In 1836, palmatine, a substance produced from palm oil, was patented as an alternative to existing waxes.

Another significant development occurred in 1850, when paraffin wax was discovered. This bluish-white wax, produced by distilling the residue left after the refinement of crude petroleum, burned cleanly with no unpleasant odor. Perhaps most significantly, it was the least expensive candle fuel ever produced. Paraffin's only disadvantage was its low melting point. However, this problem was overcome by combining paraffin with stearine. Candles made with paraffin, stearine, and braided wicks were bright, durable, and affordable.

Unfortunately, only shortly after many obstacles in the candle-making process had been overcome, the light bulb was invented in 1879. As a result, the candle-making industry declined until the turn of the century, when interest in candles revived somewhat. Although they are no longer used as a major source of light in the U.S., candles today are prized as decorations and ceremonial objects.

References for the Science Activity

Innes, M. *The Book of Candles;* Dorling Kindersley: London, 1997, pp 6–9.

National Candle Association Home Page. Candle Information. History of Candlemaking. http://www.candles.org/history.htm (accessed 17 Feb 1998).

Sherman, B. Craft Cave Home Page. Candle Cave. Candle History. http://www.craftcave.com/candhist.htm (accessed 17 Feb 1998).

WaxWorks Candle Makers Home Page. History. http://www.tascraft.com.au/WW/history.html (accessed 17 Feb 1998).

Your World at Home Home Page. Tips. Candles. A Brief History of Candles. http://www.ywh.com/Tips/Table/candles/candles-history.html (accessed 17 Feb 1998).

Part 3: Integrating with Language Arts

Featured Fiction Book: *Imani's Gift at Kwanzaa*

Author: Denise Burden-Patman   Illustrator: Floyd Cooper
Publisher: Simon & Schuster   ISBN: 0-671-79841-3
Summary: As M'dear prepares Imani's hair for the upcoming Kwanzaa celebration, the little girl learns the true meaning of Kwanzaa and the true meaning of her name.

Before reading the story, show students the cover of the book. Have them look closely at Imani's hair. Students should note that the beads are red, green, and black—the same colors as the Kwanzaa candles the class made. As you read the story, have students keep track of Kwanzaa terms by writing them and their meanings on a chart or the chalkboard as they are introduced. (A glossary in the back of the book shows definitions and pronunciations for these Swahili words.) Discuss the problem faced by Imani in the story. How does she use the principle of the day (kuumba) to solve her problem?

After reading the story, return to page 2 and discuss the song M'dear sings about the three colors of Kwanzaa and their meanings. Review and list some of the main symbolic elements in setting up a Kwanzaa table. You may want to have these elements on hand and set up the table in your classroom.

Writing Extensions

- Have students imagine that a friend has no candles for Kwanzaa. Ask students to write a set of step-by-step instructions to tell the friend how his or her family could make their own Kwanzaa candles.
- Brainstorm a list of other holidays/festivities that involve harvest time and the use of candles or lights. (Examples include the Thanksgiving dinner, which may be by candlelight; Halloween and bonfires; Obon Festival of Light; Day of the Dead and the candlelight vigil; Lucia Day and the Crown of Lights; Las Posadas and the candlelight march; Hanukkah and the menorah; and Christmas and tree lights or Advent candles.) Have students select one of these other celebrations and use a Venn Diagram to compare the rituals with those of Kwanzaa. Read some of the Additional Books to the students and model the process before having them work individually. Here is a sample:

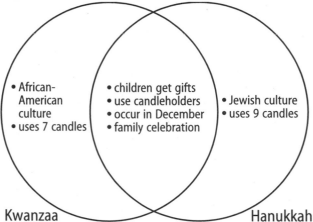

Additional Books

Fiction
Title: *Habari Gani? What's the News?: A Kwanzaa Story*
Author: Sundaira Morninghouse   Illustrator: Jody Kim
Publisher: Open Hand   ISBN: 0-940880-39-3
Summary: Kia experiences the seven principles of Kwanzaa woven into the fabric of her family and community life. Through her, we learn about Kwanzaa's cultural and political significance. Story told in journal format.

Nonfiction
Title: *Kwanzaa*
Author: A.P. Porter   Illustrator: Janice Lee Porter
Publisher: Carolrhoda   ISBN: 0-87614-668-X
Summary: Describes the origins and practices of Kwanzaa, including an explanation of each of Kwanzaa's seven principles and a practical list of items needed for readers to make their own Kwanzaa celebration.

Title: *Kwanzaa*
Author: Deborah M. Newton Chocolate   Illustrator: Melodye Rosales
Publisher: Children's Press   ISBN: 0516039911
Summary: Discusses the holiday in which Afro-Americans celebrate their roots
    and cultural heritage from Africa.

Title: *The Seven Days of Kwanzaa*
Author: Angela Shelf Medearis
Publisher: Scholastic   ISBN: 0-590-46360-0
Summary: Features authentic African recipes for a sumptuous feast, instructions
    for making meaningful craft items, and seven inspiring "celebration stories."

Title: *A Kwanzaa Celebration*
Author: Nancy Williams   Illustrator: Robert Sabuda
Publisher: Simon & Schuster   ISBN: 0-689-80266-8
Summary: An exuberant mix of symbolic holiday images, bold blocks of color and
    ingenious pop-ups. This festive book is a true celebration of a joyous
    African-American holiday.

Title: *Seven Candles for Kwanzaa*
Author: Andrea Davis Pinkney   Illustrator: Brian Pinkney
Publisher: Dial   ISBN: 0-8037-1293-6
Summary: Describes the origins and practices of Kwanzaa, the seven-day festival
    during which people of African descent rejoice in their ancestral values.

Part 4: Other Lesson Extensions

Art and Music

- Have students design and construct their own kinaras from clay, foil,
  cardboard, and other available materials. Tell students that these kinaras are
  merely decorative and are not meant to be lit.
- Have a *zawadi* gift exchange. Have each student write on a strip of paper one
  promise that he/she has kept this school year. Have the students sign their
  paper strips. Then put all the papers in a box from which students will pull a
  paper at random to determine their secret "gift pal." Select one or two
  different gifts that can be made by the students. (Bookmarks with famous
  people depicted or things to wear are ideal gifts. See *The Seven Days of
  Kwanzaa* for many more ideas.) When all the gifts are completed, have a gift
  exchange ceremony in front of the class and have the givers reveal the
  promises that the recipients kept.

Mathematics

- Make an *oware* or *mankala* game using common household objects (such as egg cartons, beans or buttons, and paint). Oware means "transferring," and the game involves logic and the movement of hasa or "playing pieces." The pieces are moved from one cup to another until there are no more left to move. The person with the most pieces at the end of the game is the winner. In some tribes, only kings are allowed to play. It is a very popular game in many regions of Africa. *The Seven Days of Kwanzaa* is an excellent resource for this activity.

Social Studies

- Set up a Kwanzaa celebration table in the classroom. (See Additional Books for references.) Have students make or donate all the necessary items. Spend seven days celebrating Kwanzaa in the classroom. Select a different student each day to pretend to "light" a candle on the kinara and to greet the class with "Habari Gani?" (What's the news?) Teach the class to respond to the greeting each day with one of the seven principles. Have the students decide their actions, behavior, or plans.
- Light the kinara and have students observe changes in the candles as they burn. You may wish to introduce the idea that the wax they observed as a solid and a liquid is now becoming a gas.
- Set up a Kwanzaa celebration using the ceremonial objects listed in the description of Kwanzaa at the beginning of this activity.

Resources

If you would like to investigate candle-making further, many resources are available to help you. Below is a list of resource books and mail-order suppliers of candle-making materials.

Books
Title: *The Book of Candles*
Author: Miranda Innes
Publisher: Dorling Kindersley   ISBN: 0-7894-1656-5

Title: *Candlemaking: Creative Designs and Techniques*
Author: David Constable   Illustrator: Steve Pawsey
Publisher: Search   ISBN: 0855326832

Title: *Candles (Keepsake Craft series)*
Author: Pamela Westland
Publisher: Sunset   ISBN: 0376042605

Title: *Candles, Naturally: A Complete Guide to Rolling Beeswax Candles*
Author: Kathy Edmonds
Publisher: Illume Press   ISBN: 0969893701

Title: *Creative Candles*
Author: Chantal Truber
Publisher: Aurum   ISBN: 1-85410-373-3

Title: *The New Candle Book: Inspirational Ideas for Displaying, Using, and Making
    Candles*
Author: Gloria Nicol
Publisher: Lorenz Books   ISBN: 1859670660

Suppliers
Candlechem Company
32 Thayer Circle
PO Box 705
Randolph, MA 02368
617/963-4161
fax 617/963-3440

Pourette Candle Making Supplies
Pourette Manufacturing Company
1418 NW 53rd
Seattle, WA 98107
800/888-9425

Part 5: National Science Education Standards

Science as Inquiry Standards:

Abilities Necessary to Do Scientific Inquiry

Students use their observations of various candles to investigate how candles are made.

Students question the melting and freezing behavior of ice (water), candles (wax), and crayons (wax).

Students observe the melting and freezing of ice, candles, and crayons.

Students use thermometers to measure the temperature of water.

Students use their observations to explain what caused the holes in the ice candles.

Students discuss their observations and conclusions as a class.

Physical Science Standards:

Properties of Objects and Materials

Students observe the changes of state of paraffin as it is heated and cooled.

Objects have observable properties, including phase, and temperature, which can be measured with a thermometer.

Candles are made from a combination of materials whose properties can be used to describe the candles.

Materials such as water and wax can exist as both solids and liquids and be changed from one state to another by heating and cooling.

Science and Technology Standards:

Abilities of Technological Design

Students question how best to make a colorful Kwanzaa ice candle.

Students decide as a group how much ice and crayon to use for their candles.

Students make sample candles from their proposed combination of wax, crayon, and ice.

Students evaluate their candles and those of other groups and modify their design as desired.

Students show their candles to the class and share the details of their designs.

History and Nature of Science Standards:

Science as a Human Endeavor

Candles have been used for more than 1,000 years.

People in various cultures contributed to improvements in candles and the process of candle-making.

Chinese New Year

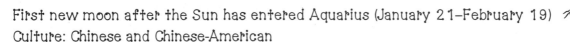

First new moon after the Sun has entered Aquarius (January 21–February 19)
Culture: Chinese and Chinese-American

Chinese festivals and customs are so closely tied to the Chinese calendar that even though the Gregorian calendar was made the official calendar of the Chinese government in 1912, the traditional lunisolar calendar is still used to determine when holidays are celebrated, just as it has been for thousands of years. The Chinese New Year begins on the day of the first new moon after the sun enters the constellation Aquarius. On the Gregorian calendar, this falls between January 21 and February 19. The celebration of the new year begins on the fifteenth day of the twelfth month of the old year, "Little New Year," and continues until the Feast of the Lanterns, the fifteenth day of the first month of the new year.

Little New Year is spent getting affairs in order, paying off debts, and buying supplies and presents for the celebrations before the shops close for the holiday. Doors and window panes are painted—usually red, the color of good omens—and homes are cleaned thoroughly to sweep away misfortune and make way for the good luck the new year brings. Houses are decorated and altars are set up to honor ancestors. The day before the new year begins, meals for the next day are made because on that day knives cannot be used (so they will not "cut" the good luck). Families spend the evening playing games, telling stories, and sharing new year's wishes and promises.

At midnight, firecrackers or whips of bamboo are lit to usher in the new year, and celebrations begin. Presents are exchanged with family and friends, and the atmosphere is warm and friendly. Traditionally, the first few days of the new year are spent at home with family, and visits to friends are made after the third day. This tradition has changed in modern times, and usually only the morning of the new year is spent with family, with parades and celebrations filling the afternoon and evening. Another tradition of the first day of the new year that is no longer widely observed is that each family member adds another year to their age, regardless of when their birthday really is.

Firecrackers are an important part of most Chinese festivals and celebrations, including weddings and anniversaries. The Chinese believe that the loud noise of the firecrackers will drive away evil spirits and bad omens. Other important symbols of the Chinese New Year, especially in America, are the dragon and lion puppets that wind their way through the streets. Both of these animals are symbols of good luck. The puppets are made out of silk or paper. Each lion is operated by one person, but the dragons may take 60 or more people standing underneath to operate them.

The end of the Chinese New Year celebration, the Feast of the Lanterns, is marked by smaller parades, and firecrackers again fill the air with noise. At night, lanterns of all shapes and sizes are lit. Small boats containing lit candles are set adrift on the water. In some areas, children parade through the streets with lanterns as they sing and dance.

One unique aspect of the Chinese calendar is its use of the Chinese zodiac: a cycle of 12 years used to organize the passage of time, with each of the years being named after a different animal. These animals are, in order, the rat, ox, tiger, rabbit, dragon, snake, horse, goat, monkey, rooster, dog, and pig. Each animal has certain characteristics, and people are said to share the characteristics of the animal during whose year they were born. Many legends tell about the Chinese zodiac. One tells of a race across a river that was held to determine the order of the animals. At the start of the race, the rat secretly climbed on the ox's back, then jumped onto the shore just before the ox did, thereby winning the race and becoming the first animal in the zodiac. The book *Why Rat Comes First: A Story of the Chinese Zodiac* (see Additional Books) offers another explanation.

Cultures that follow the Gregorian calendar celebrate the new year on January 1. The night before, on December 31, family and friends gather to count down to the new year, and at midnight they blow horns and make noise to herald the new year. In the Jewish culture, the new year, called Rosh Hashanah, occurs on the first day of the Jewish month Tishri, which corresponds to September or October of the Gregorian calendar. The Jewish calendar, like the Chinese calendar, is lunar, and the months begin with the new moon. Rosh Hashanah celebrates creation and renewal and is one of the few Jewish holidays that is more public than private. A family meal on the eve of Rosh Hashanah is one of the only observances that takes place in the home. On the morning of Rosh Hashanah, a shofar (a trumpet made from a ram's horn) is blown, the community gathers at the synagogue to read scripture passages, and the day is spent in prayer and remembrance.

References

Bredon, J.; Mitrophanow, I. *The Moon Year: A Record of Chinese Customs and Festivals;* Paragon: New York, 1966.

"Chinese New Year" Chinascape Web Site. http://www.chinascape.org/china/culture/holidays/hyuan/newyear.html (accessed 18 Feb 1998).

Latourette, K. S. *The Chinese: Their History and Culture;* MacMillan: Toronto, 1966.

Myers, R.J. *Celebrations: The Complete Book of American Holidays*, Doubleday: Garden City, NY, 1972.

Chinese New Year's Poppers

●●●●●●●●●●●●●●●●●●●●●●●●●●●●●●●●●●●●

Ring out the old year, ring in the new! Noisemakers are an important part

of the Chinese New Year celebration. In this activity, students make

their own noisemakers from film canisters and Alka-Seltzer tablets.

●●●●●●●●●●●●●●●●●●●●●●●●●●●

Key Science Topics

- chemical changes
- gases
- pressure-volume relationship in gases

Time Required

Setup   10 minutes
Performance 30–45 minutes
Cleanup   10 minutes

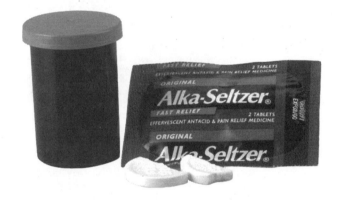

Film canister and Alka-Seltzer tablets

Part 1: Building Bridges

Building Student Knowledge and Motivation

Prior to the lesson, create a learning center containing symbols of the Chinese New Year. Let students bring in New Year's Eve items also so they can compare them with those used in Chinese New Year celebrations. Tell the students when they visit the center to look for recurring symbols associated with the Chinese New Year and New Year's Eve. Let them add symbols of both celebrations they think should be included but may be missing.

Bridging to the Science Activity

Create a Venn diagram of American and Chinese New Year celebrations using the symbols from the learning center and any others students mentioned. Since one thing they both have in common is noisemakers, have students brainstorm a list of noisemakers used at parties. Show students a package of Alka-Seltzer. Ask them if they know what it is used for and whether they think it could be used to make a noisemaker.

Drop an Alka-Seltzer tablet in a cup of water. Ask students what they observed. Discuss what the gas is and what Alka-Seltzer is typically used for. Ask the students what would happen if the mixture was placed in a small container with a lid on it. List the students' predictions.

Pour a small amount of water into a film canister, add a tablet, and snap the lid on securely. Have the students observe what happens. Ask the students to describe what they observed, then ask the students to name things they have observed that acted in a similar manner. Students will probably name such things as fireworks, a balloon full of air, and toy rockets.

Part 2: Science Activity

Materials

For Getting Ready
- Alka-Seltzer tablets

For the Procedure
Per group
- 35-mm film canister with snap-on lid that fits tightly
- Alka-Seltzer tablets (broken in half in Getting Ready)
- water
- graduated cylinder or measuring spoons
- goggles

For the Science Extension
Per student
- narrow-mouth bottle
- large balloon
- baking soda
- vinegar
- funnel
- tablespoon and ½-cup measure

Safety and Disposal

Students must wear goggles for this activity to protect their eyes in case of flying film canister lids and possible splattering of the reaction mixture. Throw any undissolved tablets in the trash. Pour liquids down the drain. The film canisters are reusable; rinse them with water.

Getting Ready

Break the Alka-Seltzer tablets in half.

Procedure

Part A: Making the Alka-Seltzer Popper

1. Give each group of students a film canister and lid. Have them check to be sure that the lid fits tightly. Have them pour 15 mL (about 1 tablespoon) water into the film canister.

2. Tell the students to put on their goggles. Tell the groups not to add their tablets until you give the signal for the whole class. Remind them it is important for the group representative to put the top on the canister immediately after the half-tablet is dropped in. Tell them to be sure to hold onto the canister after the lid is on it but be sure the lid is not close to their faces. After you give the signal, the group representatives should immediately put the half-tablets into their canisters, put the lids on, and hold the canisters in front of them.

3. Give each group half an Alka-Seltzer tablet and then give the class the signal. Have students observe as the lids pop off. Ask students what happened and why. *The lid flew off because the carbon dioxide gas that was produced created enough pressure to pop it off.*

Part B: Variables of the Pop

1. Ask students to design an experiment to determine how many times they can replace the lid on the canister and have it pop without adding more Alka-Seltzer. Let them experiment to find out and discuss the results.

2. Assign different groups to experiment and report to the class on the following topics:

   a. Determine the effect of varying the amount of water in the canister. *Added water causes the lid to pop off more quickly.*

   b. Determine the effect of varying the temperature of the water in the reaction. *The colder the water, the longer the reaction takes to pop the lid off.*

   c. Determine the effect of varying the amount of Alka-Seltzer in the canister. *The reaction takes longer when less Alka-Seltzer is used.*

   d. Determine the effect of surface area of the Alka-Seltzer. *The reaction is faster when the Alka-Seltzer is broken into small pieces or ground up (greater surface area).*

Extension for Further Science Inquiry

Create carbon dioxide gas a different way: Measure 2 tablespoons baking soda and pour it into a balloon. Put 8 tablespoons (½ cup) vinegar in a bottle that has a narrow mouth. Carefully stretch the end of the balloon over the top of the bottle without allowing the baking soda to fall into the vinegar. Mix the vinegar and baking soda by raising the balloon directly above the neck of the bottle to allow the baking soda to fall into the vinegar. (See Figure 1.) Compare this experiment to the Alka-Seltzer experiment.

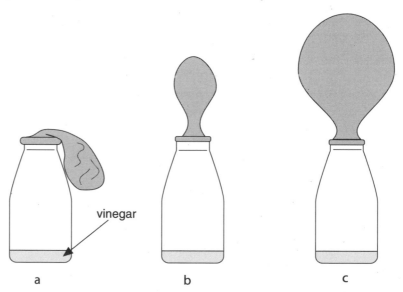

Figure 1: (a) Stretch a balloon containing baking soda over the opening of a bottle with vinegar in it. (b) Raise the balloon directly above the neck of the bottle to allow the baking soda to fall into the vinegar. (c) The balloon will begin to inflate as carbon dioxide is produced.

Science Explanation

 The following explanation is intended for the teacher's information. Modify the explanation for students as required.

Alka-Seltzer Poppers

Alka-Seltzer is a mixture of several solids, including sodium bicarbonate (baking soda), citric acid, and acetylsalicylic acid (aspirin). When mixed with water, these solids dissolve. The weak acids provide the source of hydrogen ion (H^+(aq)) when in solution and the sodium bicarbonate provides the bicarbonate ion (HCO_3^-). The hydrogen ion and bicarbonate ion react according to the following equation to produce carbon dioxide gas:

$$H^+(aq) \;+\; HCO_3^-(aq) \;\rightleftarrows\; H_2O(l) \;+\; CO_2(g)$$

$$\text{hydrogen ion} \qquad \text{bicarbonate ion} \qquad \text{water} \qquad \text{carbon dioxide gas}$$

Even though the solid Alka-Seltzer seems to be disappearing, the matter it is made from is not destroyed but rather converted to other products including carbon dioxide gas. The Law of Conservation of Mass states that matter is neither created nor destroyed in any chemical reaction. Though the gas cannot be seen, it does take up space.

This is evidenced by the bubbles that are visible as Alka-Seltzer is dropped into water. These bubbles are full of carbon dioxide gas. When this reaction is carried out in an open container, the CO_2(g) is released into the air. However, when the reaction is carried out in the closed film canister, the carbon dioxide gas is trapped. As the gas builds up, the gas pressure inside the canister increases until the lid eventually pops off.

When you add less water to the canister, there is more space available which can be filled with carbon dioxide gas; thus, it takes more time for the lid to pop off. Using colder water instead of room-temperature water also causes the lid of the canister to take longer to pop off. This is because the lower temperature of the water slows down both the dissolving process and the reaction to produce the carbon dioxide gas. Using hot water, on the other hand, causes both processes to proceed more quickly because more energy is available than there is at room temperature or a colder temperature. Decreasing the amount of Alka-Seltzer decreases the amount of solid reactants available and thus decreases the amount of CO_2 produced. Increasing the surface area of the Alka-Seltzer by breaking up or grinding increases both the dissolving and reaction rates because there is more contact between the water and the reactants.

The History of Alka-Seltzer

In 1928, the town of Elkhart, Indiana, suffered a flu epidemic that afflicted most of the residents. Strangely, the local newspaper staff seemed unaffected by the flu. A.H. Beardsley, chairman of the Miles Medical Company, was curious about this apparent phenomenon and learned that the managing editor was administering a mixture of baking soda and aspirin. Beardsley shared this secret with Maurice Treneer, a chemist at Miles, and Treneer developed a process for mass-producing the product in tablet form.

The mixture of baking soda and aspirin was effective because of the properties of the two ingredients. As far back as the late 1700s, doctors recorded that powdered willow bark, a Native American remedy, was effective in relieving the pain caused by malaria. One hundred years later, scientists were able to isolate salicylic acid, the pain-relieving ingredient, from the bark. Pure salicylic acid is toxic because of its acidity level, so chemists attempted to modify its structure to decrease its toxicity. Eventually, they created acetylsalicylic acid, which is far less acidic but retains its analgesic, antipyretic (fever-reducing) and anti-inflammatory properties. The pharmaceutical company Bayer began manufacturing acetylsalicylic acid under the name "aspirin" in 1899, and this name has become the common name for acetylsalicylic acid.

Sodium bicarbonate is a naturally occurring base that can be mined from the mineral trona, or soda ash, and is also found in the human body. The pancreas secretes sodium bicarbonate into the intestines to neutralize stomach acids that travel with food during digestion. Because it is effective in neutralizing acids in the intestines, sodium bicarbonate can also be ingested to provide relief from indigestion or upset stomach, which can be caused by an increase in stomach acids. John Dwight and Austin Church first commercially manufactured sodium bicarbonate for household use in 1846. Their company, Church & Dwight Company, Inc., still manufactures sodium bicarbonate under the brand name "Arm & Hammer®."

The combination of aspirin and baking soda, therefore, provided relief from the aches and upset stomach caused by the flu, as the staff of Elkhart's newspaper experienced. Although ingesting baking soda in its powdered form provides fast relief for indigestion, aspirin in tablet form takes longer to provide relief because it must first be digested, then absorbed into the bloodstream and sent through the body. In order to increase the speed at which the aspirin takes effect, the Miles Chemical Company designed Alka-Seltzer to be dissolved in water before ingestion, which provides faster relief in three ways:

- The time it takes to dissolve the tablet in the stomach is eliminated;
- When ingested in a solution, the medicines are more easily mixed and distributed throughout the stomach; and
- The sodium in the product causes the stomach to empty more quickly than usual, sending the pain medication to the intestines for absorption sooner.

References for the Science Activity

Alka-Seltzer Web Site. Feel Better Fast—How Does Alka-Seltzer Work? http://www.alka-seltzer.com/product/how.html (accessed 21 March 1998).

Arm & Hammer Web Site. What is Baking Soda? http://www.armhammer.com/miracle.htm (accessed 13 March 1998).

Bayer Web Site. Life & Vision. Health Care: Aspirin. http://www.bayer.com/bayer/just4u/vision/gesundheit/b_aspirin_e.htm (accessed 21 March 1998).

Brown, T.L.; LeMay, H.E., Jr.; Bursten, B.E. *Chemistry: The Central Science,* 6th ed.; Prentice-Hall: Englewood Cliffs, NJ, 1994; Chapter 14 (Chemical Kinetics).

Chang, R. *Chemistry,* 5th ed.; McGraw-Hill: New York, 1994; Chapter 13 (Chemical Kinetics).

Hayes, A. "Digestion: The Inside Story," *Exploratorium Quarterly.* Winter, 1990, 32–36.

Kostyn, J. Church & Dwight Co., Inc. Personal Communication, March 19, 1998.

Levine, J. "Fizz, fizz—plop, plop," *Forbes. 151*(13); June 21, 1993; 139.

Sarquis, A.M.; Woodward, L.M. "Alka-Seltzer Poppers: An Interactive Exploration," *Journal of Chemical Education,* in press.

"Making Aspirin and Oil of Wintergreen"; *Strong Medicine—Chemistry at the Pharmacy;* Sarquis, A.M., Ed.; Terrific Science: Middletown, OH, 1995; p 90.

"trona" *Britannica Online.* http://www.eb.com:180/cgi-bin/g?DocF=micro/604/73.html (accessed 21 March 1998).

Part 3: Integrating with Language Arts

Featured Fiction Book: *The Dancing Dragon*

Author: Marcia Vaughan   Illustrator: Stanley Wong Hoo Foon
Publisher: Mondo   ISBN: 1572551348
Summary: This rhyming story describes a typical Chinese New Year celebration.

Before reading the story, have the class brainstorm a list of New Year's traditions they or people they know follow. Items could include eating special foods, attending parties, making lots of noise, or watching parades. Tell students they are going to hear a story about the New Year's traditions of China. Read the story. After the story is finished, discuss traditions mentioned in the book. Discuss the role of the dragon in the Chinese celebration, and compare the Chinese dragon with the dragons commonly portrayed in fairy tales of European origin.

Writing Extensions

- Have students use their science journals to write a summary of the experiment they designed and the results they found.
- Have students write New Year's resolutions.

Additional Books

Fiction

Title: *Chinatown*
Author: William Low
Publisher: Henry Holt   ISBN: 0805042148
Summary: A boy and his grandmother wind their way through the streets of Chinatown, enjoying all the sights and smells of the Chinese New Year's Day.

Title: *Why Rat Comes First: A Story of the Chinese Zodiac*
Author: Clara Yen   Illustrator: Hideo C. Yoshida
Publisher: Children's Book Press   ISBN: 0-89239-072-7
Summary: This retelling of one of the many folktales about the Chinese zodiac
explains why the rat is the first animal in the twelve-year Chinese calendar
cycle. Also included is a list of the animals in the Chinese zodiac and the
characteristics and years with which these animals are associated.

Nonfiction

Title: *Fiesta Fireworks*
Author: George Ancona
Publisher: Lothrop, Lee, and Shepard   ISBN: 0688148174
Summary: Describes the preparation of fireworks as well as the festival honoring
San Juan de Dios, the patron saint of Tultepec, Mexico, which is famous for its
master pyrotechnics.

Title: *Happy New Year!*
Author: Emery Bernhard   Illustrator: Durga Bernhard
Publisher: Lodestar   ISBN: 0-525-67532-9
Summary: People around the world celebrate the new year in many different
ways. How these traditions began and what they mean is the focus of this
lively and engaging book.

Part 4: Further Lesson Extensions

Art and Music

- Have students create dragon puppets or costumes for a classroom Chinese
  New Year parade.
- Have students create and decorate their own New Year's Eve noisemakers.

Mathematics

- Measure the length of time it takes for the lid to come off the canister. Do
  10 trials and graph the results. Calculate the mean, median, and mode.
- Measure the height reached by the popping lid under different experimental
  conditions (such as different temperatures, amounts of water, and sizes of
  tablets). Do two or three trials for each condition and graph the results.
- Tilt the canister at various angles and measure the distance that the lid lands
  from the canister for each angle. Do multiple trials for each angle and average
  the results.

Social Studies

- Have students research the history of Alka-Seltzer and the various marketing strategies used to promote it. If desired, you may have students work in groups, with one group researching the introduction of new flavors and formulas and other groups studying specific advertising campaigns, such as the Speedy Alka-Seltzer character (1954–1964) and the "Plop, plop, fizz, fizz" jingle. What strategies are used to persuade people to buy the product? A brief summary of how Alka-Seltzer works and descriptions of famous advertising campaigns can be found at the Alka-Seltzer Web site, http://www.alka-seltzer.com/dev/alka/home.html.

Part 5: National Science Education Standards

Science as Inquiry Standards:

Abilities Necessary to Do Scientific Inquiry

Students question how changing variables alters how many times they can replace the lid on the film canister and have it pop off without adding more Alka-Seltzer.

Students design an investigation to measure the impact changing variables has on how many times the lids will pop off their Alka-Seltzer poppers.

Students use their data to determine the effects of and propose explanations for how and why the variables alter the popping results.

Students report their results and explanations to the class and participate in the discussion of the investigations as a whole.

Physical Science Standards:

Properties and Changes of Properties of Matter

Substances, including Alka-Seltzer, react chemically in characteristic ways to form new substances with different properties. In this investigation, carbon dioxide, a gas, is produced.

Science and Technology Standards:

Abilities of Technological Design

Students question how changing conditions changes the rate of reaction of Alka-Seltzer.

Students propose ways to test how changing conditions changes the rate of reaction of Alka-Seltzer.

Students measure the rate of reaction of Alka-Seltzer under a variety of conditions.

Students evaluate their results and those of other groups and refine their testing accordingly.

Students report on their testing design, results, and conclusions.

History and Nature of Science Standards:

Science as a Human Endeavor
Alka-Seltzer is the product of scientists working together to solve a problem.

Groundhog Day

February 2
Culture: United States

The tradition Americans know today as "Groundhog Day" has its origins in American Indian, Christian, and Pennsylvania Dutch customs and legends. The earliest component of the tradition stems from the creation story of the Delaware Indians. According to legend, the forefathers of this tribe, the Lenni Lenape, began life underground as animals, emerging later as men in order to hunt. The grandfather of the Lenni Lenape was considered to be the Oijik, or Wojak, which we know as the woodchuck, or groundhog. Because of the animal's connection to the origins of the Delaware people, the tribe respected and revered the woodchuck.

Another component of the tradition comes from the Christian holiday of Candlemas. In Europe, priests would bless candles and distribute them to the people on Candlemas Day, February 2, to help light their way through the remainder of winter. The weather on this day was very important, as is shown by this old English folk song:

" If Candlemas be clear and bright,
Come, winter, have another flight.
If Candlemas brings clouds and rain,
Go, winter, and come not again."

When Christianity reached Germany, the tradition took on a new twist. The Germans concluded that if the sun were shining on Candlemas, an animal that poked its head above ground would see its shadow and thus predict six more weeks of winter. Since hedgehogs were abundant in Germany, they became the forecasters.

When the Europeans began immigrating to America in the 1700s, many Germans settled in Pennsylvania and came to be known as the "Pennsylvania Dutch." Observing a burrowing animal similar to the hedgehogs in Germany, the immigrants named the animal the "groundhog." Thus, on Candlemas Day in America, they looked to the groundhog to see its shadow and predict the weather. They also learned that the Indians in the area esteemed the groundhog, or woodchuck, as a wise and sensible animal, and the groundhog became widely accepted as the new weather forecaster, a position it has held ever since.

Groundhog Day

February 2
Culture: United States

The most famous groundhog is "Punxsutawney Phil," a groundhog living in Gobbler's Knob in Punxsutawney, Pennsylvania. This groundhog, something of a local celebrity, is kept in a special enclosure and tended by an official keeper. When one "Phil" dies, another is obtained to replace it. The Punxsutawney Phil tradition began on February 2, 1886, when the town's newspaper reported, "Today is groundhog day and up to the time of going to press the beast has not seen its shadow." The next year, the residents of Punxsutawney made the first trek to Gobbler's Knob, where one groundhog made its home, and started a tradition that is still observed today.

Punxsutawney Phil is not the only famous groundhog prognosticator. Canada also consults its own source, an albino groundhog named Wiarton Willie. During Willie's 40-year career, he is said to have been accurate more than 90% of the time.

References

Punxsutawney Groundhog Club Home Page. http://www.groundhog.org (accessed 14 March 1998).

Myers, R.J. *Celebrations: The Complete Book of American Holidays;* Doubleday: Garden City, NY, 1972; p 350.

Groundhog Day Shadows

●●●●●●●●●●●●●●●●●●●●●●●●●●●●●●●●●

Each year on Groundhog Day (February 2), one question is in the minds of most Americans:

did the groundhog see its shadow? If the answer is yes, the legend, derived from Native American,

Christian, and Pennsylvania Dutch folklore, states that winter will last six more weeks. If no shadow

is seen, spring weather will come soon. What determines whether the groundhog sees its shadow?

Students investigate the answer to this question and others during this activity.

●●●●●●●●●●●●●●●●●●●●●●●●●●●●

Key Science Topic

- light

Time Required

Setup	10 minutes
Performance	30 minutes
Cleanup	10 minutes

A groundhog shadow puppet

Part 1: Building Bridges

Building Student Knowledge and Motivation

Set up a shadow-play learning center with puppets, a screen, and a flashlight. Let students play with making shadows with the puppets and their fingers. Include books on shadows, sundials, and eclipses and encourage students to find pictures of shadows.

Bridging to the Science Activity

Introduce the concept of shadows. Ask students to give their definitions of shadows to the class. Show students a collection of items with different transparencies. Have them predict which materials will cast dark shadows, which will cast light shadows, and which will not cast a shadow. Take students outside to experiment with the various materials. This could also be done inside with a light source. Have students observe the objects that cast dark shadows. Ask them how these objects are different from objects that cast light shadows. Explain that light passes through transparent materials. Transparent materials, like a clear, colorless drinking glass or plastic wrap, are easy to see through. Materials that let some light through, such as tissue paper or a shape made from a plastic milk jug, are translucent. Materials that block out all light are opaque. Once students have grasped the concept that all objects, even transparent ones, cast shadows, they are ready to create shadow play puppets.

Part 2: Science Activity

Materials

For Bridging to the Science Activity
Per class
- collection of items with different transparencies
- bright light source

 If the weather is unsuitable for working outside, use bright lamps or flashlights.

For the Procedure
Part A, per class
- white sheet or white bulletin-board paper
- flashlight or desk lamp with a low-wattage bulb (40 watts or less)

Part A, per group of 3–4 students
- 4 pieces of cardstock paper
- 4 pairs of scissors
- 4 Popsicle™ sticks or craft sticks
- tape

- 1 of the following (some opaque and others transparent):
  - different types of paper
  - plastic sheets of different thicknesses and colors

Part B, per class
- puppet made in Part A
- flashlight or desk lamp
- white sheet or white bulletin-board paper
- sturdy stick or dowel rod about 3–4 feet long
- (optional) can or bucket full of rocks
- sidewalk chalk
- clock or watch
- meterstick
- materials for students to make shadow clocks of their own design

For the Extensions for Further Science Inquiry
- different materials for the puppets

Safety and Disposal

Caution students not to look directly into the light source. No special disposal procedures are required.

Getting Ready

1. Hang a white sheet or white bulletin-board paper over a doorway or table.

2. Place a light source about 6 feet away from the sheet.

Procedure

Part A: Shadow Puppets

1. Have students create an original stick puppet by cutting a shape out of cardstock paper. Use tape to attach the puppet to a thin stick.

   For best results, puppets should be about the size of a hand. You may want to suggest the puppet be a groundhog in honor of Groundhog Day.

2. Divide the class into groups and assign each group to make a rectangle from the material you provide—each group's rectangle should be made of a different material, such as different types of paper, and plastic sheets of different thicknesses and colors (some opaque and others transparent). Limit the size of the rectangles to about 8½ inches x 11 inches.

3. Turn on the light, direct the beam toward the sheet, and darken the room.

4. Have students hold their puppets behind the light so that the light is between the puppets and the sheet. Ask them to look at the sheet and tell what they see. *Nothing. No shadow is cast on the sheet when the puppets are held behind the lamp.*

5. Have students move their puppets between the light and the sheet. Have them observe the sheet and record what happens. Discuss the observations and possible reasons for them. *A shadow is cast on the sheet because the light is blocked by the puppet.*

6. Ask students to predict what they would observe if different rectangles were placed between the light and the puppet. Let each group do the experiment with its rectangle while the rest of the class observes and records the results. Discuss the results.

7. Challenge students to discover ways of making their puppet's shadow larger or smaller. Have them report their results to the class.

Part B: Shadows and Time

1. Ask students whether they think other factors besides clouds might affect whether a groundhog sees its shadow on Groundhog Day. If students have trouble coming up with ideas, use a puppet and light to demonstrate what happens when light is directly overhead (the shadow is very small or covered by the standing groundhog) or in front of the groundhog (the shadow falls behind the groundhog, out of the animal's view unless it turns around). Discuss when conditions like these might occur in nature. *Around noon, the sun may be directly overhead, and at different times of day, shadows fall in different directions.*

2. Discuss the idea that the path of the sun follows a predictable pattern in a given location and season and that many people throughout history have used the sun's position to tell time. Also discuss the idea that the path appears to be different in different places and seasons. Use a globe to illustrate how the Earth tilts at different angles relative to the sun at different times of year. Tell students that they will build a device that will help them tell time by observing shadows.

3. Set up a post in an open spot in the schoolyard by pushing a sturdy stick or dowel rod into the ground or into a can or bucket of rocks that can be used on concrete or asphalt. Use chalk to mark the line of the post's shadow and write the time.

   Leave the post in the ground or in the can of rocks between observations. If you must remove the post from the ground or can of rocks, first mark on the post the ground or rock level so that you can put the post back in to the same depth. This will insure that the shadow-casting portion of the post is the same length for each observation.

4. Have students observe the location and length of shadows cast by the post at every half-hour during the school day and record this information on a class chart.

   You may need to wait for a sunny day to do this.

5. The next sunny day, have the students determine the time by observing the location of the post's shadow and measuring its length. Compare the results with a reliable clock or watch. Ask students if they think the data they gathered would help them tell time in a different season.

6. Discuss the advantages and disadvantages of the class shadow clock. Challenge students to design a better one. Have them consider issues such as portability, pointer shape, seasonal shifts in the sun's path, ways of pinpointing shadow direction, ways of determining shadow length, cost, and beauty.

7. Have students make shadow clocks according to their designs.

8. Have students observe and evaluate their shadow clocks and change the design if necessary. Have them show their clocks to the class and tell how they developed their final designs. Have students evaluate clocks made by other students and share ideas for further design changes.

Extensions for Further Science Inquiry

- Encourage students to use different materials (opaque, translucent, transparent, or any combination of the three) to make their puppet and observe the shadow cast by the puppet.
- Contact a meteorologist from a local television station and ask him or her for help in compiling a list of Groundhog Day predictions and actual results over a specified period of time (such as 20 or 30 years). Discuss whether the groundhog's predictions seem to be reliable.
- Discuss eclipses of the sun and the moon. Ask students if they have ever seen an eclipse. In a solar eclipse, the moon gets between the sun and the Earth. The moon blocks out some of the sun's light, causing a shadow to fall on Earth. When it becomes darker during one of these solar eclipses, it is because a shadow is cast on the Earth. The shadow does not fall on a very large part of the Earth. In fact, the shadow from a solar eclipse is less than 300 km in diameter. In a lunar eclipse, the Earth passes between the sun and the moon. The Earth blocks some of the sun's light, causing a shadow to fall on the moon. This is why the moon gets darker during a lunar eclipse.

Science Explanation

 The following explanation is intended for the teacher's information. Modify the explanation for students as required.

The Science of Light

Light is a form of energy that possesses a dual nature: sometimes it acts like a particle, and sometimes it acts like a wave. Until the beginning of the 19th century, light was believed to be a stream of particles emitted from a light source. This particle theory, which does explain some properties of light (such as the laws of reflection and refraction) was largely formulated by Isaac Newton. This theory held on for centuries, despite the fact that a contemporary of Newton's, a Dutch physicist and astronomer named Christiaan Huygens, showed that a wave theory of light could also explain the laws of reflection and refraction. Even though Francesco Grimaldi discovered experimental evidence for the diffraction of light (a wave property) around 1660, resistance to the wave theory continued until the early 19th century, largely because of Newton's great reputation as a scientist.

Light waves travel in a straight line until they strike an object that they cannot pass through. Light around the outside of the object can travel past the object, but some or all of the light striking the object is prevented from passing through. Therefore, a shadow in the shape of the object that is blocking the light is cast on any surface that stands in the path the blocked light would have taken. The placement of a shadow is determined by the location of the light source relative to the object. If the sun is the source and it is behind you, your shadow will be in front of you (for example, on the ground or a wall) because you are blocking the sun's rays from traveling in a straight line. If the sun is in front of you, then your shadow will be behind you. If the sun is overhead and you are standing, you will not see your shadow on the ground because your feet are covering the ground where your shadow would be. If you were suspended in the air, however, your shadow would be visible, though small, directly below you.

All objects, even transparent ones, cast shadows. Clouds are no exception. On a partly cloudy day, the shadows of clouds can be clearly seen moving across the Earth's surface. On a cloudy day, the shadows cast by all of the clouds merge into one enormous shadow that mostly obscures the shadows cast by other objects. Thus, on a cloudy day, a groundhog would not be able to see its own shadow in the midst of the shadow cast by the clouds.

The History of Shadow Clocks

Before shadows were used to forecast weather, they were used to tell time. Civilizations in the Middle East and Africa initiated clock-making more than 5,000 years ago. No evidence has been found to describe the types of clocks they used, but archeologists believe the clocks used the sun and shadows to mark the passage of time. By 3500 B.C., the Egyptians were using obelisks—slender, tapering, four-sided monuments shaped much like the Washington Monument in Washington, D.C.—as timepieces, enabling them to divide the day into two parts. When the obelisk's shadow had disappeared, the sun was overhead and it was midday, or "noon."

The first portable timepiece was also developed by the Egyptians. Built in 1500 B.C., this device divided the day into 10 parts plus two "twilight hours," one in the morning and one in the evening. The stem of this device had five variably spaced marks on it. It was oriented east and west in the morning, and an elevated crossbar on the east end would cast a shadow moving up the stem over the marks. At noon, the device was turned in the opposite direction, and the shadow would move down the stem.

Because the sun is at a different distance from the Earth each season and because of the tilt of the Earth, the sun seems to reach different heights in the sky in different seasons. In the winter, it is low in the sky, while in the summer, it is higher. Early sundials were not always accurate as the seasons changed, but sundials evolved as people began learning more about the path of the Earth around the sun. One version of the sundial included different hour-marks for each season to make the timepiece more accurate. By 30 B.C., 13 different sundial styles were in use in Greece, Italy, and Asia Minor. Pocket sundials became popular in the 10th century, but the principles employed by the ancient Egyptians were still the same.

A sundial has two parts: the plane, or dial face, and the gnomon, or style. The plane is marked with hour lines, or sometimes even half- and quarter-hour lines. The gnomon is a flat piece of metal or wood that sits in the middle of the plane. When the shadow of the gnomon falls on the plane, it crosses the hour lines and denotes the time. The accuracy of the sundial depends heavily on the user's location on the Earth and the construction of the gnomon. People in the northern hemisphere face the North Pole when reading their sundials, and people in the southern hemisphere face the South Pole. When a sundial maker constructs a gnomon, he or she must make sure that the upper edge slants upward from the plane at an angle equal to that of the latitude of his or her location on the Earth. Sundials, therefore, are most accurate at the latitude at which they are made.

References for the Science Activity

Durnie, D. *Eyewitness Science: Light;* Dorling Kindersley: London, 1992.

National Institute of Standards and Technology Physics Laboratory Web Site. http://physics.nist.gov/GenInt/Time/early.html (accessed 5 March 1998).

Serway, R.A. *Principles of Physics;* Saunders: Fort Worth, 1994, pp 711–713.

"Sundial"; *World Book Encyclopedia;* World Book: Chicago, 1992, Vol 18, p 990.

Part 3: Integrating with Language Arts

Featured Fiction Book: *Bear Shadow*

Author and Illustrator: Frank Asch

Publisher: Scholastic   ISBN: 0-590-29083-X

Summary: Bear discovers his shadow while fishing on a sunny day. He can't understand why the shadow keeps following him. Read about Bear's efforts to lose the shadow in this delightful book.

Prior to reading the story, ask students to predict what the story will be about by looking at the cover of the book. Ask them whether or not they think Bear will be able to escape his shadow. As you read the book, refer to the location of the sun for later discussion. Have students predict where the shadow will be from page to page and have them explain their answers. Ask the students how they think Bear could get rid of his shadow.

Writing Extensions

- Have students use their science journals to write a summary of the experiment they conducted and the results they found.
- Have students do a creative writing assignment about a day with their shadow. How would they try to hide from it? Could they hide? What would they do with their shadow? Where would they take it? Compile the stories into a classroom book.
- Have students write a story titled "The Day I Lost My Shadow." Have them write about the day and the weather conditions.
- Have students work in groups to write a shadow play, make puppets and background scenery, and present the show to the class.
- Have students write directions for a game of shadow tag.

Additional Books

Fiction

Title: *Geoffrey Groundhog Predicts the Weather*
Author and Illustrator: Bruce Koscielniak
Publisher: Houghton Mifflin   ISBN: 0-395-70933-4
Summary: When Geoffrey Groundhog pops out of his hole to predict the weather, he is blinded by television cameras and lights and is unable to see if he has a shadow. No one in town knows how to proceed, so Geoffrey needs help fast.

Title: *It's Groundhog Day!*
Author: Steven Kroll   Illustrator: Jeni Bassett
Publisher: Scholastic   ISBN: 059044669X
Summary: It's time for Godfrey the groundhog to wake up and see his shadow—or not. Will winter last six more weeks?

Title: *Peppe the Lamplighter*
Author: Elisa Bartone   Illustrator: Ted Lewin
Publisher: Scholastic   ISBN: 0590223100
Summary: Peppe, a young Italian immigrant, takes a job as a lamplighter to help his family make ends meet. His father teases him about his job, so one night Peppe fails to do his job. When Peppe's sister becomes lost in the dark city, his father sends him to light the lamps, and his sister is found. Illustrations throughout the story portray the contrast between light and shadow.

Title: *Punxsutawney Phil: The Tale of a Groundhog*
Author: Judy Stoehr   Illustrator: Judy Stoehr
Publisher: Warner Brothers   ISBN: 1576233758
Summary: Phil the groundhog would rather sleep in than get up and see his shadow. This educational and entertaining package provides lesson plans for cross-curricular integration, songs and accompaniments, script, and choreography, plus suggestions for costumes, setting, and staging. Titles include: "Get Up!," "Hide and Seek," "You Never Know," and more.

Title: *Time for Jody*
Author: Wendy Kessleman   Illustrator: Gerald Dumas
Publisher: Harper & Row   ISBN: 0060231386
Summary: Jody the groundhog is moving to a new field, but she is worried that
   she won't be able to wake herself up in time to wake the animals from their
   long winter sleep.

Nonfiction

Title: *Anno's Sundial*
Author: Mitsumasa Anno
Publisher: Philomel   ISBN: 0399213740
Summary: This book explains the Earth's movement around the sun and how
   shadows are used to tell time. Includes illustrations that pop up or fold out to
   demonstrate how sundials work.

Title: *Easy-to-Make Wooden Sundials*
Author: Milton Stoneman
Publisher: Dover   ISBN: 0486241416
Summary: Instructions and plans for five sundials, including suggestions for
   designing a pocket sundial, are contained in this book. Tips on correcting the
   sundials for different seasons are also included.

Title: *Me and My Shadow*
Author: Arthur Dorros
Publisher: Scholastic   ISBN: 0590427725
Summary: Arthur Dorros's hands-on approach provides easy methods to
   investigate shadow principles indoors and outdoors, at home and at school.

Title: *Science Sensations*
Authors: Diane Willow and Emily Curran   Illustrator: Lady McCrady
Publisher: Addison-Wesley   ISBN: 0201071894
Summary: These activities/experiments give a new awareness of the world
   around us. The book covers such topics as light, color, shadows, reflections,
   motion pictures, illusion, and patterns.

Title: *Shapes and Things*
Author: Tana Hoban
Publisher: Macmillan   ISBN: 0027440605
Summary: This picture book is printed as a negative rather than a shadow—great
   shapes to study.

Title: *What Makes a Shadow?*
Author: Clyde Robert Bulla   Illustrator: June Otani
Publisher: HarperTrophy   ISBN: 0060229152
Summary: When the sun is shining, everything has its own shadow—trees,
   houses, cars, and even clouds and planes way up in the sky. You have a
   shadow, too. As the sun sets, your shadow becomes part of a much larger
   one—the night!

Part 4: Other Lesson Extensions

Art and Music

- Have students make silhouettes of their profiles, cut them out, and mount them to be given as gifts.
- Have students make shadows using the following technique: Use a black marker to draw a person, animal, or other object on a piece of paper or transparency. Darken the room as much as possible. Turn on a flashlight and aim it at a light-colored wall or screen. Hold the transparency in front of the light and observe the image. Experiment with ways to change the size of the shadow image and make it move. Write a short play and draw a scene on a large piece of paper for the background scenery of your play. The scenery can be a city street, the beach, a park, another planet, or some other setting. Draw characters on transparencies and use the transparencies in front of the light to present the play to the class.

Mathematics

- Measure the height of a shadow puppet, then measure the height of the shadow cast on the cloth when the puppet is held at various distances from the sheet or paper. Determine how far away from the sheet or paper the puppet must be held for its shadow to be as large as the puppet.
- Have students work in pairs to measure each other's shadow. Using sidewalk chalk, have students take turns outlining their partner's shadow. When all students' shadows have been drawn, have the students compare their shadow size to their actual size. Take measurements once in the morning and once in the afternoon. Discuss the results.
- Have students make their own sundials using cardboard and tape. In the morning they should place the sundials on the east side of the school and make some observations. They should observe the sundials again in the afternoon, making note of any changes that have occurred. See Part 3, Additional Books, for resources on making sundials.
- Find a place outside in the sun where clear shadows can be cast. Have students work in pairs as follows: Hold a meterstick so it points straight up from the ground. Using another meterstick or tape measure, measure the length of the shadow in centimeters. Record the stick length and the shadow length. Place two metersticks together end-to-end. Overlap them and tape them together to make a stick about 1½–1¾ m long (150–170 cm). Hold this tall stick so it points straight up from the ground. Mark both ends of the shadow and measure its length. Record the stick length and the shadow length. Which is longer, the stick or the shadow of the stick? Is the answer the same for the shorter stick too? Measure the length of one partner's shadow. Now measure and record that student's height. Be sure to use the same units (centimeters) that you used when you worked with the sticks. Now plot the results on a line graph with object length as the x-axis and shadow length as

the y-axis. Draw a straight line that passes close to as many points as possible (do not simply connect the dots). Measure and record the length of the other partner's shadow. Find the corresponding number on the y-axis of the graph and move across the graph until you hit the line you drew. From this point on the line, move straight down to the x-axis. The number at this point on the x-axis should be the second partner's height. Now measure that partner's height and compare.

Just for Fun

- Have students place their hands between a light source and a wall or white screen to demonstrate hand shadows they know. See *The Little Book of Hand Shadows* by Phila H. Webb (Running Press, 0894718525) for ideas.
- Have students pair up and take turns imitating their partner's every move—being their shadow.
- On Groundhog Day, find out Punxsutawney Phil's or Wiarton Willie's prediction and ask students to predict whether the groundhog will be right or wrong. To record their predictions, students should draw a small picture illustrating winter or spring. These pictures can be displayed in a bar graph. Record the weather for the weeks following Groundhog Day to see if the students were right.
- Have students conduct research to learn more about the groundhog and its habitat.
- Investigate and discuss hibernation and estivation (similar to hibernation, but occurs in the summer) and its importance to the survival of various animals.

Part 5: National Science Education Standards

Science as Inquiry Standards:

Abilities Necessary to Do Scientific Inquiry
Students question how shadows are formed and how clouds affect shadows.

Students conduct simple experiments to learn more about shadows.

Students measure shadows (in the math extensions) using a meterstick.

Students use their experimental observations to develop an explanation for how shadows form and how they are affected by clouds.

Students report their results and discuss them as a class.

Physical Science Standards:

Properties of Objects and Materials
Objects have many observable properties, including their ability to block light and thus cast shadows.

Position and Motion of Objects

The position of an object (such as a puppet) behind or in front of a light determines whether or not it casts a shadow.

Light, Heat, Electricity, and Magnetism

Light travels in a straight line until it strikes an object and is absorbed. The light that misses the object continues until it hits a surface. The area on the surface where the light is blocked by the object is the object's "shadow."

Science and Technology Standards:

Abilities of Technological Design

Students identify the problems of using sun shadows to tell time.

Students propose ways to tell time using sun shadows and simple, inexpensive materials.

Students make "shadow clocks" and test them to see if they can be used to tell time.

Students evaluate their shadow clocks and those of other students and suggest design modifications.

Students demonstrate their shadow clocks and explain how they were developed.

History and Nature of Science Standards:

Science as a Human Endeavor

People have been using shadows to tell time for at least 5,000 years.

Valentine's Day

February 14
Cultures: North America and Europe

Beginning in the 4th century B.C., the Romans celebrated a feast on February 14 and 15 called Lupercalia, a spring festival of love and fertility. Young men would send the women they loved notes and small tokens or gifts. Valentine's Day has its roots in this festival, but the saint, or saints, this day is now named for was not born until the third century A.D. Records of early Christian martyrs list at least two men named Valentine who were associated with February 14. One was listed as a Roman priest and the other as Bishop of Interamna (modern-day Terni). Both of these men died in the second half of the third century. Few other recorded facts exist of these men's lives, and the legends surrounding them have become so interwoven that it is impossible to tell which of the Valentines was involved in which legend.

According to legend, Valentine was arrested and jailed either for helping Christians escape persecution or for performing secret marriages at a time when marriages were forbidden. (The emperor at the time, Claudius I, thought married men made poor soldiers because they would not leave their families to go to war. Needing soldiers to defend the empire, Claudius banned marriages.) One legend says that while Valentine was in jail, he befriended the blind daughter of one of the guards and cured her blindness. Before he left the jail, he sent her a farewell note, signing it "from your Valentine," a tradition that still exists today. Valentine is said to have been executed on or around February 14, during Lupercalia.

As the Roman Empire spread throughout Europe, the Romans carried the traditions of Lupercalia as well as the story of St. Valentine with them. After the empire converted to Christianity, Pope Gelasius changed the name of Lupercalia to St. Valentine's Day, in honor of the saint's commitment to lovers, and shortened the festival to one day. Even though the name changed, many of the customs did not, and people still send small gifts and wishes to their friends and loved ones. People throughout North America and Europe celebrate St. Valentine's Day; even though it has ties to the Christian religion, some non-Christians celebrate it, too.

Valentine's Day
February 14
Cultures: North America and Europe

Love, fertility, and the rebirth of life were central themes of many ancient spring festivals. Cultures that still observe these traditional festivals celebrate love and romance in the spring. In Asia, the Koreans celebrate Tet-Trung-Thu, the Mid-Autumn Festival, at the time of the full moon in mid-September. Tet-Trung-Thu is a festival of imagination and romance, and colorful lanterns line the streets as people dance and parade through the cities. Special treats are made and shared with friends and loved ones.

References

E-Cards. Valentines [sic] History. http://www.e-cards.com/occasion/valentines/history.pl (accessed 10 Feb 1998).

Flowernet. http://www.flowernet.com/v4/val.html (accessed 10 Feb 1998).

Harrowven, J. *Origins of Festivals and Feasts;* Kaye & Ward: London, 1980; pp 1–5.

Hatch, J.M. *The American Book of Days,* 3rd ed.; H.W. Wilson: New York, 1978; pp 177–179.

Ickis, M. *The Book of Festival Holidays;* Dodd, Mead: New York, 1964; pp 34–35.

Rev. Alex Stevenson. God's Valentine. http://www.carol.net/~asmsmsks/valentin.htm (accessed 10 Feb 1998).

Secret Valentine Messages

Valentine's Day (February 14) is best known for its association with friends and loved ones, but it also commemorates the death of St. Valentine, a Roman priest. On this day, cards, gifts, and good wishes are given to friends and loved ones. The heart, a symbol of Valentine's Day, has for centuries signified love and emotion. In this activity, students will make secret messages with Teflon tape to share with their Valentines.

Key Science Topics

- physical properties
- polymers

Time Required

Setup	5	minutes
Performance	20–30	minutes
Cleanup	5	minutes

Teflon-tape message, unstretched and stretched

Part 1: Building Bridges

Building Student Knowledge and Motivation

Prior to the lesson, create a learning center containing store-bought Valentines or pictures of early Valentines. Let students bring in old Valentines they may have to add to the collection. Tell the students when they visit the center to look for recurring symbols associated with Valentine's Day. Let them add symbols of Valentine's Day they think should be included but may be missing.

Bridging to the Science Activity

Ask students about ways we say, "Happy Valentine's Day," and chart their answers. Pass out candy hearts with Valentine sayings on them and talk about the custom of sending Valentine messages. Tell students that they will be investigating unique methods for sending secret messages to their Valentines.

Part 2: Science Activity

Materials

For the Procedure
Part A, per group
- plastic grocery bag
- scissors
- ruler
- permanent marker

Part B, per group
- 4- to 5-inch strip of sewing elastic
- ½- to ⅝-inch-wide rubber band (size 82, 84, or 107)
- balloon
- 4- to 5-inch strip of 1-inch-wide Teflon® tape (also called PTFE thread-seal tape)

This tape may be available at hardware stores or discount department stores in the plumbing section. If you are unable to find 1-inch-wide tape at a store, call Mill-Rose Clean Fit Products at 800/321-3598 for the name of a Mill-Rose distributor who carries this product. One-inch-wide PTFE thread-seal tape (#14-831-300B) is also available from Fisher Scientific, 800/766-7000.

- scissors

Part C, per student
- 4- to 5-inch strip of Teflon tape
- ball-point pen
- colored construction paper
- markers or crayons

For the Extension for Further Science Inquiry
- balloon
- marker

Safety and Disposal

No special safety or disposal procedures are required.

Procedure

Part A: Grocery Bag Stretch

Challenge the students to determine whether a plastic grocery bag can be stretched in both the lengthwise and widthwise directions without breaking. Have them test the bag as described in the following steps.

 Define lengthwise as being from the handles (top) of the bag toward the sealed bottom; define widthwise as around the middle of the bag.

1. Cut a lengthwise strip of plastic (about 15 cm x 10 cm) from a grocery bag; label the length and width directions with a permanent marker. Allow the marker to dry before proceeding.

2. Test the stretchability of the strip in both the lengthwise and widthwise direction by grasping the strip in the direction to be tested and gently pulling. Don't pull so hard that the piece breaks. Record your observations. Did the strip stretch to the same degree in both directions? *No, grocery bags are typically made to stretch in one direction but not the other. Plastic grocery bags typically do not show much stretch lengthwise (defined as from the handle area to the bottom of the bag), but they do stretch widthwise (across the printing area). You wouldn't want to load them with groceries only to have the bag stretch lengthwise with the weight of the groceries.*

3. Now cut a strip of the grocery bag that has letters printed on it. If words are not already present, use a permanent marker to write a word on the plastic strip. Let the ink dry before proceeding. Now gently pull the plastic strip so that the plastic stretches in the region of the printing. What do you observe? *The letters become distorted from their original shape.* Sketch what you observed.

4. Try returning the letters to their original shape by gently stretching the plastic strip in the direction opposite the one in which you pulled to distort the letters. What do you observe? *Gentle stretching in the opposite direction returns the letters to their original shapes.*

5. Use a permanent marker to draw a 2-cm x 2-cm square on the strip of plastic grocery bag. Pull to distort the square. What shape have you created? Measure and record the dimensions of this new shape. Can you get the original square shape back? Describe what you tried.

Part B: Testing Other Items

1. Give each group a strip of sewing elastic, a wide rubber band, a balloon, and a strip of Teflon tape. Tell students you want them to determine the nature of the stretch of each of these items by applying what they learned about the plastic grocery bag.

2. Challenge students to divide the materials they have tested into two or more groups and be prepared to explain their reasoning for their classification. Tell groups to record the procedures they use and their results.

3. Give the groups about 10 minutes to experiment. Then have them report their results to the class. *The sewing elastic, rubber band, and balloon can all be stretched but return to their original shape immediately after the external force is removed. The Teflon tape can be stretched, and it remains in the stretched form until it is pulled in the opposite direction.*

Part C: Writing Secret Valentine's Day Messages

1. Give each student one new strip of Teflon tape. Tell students their task will be to write a brief, secret Valentine message on this piece of Teflon tape and to use the special properties they have learned about the tape to hide the message from all but the intended reader.

2. Ask students to identify the factors they will need to consider in preparing their messages. Let them propose methods for preparing their messages and discuss ideas in small groups. After students feel confident their methods will yield the desired effect, tell them to try their methods.

3. Have students evaluate the effectiveness of their message designs and modify their designs if needed.

4. Have students design and make Valentine's Day cards containing their Teflon-tape messages and instructions for reading them.

Extension for Further Science Inquiry

Have students investigate methods of writing secret messages on balloons. One method would be to inflate a balloon and pinch the mouth shut with fingers or a twist-tie. Holding the mouth of the balloon closed, write a message in small or medium-sized handwriting on the side of the inflated balloon. Let the air out of the balloon and observe what happens to the handwriting. Students could make a card containing the balloon and instructions for reading the secret message written on it. (For health reasons, if the balloon is to be given to another person, students should insert a straw into the mouth of the balloon, pinch the mouth of the balloon firmly around the straw to prevent leaks, and blow through the straw to inflate the balloon before writing on it.)

Science Explanation

 The following explanation is intended for the teacher's information. Modify the explanation for students as required.

The Science of Polymers

The thin plastic films used in this activity are manufactured from extremely long polymer chains; during the manufacturing process these long polymer chains are aligned side by side in a specific direction, which accounts for the strength of the film in one direction and its ability to be stretched in another direction. In order to understand how the film is manufactured, it is necessary to understand the basic structure of polymers.

Polymers are giant molecules that are made up of long chains of simple molecules called monomers. ("Mono" means "one," "poly" means "many," and "mer" means "unit.") Polymers are sometimes called macromolecules because they are made of anywhere from 1,000 to 50,000 or more monomer units linked together by strong chemical bonds. In this activity, the polymers you used were polyethylene (plastic grocery bags), polytetrafluoroethylene (Teflon tape), and polyisoprene (the rubber band, sewing elastic, and balloon). Figure 1 shows the repeating units for these three polymers.

$$-CH_2-CH_2- \qquad -(C=C)_n \qquad \left[H_2C \quad CH_2 \atop C=C \atop H_3C \quad H \right]_n$$

a · · · · · · · · · · · · · · b · · · · · · · · · · · · · · · c

Figure 1: Polymers, such as (a) polyethylene, (b) polytetrafluoroethylene, and (c) polyisoprene, are made of repeating monomer units.

As previously mentioned, the machining of the thin film accounts for the direction of stretching observed in the activity. To make these films, the molten polymer is poured onto a conveyor belt and stretched in one direction. This causes the long polymer chains to align side by side in the longitudinal direction. In both the Teflon tape (polytetrafluoroethylene) and the grocery bag (polyethylene), the polymer chains are aligned parallel to each other in a lengthwise direction (the machine direction), as shown in Figure 2. Neither the Teflon tape nor the grocery bag strip stretches much in the lengthwise direction. This is because the intramolecular forces within the polymer chains are strong chemical bonds (covalent bonds).

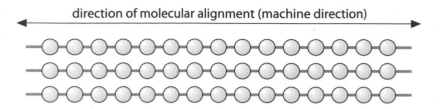

direction of molecular alignment (machine direction)

*Figure 2: Teflon and polyethylene are made of polymer chains
that are aligned parallel to each other lengthwise.*

In spite of the fact that these films appear to be very thin, they are actually many molecules thick, meaning that numerous polymer chains lie on top of and next to each other. It is this arrangement that allows the film to be stretched quite a bit in the widthwise direction. (The Teflon tape will stretch much more than the grocery bag before it breaks.) When the strips are stretched widthwise, the long polymer chains can slip and slide over one another. The film can be pulled thin as the number of chains that are in the region becomes less, but the polymer chains themselves are not broken. When the strips tear (shear), the chains have spread out to a point where the external force overcomes the intermolecular forces between the chains. The film becomes very thin at this point, and a tear results.

Elastic sewing tape, rubber bands, and balloons are made of very elastic material so that when distorted they return to their original shape once the external force is removed. This elasticity is the result of a more random orientation of the polymer molecules.

The History of Teflon and Rubber

Teflon was discovered by DuPont chemists trying to develop an alternative to Freon®, a fluorine-containing refrigerant. In 1938, Jack Rebok and Roy Plunkett were checking on small cylinders of tetrafluoroethylene (TFE) gas stored on dry ice. The pressure gauge on one of the cylinders was at zero, indicating the tank was empty. However, the cylinder weighed the same as it had when it was full of the gas. Curious, the chemists cut open the cylinder and discovered a white, waxy powder inside.

The powder was polytetrafluoroethylene (PTFE), which had been created by the spontaneous polymerization of the TFE gas. Rebok and Plunkett ran some preliminary tests on the new powder and found that it would not dissolve in common solvents. Further testing revealed that PTFE was highly resistant to corrosive chemicals, retained its strength at extreme temperatures, was an excellent electrical insulator, and was resistant to forming bonds with non-fluorocarbons. This last quality, which gives PTFE its "non-stick" property, made PTFE an important discovery. DuPont began selling PTFE under the trade name "Teflon" to manufacturing companies in the 1940s.

Today, Teflon and other PTFE products are found in military aircraft, household cookware, space rockets, and automobile engines, among other things. Teflon tape is commonly used in plumbing to seal threaded joints. It can be wrapped tightly around threads, and because it is so thin, the joint can still be screwed together. Because it is slippery, it enables metal joints to be screwed together more tightly. Its chemical properties also enable it to remain impervious to corrosive fluids and to resist drying, cracking, and melting.

Rubber bands, latex balloons, and sewing elastic are also made from a stretchy polymer, but not from the same polymer as Teflon. Instead, they are made from rubber, which is an elastomer—an "elastic polymer"—a chain of molecules capable of recovering its original shape after being stretched. Normally, the molecule chains in an elastomer are coiled irregularly. The chains straighten out when pulled and return to their compact arrangement when released.

Natural rubber is derived from latex, the milky sap of *Hevea brasiliensis,* a tree native to South America. Other trees, shrubs, and herbaceous plants (including dandelions) have also been found to produce rubber, but these sources are not harvested as easily and as safely for the plant as the Hevea source. When harvesters tap the bark of this tree, the milky latex emerges and dries to a rubbery film. The tree itself is not harmed. Although the exact biological function of latex is not known, scientists have speculated that the latex acts to protect the inner bark of the tree by sealing wounds, much as the platelets of the human blood form scabs over cuts.

Latex and rubber were originally called "caoutchouc," (pronounced COW-chook) the French spelling of a South American native word for "weeping wood." Evidence indicates that the Mayans were making rubber from the sap of trees as early as 1,000 A.D. Explorers to the New World found the natives spreading caoutchouc on their tents and cloaks to waterproof them, pouring it into earthen molds to make footwear, and forming it into bouncing balls for use in games. Columbus presented Queen Isabella with some of these balls when he returned from the New World. In 1736, French scientists brought more samples of caoutchouc to Europe, and news of the strange new substance spread. Joseph Priestly, an English scientist, noted in 1770 that dried caoutchouc was useful for rubbing away pencil marks, coining the term "rubber" still used today to describe the material.

When rubber reached the United States, it did not achieve immediate popularity. Pure rubber hardens in the cold and softens considerably in heat, making it useless in the extreme climates of North America. In 1844, Charles Goodyear, an inventor and bankrupt hardware merchant from Philadelphia, finally perfected a technique—now called "vulcanization"—of mixing rubber with sulfur and heating it to a certain temperature. This process is still used today to manufacture natural rubber.

In 1820, Thomas Hancock sliced a hard rubber bottle into bands and used these bands at the wrists of his gloves. Some historians consider this the first "rubber band." However, these bands were useless when the weather got very cold or very warm. Once Goodyear perfected vulcanization, he sent some vulcanized rubber threads to his brother-in-law, a textile merchant, suggesting he weave the threads into cloth to make it easier to create the puckered shirtfronts that were in fashion at the time. Clothing manufacturers began using vulcanized rubber threads sewn together to form "elastic" for use in waistbands, cuffs, and other parts of clothing. The "rubber band" also grew in popularity, but it wasn't until machine-driven factories were developed that the rubber band was mass-produced and became common in everyday life.

Although balloons had been around for centuries, they weren't made of latex until 1824. Early people made toy balloons by inflating animal bladders. American pioneers learned this trick from the Native Americans during the westward expansion.

Chemist Michael Faraday created the latex balloon as he was working with gases and caoutchouc. He noticed that bags made out of the caoutchouc were very elastic and could be filled with air until they were almost transparent. He also noted that a caoutchouc bag filled with hydrogen would rise in air; this discovery led to the use of helium balloons as toys. Toy balloons became exceedingly popular after Faraday's observations, and in 1931 the first modern latex balloon was created.

References for the Science Activity

Becker, R. "Teflon Tape," *Chem 13 News.* 1994, 234, 8.

DuPont Home Page. History. http://www.dupont.com/teflon/100.html (accessed 3 Dec 1997).

"Elastomers (Natural and Synthetic Rubber)" *Britannica Online.* http://www.eb.com:180/cgi-bin/g?DocF=macro/5009/31.html (accessed 18 Dec 1997).

"Elastomers (Natural and Synthetic Rubber): Production of elastomers" *Britannica Online.* http://www.eb.com:180/cgi-bin/g?DocF=macro/5009/31/1.html (accessed 18 Dec 1997).

Goodyear Home Page. The Strange Story of Rubber. http://www.goodyear.com/about/school/strange.html (accessed 3 Dec 1997).

Graham, A.; Graham, F. *The Big Stretch: The Complete Book of the Amazing Rubber Band;* Alfred A. Knopf: New York, 1985.

Grummer, A.E. *The Great Balloon Game Book;* Greg Markim: Appleton, WI, 1987.

"The Stretch Test"; *Chain Gang—The Chemistry of Polymers;* Sarquis, M., Ed.; Science in Our World Series; Terrific Science: Middletown, OH, 1995; pp 51–55.

The Wide World of Teflon. E.I. DuPont de Nemours & Co. Plastics Department: Wilmington, DE, 1963.

Part 3: Integrating with Language Arts

Featured Fiction Book: *Arthur's Valentine*

Author and Illustrator: Marc Brown
Publisher: Little, Brown   ISBN: 0-316-11062-0
Summary: Arthur is teased by his classmates about the mysterious Valentines he
    is receiving, and he finds a humorous way to get back at the teasers.

After reading the story, review and list some of the main symbols of Valentine's
Day. Mention other Arthur books that students are familiar with and discuss some
of the recurring characters.

Have students go on a "treasure hunt" like Arthur does in the book. Make nine
geoboards to hide in the classroom. Each geoboard should have one letter on it
made by stretching rubber bands on the pegs. All nine letters should spell the
word "Valentine." The backs of all the geoboards should contain instructions for
finding a Valentine "treasure." This message should be readable only when all
nine letters are arranged in order. Hide the geoboards around the room. After
reading the story, have students go on a letter hunt. When they find all nine
geoboard letters, have them arrange the geoboards to spell the word "Valentine"
and then flip all nine geoboards over and read the message giving the location of
the treasure. The treasure may be a bag of treats for the students to enjoy.

Writing Extensions

- Have students use their science journals to write a summary of the
  experiment they designed and the results they found.
- Have students write their own Valentine poems to use in their Valentine's Day
  cards.
- Have students make short stories or captioned cartoons using candy
  conversation hearts to show what the characters are saying.
- Have students make a list of school or community helpers. Using this list, have
  students create secret Valentine messages using Teflon tape or balloons to
  send to them. They should include instructions for "decoding" the messages.

Additional Books

Fiction

Title: *Henry's Secret Valentine*
Author and Illustrator: Jeffrey Dinardo
Publisher: Dell   ISBN: 0-440-40758-3
Summary: Henry is excited about sending two Valentines to a special someone.
    He is in for a surprise, because someone is sending him secret Valentines. It
    turns out to be Frieda, the new girl in class.

Title: *Love Letters*
Author: Arnold Adoff   Illustrator: Lisa Desimini
Publisher: Scholastic   ISBN: 0590484788
Summary: A collection of 20 poems written by kids and klutzes, secret admirers
    and detractors, friends, enemies, and skeptics to the objects of their
    affection—or aversion.

Title: *The Mysterious Valentine*
Author and Illustrator: Nancy Carlson
Publisher: Trumpet Club   ISBN: 0-440-84968-3
Summary: Louanne the pig has received a beautiful Valentine, mysteriously
    signed in green ink, "From your secret admirer." She tries to find out who it is
    but has no luck. The mystery continues. Will it occur again next year?

Title: *Valentine Cats*
Author: Jean Marzollo   Illustrator: Hans Wilhelm
Publisher: Scholastic   ISBN 0-590-47596-7
Summary: The author uses rhythmic style to show writer cats, artist cats, and
    postal cats creating and delivering Valentines.

Title: *Winnie the Pooh's Valentine*
Author: Bruce Talkington   Illustrator: John Kurtz
Publisher: Disney   ISBN: 0-7868-3017-4
Summary: Pooh and his friends help Roo come up with a special Valentine for his
    mother. However, the Valentine is much too big to send because it is made
    from a boulder. At the end, Roo decides to give his mother a handful of
    beautiful wildflowers because they say, "I love you."

Nonfiction

Title: *Valentine's Day*
Author and Illustrator: Gail Gibbons
Publisher: Holiday House   ISBN: 0-8234-0764-0
Summary: This book explains the traditions and customs involved in Valentine's
    Day.

Part 4: Other Lesson Extensions

Art and Music

- Have students design and construct their own Valentine's Day cards. Have a
  Valentine's Day card exchange using these cards.
- Have students create a folded Valentine's Day card with a special message
  inside and a head and arms that fold out to display the message.
- Have a Valentine's party including different symbols of Valentine's Day.

- Have students learn the song, "On Valentine's Day," from *Holiday Songs for All Occasions,* by Jill Gallina (cassette by Kimbo Educational, Long Branch, NJ; Music Number KIM 0805C).

Mathematics

- Integrate this activity with patterns and measurement (amount of stretch and percentage of stretch).
- Have students create a math book of story problems using candy conversation hearts or Hershey's® Kisses to illustrate various number sentences. If you prefer not to use three-dimensional items, students may make construction-paper hearts or foil cutouts in the shape of Hershey's kisses and glue them in the book.
- Have students estimate the number of heart candies in a bag, and as a class, graph the colors in the bag. Ask each student what his or her favorite color is and graph the favorites using the candies as markers.

Social Studies

- Have students create a heart-shaped book containing ways to say "I love you" in different languages. (It may be helpful for students to learn the song "On Valentine's Day," listed in Art and Music Extensions, before writing this book.)

Part 5: National Science Education Standards

Science as Inquiry Standards:

Abilities Necessary to Do Scientific Inquiry

Students question whether stretchy materials will stretch by the same degree both lengthwise and widthwise and whether the materials will return to their original shape.

Students test the ability of several materials to stretch and to return to their original shape.

Students measure the materials in both their stretched and unstretched positions.

Students use mathematics to calculate the stretch and percent stretch in each direction.

Students use their data to draw conclusions about how materials stretch and which of the tested materials is the most elastic.

Physical Science Standards:

Properties of Objects and Materials
The materials investigated have many observable properties, including the ability to stretch in one or more directions.

Science and Technology Standards:

Abilities of Technological Design
Students question how they can use the properties they have investigated to write a secret message on Teflon tape.

Students identify the factors they must consider and determine their approach to making the secret message.

Students try their designs for secret messages on Teflon tape.

Students test their products, evaluate their effectiveness, and modify their designs as needed.

Students write out instructions explaining the secret messages and how to read them.

History and Nature of Science Standards:

Science as a Human Endeavor
Humans have used rubber for more than 1,000 years. People from various cultures have contributed to discoveries that have made rubber and Teflon useful products today.

St. Patrick's Day

March 17
Cultures: Irish, Irish-American

Patrick, the patron saint of Ireland, was actually the son of a Roman deacon who was living in Wales. When Patrick was 16, he was kidnapped by pirates and taken to Ireland to be sold as a slave. He worked for six years in County Antrim as a herdsman before he escaped and returned to his homeland. During his time of slavery, he felt an increasing awareness of God, and after his escape he went to France and became a Christian priest. He returned to Ireland and became its bishop in 432 A.D.

The symbols associated with Patrick come from the many stories and legends about him in Irish folklore. The most popular tells how Patrick drove the snakes out of Ireland by banging a drum. Although there is no proof that he did this, the Irish will tell you that you won't find a single snake in their country. The drum is also tied to another story about St. Patrick. When Patrick walked through the Irish countryside, he was preceded by a drummer boy who announced his coming. Today, many people associate the drum with St. Patrick. A third legend says that the sun refused to set for twelve days and nights after Patrick's death, standing still in the sky as if it wouldn't bring a new day without him. The shamrock, one emblem of the Irish, is also associated with the patron saint. Patrick is supposed to have used the shamrock in his teachings to illustrate the Holy Trinity of the Christian faith.

The Irish have commemorated St. Patrick's death since the year he died. At first, people would journey to his gravesite in County Down to pray and reflect upon Patrick's teachings. As the Irish emigrated, it became more difficult to visit the grave, so they organized other festivities to honor their saint. Over the years, St. Patrick's Day has become a national holiday in Ireland. Church services are held in the morning, with parades and other festivities following. The parade in Dublin, Ireland, is one of the largest St. Patrick's Day parades in the world, as people from all over Ireland and the United States travel to Dublin to take part.

The Irish in America began organizing parades as early as 1684. Boston's parades were so popular that when General George Washington was leading the Boston evacuation on March 17, 1776, he used "Boston" as the password and "St. Patrick" as the response. In 1965, the mayor of Chicago ordered that hundreds of gallons of green dye be poured into the Chicago River as part of the celebration. This tradition continues today. Many people, whether they are Irish or not, wear green on St. Patrick's Day to take part in the festivities.

Other countries and regions celebrate the feast days of patron saints, as well:

- August 30 is the feast day of St. Rose of Lima, Peru's patron saint. Shrines to the Rose are decorated with flowers and special church services are held.
- Some Christians celebrate Michaelmas for the Archangel Michael with special church services and prayers. Michaelmas occurs on September 29.
- In the Netherlands, December 6 is the feast day of St. Nicholas, the patron saint of this country and of children. Special church services are held, and children fill their shoes with hay and leave them on the doorstep. According to tradition, when St. Nicholas passes by, his reindeer eat the hay, and Nicholas leaves small gifts for the children.
- December 26 marks the death of St. Stephen, the first Christian martyr. Christians in central Europe commemorate the day with prayers and services.

References

Hatch, J.M. *The American Book of Days,* 3rd ed.; H.W. Wilson: New York, 1978; pp 262–264.

Ickis, M. *The Book of Festival Holidays;* Dodd, Mead: New York, 1964; pp 24, 45.

NJWeb, Inc. Everything You Wanted to Know About St. Patrick's Day. http://www.njweb.com/stpats.html (accessed 23 Feb 1998).

Personal communications with the people of Tully Cross, Co. Galway, Ireland.

Spicer, D.G. *The Book of Festivals;* Women's Press: New York, 1937; p 55.

St. Patrick's Day Spuds

The Irish and Irish-Americans celebrate St. Patrick's Day (March 17), the anniversary of the death of Ireland's

patron saint, with parades, festivities, and the "wearin' of the green." St. Patrick is an important figure in

Irish history, and the anniversary of his death is important for many reasons. On St. Patrick's Day, Irish

farmers let their stock out to pasture and plant potatoes, an important crop in Irish history. In this lesson,

students will examine some properties of potatoes and even use them as toys.

Key Science Topics

- air takes up space
- chemical changes
- gases
- pressure-volume relationships in gases

Time Required

Setup	20–30	minutes
Performance	30–45	minutes
Cleanup	10	minutes

Materials for the potato investigations

Part 1: Building Bridges

Building Student Knowledge and Motivation

Prior to beginning the lesson, create a classroom center containing items related to Irish culture and to the celebration of St. Patrick's Day. Sample items might include a rubber snake; picture of the sun; shamrock; shillelagh; harp, flute, or violin; leprechaun; gold-covered candy coins; book of poetry; picture of a parade; rainbow; pot of gold; and potato. The resources listed in Part 3, Additional Books, offer explanations of the importance of these and other symbols. Allow students to examine the items and to make written contributions to a chart entitled "What I Believe These Items Have in Common." Depending upon the familiarity of the students with the real significance of these items and/or their interest in the holiday, you may elect to read aloud to the class *St. Patrick's Day* by Gail Gibbons. (See Part 3, Additional Books.) Reveal that the items in this display all deal with Irish history and culture.

Bridging to the Science Activity

Point out the role the potato has played in Irish history. Ask students if they know how potatoes grow (green part above ground, potato underground). Show them pictures of potatoes being grown or harvested. Ask them if they know of different types of potatoes: russet, red, round white, baking, and gourmet specialty potatoes. These potatoes are all major types of Irish, or white, potatoes, and include many specially bred varieties. (Sweet potatoes and yams are two similar vegetables that also grow as tuberous roots, but they are not closely related to Irish potatoes or to each other.) Discuss and show examples of these different types. Discuss different ways potatoes are cooked, and if permissible by school policy, invite parents to make and bring in their favorite foods made with potatoes for the class to sample.

After discussing different ways potatoes are cooked, have students create riddles to describe various potato dishes, such as the following: mashed potatoes, baked potatoes, french fried potatoes, potato pancakes, potato salad, and twice-baked potatoes. See the following example.

Riddle: They are flat and often served with German meals.
Answer: potato pancakes

Tell students this science lesson includes four different activities with potatoes—two look at the chemicals in potatoes, and two use potatoes as a material for fun challenges.

Part 2: Science Activity

Materials

For Bridging to the Science Activity
- pictures of potatoes being grown or harvested
- samples of different types of potatoes, such as russet, red, round white, baking, and gourmet specialty potatoes

For Getting Ready
Part A, per class
- ¼ teaspoon tincture of iodine

  This solution, available in drugstores, must be the brown type, NOT the colorless type.

- water
- container to mix the iodine solution
- old newspapers

Part A, per group
- dropper bottle, or small bottle with a dropper attached

Part D, per class
- pliers
- scissors, sharp knife, or small saw (unless the pens have removable tips and ends)

  The teacher should be the only one to use this item.

- sandpaper
- (optional) clay, putty, or tape

Part D, per student
- 1 of the following:
  - ball-point pen without a hole in the side

    If a hole is present, fill it with clay or putty and tightly cover the hole with tape so it is airtight and completely sealed.

  - narrow piece of rigid aquarium tubing approximately 5–10 mm in diameter and at least 15 cm long

For the Procedure
Part A, per group
- bottle of dilute iodine solution prepared in Getting Ready
- wax paper
- water
- toothpick
- corn starch
- raw potato
- raw apple
- sheet of notebook paper

- paper towel
- half sheet of newspaper
- coffee filter

Part B, per group
- 3% hydrogen peroxide solution

  This product is available at drug and discount stores.

- 2 small, clear containers, such as plastic cups or test tubes
- small piece of raw potato
- small piece of raw apple
- small piece of boiled potato
- small piece of boiled apple
- (optional) magnifying lens

Part C, per class
- (optional) knife (for teacher use only)
- (optional) potato peeler

Part C, per student
- 2 or more transparent plastic drinking straws

  McDonald's® straws work very well. Make sure to have plenty of extra straws on hand, because many straws are likely to be bent or broken.

- raw potato

  An extremely firm potato may be too hard for thin-walled straws to penetrate without bending. Using thick-walled straws such as those from McDonald's and peeling the potato before doing the activity may solve the problem. If the potato is still too firm, allow it to sit for a day or two to soften slightly. Test a potato with one of the straws before doing the activity with the class to determine if this will be a problem.

Part D, per class
- (optional) piece of rigid aquarium tubing 2–5 times longer than the student poppers

Part D, per group
- stabbed potato from Part C
- extra drinking straws
- chopstick, wooden dowel rod, or plastic drinking straw that will slide easily into the straws listed in Part C and into the pen barrel
- pen barrel or aquarium tubing prepared in Getting Ready

For the Extension for Further Science Inquiry
Per student or group
- newspaper
- raw potato
- dilute iodine solution prepared in Getting Ready
- variety of packaged foods, some containing starch and some containing no starch

Safety and Disposal

Tincture of iodine used to make the dilute iodine solution in this activity should be handled with care to prevent spillage, eye contact, or ingestion. Iodine solution can cause stains.

When using any launcher or projectile toy, use caution and point it away from people or breakable objects. In Part D, you may want to allow just one student to launch a potato popper at a time. The potato piece is propelled out of the launcher with considerable force.

No special disposal procedures are required.

Getting Ready

For Part A

Make the dilute iodine solution as follows:

Handle tincture of iodine and the dilute iodine solution carefully. See Safety and Disposal. Prepare a dilute iodine solution by adding ¼ teaspoon tincture of iodine solution to about ¼ cup (60 mL) water until the solution is the color of weak tea. Pour this dilute solution into dropper bottles or small bottles with droppers attached.

For Part D

If using a pen barrel, prepare it as follows:

1. Use a pair of pliers to remove the tip and ink tube from the pen. (See Figure 1.) If the pen has a small hole near the tip, either cut that end off or fill the hole with clay or putty and tightly cover the hole with tape so it is airtight and completely sealed.

 Plugging the hole is recommended. Cutting off the hole can make the barrel too short and cause the activity not to work.

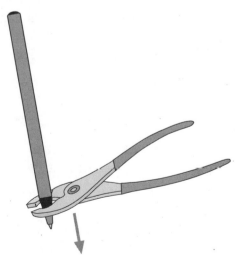

Figure 1: Use a pair of pliers to remove the tip and ink tube from the pen.

2. If possible, pry off the plug at the other end of the pen. If the plug cannot be pried out, cut off the end with a pair of scissors, a sharp knife, or a small saw. You should now have a straight plastic tube with no holes in the side. Sand the cut end(s) to remove sharp edges.

Procedure

 The individual parts of the following procedure are independent of each other and can be done in any order or combination.

Part A: Starch Test

1. Have each group use a dropper to place 1 or 2 drops of dilute iodine solution on a piece of wax paper. What do they observe? *A drop of yellow-brown liquid.*

2. Have each group add 1–2 drops of water on top of the drops of dilute iodine solution. Use a toothpick to mix. Have students record what they see. *The yellow-brown color becomes lighter but is still present.* Tell the students to sprinkle a pinch of corn starch powder over the liquid mixture and record their observations. *The solid turns blue-black.* Tell students that the blue-black color results from a chemical reaction between the iodine and the starch. Wax paper and water do not contain starch, and thus the blue-black color did not develop when the dilute iodine solution came into contact with them.

3. Tell the groups to place a few drops of dilute iodine solution on small pieces of raw potato and apple. Have them record their observations. *A dark blue-black color results on contact with the potato and apple.* Ask students what this means. *The pieces of potato and apple contain starch.*

4. Try testing several other items for the presence of starch. These items might include white notebook paper (*turns blue-black*), a white paper towel or napkin (*turns blue-black*), newspaper (*no blue-black*), and a coffee filter (*no blue-black*).

5. Ask students to consider whether boiling the potato or the apple makes them lose starch. Ask them how they would test this, and then do the experiment. (*The potato and apple again turn blue-black.*)

6. Have students discuss their results with the class.

Part B: The Peroxide Test

1. Have each group pour 3% hydrogen peroxide solution about ¼ inch deep into two small, clear containers such as plastic cups or test tubes.

2. Have students place a small piece of potato in one container and a small piece of apple in the other. What do they observe? Have them use a magnifying lens if needed. *Although few, if any, bubbles are visible around the apple, numerous bubbles form around the potato.*

3. Ask the students to consider whether boiling the potato and the apple will affect the reaction with hydrogen peroxide. Discuss. Provide them with a boiled piece of each. What do you observe? *No bubbles in either case.*

4. Ask students to draw some conclusions from this peroxide test. *The raw potato contains something the other items did not. But cooking the potato must have done something to the chemicals that were in the raw potato. Boiling removed or destroyed the active component.* Ask the students if starch could be the component of the potato that is responsible for the bubble formation. Discuss. *No, the apple contains starch and no bubbles were seen with it.*

Part C: Straw Spud-Stabber

1. Have students examine their drinking straws and raw potatoes. Ask them to predict what will happen when they stab the end of the straw against the potato.

2. Have students hold a straw in one hand (all fingers around the straw, leaving the end open) and attempt to stab the straw into a raw potato. Discuss results. *The straw bends and will not pierce the potato.*

3. Ask students to predict what will happen if they put one finger firmly over one end of the straw and stab the free end against the potato.

4. Have students hold their thumb or one finger firmly over the top end of a new straw and try to stab the potato again. Discuss results. *Most students should succeed in piercing the potato.* Ask why the second method works. *Sealing the end of the straw with a finger traps air inside. This trapped air makes the straw more rigid and less likely to bend.* If the straw does bend, it may be too long for small hands to control, or the potato may be too thick. Cut 1-inch-thick slices from the potato and have the previously unsuccessful students try using a slice instead of a whole potato. If they still have problems, cut the straw in half and repeat. When students have succeeded in piercing the potato, have them leave the straws stuck in the potatoes for Part D.

Part D: Potato Popper

1. Tell students that they will use the principle that air takes up space, which they just observed in Part C, to make a potato popper. Using the straw stuck in the potato from Part C, have them continue to push the straw all the way through the potato (or slice) and observe the plug of potato in one end. (See Figure 2.)

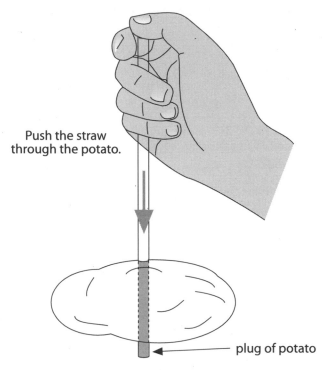

Push the straw through the potato.

plug of potato

Figure 2: Push the straw through the potato to make a plug in one end of the straw.

2. Tell the students to use a narrower straw, chopstick, or wooden dowel to push the potato plug about 1 cm (½ inch) farther into the straw. (See Figure 3.)

Figure 3: Push the potato plug a short way into the straw.

3. Have them turn the straw around and stab the other end completely through the potato as in step 1. Their straws should now have a potato plug at each end. (See Figure 4.)

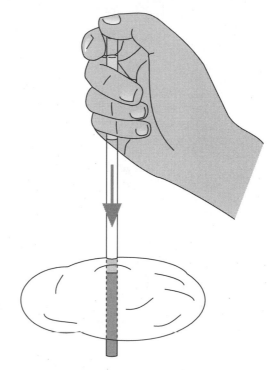

Figure 4: Plug the other end of the straw with another potato plug.

4. Have students point their straws away from themselves and their neighbors and place a narrower straw, chopstick, or wooden dowel against the plug that was pushed into the straw in step 2. (See Figure 5.) Have them push this plunger into the straw with a quick, sharp motion. The potato plug at the far end should shoot out of the straw if the straw and plugs are airtight. Have students retrieve the potato plugs.

Figure 5: With a quick, sharp motion, push the plunger into the straw. The far potato plug should shoot out.

5. Compare results as a class. Probably at least half of the class will not have been able to make their straw potato poppers work. Talk about reasons some may have worked and others not. Lead them to the idea that a sturdier column might work better. Tell students that they will now make sturdier poppers using different materials.

6. Give each student a sanded ball-point pen barrel (be sure it has no sharp edges) or piece of rigid plastic aquarium tubing. Challenge them to build and test a potato popper with this tube. Have them evaluate their results, compare them with other students in small groups, and discuss results as a class. (The success rate should be much higher than it was with the straws.)

7. Discuss how reproducible results with the straw and with the pen barrel are within the class. In other words, does each method give fairly consistent results? Students can express success rates as "X tries out of Y [number of students in the class] were successful."

8. Have students investigate the following questions:

   - Can you reuse the drinking straw for the popper? *Probably not, because the straws tend to weaken after stabbing and thus cannot maintain an airtight seal.* Can you reuse the pen barrel? *Yes, because it is much sturdier and maintains an airtight seal.*

   - Can you reuse the potato plugs? *The second plug can be left in and reused for another time. However, the fired plug can't be easily reused because it is very difficult to push it back into the popper and achieve an airtight seal.*

   - How far do the poppers shoot? (Answers will vary.)

9. (optional) You may wish to demonstrate a larger potato popper using a piece of rigid aquarium tubing 2–5 times longer than the student poppers. Have students predict the distance a potato plug will travel with this larger popper and discuss reasons for the results. (Typically, the greater the amount of air trapped in the popper, the farther the potato plug will travel, assuming all other factors are equal.)

Extension for Further Science Inquiry

Mark a piece of newspaper with starch by stamping it in spots with a slice of potato. Allow the potato spots to dry so they are invisible. Challenge students to find the "starch prints" on the newspaper. If desired, create a scenario for a "crime investigation" involving the potato popper, where the student "detectives" must determine whether this "weapon" was used. The challenge can be further extended by having students test packaged foods whose contents indicate they may contain starch.

Science Explanation

 The following explanation is intended for the teacher's information. Modify the explanation for students as required.

The Starch Test

When tincture of iodine solution comes in contact with starch, a characteristic blue-black color is produced. Many types of foods, including potatoes, apples, and pasta, contain starch. Many types of paper also contain starch. However, newspaper and coffee filters contain no starch. In the case of the wax paper, the paper does not turn blue-black, because the wax keeps the iodine solution from reaching the starch in the paper. Boiling the potato and apple does not destroy the starch, so these materials still turn blue-black when treated with the iodine solution.

The starch-iodine reaction can be used to detect counterfeit paper money. Ordinary paper contains starch, which is added near the end of the papermaking process to stiffen the paper. However, genuine U.S. currency contains no starch. When a special Counterfeit Detector Pen containing a solution of iodine is used to mark on a bill, it makes a yellow line. If the mark stays yellow, the bill may be genuine. If the mark turns blue-black, the bill is counterfeit.

The Peroxide Test

Raw potatoes contain the enzyme peroxidase. Enzymes are chemical catalysts found in living cells. One of their functions is to speed up the breakdown of complex food compounds into smaller compounds. Peroxidase from the potato's cells causes the hydrogen peroxide to quickly react to form water and bubbles of oxygen gas. Boiling the potato causes the peroxidase to break down, so no reaction occurs when the boiled potato is placed in hydrogen peroxide.

Straw Spud-Stabber

With no finger over the top, a straw stabbed against a potato will simply bend, because the thin plastic walls are flimsy compared to the potato. However, when a finger is held firmly over the top and the straw is stabbed against the potato, air is trapped inside the straw. The pressure of the air keeps the walls of the straw rigid, so the straw generally is able to penetrate the potato.

Potato Popper

In Part D, air is trapped in the tube between the two potato plugs. When one plug is quickly pushed farther into the tube with the rod, it decreases the volume of the trapped air and increases the air's pressure. This greater air pressure pushes back on both plugs, but one is held in place by the rod. The other plug is pushed out of the tube by the increased air pressure. The greater the air pressure (the more the air has been compressed), the greater the force pushing the potato plug out of the tube, and the farther the plug will travel.

History of Potatoes

Potatoes (common potatoes, white potatoes, or Irish potatoes) were cultivated in South America as early as 1,800 years ago, probably in a mixture of varieties. Most botanists consider the plant to be a native of the Peruvian-Bolivian Andes. Invading Spaniards in the 16th century brought potatoes back to Europe, and the vegetable became a major crop in Ireland by the end of the 17th century. Within 100 years the potato became a major crop in continental Europe as well. During the first half of the 19th century the potato continued to spread, but in the mid-19th century a disastrous potato blight struck Ireland, whose economy had become dependent on the potato. The resulting famine discouraged other nations from becoming too dependent on the crop.

Potatoes are very useful and versatile vegetables. They can be cooked in a variety of ways, ground into flour, and used as a thickener for sauces. They are easily digested and contain carbohydrates, including starch; vitamin C; amino acids; proteins; thiamine; and nicotinic acid.

References for the Science Activity

McClure, M. "Chemical Counterfeit Catcher," *ChemMatters*. October 1997, *15*(3), 13–15.

"potato" *Britannica Online*. http://www.eb.com:180/cgi-bin/g?DocF=micro/478/12.html (accessed 17 Dec 1997).

Sarquis, M.; Kibbey, B.; Smyth, E. "Pull it in/Push it out"; *Science Activities for Elementary Classrooms;* Flinn Scientific: Batavia, IL, 1989; p 59.

Part 3: Integrating with Language Arts

Featured Fiction Book: *The Hungry Leprechaun*

Author: Mary Calhoun   Illustrator: Roger Duvoisin
Publisher: William Morrow   ISBN: 62-7214
Summary: The spirit of Ireland pervades this tale about a poor man and an equally poor leprechaun who seems to have lost his magic touch.

Show students the cover of *The Hungry Leprechaun*. Ask, "What is a leprechaun? What is its significance in Irish culture?" Read the story aloud, pausing on page 24 where it says, "And he gave one of the rocks a mighty whack with his dandelion shovel. But what was that?" Ask the students to predict what "it" was. Continue to read until page 26 where Tippery says, "We put them in the *pot*, and we *ate* them. We'll call them..." Have the students name the mystery item.

Writing Extensions

- Have students use their science journals to write a summary of the experiment they designed and the results they found.
- Have students write instructions for making the potato popper.
- Read aloud *Jeremy Bean's St. Patrick's Day* (see Additional Books) and have students write about a time when they were subjected to a lot of teasing or felt uneasy in a situation and a friend came to their rescue.

Additional Books

Fiction

Title: *Jamie O'Rourke and the Big Potato: An Irish Folktale*
Author and Illustrator: Tomie De Paola
Publisher: G.P. Putnam's Sons   ISBN: 0-399-22257-X
Summary: The laziest man in all of Ireland catches a leprechaun, who offers a potato seed instead of a pot of gold for his freedom.

Title: *Jeremy Bean's St. Patrick's Day*
Author: Alice Schertle   Illustrator: Linda Shute
Publisher: Lothrop, Lee, and Shepard   ISBN: 0-688-04813-7 or 14-5
Summary: Shy Jeremy Bean forgets, much to his humiliation, to wear green to
    school for St. Patrick's Day. He finds solace and companionship from a new
    and unexpected friend.

Title: *Leprechauns Never Lie*
Author and Illustrator: Lorna Balian
Publisher: Abingdon   ISBN: 0-687-21371-1
Summary: Gram is ailing and Ninny Nanny, too lazy to care for their simple needs,
    says she'll catch a leprechaun to discover his hidden gold. Gram thinks it
    won't work—but does it? Delight in the dialogue written in Irish dialect.

Nonfiction

Title: *One Potato: A Counting Book of Potato Prints*
Author: Diane Pomeroy
Publisher: Harcourt Brace   ISBN: 0152003002
Summary: A counting book which uses potato-print images of fruits and
    vegetables to illustrate numbers from 1 to 100 and includes an explanation of
    how to do potato printing.

Title: *St. Patrick's Day Magic*
Author: James W. Baker   Illustrator: George Overlie
Publisher: Lerner   ISBN: 0-8225-2234-9
Summary: Directions for 10 magic tricks with a St. Patrick's Day theme; exercises
    in logic and math reasoning.

Title: *St. Patrick's Day*
Author and Illustrator: Gail Gibbons
Publisher: Holiday House   ISBN: 0-8234-119-2
Summary: Information about St. Patrick's life, his legends, and the meaning of the
    holiday symbols is given in delightful story form; particularly well suited for
    lower elementary.

Title: *St. Patrick's Day*
Author: Joyce K. Kessel   Illustrator: Cathy Gilchrist
Publisher: Carolrhoda   ISBN: 0-87614-193-9
Summary: Presents a brief account of the life of the Roman aristocrat who
    became Ireland's patron saint and discusses the annual holiday that honors
    him; suitable for middle elementary.

Title: *Shamrocks, Harps, and Shillelaghs, The Story of the St. Patrick's Day Symbols*
Author: Edna Barth   Illustrator: Ursula Arndt
Publisher: Houghton Mifflin/Clarion   ISBN: 0-395-28845-2 or 14-5
Summary: A very fascinating and thorough exploration of the origins and
    meanings of symbols and legends associated with St. Patrick's Day; well suited
    for upper elementary. Excellent teacher background information.

Part 4: Other Lesson Extensions

Art and Music

- Have students make potato prints by cutting raw potatoes in half and cutting the flat sides to create a raised shape on each half. They can use these potato halves as they would rubber stamps to make patterns or pictures with green paint. Have them create decorative paper items such as St. Patrick's Day cards or bookmarks.
- Give each student a raw potato to decorate. This will be their potato "bud"dy for the day. When all students have finished creating their "bud"dies, have a tabletop parade.
- Have a guest knowledgeable about Irish culture teach the students an Irish jig. Have students teach other classes the jig. Have a St. Patrick's Day parade through the school.

Mathematics

- *St. Patrick's Day Magic* contains many activities that challenge readers' sense of logic. Each activity is explained well enough for students to be able to replicate the feats, which are not really magic but rather scientific or mathematical concepts yet to be understood.
- Have students share how they like to eat potatoes, and graph the results.

Social Studies

- Learn about the history of Ireland and the real St. Patrick by reading to the students from *St. Patrick's Day* by Joyce K. Kessel and/or *Shamrocks, Harps, and Shillelaghs: The Story of the St. Patrick's Day Symbols* by Edna Barth. (See Part 3, Additional Books.)

Just for Fun

- Hold potato-sack races and leprechaun leap contests.

Part 5: National Science Education Standards

Science as Inquiry Standards:

Abilities Necessary to Do Scientific Inquiry

Students conduct investigations of potatoes and other substances to determine their properties and how heating affects these properties.

Students use their observations to identify substances containing starch and to explain how heat changes some properties.

Students discuss their results and conclusions as a class.

Physical Science Standards:

Properties of Objects and Materials

Objects will sometimes react with other substances, as the raw potato does with the iodine and hydrogen peroxide.

Objects, such as potatoes, are made from one or more materials and can be described by the properties of the materials. Potatoes contain starch, which reacts with iodine, and peroxidase, which catalyzes the decomposition of hydrogen peroxide.

Properties and Changes of Properties in Matter

When substances, such as the starch in a potato, react, they produce new substances with different characteristic properties. The potato turns a blue-black color when the starch in it reacts with iodine.

Position and Motion of Objects

The position and motion of objects, such as the potato plug, can be changed by pushing or pulling. The length of the tube of the potato popper affects the force of the push.

Science and Technology Standards:

Abilities of Technological Design

Students question ways to put a straw through a potato and ways to make an effective potato popper.

Students propose ways to make a potato-popper barrel that works better than a straw.

Students test their proposed changes in the potato popper within their groups.

Students evaluate the results of their design changes and those of other groups. They use the information to make further modifications.

Students discuss their design changes and conclusions, including success rates of their potato poppers, with the class.

Spring

Spring is the first season of the astronomical year, and to the early peoples who depended upon agriculture for their well-being, it was also the most important. The ancient people regarded winter as a season of darkness, death, and chaos, while spring symbolized the return of light and order. Just as they held festivals to encourage the sun to return from the dark winter (see the introduction to Winter for more information), early peoples held festivals to welcome the sun and the spring.

Spring festivals were marked by flowers and dancing as people rejoiced in the warm weather and the promise of the growing season. Special rites, such as the powwows and dances of Native American cultures, were performed to ensure the fruitfulness of fields, animals, and people. Weddings were often held in the spring as a symbol of new life and new beginnings. Even today, spring is considered a season of new beginnings, as weddings and graduations are traditionally held during this time.

Two of the major religious holidays that occur in this season also epitomize the nature of spring. The Jewish Passover commemorates the release of the Jewish people from Egyptian slavery and also from the labors of winter. In fact, the Torah, the Jewish Scripture upon which Jewish law is based, dictates that Passover be held in the spring. Easter, a Christian holiday, celebrates resurrection and eternal life, and some modern Easter traditions were actually developed from spring festivals (see the introduction to Easter for more information).

Officially, the first day of spring is either March 20 or March 21 in the northern hemisphere, depending upon the position of the Earth in its orbit around the sun (see the introduction to Winter for more information on the seasons in the Earth's hemispheres). Spring begins at the vernal equinox, when the sun passes through the intersection of the "ecliptic" (the path of the Earth's orbit around the sun) and the celestial equator. The celestial equator is the "equator" of the universe, whose position was determined by observing the motion of the stars, planets, and galaxies with relation to each other. The equinox is marked by a day that has 12 hours of sunlight and 12 hours of darkness, and there are two—one in the spring and one in the fall.

In the second century B.C., the Greek astronomer Hipparchus calculated the position of the sun at the exact moment of the vernal equinox and found that the sun was entering the constellation Aries. His calculations eventually led to the present Zodiac system. Because of the retrograde motion of the equinoxes (the equinoctial points move backwards in relation to the Earth's movement through space), the vernal equinox moves slightly westward each year. Today, the vernal equinox happens when the sun is in Pisces, the constellation immediately to the west of Aries.

Twice a year, the Earth crosses the region where the ecliptic and the celestial equator meet, marking the beginning of spring and fall. As the Earth passes this intersection, the pole that is tilted toward the sun begins to tilt away from the sun, and vice versa. As spring begins in the northern or southern hemisphere, the pole in that hemisphere begins tilting toward the sun. This causes more solar rays to hit this hemisphere directly, increasing the amount of solar energy absorbed. Since plants and flowers need this solar energy to grow and develop, spring is the first season of growth, because the supply of solar energy begins to increase. By June 21, the summer solstice in the northern hemisphere, (or December 21 for the southern hemisphere) the North Pole (or South Pole) is pointing directly at the sun, and the solar rays hitting the hemisphere directly are at a maximum, causing warmer temperatures and an increase in solar energy.

Reference

Hatch, J.M. *The American Book of Days,* 3rd ed.; H.W. Wilson: New York, 1978; pp 276–277.

Spring into Capillary Action

• •

Spring is a colorful time of year, when plants begin to grow again and flowers bloom. An important chemical

principle that helps plants grow is capillary action, a process that causes liquids to rise up very narrow tubes.

In this activity, students observe this process using celery and food color.

• •

Key Science Topic

• capillary action

Time Required

Setup   5 minutes
Performance   5–10 minutes day 1, plus overnight
                          20–30 minutes day 2
Cleanup   5–10 minutes

A celery stick in red food color

Part 1: Building Bridges

Building Student Knowledge and Motivation

Create a center where you have placed several symbols of spring, including plants and flowers. Ask students to think about what relationship these symbols have to spring. Allow them to add other symbols of spring they feel should be included in the collection.

Bridging to the Science Activity

"April showers bring May flowers." Discuss this saying and also the importance of water in keeping flowers fresh once they are cut. Bring in several fresh flowers. Leave one out of water and place the others in water. Ask students to discuss the importance of water to these flowers. Ask them to predict what they will observe over several days. Each day observe all of the flowers. Discuss the differences between the flowers in water and the flower not in water.

Part 2: Science Activity

Materials

For Bridging to the Science Activity
Per class
- several flowers
- vase
- water

For the Procedure
Part A, per student or group
- water
- 2 clear, colorless narrow cups or jars
- 2 celery sticks
- spoon or stirring stick
- ½ teaspoon food color (Red or blue work best; yellow does not work.)

   If possible, buy food color in bottles of 30 mL or 1½ ounces; this is less expensive than buying many small vials.

Part B, per class
- fine glass tubes (capillary tubes) or a pair of microscope slides
- ½ teaspoon food color
- clear, colorless glass or jar

For the Science Extension

Per class

- white carnation or rose
- 2 clear, colorless glasses or jars
- ½ teaspoon each of 2 colors of food color
- water
- knife or pair of scissors
- ringstand or other tall object, such as a box, to support the flower
- (optional) tape

Safety and Disposal

Care must be exercised when using the knife. No special disposal procedures are required.

Procedure

Part A: Celery Color Test

1. Have each student or group stir ½ teaspoon food color into 1 cup water in a narrow cup or other container. Have them pour the same amount of plain water into a second container.

2. Cut the end off 2 sticks of celery about ½ inch from the bottom. Place one piece of freshly cut celery in the container of colored water and the other in the plain water. Allow both pieces to sit overnight undisturbed.

3. The next day allow students to examine both pieces of celery and describe any differences they observe.

4. Have students break both pieces of celery in half and carefully observe the veins. Have them peel a red vein from this tinted stalk to observe more closely. (This can be done easily if they pick a vein near the perimeter.)

5. Challenge students to pose possible explanations for the observations.

Part B: Observing Capillary Action

1. Demonstrate capillary action using fine glass tubes (capillary tubes) of various diameters or a pair of microscope slides. Put the end of a glass tube in a solution of ½ teaspoon food color in 1 cup water, or place two flat slides together tightly and put one end in the solution of colored water.

2. Ask your students what they observe. *The water will be drawn up the tube or into the space between the glass slides.*

3. Have the students compare their observations in step 2 to their observations in Part A.

4. As a class, discuss possible explanations for the behavior of the liquid.

Extension for Further Science Inquiry

1. Show students a white carnation or rose. Encourage students to propose ways to use capillary action to color the flower. Have them test their proposals and evaluate their results.

2. Have students try the following method and compare the results of their methods with it. Have them share their results with the class.

   a. Stir ½ teaspoon food color into ½ cup water. Stir ½ teaspoon of another food color into ½ cup water in a second cup. Alternatively, just remove the caps from two vials of different colors of food color and use them as the containers in step 3.

   b. Use a knife or scissors to make a fresh cut perpendicular to the length of the stem at its tip. Then carefully split the stem in half lengthwise—that is, parallel to the stem. The split portion of the stem must be long enough to allow each half of the split stem to reach the bottom of one of the containers of food color. (See Figure 1.)

      You may wish to wrap a piece of tape carefully just above the split in the stem to prevent further splitting.

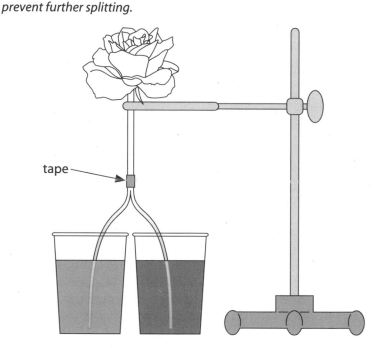

Figure 1: After splitting the stem, put each half into a container of food color so that the stems reach the bottom of the container. Fasten the flower to a ringstand or another object.

   c. Ask students to predict what will happen when one of the stem halves is placed in one container of food color and the other stem half in the other container. After they have made their predictions, do the experiment, being sure to fasten the flower to a ringstand or another object to prevent it from tipping over.

   d. Leave the flower stems in the solutions until the next day. Observe and record observations.

Science Explanation

The following explanation is intended for the teacher's information. Modify the explanation for students as required.

Capillary action can make a liquid appear to defy gravity by causing the liquid to creep up thin gaps, tubes, or nooks and crannies. This phenomenon is caused by an attraction between the walls of the tube and the liquid within. Capillary action in the wood fibers in paper allows a paper towel or blotter to absorb liquids. Capillary action plays a part in the growth of plants by enabling water to move from the soil into the roots and by enabling sap to move up into the stems and leaves. (Transpiration and osmotic pressure also contribute to the movement of water within the stem.)

While the Extension for Further Science Inquiry involves creating colorful flowers, the technique students use is not the one used by florists to make color highlights. Most often, florists dip or spray flowers to color them.

References for the Science Activity

Allison, L.; Katz, D. *Gee Whiz!: How to Mix Art and Science or the Art of Thinking Scientifically;* Little, Brown: Boston, 1983; p 40.

Arnov, B. *Water: Experiments to Understand It;* Lothrop, Lee and Shepard; New York, 1980; pp 56–59.

"Two-Toned Flower"; *Fun with Chemistry: A Guidebook of K–12 Activities;* Vol. 2; Sarquis, M.; Sarquis, J.L., Eds. Institute for Chemical Education: Madison, WI, 1993; pp 9–12.

Part 3: Integrating with Language Arts

Featured Fiction Book: *The Sunflower That Went FLOP*

Author: Joy Cowley   Illustrator: David Cowe
Publisher: The Wright Group   ISBN: 1-55911-491-6
Summary: Mrs. Brown's prize sunflower keeps *flopping* in the hot summer sun.
    Mr. Brown's efforts to fix it continue to fail until one night it rains.

Use a real or plastic sunflower to demonstrate the flower's plight in the story. Have a student hold the sunflower as the story is read. Every time the sunflower in the story goes *flop,* have the student make the real or plastic sunflower flop, too. At the end of the story, discuss what was happening to the sunflower in the story and how the rain solved the problem.

Writing Extensions

- After reading and acting out *The Sunflower That Went FLOP,* discuss the author's use of the word "flop." Introduce the concept of onomatopoeia (words that imitate sounds, such as "buzz," "hum," "slap," and "splash"). Have students brainstorm other such words that could be added to the story. Have students act out the new version of the story using their onomatopoeia.
- Have students write a letter to the Browns explaining what is happening to the sunflower and what they can do to solve the problem.

Additional Books

Nonfiction

Title: *Flowers*
Author: Peggy Roalf
Publisher: Hyperion   ISBN: 1562823582
Summary: Explores 2,000 years of art history by looking at paintings of flowers by various artists.

Title: *Gather Up, Gather In*
Author: M.C. Helldorfer   Illustrator: Judy Pedersen
Publisher: Viking   ISBN: 0-670-84752-6
Summary: Presents a child's-eye view of the seasons through luminous illustrations and evocative prose-poetry.

Title: *Spring Across America*
Author: Seymour Simon
Publisher: Hyperion   ISBN: 0786800690
Summary: Describes the natural history of spring in various parts of the United States.

Part 4: Other Lesson Extensions

Art and Music

- Have students make "capillary flowers" as follows: Cut out a circle approximately 9–15 cm in diameter from a piece of filter paper. (You can use a coffee filter instead, but the separation won't be as good.) Poke a small hole though the center of the filter-paper circle. Make a coin-sized ring of small dots around the hole in the filter-paper circle using two different colors of water-soluble fine- or medium-point felt-tip pens. (Be sure to try at least some black ink; Vis-a-Vis® brand works well.) Use one pen to make five or six equally spaced dots, then use the second pen to make dots at equal intervals between the first ones. Wet a 4- to 6-inch-long piece of pipe cleaner thoroughly. Pull it through the hole in the filter-paper circle (from the bottom) until 1–2 inches extend above the paper. Put enough water in a cup so that the bottom of the pipe cleaner will dip into the water. Dry the rim of the cup. Set the paper circle on the rim of the cup with the pipe cleaner extending into the water. Record observations of any changes until the fastest-moving color comes near the edge of the paper circle. Lift the paper off the cup, remove the pipe cleaner, and set the paper on another cup to dry. If desired, have students use different varieties of pens and compare color patterns to determine which students used the same brand of pen.

- Make dried flowers.
- Show students some paintings from *Flowers* by Peggy Roalf (see Part 3, Additional Books). Discuss some key terms such as "background" and "shadows." Bring in some flowers and have students make their own flower drawings or paintings.
- Have students write a song that a flower might sing to the rain, such as "Rain, rain, come to me! I am thirsty, can't you see? Up my stem you will flow. Capillary on the go!"

Mathematics

- Use a single food color to color flowers with stems of different lengths. Measure the length of the stem and compare this to the time required for the color to show in the flower.
- Make a paper flower garden by having each student measure his or her own height and use green construction paper to make a stem of equal height. Have students use a variety of art materials to create the petals and other parts of the flower. Students may choose to put their pictures or drawings of themselves in the centers of the flowers. Using measurement and geometry skills, have students compare and contrast the various flowers they have made. Discuss geometry terms such as circumference, length, and width. This garden could be displayed in the hall or classroom with the title, "We have really bloomed in math this year!"

Social Studies

- Gather information about how various cultures celebrate spring and the growing season. Have a Native American powwow and dance. Have students learn about rain dances to celebrate the growing season. Have the students create their own rain dances and perform for other classes.
- Research the meanings of various kinds of flowers in different cultures.

Just for Fun

- Have a spring party with edible art. Make a "dirt dessert" flowerpot according to the following recipe:
  - large (5.1 ounce) package instant vanilla pudding mix
  - 3 cups cold milk
  - large (8 ounce) container frozen whipped topping, thawed

- 6-ounce package miniature chocolate chips
- new child's sand bucket and shovel, cleaned thoroughly, or plastic cup, or new flowerpot
- large package Oreo® cookies, crushed to crumb consistency
- gummi worms
- silk or paper flower

Mix the pudding according to the package directions and allow it to set for a few minutes. Then fold the whipped topping and chocolate chips into the pudding. Put half of the pudding mixture in the bucket. Top with half of the cookie crumbs. Layer with the rest of the pudding and top with cookie crumbs. Add gummi worms and chill. "Plant" an artificial (silk or paper) flower in the pot. Use the shovel to serve.

- Make edible sunflowers according to the following recipe:
  - 2 vanilla wafers
  - 1 spoonful peanut butter
  - 8 miniature chocolate chips
  - 10 pieces candy corn
  - ½ celery stalk
  - vanilla icing tinted with green food color

Spread peanut butter on one vanilla wafer. Put a few miniature chocolate chips on top of the peanut butter. Place the tips of the candy-corn pieces around the edge of the wafer with the wide ends sticking out beyond the edge of the wafer to resemble petals. Place the celery stalk at the bottom of the flower to represent the flower's stem. Cut the other vanilla wafer in half. Spread the green icing on each half of the wafer. Place the wafer halves on opposite sides of the stalk at the bottom to represent leaves.

Part 5: National Science Education Standards

Science as Inquiry Standards:

Abilities Necessary to Do Scientific Inquiry

Students question why plants left out of water wilt much more quickly than those in water.

Students use celery to investigate the movement of water up plant stems.

Students use their observations of the behavior of celery in colored water to explain why plants in water do not wilt immediately.

Students discuss their observations and conclusions about capillary action and prevention of wilting.

Physical Science Standards:

Properties of Objects and Materials

Water evaporates from plant cells, and the plants will wilt if the water is not replaced.

Water moves up small tubes by capillary action.

Science and Technology Standards:

Abilities of Technological Design

Students question how capillary action can be used to color a white flower.

Students propose ways to use capillary action to color a white flower.

Students test their proposals.

Students evaluate their results, compare their methods with methods used by other students, and modify their designs as needed.

Students show their colored flowers to the class and explain how they made them. The class discusses why each approach did or did not work well.

Earth Day

March 21, April 22
Culture: United States and other countries

Since 1970, Earth Day has been an important environmental holiday for the United States and other countries around the world. The origin of Earth Day, however, is credited to two different individuals, each of whom devised the holiday independently of the other.

Gaylord Nelson, a U.S. Senator, first conceived of an Earth Day in the 1960s as a way to move the environment into the political limelight. Nelson's campaign for the environment began with a presidential national conservation tour, which President Kennedy did in 1963. However, the tour did not succeed in making the environment a national issue, and Nelson went back to the "drawing board." Six years later, as he was reading an article on "teach-ins" during the Vietnam War, he conceived the idea of having a "teach-in" about the environment, and the idea of Earth Day was born.

Nelson met with other political leaders and grassroots organizations to plan the events for the first Earth Day, scheduled for April 22, 1970. People across the country met to discuss the environment and human impact on it. They spoke with community and state leaders, voicing their concerns about the environment. As this tradition continued, additional activities were incorporated into Earth Day, including neighborhood cleanups, tree planting, and other environmental awareness activities.

John McConnell also wanted to have a holiday during which people around the world would celebrate life and nature. As he thought about the idea, one of his greatest concerns was when to have it. He wanted the day to have meaning and significance for the entire world, not just for the United States. In the spring of 1969, the perfect day came to mind: the vernal equinox, the first day of spring.

On March 21, 1970, the first Proclamation of Earth Day came from San Francisco, the city named for St. Francis, the patron saint of ecology. The United Nations showed their support for this day by officially sanctioning March 21 as Earth Day, a date which is still observed today.

Although two "Earth Days" are observed in the United States, each community and culture around the world celebrates the Earth at a time appropriate for its climate. In some parts of the northern hemisphere, for example, the winter snow has not melted completely by the end of March, making planting and cleaning difficult. In the southern hemisphere, March 21 is actually the beginning of autumn due to the tilt of the Earth (see the introduction to Autumn for further explanation), and some cultures in this hemisphere celebrate the Earth during their spring season, September–December.

No matter when you celebrate Earth Day, taking care of the environment is a responsibility that should be considered all year round. One of the leading issues in environmental awareness is recycling. Each year, Americans throw away an average of 1,562 pounds of trash per person; much of this trash is placed in landfills. However, many items commonly thrown away can be recycled, especially paper, including newspaper, notebook paper, and cardboard. In fact, many new companies have been created specifically to recycle paper or other products.

References

Earth Trustees, Earth Site, http://www.earthsite.org/day.htm (accessed 9 Feb 1998).

Kaufman, D.G., Franz, C.M. *Biosphere 2000: Protecting Our Global Environment,* 2nd ed.; Kendall/Hunt: Dubuque, IA, 1996, p 446.

Wilderness Society Web Site. Earth Day '98 Online. History of Earth Day. http://www.envirolink.org/earthday/history.html (accessed Feb 1998).

Recycling Paper For Earth Day

Earth Day is one of the few secular holidays celebrated around the world. The United States celebrates

Earth Day on March 21 and April 22, and other countries celebrate it on different days in the spring. Recycling

and planting are two themes of Earth Day activities, and in this lesson, students do a little of both. They will

make their own recycled paper that contains seeds and then use the paper to write a letter to a friend

containing instructions for planting the paper and watching the seeds grow!

Key Science Topics

- physical properties
- recycling

Time Required

Setup	15	minutes
Performance	45–60	minutes plus drying time spread over several days
Cleanup	15	minutes

A piece of recycled paper

Part 1: Building Bridges

Building Student Knowledge and Motivation

Prior to the lesson, create a learning center containing many items relating to Earth Day. Let students bring in Earth Day items they may have to add to the collection. Tell the students when they visit the center to look for recurring symbols associated with Earth Day. Let them add symbols of Earth Day they think should be included but may be missing.

Bridging to the Science Activity

Pass around examples of several different kinds of paper, including photocopy paper, "ragg" paper, "linen" paper, and different kinds of art paper. Allow students to examine the different papers with a magnifying lens. Ask them if they know what paper is usually made from. *Trees.* Ask students how many pounds of paper can be made from one tree, on average. *An average 30-year-old pine tree yields 117 pounds of paper.* Discuss the importance of trees to our environment. *Trees produce oxygen, remove carbon dioxide (a "greenhouse gas") from the air, provide shade, prevent soil erosion, provide homes and food for wildlife, and help regulate climate.*

Display a recycling bin and ask students whether they have ever heard the term "recycling." What does it mean? What is the significance of the three-sided arrow? *Resources, manufacturer, consumer, and back through the cycle.* How does recycling fit with Earth Day? Ask students if paper can be recycled. *Yes.* Ask them how they think recycled paper is made. What might be some advantages of recycling paper? Show students some products made from recycled paper, such as a greeting card, theater ticket, paper bag, or paperboard container (make sure the label says the product contains at least some recycled paper). If possible, show students a sheet of paper with small flowers or leaves embedded in it and tell them that they will be making paper that contains seeds and can be planted. They will use this paper to make an Earth Day card.

Part 2: Science Activity

Materials

For Bridging to the Science Activity
Per class
- examples of several kinds of paper, such as photocopy paper, "ragg" paper, "linen" paper, and different kinds of art paper
- several magnifying lenses
- recycling bin with three-sided arrow logo
- various products made from recycled paper
- sheet of paper with small flowers or leaves embedded in it

For Getting Ready

Per class
- scissors
- blender
- (optional) string

Per group
- 6 reusable wiping cloths, such as Handi Wipes® or Easy Wipes®
- 2 identical 2-piece wooden or plastic embroidery hoops 4–5 inches in diameter
- plastic window screen to fit hoop
- 1 of the following:
  ○ 2 double sheets of newspaper (1 double sheet is approximately 26 inches x 23 inches) and a scrap sheet of colored copy or construction paper
  ○ scrap sheets of colored copy or construction paper (Green and blue look nice for Earth Day.)
- oblong plastic dish pan
- water

For the Procedure, Part A

Per class
- clear plastic jar
- quarter sheet of newspaper

Per group
- quarter sheet of newspaper
- magnifying lens or 10x jeweler's loupe
- clear plastic jar
- water
- small, rigid screen such as a piece of plastic needlepoint canvas
- bucket or dish pan

For the Procedure, Part B

Per class
- (optional) "clotheslines" and clothespins (See Getting Ready.)

Per group of 3–4 students
- the following materials prepared in Getting Ready
  ○ mold
  ○ deckle
  ○ dish pan filled with slurry
  ○ reusable wiping cloths cut in half
- extra newspaper (for making "couch")
- mixing spoon or stirring stick
- magnifying lens or 10x jeweler's loupe

- pressing board made from 1 of the following:
  - piece of wood approximately 9 inches x 12 inches
  - hardback book inside a 1-gallon zipper-type plastic bag
- small pieces of paper and paper clips for labels

For the Procedure, Part C
- all materials listed for Part B
- package of small flower seeds

For the Extensions for Further Science Inquiry
- all materials listed for the Procedure, Parts B and C
- additional materials as requested by students
- disposable cups

Safety and Disposal

Use caution when operating the blenders. Blenders should be used only by an adult.

Do not pour leftover slurry down the drain, as it may cause a blockage. Flush the slurry down a toilet.

Getting Ready

1. Cut the reusable wiping cloths in half to make rectangles approximately 10 inches x 13 inches.

2. (optional) Use string to make one or more "clotheslines" for hanging the paper up to dry.

3. Make a mold and deckle for each group as follows:

   a. Cut a square of window screen for each embroidery hoop with a length and width about 2 inches greater than the diameter of the inner ring of the embroidery hoop.

   b. Separate the rings of one embroidery hoop.

   c. Set the screen over the smaller ring and gently slide the larger ring into place (see Figure 1), keeping the screen taut. If the screen wrinkles, pull it firmly to smooth it.

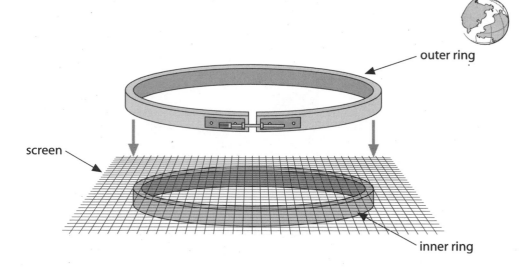

Figure 1: Gently slide the outer ring into place over the screen and inner ring.

d. If the outer ring has a screw, tighten it. Trim the window screen to extend about half an inch outside the hoop. This is the mold.

e. Keep the inner and outer rings of the second embroidery hoop together. (See Figure 2.) This is the deckle. It sits on top of the mold, with the hoops aligned with each other.

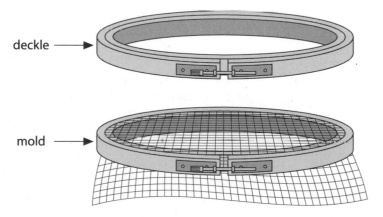

Figure 2: The mold and deckle go together.

4. Prepare batches of pulp ahead of time so that students do not have to use the blender. Make one dishpan of slurry for each group of students as follows:

a. Tear the paper into pieces about 1 inch square. If using newspaper, tear up two double sheets plus a sheet or two of colored paper (green and blue look nice for Earth Day). Keep the colored paper separate from the newspaper.

b. Fill the dish pan about half full of clean water.

c. Put a handful of torn paper into the blender. (If you are using newspaper plus colored paper, put only the newspaper into the blender now.)

d. Fill the blender about two-thirds full of water.

e. Blend in 10-second bursts for a total of about 30 seconds.

f. Pour the pulp into the dish pan of clean water.

g. Repeat steps c–e three or four times more.

h. If you previously blended newspaper, put a handful of colored paper into the blender, blend for only 10 seconds (leaving intact chunks of paper), and pour this pulp into the dish pan.

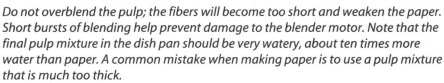

Do not overblend the pulp; the fibers will become too short and weaken the paper. Short bursts of blending help prevent damage to the blender motor. Note that the final pulp mixture in the dish pan should be very watery, about ten times more water than paper. A common mistake when making paper is to use a pulp mixture that is much too thick.

Procedure

Part A: Introduction to Pulp and Paper

Do steps 1–9 in one day. As noted in step 10, you should allow the paper to dry overnight.

1. Instruct students to tear the quarter sheet of newspaper into small pieces (about 1 inch x 1 inch).

2. Have students use a magnifying lens or loupe to carefully observe a piece of torn paper, especially the edges. Tell them to draw what they see and describe it in words.

3. Tell each group to put a handful of the torn paper in a jar, fill the jar about half full of water, and tightly cap the jar. Have students take turns shaking the jar for a few minutes and then repeat their observations, drawing and describing the paper.

4. Put another handful of paper in another jar, but do not add water. Explain that this jar will serve as a control for the entire class. Discuss reasons for having a control in an experiment.

5. Tell students to shake the jars of paper and water for a few minutes every hour or so and note any changes in the appearance of the paper in each.

6. Give students a final chance to shake and check their jars near the end of the day and note any changes. As a class, discuss what happened to the paper in the jars with water and in the jar without water. Introduce the idea that paper is made of fibers that are pressed together into a sheet. Explain that the fibers come apart again when the paper is wetted and shaken. These separated fibers are called pulp. Have students swirl the jars and look carefully for the paper fibers.

7. Ask the students to predict what would happen if you could pour the water off the fibers and let them dry again.

8. Give each group a small screen and instruct them to pour the contents of the first jar (paper and water) over the screen, collecting the water in a bucket or dish pan.

9. Tell students to observe and draw the filtered pulp. You may want to have them use a magnifying lens or loupe.

10. Let the pulp dry on the screen overnight and observe the next day. Have students compare the result to their predictions in step 7.

11. Tell students that once the paper fibers come apart they can be reused to make new paper. Explain that an electric blender can be used to make pulp much more quickly than students could do by shaking the paper in a jar and that they will be making new paper from pulp produced in a blender.

Part B: Demonstrating Some Paper Technology

1. Introduce the words "mold" and "deckle," explaining that a mold is a frame with a screen that catches and drains the pulp, and a deckle is a matching frame with no screen that gives the paper its edge. Demonstrate how to make a mold and deckle using embroidery hoops and plastic window screen, as in Getting Ready, step 3.

2. Introduce the word "slurry." Explain that slurry is a mixture of paper pulp and water; you prepared slurry by adding water to small pieces of newspaper and mixing the solution in a blender.

3. Introduce the words "pulling" and "couching," explaining that pulling is gathering a sheet of pulp on the mold and couching is transferring the sheet of pulp to a cloth so it can dry. Demonstrate the following steps.

   a. Place a clean, damp, reusable wiping cloth on a small stack of newspaper. Roll up several additional sheets of newspaper into a cylinder and put the cylinder underneath the first stack of newspaper to prop up the stack at one end. This cloth-covered stack of paper, called a couch, should now form an even slope. Position the couch with the elevated edge near you. (See Figure 3.)

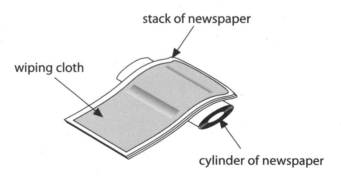

Figure 3: Assemble the couch.

   b. Vigorously stir up the pulp mixture in the dish pan. Explain that you do not want the fibers to settle on the bottom of the dish pan.

   c. Hold the mold and deckle together with both hands, keeping the deckle on top and the screen side of the mold facing up. Dip the mold and deckle into the pulp mixture at about a 45° angle, and then level them (while still in the pulp mixture). (See Figure 4a.)

d. Keeping the mold and deckle level, lift them straight up out of the pulp mixture, and let the water drain away. (See Figure 4b.) While the pulp is still wet, gently shake the apparatus to help the fibers settle. Carefully lift off the deckle and set it aside.

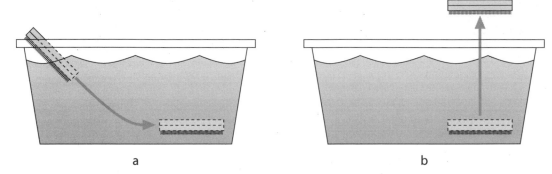

a   b

Figure 4: Pulling pulp involves (a) dipping the mold and deckle into the pulp mixture at a 45° angle and leveling them, and (b) lifting the mold and deckle straight up out of the mixture.

e. Place the mold on its edge at the top of the slope on the couch, with the pulp facing down the slope. (The pulp will not fall off the screen.) Carefully tilt the mold down the slope (away from you) until it lies screen down on the cloth. Gently press the screen against the cloth. Lift the mold slowly; the pulp will remain on the cloth. Place another cloth over the pulp. (See Figure 5.)

If the sheet is too thin (transparent or falling apart), you may not have dipped your mold and deckle deeply enough in the dish pan. Try dipping it almost to the bottom before bringing it up. If this doesn't work, make another blenderful of pulp and add it to the dish pan. If the paper sticks to the mold, scrape up the pulp and put it back in the dish pan.

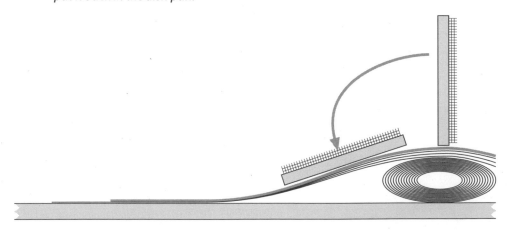

Figure 5: Couch the paper by tilting the mold until it rests on the cloth. Gently press the screen against the cloth and slowly lift the mold.

f. Repeat steps b–e, layering up to 10 sheets of paper. End the stack with a cloth and then a small stack of newspaper. Remove the rolled-up newspaper. Press the whole stack under the pressing board or roll with a rolling pin.

g. Carefully peel off each layer (cloth and the pulp sheet on top of it together) and clip it to the "clothesline" or lay it out to dry overnight. The paper will peel off the cloth when dry.

4. If desired, give students a chance to practice pulling and couching paper before continuing with Part C. Have them label their creations by writing their names on small slips of paper and attaching them to the cloth with paper clips.

Part C: Making Seed Paper

1. Remind students that they will be making paper for a special Earth Day card. Challenge groups to propose a method for making paper that has flower or vegetable seeds in it using the basic technique you demonstrated and the molds, deckles, and pans of slurry provided. Tell students that since the paper is to be used for a card, the seeds need to stay on the paper when it is put in an envelope, and students must be able to write on the card.

2. Have each group tell you their plan; guide them as needed to avoid major problems, but do not recommend a solution.

   Students may suggest one of the following ideas or something completely different: a) sprinkling the seeds in the slurry, b) sprinkling the seeds on each sheet while it is draining on the screen, c) sprinkling seeds on the couched sheet, d) sandwiching seeds between two sheets of wet paper by couching one sheet right on top of another, and e) spreading a bit of pulp over the seeds after they are sprinkled on the couched sheet. In our testing, methods d and e worked best.

3. Have groups make one test sheet to try their plan and then lay it out or hang it up to dry overnight. (The paper must dry before they can fully evaluate the product.) Once dry, have the group design a test to evaluate the usefulness of the paper as a card. (Encourage them to try handling the dry paper and writing on it.) Ask, "How well do the seeds stay on or in the paper? Can you write on the paper? What else do you like or dislike about your paper?"

4. Have each group share their results and products with the class.

5. Allow groups to modify or repeat their procedure while each student makes a piece of paper. Tell students to label their sheets of paper (by writing their names on small slips of paper and attaching them to the cloths with paper clips) and lay them out or hang them up to dry.

6. Have students carefully observe the dry paper they have made, using the magnifying lenses or loupes. Have them compare and contrast their paper with the newspaper they observed originally and the pulp they observed in the jar. Have them draw and write their observations.

7. Have students use their paper to create Earth Day cards. In addition to the personal message, have them include the following instructions for planting the embedded seeds: "Tear up the card and spread it out under ¼ inch of soil. Pick a favorite spot that receives at least 6 hours of sun a day. Keep the soil fairly moist with regular watering and good drainage."

   Students may phrase these instructions in their own words if desired. See Part 3, Writing Extensions, and Part 4, Art and Music Extensions, for ideas about making Earth Day cards from the seed paper.

8. (optional) Have students make envelopes for their cards according to the envelope pattern (provided at the end of this lesson).

Extensions for Further Science Inquiry

- Have students list all the general characteristics of paper that they can name. For example, they might list color, texture, thickness, shape, and stiffness. Through a facilitated discussion, have students think of ways to alter the paper-making process they have learned to change the qualities of the paper. For example, using a different kind of paper for the pulp (or adding another material altogether, such as straw) would change the color, texture, and stiffness of the product. Using more pulp or less water in the slurry would change the thickness. Using a different shape of screen and deckle or a different screen material would change the shape and/or the texture of the product.

  Have groups of students work together to develop short written proposals for modifying the paper-making process. The proposals should include a list of materials, what steps students will follow to make their paper, and what outcome they expect. Have each group present their plan to you; guide them as needed to avoid major problems. For example, if they propose using heavy papers and cardboard, they should be told that this material must be soaked overnight before being blended. After proposals are approved, you may wish to have groups work together to plan who will bring in the materials. Alternatively, you may want to provide the materials yourself.

  Give groups an opportunity to test their ideas and evaluate their finished products. Have each group share methods and products with the class.

- Have students line cups with extremely thick pulp. Let the pulp dry and then take away the cups, leaving paper-pulp "cups." Use these paper-pulp cups like flowerpots, filling them with dirt and planting seeds. When the seeds are seedlings, plant them, cup and all, in the ground.

Science Explanation

 The following explanation is intended for the teacher's information. Modify the explanation for students as required.

The Paper-Making Process

Most virgin paper is made today from cellulose fibers from plants, primarily trees. After the trees are cut and the bark is removed, the logs are cut into small chips, which are pulped. The most common pulping process, the kraft process, involves cooking the wood chips under pressure in a chemical bath of water, sodium hydroxide, and sodium sulfide (which gives pulp mills their unpleasant "skunky" smell). The pulp is then separated from the cooking liquid, washed, and in most cases bleached. The white pulp is beaten to rough up the fibers, changing their surface and causing them to stick tightly to one another. Water is added to make a slurry, which is placed on a moving screen where it forms a sheet as the water drains off. This continuous sheet moves through rollers which press out more water, heat-dry the paper, and give it a smoother finish.

The pulping step in the process described above is a type of chemical pulping and involves chemical changes. Pulping can also be done mechanically by grinding fibers off the logs. This is a physical change, as only the size of the fibers is being changed. Paper made from this pulp is weak and yellows easily. However, it is also cheap and produces less waste. Newsprint is an example of paper made by mechanical pulping.

Most papers are made from a combination of hardwoods and softwoods. The trunks of both of these types of trees contain about 50% cellulose fibers. Softwoods contain more lignin, which is difficult to remove, but they have the advantage of containing longer cellulose fibers, which give the paper strength. Hardwoods, with their shorter fibers, give the paper body. Most of the lignin and some of the hemicellulose (the other major component of wood) are broken down, dissolved, and removed during the pulping process. The remainder of the lignin (which gives the pulp its color) is removed during the bleaching step.

Production of recycled paper (whether handmade or in a paper mill) begins with the pulping process. The chemical bath is not needed; the paper is pulped in water. The remainder of the process is similar to that described above for virgin paper. Making and using recycled paper has the advantages of not requiring the destruction of more trees and of reducing waste. The problems involved with its production include fluctuations in the availability of used paper, extra work required to separate different types of used papers and other material to produce recycled paper of consistent quality, and the shortening of the cellulose fibers as they are reprocessed. Individuals can help solve the first of these problems by regularly recycling their own waste paper. The other two problems require industrial solutions.

The History of Papermaking

More than 4,000 years ago, the Egyptians were making a paper-like writing surface from the stems of papyrus, an aquatic plant that grows on the banks of the Nile. Their technique involved splitting the stems, weaving them together in mats, beating them into flat sheets, and coating them with a glue-like material. This technology was adopted by the Greeks and Romans.

While the name "paper" probably came from the word "papyrus," the product made by the Egyptians is not considered to be true paper of the kind made today. Modern papermaking involves separating fibers and then pressing them together; the papyrus fibers were not separated. Paper as we know it today was invented in China. In A.D. 105, an Imperial Court official named Ts'ai Lun patented a kind of paper made by beating fibrous materials into a pulp in water, then draining the pulp and pressing it into sheets that were dried in the sun. At first he used ropes and old fishing nets for pulp, but later he started using plant fibers and silk. Ts'ai Lun also discovered how to make paper from wood fibers, but this technology did not gain immediate widespread acceptance and was subsequently lost for the next 2,000 years.

Although the Egyptians were the first to make a kind of paper, the Japanese also have a long history of papermaking technology. They experimented with many different plant materials and developed a wide variety of papers with different properties and different uses.

Papermaking was not a widely practiced craft in ancient times because very few people could read and write. But after Johann Gutenberg invented the printing press in 1450, demand for paper grew rapidly—so rapidly that rag fibers, one of the most common materials used for paper at the time, became scarce. In the mid-18th century, a French scientist named Rene de Reaumur suggested using wood as a source of pulp. He had observed paper wasps building nests with pulp made from chewed-up wood and saliva, and he figured that humans could make paper from wood, too. However, like Ts'ai Lun's idea, Reaumur's idea did not gain immediate acceptance, since suitable technology for pulping wood had not yet been invented.

Until the late 18th century, the method most commonly used for making paper was hand dipping. However, around that time, demand increased so much that the hand-dipping method could no longer keep up. A Frenchman named Nicholas Louis Robert invented a hand-cranked machine that produced paper in a continuous roll, but since he lacked financial backing to put his invention into practice, he sold the patent to two brothers from London, the Fourdriniers. The Fourdriniers made their own improvements to the design, and their machine, which is named after them, is still used today.

Over the next century, scarcity of rag fibers continued to be a problem, and papermakers began to experiment with wood pulp in earnest, since trees were plentiful and renewable. Several methods of chemical pulping, in which wood chips were cooked with various chemicals, were tested. Around 1879, a Swedish man named C.F. Dahl developed a process for cooking wood chips under pressure with sodium hydroxide and sodium sulfide. This process, which became known as the kraft process (from the Swedish word for "strength") produces strong paper. The kraft process is still used. In fact, most paper today is produced through this chemical pulping process, although several other methods are used for making different types of paper.

Most sheets of paper contain more than just wood pulp; they also contain various additives that give the paper desired qualities, such as color, bulk, water resistance, and ability to hold ink. Paper may also be coated with wax. Additives and coatings make paper useful for many different applications besides writing, such as food wrapping, gift wrapping, packaging, product labels, napkins and paper towels, and disposable plates, to name just a few.

The average 30-year-old pine tree yields 117 pounds of paper. Each year the average American consumes 730 pounds of paper, for a national total of about 90 million tons of paper a year. As a result of this high demand for paper as well as for building materials and fuel, some once-forested regions of the world are now treeless. Such widespread destruction is very harmful to the environment because trees produce oxygen, remove carbon dioxide (a "greenhouse gas") from the air, provide shade, prevent soil erosion, provide homes and food for wildlife, and help regulate climate. Recycling paper products means that fewer trees need to be cut down to be used for paper. Estimates of tree conservation range from 17–24 trees saved for every ton of paper either recycled or not consumed. (The fact that trees used in paper production vary widely in height and diameter makes it difficult to give more than a broad estimate.) Some companies have also developed alternatives to using wood for paper, including kenaf (a hardy annual plant native to Africa and Asia), hemp, seaweed, banana peels, grass clippings, bottle labels, hop and barley waste, leaves, cotton, textile trimmings, and shredded currency.

References for the Science Activity

Burdette, J.; Conway, L.; Ernst, W.; Lanier, E.; Sharpe, J. *The Manufacture of Pulp and Paper: Science and Engineering Concepts;* TAPPI: Atlanta, 1988; pp 11–14.

Lehmer, A. ReThink Paper, personal communication, January, 1998.

ReThink Paper Web Site, http://www.igc.apc.org/ei/paper/paperstats1.html (accessed 9 Feb 1998).

Richardson, F. "Yes, We Have No Trees." *Circle Reader Service,* No. 125, February 1997; 36, 39.

Watson, D. *Creative Handmade Paper;* Search: Tunbridge Wells, Kent, 1991; pp 6–7.

Part 3: Integrating with Language Arts

Featured Fiction Book: *The Lorax*

Author and Illustrator: Dr. Seuss
Publisher: Random House   ISBN: 0394823370
Summary: The remorseful Once-ler describes the results of pollution and the loss of Truffula Trees. At the end, he presents his visitor with the very last Truffula seed, with which the forest may be restored.

As you begin the story, show students the pictures of the town and the Once-ler's house. Discuss whether it looks like a nice place to live. Compare these pictures with the ones at the beginning of the Once-ler's story (page 12). How are the pictures different? As you continue reading, discuss the benefits the Truffula Trees provide and what happens when too many are cut down. What reasons and excuses does the Once-ler give for continuing to expand his business? Discuss the concept of Thneeds. Do students think that people in the story really needed them? Ask students if they can think of any products in real life that might be comparable to the Thneeds.

Writing Extensions

- Have students use their science journals to describe and sketch their initial design for the papermaking process, record evaluations by other students, and describe and sketch design modifications.
- Have students write a message in the card in poetry or prose form explaining why and how the card was made of recycled materials.
- Have students write letters to a pen pal on paper they have made.

Additional Books

Fiction

Title: *Just a Dream*
Author and Illustrator: Chris Van Allsburg
Publisher: Houghton Mifflin   ISBN: 0-395-53308-2
Summary: Walter has a dream about a future Earth devastated by pollution and careless resource management. He awakens from his nightmare with a new commitment to the environment.

Title: *The Paper Bag Prince*
Author: Colin Thompson
Publisher: Knopf   ISBN: 0679885463
Summary: A wise old man who visits the town dump every day moves into an abandoned train there and watches as nature gradually reclaims the polluted land.

Title: *Where Once There Was a Wood*
Author: Denise Fleming
Publisher: Henry Holt   ISBN: 0805037616
Summary: Examines the many forms of wildlife that can be displaced if their
environment is destroyed by development and discusses how communities
and schools can provide spaces for them to live. Illustrations are made of
handmade paper.

Nonfiction

Title: *Painting with Paper: Easy Papermaking Fun for the Entire Family*
Author: Denise Fleming
Publisher: Henry Holt   ISBN: 0805035281
Summary: Caldecott Honor-winning author and illustrator Denise Fleming shares
her secrets for "painting" with paper pulp. This papermaking kit includes the
basic materials needed to make handmade paper and comes with clear, step-
by-step instructions. Full-color photos of the papermaking process from start
to finish are provided.

Title: *The Paper Book and Paper Maker*
Author: Shar Levine   Illustrator: Joe Weissmann
Publisher: Somerville House   ISBN: 0921051751
Summary: With this collection of more than 20 paper-making activities, children
can turn yesterday's newspaper into a birthday card, create embossed
stationery from discarded junk mail, and learn to make paper with grass,
plants, flowers, and fabric. Includes a plastic mold and deckle.

Title: *Recycle*
Author and Illustrator: Gail Gibbons
Publisher: Little, Brown   ISBN: 0-316-30943-5
Summary: This book explains the process of recycling from start to finish for
paper, glass, aluminum, and plastics.

Part 4: Other Lesson Extensions

Art and Music

- Have students make paper that is itself decorative. They could use materials
besides paper, such as straw, grasses, flowers, and leaves. Also, they could
manually spread pulp of different colors and textures in patterns on the mold
to create designs.
- Have students design posters with themes such as "Earth Day" or "Save a
Tree," or make paper products such as puppets, mobiles, or wrapping paper
from waste paper.
- Read aloud or have students read *Big Band Sound* by Harriet Diller (Boyds
Mills, 1996). In this story, a young girl named Arlis makes "recycled" musical
instruments from items such as old paint cans. Have students create their own
musical instruments from "trash." Review designs beforehand for safety.

Mathematics

- Have students keep a tally of how much paper they use in a week and graph individual and class results. If desired, have them tally how much newspaper, glass, and aluminum they and their families use in a week (or other period of time). Have them use their one-week totals to calculate how much of each material individuals and the class (and their families) would use in a month, year, or other time period at that rate of consumption. Discuss ways to reduce the amount of waste produced.
- Have students measure the mass in grams and radius in centimeters of their circle of handmade paper and calculate its area using the following formula:

$$A = \pi r^2 \quad or \quad Area = (3.14)(radius)^2$$

Explain that the "basis weight" of paper is a measure of the mass of the fibers and additives per unit area. The standard area for comparison is 1 m² (10,000 cm²). It is calculated as follows:

$$basis\ weight\ (g/m^2) = mass\ of\ paper\ (in\ g) \times \frac{10,000\ cm^2/1m^2}{area\ of\ paper\ (in\ cm^2)}$$

They can then compare the basis weight of their paper with other papers.

Paper Weight Table	
Paper Type	Basis Weight (g/m²)
tissues and paper towels	16 to 57
newsprint	45 to 70
grocery bags	49 to 98
fine paper	60 to 150

Social Studies

- Have students write an article for the school newsletter on the value of recycling.
- Study the history of paper.
- Have students pick a real-life product that they think is comparable to the Thneed mentioned in *The Lorax*. Have them explain their choice and research the strategies used by the company to persuade people that they need this product. To accompany this project, you may want to read *Arthur's TV Trouble,* by Marc Brown (Little, Brown; ISBN 0-316-11047-7).

Just for Fun

- Contact a local environmental or recycling organization and have representatives come to the class to make a presentation or put on a play about recycling.
- Have students make recycled-paper puppets, write a play for a puppet show about recycling, and present the show to younger students.

Part 5: National Science Education Standards

Science as Inquiry Standards:

Abilities Necessary to Do Scientific Inquiry

Students question how paper can be recycled.

Students use magnifying lenses to observe the detail of torn commercial paper, pulp, and recycled paper.

Students share their results and products with the class.

Students propose a method for making paper that has flower or vegetable seeds embedded in it.

Physical Science Standards:

Properties of Objects and Materials

Objects have many observable properties. The commercial paper, pulp, and recycled paper have some common properties and others that differ.

Objects are made from one or more materials and can be described by the properties of the materials from which they are made. The characteristics of the recycled paper depend not only on the techniques used to produce it but also on the properties of the original paper.

Science and Technology Standards:

Abilities of Technological Design

Students propose a method for embedding seeds in their paper so that the paper can be written on and hold the seeds tightly.

Students use their proposed method, along with the paper-making techniques they have been shown, to make seed paper.

Students evaluate their seed paper product along with those of the other groups and modify their techniques accordingly.

Students share their experiences and products with the class.

History and Nature of Science Standards:

Science as a Human Endeavor

Paper-making technology has existed for at least 4,000 years. People in many cultures have continued to refine the paper-making process over the years.

Envelope Pattern

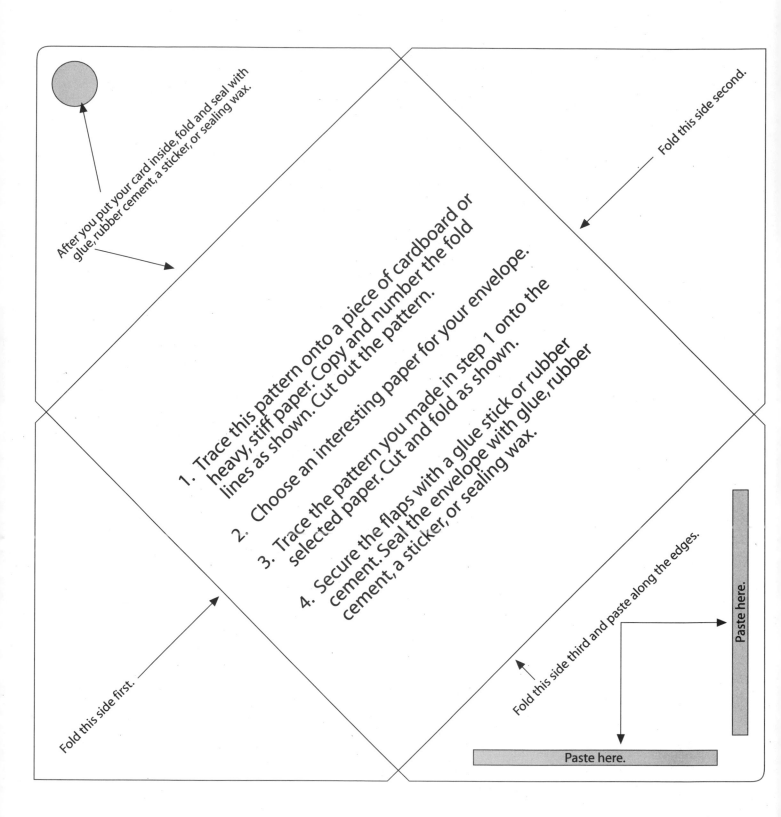

After you put your card inside, fold and seal with glue, rubber cement, a sticker, or sealing wax.

Fold this side second.

1. Trace this pattern onto a piece of cardboard or heavy, stiff paper. Copy and number the fold lines as shown. Cut out the pattern.

2. Choose an interesting paper for your envelope.

3. Trace the pattern you made in step 1 onto the selected paper. Cut and fold as shown.

4. Secure the flaps with a glue stick or rubber cement. Seal the envelope with glue, rubber cement, a sticker, or sealing wax.

Fold this side first.

Fold this side third and paste along the edges.

Paste here.

Paste here.

Easter

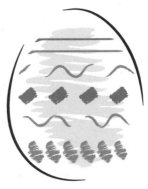

First Sunday after the first full moon appearing on or after the vernal equinox
Culture: Christian

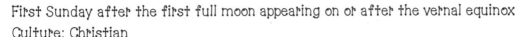

Along with Christmas, Easter is one of the two most important Christian holidays. Easter is the celebration of Jesus' resurrection from the dead, and the holiday is one of both solemnity and rejoicing. Like many of the spring festivals, Easter's date is tied to the vernal equinox. Easter is the first Sunday following the first full moon appearing on or after the vernal equinox, which is either March 20 or March 21 (see the introduction to Spring in the activity "Spring into Capillary Action" for more information). Venerable Bede, an Anglo-Saxon priest who lived in the 8th century A.D., is credited for giving this Christian holiday the name "Easter," which he derived from "Eostre," a goddess of spring.

The observation of Easter varies among Christian denominations. The Easter season begins 40 days before Easter Sunday on a day called "Ash Wednesday," which marks the beginning of Lent. During Lent, Christians may fast and pray, preparing for Easter. The members of some Christian denominations also make Lenten promises, vowing to go without something they like during the 40 days. On Easter Sunday, they can once again have what they went without for Lent.

The final days of Lent especially are solemn days of fasting and prayer, culminating on Good Friday, the Friday before Easter, the day Jesus was crucified. According to the Bible, Jesus rose from the dead three days later, on a Sunday, and it is this restoration to life that Christians celebrate in their Easter festivities. The Easter celebration may include a special service, the lighting of the Easter candle (from which all other candles in the church are lit throughout the next year), and joyous songs. Many families gather together for Easter dinner.

With both secular and religious origins, Easter has traditions and symbols borrowed from many different cultures. During the early days of Christianity, the Christians celebrated the Jewish holiday of Passover, which was held in the spring. Gradually, however, the Christians created their own holiday to commemorate events unique to their faith. As the Roman Empire spread through Europe, bringing the Christian faith with it, the Romans encountered people who were unfamiliar with Christianity. These indigenous people

Easter

celebrated their own spring festivals at the same time the Romans observed Easter. Many of these traditions became part of the Easter celebration:

- Eggs: Romans, Gauls, Chinese, Egyptians, and Persians all cherished the egg as a symbol of the universe and rebirth. To the native Europeans, the egg was a symbol of life. The Christians used the egg as a symbol of the tomb and Jesus' resurrection.

- Colored eggs: People in the northern regions of Europe dyed the eggs they used for spring festivals with bright colors to symbolize the aurora borealis (the "northern lights") or the rays of the sun.

- Rabbits: Because rabbits are known for their rapid reproduction, especially in the spring, rabbits were a symbol of many of the ancient spring festivals. One legend states that the goddess of spring, Eostre, turned a bird into a rabbit to help it escape from a foe. The rabbit continued to lay eggs after the transformation. This story gave rise to the legend of the Easter bunny.

- Flowers: Spring is also the time when many flowers bloom, and many cultures decorated with floral wreaths and garlands. One type of lily, called the Easter lily, became associated with the Christian holiday because of its pure-white flowers and because it blooms in the early spring, usually on or near Easter.

References

Zia Holiday Pages. Easter History. http://www.zia.com/holidays/easter/history/ (accessed May 1997).

Zia Holiday Pages. Easter Symbols. http://www.zia.com/holidays/easter/cards/eggs/hist.htm (accessed May 1997).

"Easter" *Britannica Online*. http://www.eb.com:180/cgi-bin/g?DocF=micro/184/21.html (accessed 05 March 1998).

Hatch, J.M. *The American Book of Days*, 3rd ed.; H.W. Wilson: New York, 1978; p 302.

Harrowven, J. *Origins of Festivals and Feasts;* Kaye & Ward: London, 1980; pp 41, 58.

Ickis, M. *The Book of Festival Holidays;* Dodd, Mead: New York, 1964; p 55.

Easter Egg Geodes

Easter is a Christian holiday commemorating Jesus' resurrection from the dead and new life. Many symbols are associated with Easter, including the Easter bunny and the brightly colored eggs that are hidden for children to find. In some countries, the eggs are made out of sugar, chocolate, or wood and have small toys hidden inside. In this activity, students will fill plastic eggshells with crystals to make their own special eggs.

Key Science Topics

- crystals, crystallization
- evaporation
- solutions

A rock geode and two Easter egg geodes

Time Required

Setup	30	minutes
Performance	30	minutes for Part A, plus 5 minutes daily for a week
	45–60	minutes for Part B
Cleanup	10	minutes

Part 1: Building Bridges

Building Student Knowledge and Motivation

A few days prior to doing the activity, set up a learning center displaying various eggs in two categories: real and collectible. Real eggs could include chicken, goose, turkey, robin, and fish eggs (bait). Collectible eggs could include ones made of plastic, tin, china, wood, or marble, or egg-shaped containers that stack or have hinges.

Bridging to the Science Activity

Have the class create an egg word map like the one in Figure 1.

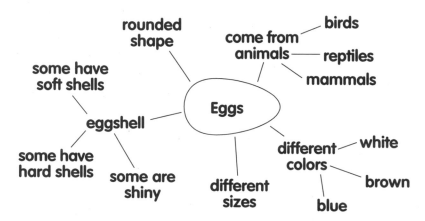

Figure 1: Make an egg word map.

Add a collection of rock geodes to the science table and ask students to compare geodes to eggs. Tell the students they will be making their own "geodes" using plastic eggshells.

Part 2: Science Activity

Materials

For Getting Ready
Per 5–10 eggs
- 1-cup graduated measuring cup
- 2 cups water
- 1- to 2-L beaker or other container (not aluminum) for heating solution
- hot plate or other heat source
- heat-resistant spoon or stirring stick
- 1 of the following solids:
  - for younger students—2 cups (about 420 g) food-grade alum (potassium aluminum sulfate dodecahydrate {$KAl(SO_4)_2 \cdot 12H_2O$}), available at grocery stores or pharmacies

○ for older students—1¼ cups copper(II) sulfate pentahydrate ($CuSO_4 \cdot 5H_2O$) crystals [also called cupric sulfate pentahydrate]

Cupric sulfate pentahydrate (#F73300 for 500 g) is available from lawn and garden stores as copper sulfate. It can also be ordered from Frey Scientific, 100 Paragon Parkway, Mansfield, OH 44903, 888/222-1332, fax 888/454-1417, and other science education suppliers. Before ordering this chemical, check local ordinances for disposal. If you do not feel comfortable following your local disposal procedure, use alum instead. The advantage of copper sulfate is that it produces larger, more spectacular crystals. You may want to make just one geode with this substance and have students compare it with the alum geodes they make.

- (optional) rubber gloves

For the Procedure

Part A, per class
- (optional) straight pins, tape, and pen for labels

Part A, per group
- egg carton

Part A, per student or group
- small plastic egg

    Plastic eggs are readily available at Easter time.

- plastic teaspoon
- 2 teaspoons plaster of paris
- 1 teaspoon fine copper(II) sulfate pentahydrate or alum crystals

    This should be the same material used in Getting Ready.

- 1, 3-ounce disposable plastic bathroom cup
- craft stick or plastic knife
- water
- ¼–½ cup saturated copper(II) sulfate solution or ¼–½ cup saturated alum solution (See Getting Ready.)
- magnifying lenses
- (optional) permanent markers, or sequins and glue

Part B
- all materials listed for Part A

For the Extensions for Further Science Inquiry

❶ Per class or per group
- all materials listed for the Procedure, Part A
- access to a refrigerator and a heater
- paper
- plastic wrap

Safety and Disposal

Copper(II) sulfate pentahydrate is a strong irritant to the skin and mucous membranes. To avoid inhaling its dust, use copper(II) sulfate only in an area with adequate ventilation. It can be harmful or fatal if taken internally; use caution when handling it. If contact with the skin occurs, flush with running water. Wash your hands after use. We strongly recommend that copper sulfate not be used with younger children, with whom the chance of ingestion is higher; instead, we recommend substituting food-grade alum.

Follow local ordinances for disposing of copper(II) salts and alum. It is recommended that unused copper(II) sulfate solution be left to evaporate to dryness. Near the end of the evaporation process, the crystals tend to stick to the container. Stirring the crystals in solution before evaporation is complete aids in freeing them from the evaporation container. Place the resulting crystals in a sealed, labeled jar for reuse. Unused alum solution may be allowed to evaporate to dryness. The resulting crystals can be stored in a labeled, covered container for future use.

Getting Ready

1. Pour 2 cups water into a beaker or other suitable, heat-resistant container. Heat the water until a visible "cloud" comes from the surface but the water is not yet boiling, and cautiously remove the container from the heat source.

2. While stirring, add 2 cups alum or 1¼ cups copper(II) sulfate to the hot water in the container. Continue stirring for 3–4 minutes to dissolve as much of the solid as possible. Some solid should remain undissolved.

3. Keep the solution hot or reheat to almost boiling as before and stir immediately before filling the cups in step 8.

Procedure

Part A: Making Easter Egg Geodes

1. Have students separate the plastic eggs, setting aside the more pointed ends and placing the rounder (less pointed) ends (bottoms) in egg cartons. They will use these bottom halves to make their geodes.

2. Have students measure 2 level teaspoons plaster of paris and 1 level teaspoon copper(II) sulfate pentahydrate or alum into the small plastic cup. Have them stir with a craft stick or plastic knife to mix.

3. Have the students measure 1 teaspoon water and stir it into the solids in the cup. The mixture will harden quickly, so step 4 should be done promptly.

4. Have students quickly coat the inside of the rounder end of the plastic egg with the plaster of paris mixture. The craft stick or plastic knife can be used to smooth it out. If the mixture is too runny, students should wait briefly and it

will harden to a more usable consistency. However, if they wait too long, it will solidify, and further spreading will be impossible.

5. Have students wait several minutes for the mixture to solidify, and then place their egg bottoms back in the egg cartons. The lip of the egg bottom should be up and as level as possible.

6. (optional) Have students write their names on small pieces of tape and affix the tape like a flag to a straight pin. Students should stand their pins beside their eggs in the cartons.

7. Place the cartons in a location where they will not be disturbed.

Do the following step yourself, and only in a well-ventilated area.

8. Fill each egg almost to the top with the hot alum or copper(II) sulfate solution (see Getting Ready).

9. Have students answer and explain their answers to the following questions:
   • What do you think will happen? Why?
   • How many crystals do you think will form?
   • Will everyone have the same number of crystals? Why or why not?

10. Have the students observe the eggs daily and record the progress of crystal formation until all the water has evaporated or most of the copper sulfate or alum has precipitated out (up to a week).

If only a few crystals have formed, steps 8 and 10 can be repeated with additional hot, saturated copper(II) sulfate or alum solution. If a thin film of crystals forms over the solution, break it gently and push the crystals under the solution.

11. Have students use magnifying lenses to observe their crystals closely and draw what they see. Have students describe the crystals in terms of size, shape, number, color, and any other qualities they consider important.

12. Have students use the more pointed ends of the plastic eggs as covers for the geodes. If desired, have students decorate the outside of the eggs with permanent markers or by gluing on sequins.

Part B: What Role Does the Plaster of Paris Play?

1. Discuss possible reasons for using plaster of paris in the eggshell geodes.

2. Divide the class into groups. Challenge the students to design experiments to determine if plaster of paris is in fact necessary. Have groups share their ideas with the class.

3. Allow each group to try a different experiment. Monitor groups carefully to ensure that proper safety precautions are followed.

4. Have the groups report the results of their experiments and their conclusions about the role of the plaster of paris to the class.

Extensions for Further Science Inquiry

- Test the effect of temperature on crystal formation by putting some eggshells in a refrigerator and some near a heater after they are filled with hot solution. Also test the effect of covering the drying eggs with paper or plastic wrap.
- See the book *Science Is* by Susan V. Bosack (Scholastic Canada, ISBN 0-590-74070-0) for ideas on how to do the following activities:
  ○ Making rock candy with sugar water and string,
  ○ Growing salt crystals, and
  ○ Making a charcoal crystal garden.

Science Explanation

The following explanation is intended for the teacher's information. Modify the explanation for students as required.

Geodes are roughly spherical, hollow rocks with diameters of up to 60 cm. They look like ordinary, round rocks from the outside, but the cavity inside is coated with crystals. In nature, water containing dissolved mineral salts can seep into the inner cavities of hollow rocks. After long periods of time, if conditions are favorable, the mineral salts can crystallize and be deposited on the inside of the hollow rock, forming a geode. Typical crystals lining the cavities of natural geodes are quartz (SiO_2), calcite ($CaCO_3$), dolomite ($CaMg(CO_3)_2$), and hematite (Fe_2O_3).

In this activity, half of a plastic eggshell acts like part of a rounded, hollow rock. The crystals inside the plastic "geode" form from a saturated aqueous solution of copper(II) sulfate or alum. As the solution cools and the water evaporates, the amount of salt that can stay in solution decreases, and crystals of copper(II) sulfate pentahydrate or alum begin to form. When the solution is exposed to the air, the water takes about a week to evaporate; however, the evaporation process would take much longer if the container were sealed. Such is the case with natural geodes as they form in closed, hollow rocks underground.

The crystal-growing solution used in this activity is a saturated solution of a mineral salt. A saturated solution is one that contains as much of a solute (the alum or copper(II) sulfate in this case) as can be dissolved in the solvent (water) at a given temperature. The amount of copper(II) sulfate or alum, as well as the majority of other salts, that can dissolve in a given volume of water increases as the temperature of the water increases. Thus, increasing the temperature of the solution allows more salt to go into solution. Stirring the solution also speeds the dissolving process. As the solution cools and the solvent (water) slowly evaporates, the salt that can no longer remain in solution begins to come out of solution (precipitate), often as crystals.

During crystallization, atoms, molecules, and/or ions align themselves in a specific three-dimensional pattern called a crystal lattice; this lattice is a characteristic property of crystalline substances. The alum crystals or solid copper(II) sulfate crystals in the plaster of paris coating the inside of the plastic egg function as seed crystals. That is, they provide a pattern for the continued growth of the crystals as the solid comes out of solution.

The plaster of paris forms a bed for seed crystals all around the inside of the plastic shell and provides a rough surface on which larger crystals can form.

References for the Science Activity

Sarquis, J.L.; Sarquis, M.; Williams, J.P. "Crystal Pictures"; *Teaching Chemistry with TOYS: Activities for Grades K–9;* McGraw-Hill: New York, 1995; pp 19–23.

"Eggshell Geodes"; *Fun with Chemistry: A Guidebook of K–12 Activities;* Sarquis, M., Sarquis, J., Eds.; Institute for Chemical Education: Madison, WI, 1993; Vol. 2, pp 281–286.

Part 3: Integrating with Language Arts

Featured Fiction Book: *The Talking Eggs*

Author: Robert D. San Souci   Illustrator: Jerry Pinkney
Publisher: Scholastic   ISBN: 0-590-44189-2
Summary: A young girl named Blanche befriends a mysterious elderly woman who gives her a basket of eggs filled with treasures. When Blanche's selfish sister and mother try to get more eggs for themselves, they get a real surprise!

Discuss the characteristics of the talking eggs in this book. How do both kinds of eggs compare with decorated Easter eggs? How are they similar to the eggshell geodes students made in the activity? If desired, have students make a basket of "talking eggs," some decorated and some plain. They could fill the decorated eggs with plastic creepy-crawly toys and fill the plain eggs with treats. (They could even close up some eggshell geodes and include them.) Volunteers could re-enact the parts of the story in which Blanche and her sister gather the eggs and break them. (Instead of actually breaking the plastic eggs, students should just open them.)

Writing Extensions

- Have students use their science journals to write a summary of the experiment they designed and the results they found.
- Have students write a story entitled "Not Eggs-actly What I Expected." As in *The Talking Eggs,* the story should include eggs that contain a welcome—or unwelcome—surprise.
- Have students write instructions for this activity on egg-shaped pieces of paper and bind them into a small book.
- Have students imagine that they will give their eggshell geodes to someone special. Have them write about who this individual is and why they selected him or her.

Additional Books

Fiction

Title: *The Baby Uggs Are Hatching*
Author: Jack Prelutzky   Illustrator: James Stevenson
Publisher: Mulberry   ISBN: 068809239X
Summary: A collection of 12 humorous poems about such strange creatures as
the sneepy and the quossible.

Title: *The Best Easter Egg Hunt Ever*
Author: John Speirs
Publisher: Cartwheel   ISBN: 0-590-95624-8
Summary: Readers will have hours of fun as they search for different Easter
objects, following John Speirs' delightful, full-color rebus pictures as clues.

Title: *The Easter Egg Farm*
Author: Mary Jane Auch
Publisher: Holiday House   ISBN: 0-823-41076-5
Summary: Pauline the hen can't concentrate well enough to lay an egg. The other
hens call her lazy. But then a wonderful thing happens. Pauline concentrates
very hard and lays a most unusual egg—one with a pattern on it. Soon she
lays many colorful eggs, and Mrs. Pennywort, her owner, wants to sell the
eggs for the town's annual Easter egg hunt. Then, the unexpected happens...

Title: *The Egg Tree*
Author: Katherine Milhous
Publisher: Aladdin   ISBN: 0689715684
Summary: Katy's Easter morning discovery renews the tradition of the Easter egg
tree.

Title: *The Enormous Egg*
Author: Oliver Butterworth   Illustrator: Louise Darling
Publisher: Little, Brown   ISBN: 0316119202
Summary: Nate, a 12-year-old boy living in New Hampshire, takes over the care of
an enormous egg laid by one of the family's hens, and the last thing he
expects to hatch from it is a triceratops!

Title: *Nina's Treasures*
Author: Timothy Rhodes   Illustrator: Stefan Czernecki
Publisher: Hyperion   ISBN: 1562824872
Summary: When Katerina runs out of food at the end of winter, her beloved hen
Nina saves them both by laying marvelous multicolored eggs.

Title: *Rechenka's Eggs*
Author: Patricia Polacco
Publisher: Putnam   ISBN: 0-698-11385-3
Summary: Old Babushka is collecting eggs for the Easter festival when she takes
    in Rechenka, an injured goose, who shows her that miracles really can
    happen.

Title: *Two Bad Ants*
Author: Chris Van Allsburg
Publisher: Houghton Mifflin   ISBN: 0-395-4866-88
Summary: A group of ants sets out to retrieve a marvelous and delicious crystal
    from a faraway place. But two of the ants, overwhelmed by the treasure,
    remain behind when their fellow ants head home. And so begins a terrible
    ordeal for the two ants. Are the crystals worth the risk?

Nonfiction

Title: *The Amazing Egg Book*
Author: Margaret Griffin and Deborah Seed Illustrator: Linda Hendry
Publisher: Addison-Wesley   ISBN: 0201523345
Summary: Which comes first, the chicken or the egg? While sampling recipes for
    egg drop soup, eggnog, and baked Alaska, kids discover why eggs exist and
    what happens inside them. Includes recipes and instructions for egg-dyeing
    and other craft projects.

Title: *An Easter Celebration: Traditions and Customs from Around the World*
Author: Pamela Kennedy
Publisher: Ideals   ISBN: 0824985060
Summary: Easy-to-understand text relates the symbols and customs of Easter to
    their Christian origins and explains the beginnings of those which are not
    religious in nature. Beautifully illustrated with fine art reproductions, line
    engravings, and vintage photography.

Title: *Egg: A Photographic Story of Hatching*
Authors: Robert Burton, Jane Burton, Kim Taylor
Publisher: Dorling-Kindersley   ISBN: 1564584607
Summary: Here, in more than 500 astonishing, life-size, full-color photos and
    fascinating text, is the "inside story" of the beginning of life, from the first
    glimmerings of growth inside the eggshell to the animal's struggle to be free.
    This book shows a diversity of bird, reptile, insect, fish, and amphibian eggs
    hatching.

Title: *The Egg*
Authors: Gallimard Jeunesse, Pascale De Bourgoing
Illustrator: Rene Mettler
Publisher: Cartwheel   ISBN: 0590452665
Summary: Follows a hen's egg from the moment it is laid to the time the chick
    hatches. Also introduces various egg-laying animals, such as birds, snails, and
    snakes.

Title: *We Celebrate Easter*
Author: Bobbie Kalman   Illustrator: Maureen Shaughnessy
Publisher: Crabtree   ISBN: 0-865-05042-2
Summary: Describes the secular and religious origins of Easter and Easter symbols
such as eggs, bells, and the Easter bunny. This book includes games, recipes,
stories, and related projects.

Part 4: Other Lesson Extensions

Art and Music

- Decorate the outside of the eggs in the Procedure, Part A, step 12.
- Have students make spinning-marker designs for an egg book cover or greeting cards as follows: Place an egg-shaped piece of construction paper in a box. Insert a pen into a Doodle Top and spin the top in the box to create beautiful designs.
- Have students paint with cotton-tipped swabs dipped in salt-water (made from table salt or Epsom salts) on dark construction paper. (For more complete instructions, see the activity "Magic Trees for Arbor Day.")
- Design crystal patterns.
- Have students make egg-shaped cards containing simple pop-ups of appropriate birds or animals. (See Part 3, Additional Books, for a list of nonfiction books that describe various kinds of egg-laying animals.)

Social Studies

- Study crystals that are gems, such as diamonds, sapphires, emeralds, and rubies. Discuss why they are valuable. Ask a jeweler to speak to the class about gems for retail or industrial use. Have students research famous gems such as the Hope Diamond, the Star of Africa, and the Crown Jewels of England.

Part 5: National Science Education Standards

Science as Inquiry Standards:

Abilities Necessary to Do Scientific Inquiry

Students question reasons for using the plaster of paris inside their Easter egg geodes.

Students design and conduct investigations to determine if plaster of paris is needed to make the Easter egg geodes.

Students use volume measuring devices to measure water, plaster of paris, and copper sulfate or alum. They use magnifiers to observe their crystals.

Students use their results to answer the question of whether plaster of paris is necessary and why.

Students share information between groups and modify their conclusions as appropriate.

Physical Science Standards:

Properties of Objects and Materials

The Easter egg geodes can be described by the properties of the eggshells and the crystals. The eggshells will probably differ only in color, but the crystals will vary greatly in such qualities as size, shape, and number.

Science and Technology Standards:

Abilities of Technological Design

Students question whether plaster of paris is necessary for making the Easter egg geodes.

Students propose ways the procedure might be modified to make a better product.

Students test their proposed modifications to the procedure for making Easter egg geodes.

Students compare the results of their modified procedures with their original geodes and with other groups' products. They use this information to evaluate the role of plaster of paris in making the Easter egg geodes.

Groups present their results and conclusions to the class.

April Fool's Day

April 1
Cultures: Various

Although no one knows for sure how April Fool's Day began, three stories offer plausible theories:

- In ancient Rome, April 1 was the first day of spring and also of the new year. It was a time of great rejoicing and merriment. When Christianity was declared the official religion of the Roman Empire, Easter replaced the spring and new-year festivals. Some people still followed the old ways for a few years as they adjusted to the changes. Those who had adjusted would play pranks on those who hadn't to trick them into thinking that nothing had changed.

- Early April was also the time for the Roman festival of Cerealia. This festival recalls the story of Ceres' search for her daughter, Proserpina, who was kidnapped by Hades. Ceres tried following her daughter's screams, but they echoed off the cave walls, making Ceres' errand a foolish one. In commemoration, people would send others out on "fool's errands" during Cerealia.

- In 1582, the Gregorian calendar, still in use today, came into use in Europe. This calendar officially moved New Year's Day to January for all cultures in the Roman Empire. In France, gifts had traditionally been exchanged on April 1 in celebration of the new year. After the calendar was redesigned, French people would send their friends gag gifts and play pranks on April 1, hoping to confuse them into believing it was New Year's Day. The hoaxes are called poisson d'avril, or "April fish," in France, because the fish in spring are supposed to be easily caught, just as the April fools are. Chocolates shaped like fish and postcards with fish on them are often given as part of the joke.

April Fool's Day spread throughout Europe with the Roman empire and eventually came to America through the European settlers. The earliest record of the custom in Britain was in an April 2, 1698, newsletter that included a story about a "lion washing" at the Tower of London's ditch that supposedly had taken place the day before. This became an annual prank, with some people printing tickets for the lion washing to give to their unsuspecting friends. Today, April Fool's Day is celebrated by people in the United States, France, England, Ireland, Australia, Sweden, Japan, and Portugal, as well as in other places around the world.

April Fool's Day
April 1
Cultures: Various

Although people in India do not celebrate April Fool's Day as we do, they do have a holiday in which pranks and foolish errands play a part. The holiday is called Holi, or Huli, and it is a five-day fire festival celebrating spring and fertility. Holi culminates on March 31, and this day is set aside to send people on foolish errands.

References

Gaer, J. *Holidays Around the World;* Little, Brown: Boston, 1953; p 57.

Harrowven, J. *Origins of Festivals and Feasts;* Kaye & Ward: London, 1980; pp 56–57.

Hatch, J.M. *The American Book of Days,* 3rd ed.; H.W. Wilson: New York, 1978; pp 314–316.

Ickis, M. *The Book of Festival Holidays;* Dodd, Mead: New York, 1964; p 96.

Spicer, D.G. *The Book of Festivals;* Women's Press: New York, 1937; p 17.

Tricky April Fool's Day Toys

● ●

April Fool's Day (April 1), which dates back to the first century, B.C., is a holiday dedicated

to pranks, jokes, and foolish errands. Some customs of April Fool's Day began in Rome and

others in France, but all are marked by humor and clever pranks. This lesson includes

three activities in which students make toys to fool their friends.

● ●

Key Science Topics

- air takes up space
- gases
- hydrophobic and hydrophilic
- light
- physical properties
- pressure-volume relationships in gases

Time Required

Setup   10–20 minutes
Performance   45–60 minutes
Cleanup   10 minutes

A balloon in a bottle, Sandy and Magic Spoons, and the
Double Your Money trick

Part 1: Building Bridges

Building Student Knowledge and Motivation

Have students share tricks they have played on people or that others have played on them. What kinds of tricks were enjoyed by both parties? What kinds were not?

Bridging to the Science Activity

Demonstrate one of the following discrepant events. (A discrepant event is a phenomenon that seems to defy the laws of science.) In front of the class, fasten a piece of flexible screen securely over the mouth of a jar or drinking glass and fill the container completely to the rim with water. Working over a bucket, put a piece of cardboard or an index card over the mouth of the container, turn the container upside down, and remove the cardboard. Have students observe the surprising behavior of the water—it stays in the jar. Alternatively, instead of using a screen, just hold a piece of cardboard over the mouth of the full container, turn the container upside down, and let go of the cardboard while still holding the container. Have students observe that the cardboard stays against the mouth of the container and that the water doesn't run out. Tell students that the properties of some materials can cause them to behave in surprising ways under certain conditions and that we can use science to play fun "tricks." Tell students that they will learn three fun ways to use science for April Fool's Day amusement.

Part 2: Science Activity

Materials

For Getting Ready
Part A, per class
- ordinary children's play sand

  Sand is available at hardware, toy, and discount stores.

- Magic Sand™ or Sqand™

  These products are available at toy stores. A similar product, Mystic Sand (#AP4304), is available from Flinn Scientific, P.O. Box 219, Batavia, IL 60510–0219; 800/452-1261, fax 708/879-6962.

- clear acrylic spray coating

  Clear acrylic spray coating is available at hardware and discount stores.

Part A, per group
- 2 plastic spoons

Part B, per class
- clear plastic 1-L soft-drink bottle

  Flavored water sometimes comes in 1-L bottles. Although 1-L bottles work best, 2-L bottles can be substituted.

- pushpin, thumbtack, or nail

  The sharp object, intended for teacher use only, is needed to make holes in some of the soft-drink bottles the first time the activity is done.

For the Procedure
Part A, per group
- ¼ cup ordinary children's play sand
- ¼ cup Magic Sand or Sqand
- 4 clear plastic cups
- water
- Sandy Spoon (prepared in Getting Ready)
- Magic Spoon (prepared in Getting Ready)

Part A, per student
- plastic bag (to transport spoons home)
- (optional) Sandy Spoon and Magic Spoon to take home

Part B, per class
- extra balloons
- clear plastic bottle with hole (prepared in Getting Ready)
- pushpin, thumbtack, or nail

Part B, per student
- balloon
- clear plastic 1-L soft-drink bottle

  Although 1-L bottles work best, 2-L bottles can be substituted. Ask students to bring in empty, clean bottles.

Part C, per group
- clear plastic cup
- water
- coins

For the Extension for Further Science Inquiry
Per class
- clear, plastic bottle with hole (prepared in Getting Ready)
- 2 balloons

  These balloons must be the same size as those used in Part B. The Extension may not work if the inner balloon has been inflated repeatedly and the outside one has not.

Safety and Disposal

When making Sandy Spoons and Magic Spoons, work in a well-ventilated area, avoid inhaling the acrylic spray fumes, and follow the directions on the can. Caution students that the coated spoons must never be used for eating.

For health reasons, each student blowing up a balloon must have his or her own previously unused balloon. No special disposal procedures are required.

Getting Ready

For Part A

> Prepare one Sandy Spoon and one Magic Spoon per group as follows.
> *Do this step in a well-ventilated area or outside.*

1. Sandy Spoon: Apply a thin layer of acrylic coating evenly inside the bowl of a plastic spoon. Immediately dip the spoon into a cup of ordinary sand to coat the bowl, and pull out the spoon. Allow the spoon bowl to dry for a few minutes before touching it.

2. Magic Spoon: Repeat step 1, substituting Magic Sand for the ordinary sand.

For Part B

In one plastic bottle, make a hole about 2 mm in diameter in the side near the bottom by pushing a pushpin or nail through the side several times if needed to make the hole big enough. (See Figure 1.)

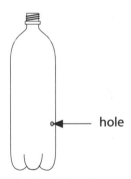

Figure 1: Make a hole in the side of one plastic bottle.

Procedure

> *The individual parts of the following procedure are independent of each other and can be done in any order or combination.*

Part A: The Magic Spoon Trick

1. Show the class about ¼ cup ordinary children's play sand and ¼ cup Magic Sand or Sqand in clear plastic cups. Ask for one helper to touch each type of sand and report what it feels like. *Both feel like sand, and neither is wet.*

2. Tell students you want to determine what happens when each kind of sand is poured into water. Allow them to speculate about possible outcomes based on trips they may have taken to the beach or experiences while playing in a sandbox.

3. Pour the ordinary children's play sand into a clear plastic cup containing about 1 cup water and ask students to observe. *The sand will sink to the bottom.* Ask for a volunteer to help you pour the water off the sand and into the cup that originally held the sand. Allow the helper to touch the sand and report what it feels like. *Wet.*

4. Repeat step 3, pouring the Magic Sand into another cup of water. Ask how the Magic Sand or Sqand behaves. *When poured, it tends to build a column instead of spreading out like the regular sand. The Magic Sand also stays dry.* You may wish to practice pouring Magic Sand into the cup of water. Pouring in a slow, steady stream will allow the sand to form a tall column.

5. Give each group a Sandy Spoon (prepared in Getting Ready). Ask them to predict what will happen if a drop of water is placed in the bowl of this spoon. Have them do the experiment and report what happens. *The water drop wets the sand.*

6. Give each group a Magic Spoon (prepared in Getting Ready). Ask them to predict what will happen if a drop of water is placed in the bowl of the Magic Spoon. Have them do the experiment and report what happens. *The water drop remains a drop and rolls around on the sand without wetting it.* Discuss differences in the behavior of the water drops in the two spoons.

7. Have students discuss reasons why one sand might make water behave differently than the other.

8. Challenge the groups to design some water tricks that might be done with the Magic Spoon. (Possibilities include tossing water drops between pairs of Magic Spoons, or challenging a friend to determine the number of drops of water that can be contained in the bowl of a Magic Spoon.)

9. Have the groups evaluate how well their water tricks work and modify them based on the evaluation. Once the tricks are modified to the group's satisfaction, groups should share their water tricks with the class.

10. (optional) Make a set of coated spoons (one Sandy Spoon and one Magic Spoon) for each student to take home; follow the procedure in Getting Ready, For Part A. Seal the spoons in plastic bags for transport.

Part B: The Balloon in a Bottle Trick

Make sure the students understand that only one student should blow into each balloon (to prevent the spread of germs).

1. Give each student a balloon and an empty plastic soft-drink bottle. Demonstrate how to place the deflated balloon in the plastic bottle by holding the neck of the balloon, pushing the rest of the balloon into the

bottle, and stretching the neck of the balloon back over the bottle's mouth. (See Figure 2.)

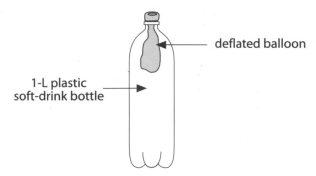

deflated balloon

1-L plastic
soft-drink bottle

Figure 2: Prepare the balloon in a bottle.

2. Ask the students to blow up the balloon in the bottle. Stop them after a brief time and ask them what they observed. Have them describe any resistance they felt when trying to blow up the balloon.

3. Have students pair up, with one partner blowing while the other observes, and try again.

   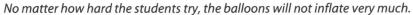
   No matter how hard the students try, the balloons will not inflate very much.

4. Have the students who tried to blow up the balloons in step 3 remove the balloons from their bottles and blow up the balloons to show that the balloons themselves are capable of being inflated.

5. Have the students work in groups to propose explanations for what happened, supporting their explanations with observations. Challenge them to suggest ways to make it possible to blow up the balloon inside the bottle.

6. Bring out the bottle with the hole in the side that was prepared in advance. Place a deflated balloon into the mouth of the bottle as before. (See Figure 2.) With the hole uncovered, blow up the balloon. Stop blowing and allow the balloon to deflate. Ask the students to describe what they observed.

7. Blow up the balloon again, but this time place your finger over the hole after the balloon is blown up. Ask students what they observed. *The balloon stays inflated.*

8. Challenge the students to come up with explanations for their observations in steps 6 and 7. Have them work in small groups, first writing down the problem in their own words and then discussing possible solutions. Working with each group individually, have them plan ways to test their ideas, and help them to do so.

9. After the students have had time to work on the problem, bring them together to discuss their investigations and results. Have successful groups demonstrate their solutions, and discuss as a class why they worked.

10. Help each student make his or her own trick bottle by making a hole near the bottom as you did in Getting Ready.

11. Have each student experience trying to blow up the balloon with the hole uncovered and with it covered. Also have them hold their hand next to the hole while another student blows up the balloon as quickly as possible. What do they observe that can help explain the behavior of the balloon? *They will be able to feel air coming out of the hole in the bottle as the balloon is blown up.*

12. Have each student record, in words or pictures, why the balloon can be blown up when the bottle has a hole in it but not when the bottle is sealed.

Part C: The Double Your Money Trick

1. Have each group pour about 2 cm (1 inch) of water into a clear plastic cup and drop one coin into the water.

2. Tell them to look into the cup from the side. Ask, "How many coins do you see?" *They should see one.*

3. Now have students hold the cup about 5 cm (2 inches) above their eye level. Ask, "Now how many coins do you see?" *A big coin should appear at the bottom with a small coin directly above it in the water.* (The cup may need to be maneuvered to see this trick.)

4. Ask, "Are there really two coins in the cup?" *No.* "Why do two coins appear to be in the cup?" *When you look from the bottom, you see the reflection of the coin on the underside of the water surface.*

5. Have students test different kinds and numbers of coins.

Extension for Further Science Inquiry

Partially blow up a balloon inside the trick bottle (with the hole) made in Part B. Place a finger over the hole once the balloon is blown up, and remove your mouth. At the same time, have an assistant blow up a second balloon. This balloon, outside the bottle, should be inflated to a larger volume than the one inside. With both balloons still blown up, have the assistant twist the neck of the second balloon to seal it, stretch the neck of this balloon over the outside of the mouth of the bottle, and hold the neck of the balloon to keep it in place. The neck should still be sealed. Release your finger from the hole in the bottle. Ask students to predict what will happen when the neck of the second balloon is untwisted so the two balloons are connected. Untwist the neck of the second balloon and have students observe. *The air in the smaller balloon inside the bottle should flow into the larger balloon outside the bottle, inflating it even more.*

Science Explanation

 The following explanation is intended for the teacher's information. Modify the explanation for students as required.

Magic Sand Trick

In this activity, students observe the behavior of different types of sand in water. Regular (untreated) sand becomes wet when placed in water; Magic Sand or Sqand stays dry. Such behavior is an example of a general phenomenon involving water. A substance attracted to water is hydrophilic. ("Hydro" means "water" and "philic" means "loving.") A substance repelled by water is hydrophobic. ("Phobic" means "fearing.") Grains of regular sand become wet because they have hydrophilic portions on their surface and thus are attracted to water. In contrast, the surfaces of grains of Magic Sand have been coated with a hydrophobic substance, so they are not "wetted" by water; that is, they tend to stay in contact with each other. When the water is removed, the grains are observed to be dry.

Balloon in a Bottle Trick

Blowing up a balloon involves forcing additional air into the balloon. The gas molecules blown into the balloon hit the inside walls of the balloon, creating enough pressure to force the rubber of the balloon to expand and the balloon to inflate. Pressure is also being exerted on the outside of the balloon (atmospheric pressure). Atmospheric pressure is a result of molecules of gas in the atmosphere pushing on an object. For the balloon to stay inflated, the pressure inside the balloon must be greater than atmospheric pressure. Additional pressure is necessary because the pressure inside the balloon must not only counter the atmospheric pressure but also stretch the elastic rubber when a balloon is inflated. If the mouth of the inflated balloon is opened (or the balloon pops), the extra air inside will quickly flow out because gases move from areas of higher pressure to areas of lower pressure.

The activity shows that it is impossible to significantly inflate the balloon by mouth when the balloon is inside a closed bottle. (See Figure 3.) The pressure of the air trapped inside the bottle prevents you from inflating the balloon.

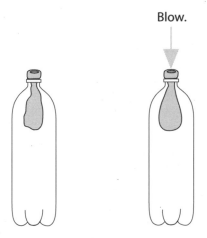

Blow.

Figure 3: It is impossible to significantly inflate a balloon by blowing into it when it is inside a closed bottle.

In order to actually inflate the balloon in the bottle, you not only need to blow enough air into the balloon to provide the pressure needed to stretch the rubber of the balloon, but you also must apply enough pressure to compress the air trapped in the bottle. This compression is needed to make room for the inflated balloon. Even though gases are compressible, it is difficult for most of us to exert enough pressure just by blowing to compress the trapped air very much. (See Figure 4a.)

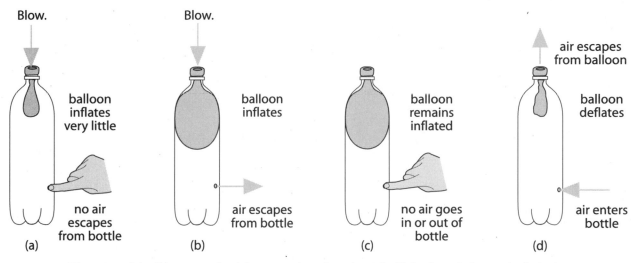

Figure 4: A balloon can be blown up in a bottle only if the bottle has a hole in it.

A balloon can be blown up in a bottle if the bottle has an opening to allow the air initially inside the bottle to escape to make room for the expanding balloon. (See Figure 4b.) If you seal the hole with your finger after inflating the balloon, the balloon will remain inflated even after you remove your mouth. (See Figure 4c.) The careful observer may notice that the bottom part of the plastic bottle contracts slightly around the inflated balloon or the balloon shrinks very slightly. The atmospheric pressure exerted on the open end of the balloon is greater than the pressure in the region between the balloon and the bottle. This greater pressure keeps the balloon inflated.

The balloon will deflate to its original size when the hole in the side of the bottle is opened again. (See Figure 4d.) This is because opening the side hole allows the air pressure on both sides of the balloon to equalize.

Double Your Money Trick

When light hits a mirror or other shiny surface, much of the light is reflected back. Light is also reflected when the medium it is traveling in abruptly changes. For example, light that is traveling through air will reflect off the surface of water. In this activity, light that is traveling through water will be reflected at the water-air surface. As a result the light will then be reflected back into the water. This reflection is what causes the duplicate image of the coin to appear in the glass of water when viewed from the bottom.

The Extension for Further Science Inquiry

Most people would probably predict that the air in this demonstration will flow from the larger balloon into the smaller balloon to equalize the volumes. Instead, air flows from the smaller to the larger, increasing the size difference but decreasing the total surface area of the balloons to the minimum for the system. This phenomenon occurs because with a balloon system as described at a constant temperature and with a constant total volume of air, a single more-inflated balloon has less surface area than two less-inflated balloons. To attain the minimum surface area, the total surface area is reduced as the air flows from the smaller to the larger balloon. Air does not flow from larger to smaller because this transfer would result in an increase in the total surface area. (See Figure 5.)

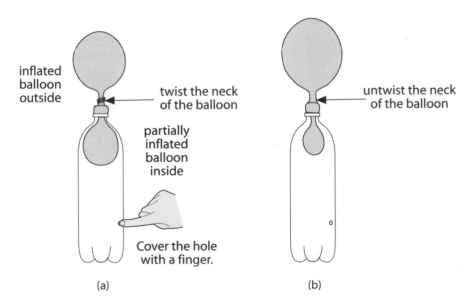

Figure 5: In the Extension, air flows from the smaller balloon to the larger when the hole is uncovered.

If students think having the balloon in the bottle is responsible for the direction of air flow, demonstrate or have them try the following. Cut off the neck of the bottle, again place one balloon over the bottle opening, push it through the bottle neck, blow it up, and hold it closed by twisting the neck of the balloon where it comes out of the bottle neck. Then proceed as in the Extension for Further Science Inquiry.

References for the Science Activity

Becker, R. "Two-Balloon Demo Revisited"; *Chem 13 News;* #49; University of Waterloo: Waterloo, Ontario, September, 1988; p 7.

Sarquis, J.L.; Hogue, L.M.; Sarquis, A.M.; Woodward, L.M. "Balloon In A Bottle"; *Investigating Solids, Liquids, and Gases with TOYS;* McGraw-Hill: New York, 1997; pp 71–79.

Sarquis, M.; Kibbey, B.; Smyth, E. "Light Tricks; Double Image"; *Science Activities for Elementary Classrooms;* Flinn Scientific: Batavia, IL, 1989; p 79.

Sarquis, J.L.; Sarquis, A.M.; Williams, J.P. "Mysterious Sand"; *Teaching Chemistry with TOYS: Activities for Grades K–9;* McGraw-Hill: New York, 1995; pp 183–188.

Part 3: Integrating with Language Arts

Featured Fiction Book: *Harvey Potter's Balloon Farm*

Author: Jerdine Nolen   Illustrator: Mark Buehner
Publisher: Lothrop, Lee & Shepard   ISBN: 0-688-07887-7
Summary: This book is an enchantingly original tall tale about a farmer who grows an unusual crop—balloons. Set in the rural south and populated with a truly unforgettable cast of characters—including, if you look very carefully, a rabbit, *a Tyrannosaurus rex,* a cat, a chicken, a cow, and a pig hidden in each illustration—this book is filled with wonderful impossibilities and magical imagination.

Ask students if they know what a "tall tale" is. Discuss some famous tall tales and their heroes from American legends, such as Paul Bunyan and Pecos Bill. Ask students, "Why might people tell such stories?" Discuss what makes some silly stories and tricks funny and what makes others hurtful.

Writing Extensions

- Have students use their science journals to describe and sketch the initial design for their Magic Spoon tricks, record evaluations by other students, and describe and sketch design modifications.
- Have students write a class tall tale, with students taking turns contributing a few sentences.

Additional Books

Fiction

Title: *Cut from the Same Cloth*
Author: Robert D. San Souci   Illustrator: Brian Pinkney
Publisher: Philomel   ISBN: 0-399-21987-0
Summary: A collection of 20 stories and tall tales about legendary American
women, drawing from folktales, popular stories, and ballads.

Title: *It's April Fool's Day!*
Author: Steven Kroll   Illustrator: Jeni Bassett
Publisher: Holiday House   ISBN: 0-8234-0747-0
Summary: Horace is friends with Alice, yet he plays tricks on her. On April Fool's
Day, Alice is scared to leave her home because of the mean tricks that await
her. So Alice has some tricks of her own for Horace.

Title: *Reflections*
Author and Illustrator: Ann Jonas
Publisher: Greenwillow   ISBN: 0-688-06140-0
Summary: Chronicles a child's busy day by the sea, in a forest, at a carnival, and
then to dinner and a concert. The illustrations change when the book is
turned upside down.

Part 4: Other Lesson Extensions

Art and Music

- Have students create underwater sand sculptures using Magic Sand or Sqand.

Mathematics

- Estimate the surface areas of the balloons at the beginning and end of the
Extension for Further Science Inquiry.

Just for Fun

- Have students research how the lungs work and compare this to the action of
a balloon in a bottle.
- Have students research mirages and trick mirrors and try to create such effects
in the classroom.

Part 5: National Science Education Standards

Science as Inquiry Standards:

Abilities Necessary to Do Scientific Inquiry

Students question how regular sand and Magic Sand or Sqand differ and why.

Students investigate how water acts on Sandy Spoons and on Magic Spoons.

Students use their observations to discuss reasons why one sand might make water behave differently than the other.

Students discuss their observations of the two types of sand and their ideas about why the behavior differs.

Students question if and how a balloon can be blown up inside a bottle.

Students work in groups to plan and conduct a simple investigation to determine how to blow up a balloon inside a bottle.

Students use the results of their investigations to explain what conditions make it possible to blow up a balloon in a bottle.

Students record their results and explanations in words or pictures.

Students question why a cup of water appears to contain two coins when it only contains one.

Students observe the coin in the glass from different angles.

Students use their observations to develop an explanation of why two coins are visible instead of one.

Physical Science Standards:

Properties of Objects and Materials

Materials, such as the two types of sand, have distinguishing properties.

Objects, such as the coin, have observable properties.

Position and Motion of Objects

The position and motion of objects, such as the balloon, can be changed by pushing. The size of the change is related to the strength of the push and the resistance it meets.

Light, Heat, Electricity, and Magnetism

Light can be reflected by a mirror or similar surface, such as the surface of water.

Science and Technology Standards:

Abilities of Technological Design

Students question how to use the Magic Spoons for water tricks.

Students use their experience with the Magic Spoons to propose a water trick.

Students use their Magic Spoons to do their water tricks.

Students evaluate how well their water tricks work and modify them based on the evaluation.

Students share their water tricks with the class.

Students question how to design a balloon-in-a-bottle device that will enable the balloon to be blown up.

Students propose ways to blow up a balloon in a bottle.

Students test their proposals by trying out their designs.

Students evaluate their results and those of other groups and modify their designs accordingly.

Students demonstrate how they were able to blow up balloons in their bottles and discuss why their methods worked.

Arbor Day

April 22
Culture: United States

In 1854, J. Sterling Morton and his wife Caroline moved from Detroit, Michigan, to the treeless Nebraska Territory with many other pioneers. They loved greenery and quickly planted trees, shrubs, and flowers around their new home. As editor of Nebraska's first newspaper, Morton spread agricultural information and his knowledge of trees among his fellow pioneers. Trees not only were important sources of shade and building materials but also served as windbreaks to keep the farmers' soil from blowing away. Through the newspaper, Morton advocated the planting of trees by individuals and civic groups in the Nebraska Territory.

On January 4, 1872, Morton proposed a tree-planting holiday to the State Board of Agriculture. Prizes would be awarded to the counties and individuals who could properly plant the most trees during the one-day holiday. It has been estimated that more than one million trees were planted in Nebraska on the first Arbor Day, April 10, 1872. Morton thought it was very important to involve children in Arbor Day, and he encouraged schools to join the festivities each year. Two years later, Nebraska Governor Robert W. Furnas proclaimed Arbor Day a state-wide holiday. In 1885, April 22 was selected as the permanent date for Nebraska's Arbor Day because it was Morton's birthday.

During the 1870s, other states began celebrating Arbor Day at the time of their best tree-planting weather—from January and February in the south to May in the north. Although the last Friday in April is National Arbor Day, many individual states and U.S. territories continue to hold their own Arbor Day celebrations during prime tree-planting weather. The following is a list of U.S. states and territories, state trees, and Arbor Day celebrations:

State	State Tree	Arbor Day
Alabama	Southern Pine	Last full week in February
Alaska	Sitka Spruce	Third Monday in May
Arizona	Paloverde	Last Friday in April
Arkansas	Pine	Third Monday in March
California	California Redwood	March 7–14
Colorado	Blue Spruce	Third Friday in April
Connecticut	White Oak	April 30

Arbor Day

April 22
Culture: United States

Delaware	American Holly	Last Friday in April
District of Columbia	Scarlet Oak	Last Friday in April
Florida	Cabbage Palmetto	Third Friday in January
Georgia	Live Oak	Third Friday in February
Hawaii	Kukui	First Friday in November
Idaho	Western White Pine	Last Friday in April
Illinois	White Oak	Last Friday in April
Indiana	Yellow Poplar	Last Friday in April
Iowa	Oak	Last Friday in April
Kansas	Cottonwood	Last Friday in March
Kentucky	Kentucky Coffee Tree	Last Friday in April
Louisiana	Bald Cypress	Third Friday in January
Maine	Eastern White Pine	Third full week in May
Maryland	White Oak	First Wednesday in April
Massachusetts	American Elm	April 28–May 5
Michigan	Eastern White Pine	Last Friday in April
Minnesota	Red Pine	Last Friday in April
Mississippi	Southern Magnolia	Second Friday in February
Missouri	Flowering Dogwood	First Friday in April
Montana	Ponderosa Pine	Last Friday in April
Nebraska	Cottonwood	Last Friday in April
Nevada	Singleleaf Piñon	February 28 (South); April 23 (North)
New Hampshire	Paper Birch	Last Friday in April
New Jersey	Northern Red Oak	Last Friday in April
New Mexico	Piñon	Second Friday in March
New York	Sugar Maple	Last Friday in April
North Carolina	Pine	First Friday after March 15
North Dakota	American Elm	First Friday in May
Ohio	Ohio Buckeye	Last Friday in April
Oklahoma	Eastern Redbud	Last full week in March
Oregon	Douglas Fir	First full week in April
Pennsylvania	Eastern Hemlock	Last Friday in April
Rhode Island	Red Maple	Last Friday in April
South Carolina	Cabbage Palmetto	First Friday in December
South Dakota	White Spruce	Last Friday in April
Tennessee	Yellow Poplar	First Friday in March
Texas	Pecan	Last Friday in April
Utah	Blue Spruce	Last Friday in April
Vermont	Sugar Maple	First Friday in May
Virginia	Flowering Dogwood	Second Friday in April
Washington	Western Hemlock	Second Wednesday in April
West Virginia	Sugar Maple	Second Friday in April
Wisconsin	Sugar Maple	Last Friday in April
Wyoming	Cottonwood	Last Monday in April

References

Arbor Lodge State Historical Park Web Site, http://ngp.ngpc.state.ne.us/parks/arbor.html (accessed 6 March 1998).

National Arbor Day Foundation, http://www.arborday.org/what/history.html (accessed 11 Feb 1998).

Magic Trees for Arbor Day

• •

Trees are special and beautiful plants that give us many benefits throughout their long lives. Arbor Day is a

great time to plant trees and celebrate what they do for us. Real trees take many years to grow, but in this

activity, students "plant" trees that "grow" in just a few hours.

• •

Key Science Topics

• capillary action
• crystals, crystallization
• evaporation
• solutions

Time Required

Setup	15	minutes
Performance	5	minutes for Part A
	10–15	minutes for Part B plus 10–30 minutes for pictures to dry
	10–15	minutes for Part C plus 2 or more hours for crystals to form
Cleanup	5	minutes

A homemade Magic Tree

Part 1: Building Bridges

Building Student Knowledge and Motivation

Set up a classroom center with a number of wood and fiber products such as chewing gum, pencils, tongue depressors, cardboard, rayon (fabric), and corks. Prior to the lesson, have groups of students visit the center and examine the wood products. Encourage them to bring in wood and fiber products to add to the center. Discuss other uses of wood such as building materials and paper.

Bridging to the Science Activity

Prepare a commercial Magic Tree by following the package directions. Show the students a variety of crystals. Give them the opportunity to observe several different crystals, such as sugar and salt, with a magnifying lens or microscope. Explain that crystals are solids whose particles are arranged in a fixed, regular pattern. Examples include salt, sugar, diamonds, and ice. No matter how big or small a piece of crystalline solid is, its particles are always arranged in the characteristic pattern of that solid. Tell students that they will be growing very tiny crystals that will not look as regular as, for example, salt, but more like powdered sugar.

Discuss the functional and aesthetic value of trees. They add beauty and interest to our environment, provide sound control for traffic areas, shield buildings and fields from harsh winter winds, provide erosion control and shade, and give off oxygen for us to breathe. They also provide food and shelter for birds and animals.

Show the students the "Snowy Tree" in the Featured Fiction Book, *Sky Tree*, and tell them they are going to transform a plain tree made of construction paper to a beautiful crystalline tree as shown in the illustration.

Part 2: Science Activity

Materials

For Bridging to the Science Activity
Per class
- commercial Magic Tree®

  Magic Tree kits are available from Toysmith (#8309), 6250 S. 196th St., Kent, WA 98032; 800/356-0474.

- samples of various crystals, including salt and sugar
- magnifying lenses or microscope

For Getting Ready

Per group
- salt solution ingredients:
  - 1 tablespoon Morton Lite Salt® or table salt

    Since the additives in table salt tend to make the solution cloudy, Morton Lite Salt is preferable.

  - 3 tablespoons hot tap water
- small plastic glass

Per class
- Growing Solution ingredients:
  - 180 mL (12 tablespoons) laundry bluing (can be found in or ordered by most grocery stores)
  - 90 mL (6 tablespoons) table salt
  - 180 mL (12 tablespoons) water
  - 48 mL (3 tablespoons) household ammonia
- container(s) with a tight-fitting lid for Growing Solution
- spoon or stirring stick
- goggles

For the Procedure

Part A, per student or group
- strip of paper towel
- small clear plastic glass
- water

Part B, per student
- piece of black or dark-colored construction paper
- cotton swab
- (optional) magnifying lens

Part B, per group
- 3 tablespoons salt solution in a plastic cup (prepared in Getting Ready)

Part C, per student
- blotter paper
- goggles
- 15–30 mL (1–2 tablespoons) Growing Solution (prepared in Getting Ready)
- McDonald's® sundae cup with lid

 Local McDonald's restaurants may donate sundae cups or sell them at a low cost.

- scissors

Part C, per group
- tablespoon measure or 50-mL graduated cylinder
- water-soluble ink pens of 3 or 4 different colors
- magnifying lens
- (optional) masking tape and pen for labels

For the Extensions for Further Science Inquiry
- all materials required for the Procedure except
  - ° use a porous surface for the crystal growing surface
  - ° other materials as suggested by students

Safety and Disposal

Household ammonia and its vapor can damage the eyes. Eye protection is required even when using dilute solutions. Use only in a well-ventilated area. Should contact with eyes occur, rinse the affected area with water for 15 minutes. Medical attention should be sought while rinsing. The household ammonia and the Growing Solution can be diluted with water and flushed down the drain, or they can be saved for future use.

Laundry bluing alone or in the Growing Solution will stain hands, clothing, and utensils. Use appropriate caution.

Getting Ready

1. Prepare the salt solution using the proportions listed in Materials. Use hot tap water if possible and heaping spoonfuls of salt. Stir to dissolve, which may take 5–10 minutes. Residual solid on the bottom of the cup will not interfere with the investigation.

2. Prepare the Growing Solution as follows:

   The amounts listed in step 2a should make enough solution for a class to do the Procedure as a hands-on activity.

   a. While wearing goggles, place the following Growing Solution ingredients in a container and mix:
      - 180 mL (12 tablespoons) laundry bluing
      - 90 mL (6 tablespoons) table salt
      - 180 mL (12 tablespoons) water
      - 48 mL (3 tablespoons) household ammonia

   b. Stir well to dissolve as much of the salt as possible.

   c. Cover the solution so that it will not evaporate before use.
      The Growing Solution may discolor with time but is still usable.

Procedure

Part A: Capillary Action

1. Have students hold a strip of paper towel at one end while they lower the other end into a cup of water to a depth of about 1 cm and observe the water as it moves up the towel.

2. Explain that the motion is called capillary action.

Part B: Crystal Pictures

1. Give each student a sheet of black or dark-colored construction paper and a cotton swab. Divide the students into groups and give each group a cup containing the salt solution prepared in Getting Ready.

2. Instruct the students to draw a tree with the salt solution on the paper by dipping the cotton swab in the solution and using it as a pen.

3. Let the papers dry for 10–30 minutes.

4. After papers are dry, have students observe the crystal pictures and compare them. If desired, have them use magnifying lenses.

Part C: Making a Crystal Tree

1. Have students cut out a pair of Tree Templates (provided at the end of this lesson), trace them onto blotter paper, and cut out the blotter-paper shapes.

   Each template has two tree shapes, one with a slit at the top, and one with a slit at the bottom. Students will need to cut out these slits.

2. Have students use water-soluble marking pens to color the tips of the "tree branches."

   This color will be picked up by the crystal solution and will color the crystals.

3. Have students fit the tree shapes together by sliding the slit on one tree shape into the slit on the other to make three-dimensional trees that can stand by themselves.

4. Tell the students you will provide them with 1–2 tablespoons of Growing Solution and the lid of a sundae cup. Have students brainstorm methods for decorating the trees with crystals using the information they learned in Parts A and B about capillary action and crystals—without painting as in Part B.

5. Lead groups to try the following procedure.

   a. Have students put on goggles.

   b. Have students pour 1–2 tablespoons of the Growing Solution (prepared in Getting Ready) into the lids of the sundae cups. (See Figure 1.)

   c. Have students carefully stand their trees in the center of their lids. (See Figure 1.)

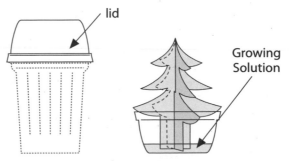

Figure 1: Pour Growing Solution into the lid of the sundae cup and "plant" your magic tree in the lid.

d. Have students label their lids with masking tape and pens and place the trees in a location where they will not be disturbed. Let the tree systems stand undisturbed for several hours.

> *It will take at least several hours for the crystals to grow. High humidity or cold room temperature may slow the evaporation rate and increase the time required to grow the crystals.*

6. Once the crystals have formed, have the students observe their crystals with a magnifying lens. Ask them to compare their crystals with the crystals they observed in Bridging to the Science Activity.

7. To preserve the trees, have students place the sundae cups upside down over the trees to make a protective carrying case.

> *The trees must be completely dry before they are covered, or the crystals will disappear.*

Extensions for Further Science Inquiry

- Have students develop modifications for the Procedure, predicting the effects of the changes and then testing. For example, compare the rate of crystal formation in a sunny window with the rate of formation in a cooler, darker area. What happens if water is left out of the Growing Solution? Try using a different porous object, such as a piece of sponge, as the crystal growing surface. Challenge your students to come up with other factors to test.
- Make a chart of tree species that grow in different environments. Include average size, distinguishing characteristics, and reasons why the tree might grow as it does. Also list wildlife that use the trees for shelter and food.

Science Explanation

> *The following explanation is intended for the teacher's information. Modify the explanation for students as required.*

A crystal is a solid that has a definite geometric shape due to the regular repeating pattern of the atoms, molecules, or ions that make up the substance. During crystallization, atoms, molecules, and/or ions align themselves in a specific three-dimensional pattern called a crystal lattice; this lattice is a characteristic property of crystalline substances. The crystal lattice is responsible for the geometric patterns found in many crystals but is present even when obvious crystal shapes are not observed (as in this activity).

Crystals can be grown from saturated solutions, solutions that contain the maximum amount of solute (salts in this activity) that the solvent (water) can dissolve at a given temperature. The blotter paper provides a surface on which crystallization can occur.

The solution moves up the paper by a type of capillary action called wicking. Capillary action occurs when a liquid moves through the pores of a substance. Wicking is a process similar to that occurring in candles, where the melted wax travels up through the pores of the wick as the candle burns. Wicking is not possible with nonporous materials. When the ammonia/bluing/salt solution reaches the surface of the paper tree, the water in the solution begins to evaporate. As the water evaporates, the salts in the solution are left behind as soft, flower-like crystals.

References for the Science Activity

Sarquis, J.; Hogue, L.; Sarquis, M.; Woodward, L. "Crystals from Solutions"; *Investigating Solids, Liquids, and Gases with TOYS: States of Matter and Changes of State;* McGraw-Hill: New York, 1997; p 141.

Sarquis, J.; Sarquis, M.; Williams, J.P. "Crystal Pictures"; *Teaching Chemistry with TOYS;* McGraw-Hill: New York, 1995; pp 19–21.

Part 3: Integrating with Language Arts

Featured Fiction Book: *Sky Tree*

Authors: Thomas Locker and Candace Christiansen
Illustrator: Thomas Locker
Publisher: HarperCollins   ISBN: 0-06-024883-1
Summary: A tree stands on a hill by a river. As the sky changes, so does the tree, its branches filling with clouds, stars, snow, birds, mists, and the golden spring sun. One tree can mean many things.

This book contains thought-provoking questions at the end of each description. Pause at each tree painting and discuss the art or science issue raised by the question on that page. When you have finished the story, you may want to lead the class through "Connecting Art and Science in *Sky Tree*," a section at the back of the book. This section addresses the questions asked in the story and provides interesting information about the techniques the artist used to create each painting.

Writing Extensions

- If you did the first Extension for Further Science Inquiry, have students use their science journals to write a summary of the crystal-growing experiment they designed and the results they found.
- Ask students to pretend they are trees and have them describe one day in their life and their most unusual visitor.
- Have students keep records in their science journals of their observations of trees in the schoolyard or near the school. The record could include observations of animals that live in the tree; organisms that use the tree for shelter, shade, or food; the time of year when buds, flowers, and leaves appear and are shed; and other information the students consider important. Have students find out how many different kinds of trees live near the school and then make a chart of bark rubbings, leaves, and journal observations.

- Have students develop a list of "tree language," including words and phrases such as "out on a limb," "up a tree," "branch out," and "trunk." Have students use these words and phrases in a story.

Additional Books

Fiction

Title: *The Alphabet Tree*
Author and Illustrator: Leo Lionni
Publisher: Trumpet Club   ISBN: 0-440-84361-8
Summary: A strong wind blows most of the letters off the alphabet tree, and those that remain hide among the branches. Then a bug and a caterpillar come along and teach them how to arrange themselves into words and sentences to form a special message.

Title: *Cherry Tree*
Author: Ruskin Bond   Illustrator: Allan Eitzen
Publisher: Caroline House   ISBN: 1-878093-21-5
Summary: This story from India, in which a little girl plants a cherry seed and cares for the cherry tree through its difficult life, is about life and growing older.

Title: *Someday a Tree*
Author: Eve Bunting   Illustrator: Ronald Himler
Publisher: Clarion   ISBN: 0-395-61309-4
Summary: A young girl, her parents, and their neighbors try to save an old oak tree that has been poisoned by pollution.

Title: *The Tree That Would Not Die*
Author: Ellen Levine   Illustrator: Ted Rand
Publisher: Scholastic   ISBN: 0-590-43724-0
Summary: The story of the 500-year-old Treaty Oak in Austin, Texas, is told from the tree's point of view, covers the nation's history that took place during the tree's lifetime, and describes the malicious 1989 poisoning that nearly destroyed it.

Nonfiction

Title: *A B Cedar: An Alphabet of Trees*
Author: George Ella Lyon   Illustrator: Tom Parker
Publisher: Orchard   ISBN: 0-531-05795-X
Summary: A tree, any tree, is a miracle. Here are 26 of them from Aspen to Zebrawood. Lined up, they make an alphabet. You've never seen letters or trees in quite the way this book presents them, in grand companionship.

Title: *A Gift of a Tree*
Author: Greg Henry Quinn   Illustrator: Ronda Krum
Publisher: Scholastic   ISBN: 0-590-48092-8
Summary: This book describes the gifts trees give to all other creatures on Earth, such as oxygen, shelter, wood, food, and beauty. It also describes things we can do to help trees and includes a seed kit for planting your own tree.

Part 4: Other Lesson Extensions

Art and Music

- Have students adopt trees and sketch them on light-colored construction paper. Have them make bark and leaf rubbings by placing large pieces of paper against the bark or one leaf of their trees. Have them gently rub over the paper with a crayon and glue the bark and leaf rubbings to the tree sketch.
- Have students research musical instruments that are made of wood.

Mathematics

- Have students gather leaves from several different kinds of trees, trace the outline of the leaves on graph paper, count the squares, and compare the sizes of the leaves.
- Research the life spans of various tree species. Have students calculate the year that a tree of a given age would have sprouted. What historical events occurred in that year? What people(s) could have used the tree for shade? Make a timeline for the life of the tree.

Social Studies

- Have students adopt a tree near the school grounds and then draw a map with their tree identified. Go on a nature walk with a buddy using the student-created map to locate the trees.

Part 5: National Science Education Standards

Science as Inquiry Standards:

Abilities Necessary to Do Scientific Inquiry
Students make systematic observations of crystal-growing systems.

Students decide how to collect and organize their data.

Students use their observations to develop explanations of crystal-growing.

Students question how they can transform their plain "trees" into crystalline trees.

Students design an investigation to find out if their trees will soak up the crystal solution and grow crystals as the water evaporates.

Students use magnifying lenses to observe their trees and crystals more closely.

Students observe their trees as the crystals form and use these observations to propose an explanation of how the crystals form.

Students share their project designs, products, and explanations with the class.

Physical Science Standards:

Properties of Objects and Materials

A characteristic property of crystalline substances is the specific three-dimensional pattern of the crystal lattice, which determines the shape of the crystals.

Objects, such as the trees and crystals, have observable properties such as size, shape, and color.

The tree is made of blotter paper, so like blotter paper, it will absorb water.

Water changes from the liquid to the gas state.

Science and Technology Standards:

Abilities of Technological Design

Students question how to improve their tree design.

Students propose changes in the tree-growing procedure that might produce an improved tree.

Students test their ideas by repeating the crystal-growing procedure with their changes incorporated.

Students evaluate their original and altered trees and those of other students. They modify their designs based on this evaluation.

Students present their designs and products to the class and participate in a discussion of what techniques make the best trees.

Tree Templates (three pairs)

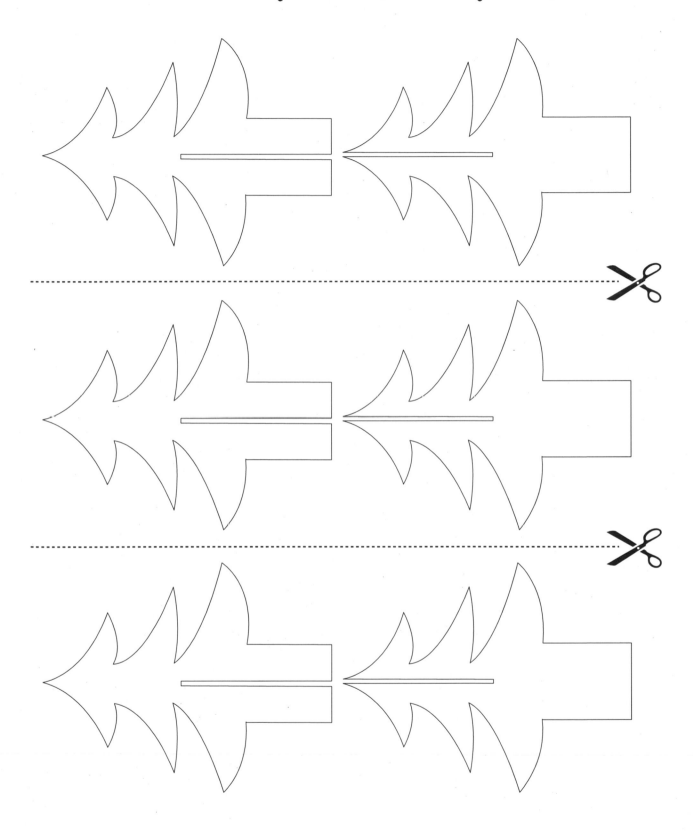

Cinco de Mayo

May 5
Culture: Mexican

Cinco de Mayo (Spanish for "the fifth of May") commemorates the Mexican victory at the Battle of Puebla on May 5, 1862. The events leading up to this battle began on August 24, 1821, when Spain and Mexico signed the Treaty of Cordoba that ended 300 years of Spanish rule in Mexico. Although the Mexican people had fought together for independence, they could not agree on a form of government to replace the Spanish monarchy. During the years following independence, the southern part of the new "Mexican Empire" broke off to rule themselves, eventually becoming the present-day countries in Central America. The rest of the Mexican Empire went through decades of rebellion and instability.

To raise money for civil wars and rebellions, contending political groups negotiated international loans from England, France, and Spain. However, Mexico still had no stable government or plan for survival as a country. After the United States won the land now known as Texas, many Mexican people realized that a fundamental reform had to take place in order for the country to survive. The reformists, led by Benito Juárez, set up government in Veracruz, the main port city. Their opponents, the conservatives, took control of Mexico City and formed their own government. In December 1860, the conservative government collapsed and Juárez became president of a united Mexico.

After winning the presidency, Juárez had to deal with the troubled finances and bankrupt treasury of the country. He proposed suspending payment of the foreign debt for two years, hoping to use that time to rebuild Mexico's economy and treasury. England, France, and Spain refused to accept this proposal and signed the Treaty of London, in which the three nations agreed to occupy the port of Veracruz until the debts were repaid. The three nations would control the customs house in Veracruz, applying customs and taxes to the debt. The treaty specifically stated that the nations would not try to control the Mexican government or Mexico's right to rule themselves.

England and Spain honored the treaty, but France launched an invasion of Mexico in 1862, hoping to establish a French empire in the Americas. The French troops were among the best-trained and best-equipped in the world and quickly marched inland toward Mexico City, the capital of the Mexican Empire. When they reached the city of

Puebla, however, they were met by General Ignacio Zaragoza and his army of Mestizos and Zapotec Indians. Despite the fact that the French army's equipment and training were superior, the Mexican army defeated the French on May 5, 1862. Although the French captured Mexico City the following year, the victory at Puebla inspired the Mexicans with a growing sense of nationalism and self-esteem. The Mexican republican forces reconquered Mexico in 1867, forcing the French out of the country. This victory marked the end of European dominance over Mexico and the beginning of a united, stable, independent Mexico.

Although the victory at Puebla is still commemorated in Mexico on the fifth of May, Cinco de Mayo has taken on a new significance among Hispanics in America. Whether of Mexican heritage or not, many Hispanic-Americans celebrate Hispanic culture on Cinco de Mayo, organizing parades, folklorico dancing, and other festivities. While the focus is on the culture as a whole, reenactments of the Battle of Puebla are often held.

An important part of many Hispanic celebrations is the piñata, a pineapple-shaped earthenware pot full of sweets. The piñata originated during the sixteenth century in Italy, where it was called a "pignatta" (from the Italian word "pigna" meaning "cone-shaped"). The pignatta was suspended by a rope in mid-air, and as a blindfolded person tried to hit the pot with a stick to get at the sweets, someone would pull on the rope, causing the pignatta to move. During the middle of the 16th century, Italian adventurers took their pignatta traditions to Spain. The Spanish adopted the game, changing the name to "piñata" and using a jar called an "olla." To make the plain, earthenware ollas more festive, paper figures were built around them.

The Spanish in turn brought the piñata game to Mexico. At first, the Mexicans used the piñatas for religious celebrations, especially Christmas, but through the years piñatas began being used for all celebrations. Today, Hispanic-Americans continue the tradition, using piñatas for all festive occasions.

References

Hatch, J.M. *The American Book of Days,* 3rd ed.; H.W. Wilson: New York, 1978.

"Mexico: History" *Britannica Online.* http://www.eb.com:180/cgi-bin/g?DocF=macro/5004/17/toc.html (accessed 22 Oct 1997).

"Mexico"; *World Book Encyclopedia;* World Book: Chicago, 1995; Vol. 13, p 457.

"Puebla, Battle of" *Britannica Online.* http://www.eb.com:180cgi-bin/g?DocF=micro/485/78.html (accessed 21 Oct 1997).

Vega, E.R. Frequently Asked Questions (FAQ) of the Newsgroup soc.culture.mexican. "What do Mexicans celebrate on Cinco de Mayo (May 5th)?" http://www.public.iastate.edu/~rjsalvad/scmfaqindex.html (accessed 23 March 1998).

Piñata-Making for Cinco de Mayo

* *

Originally from Italian culture, today the piñata is a fixture at almost every Hispanic celebration. Children love to break these beautiful figures open and race for the treats that fall. In America, clay jars (ollas) have largely been replaced with other types of containers. In this activity, students test the strength of papier-mâché baskets made with different pastes.

* *

Key Science Topic

- physical properties

Time Required

Setup	10	minutes
Performance	30–45	minutes for construction
	4–6	days for drying
	30–60	minutes for testing
Cleanup	10	minutes

A papier-mâché basket around a balloon mold

Part 1: Building Bridges

Building Student Knowledge and Motivation

Read the book *Fiesta! Cinco De Mayo* (see Additional Books) and briefly explain the similarities and differences between the Mexican victory over France (May 5, 1862) and U.S. independence from England (September 3, 1783, but celebrated on July 4 to commemorate the adoption of the Declaration of Independence). Use a globe to point out the United States, England, Mexico, and France. Show pictures depicting U.S. Independence Day celebrations. Discuss the Fourth of July and the role parades and fireworks play in this celebration. (If the book *Fourth of July Bear*, by Kathryn Lasky (Morrow, ISBN 0688082874) is available, read it to the class.) Mexico also celebrates its independence with parades.

Bridging to the Science Activity

Show the students a store-bought piñata or a picture of a piñata. Tell the students that they will be making their own piñatas. (Piñatas are often part of Mexican celebrations.) Discuss with the students that a piñata is a sculpture. Brainstorm ideas on how piñatas are made and what materials are needed for making them. Then read *The Piñata Maker*, by George Ancona. (See Part 3, Featured Nonfiction Book.)

After reading the story, show the students a papier-mâché basket made from wheat flour and water. (See Getting Ready.) Have students feel the basket, observe its appearance, and determine how many treats it holds.

Part 2: Science Activity

Materials

For Bridging to the Science Activity
- store-bought piñata or a picture of a piñata
- papier-mâché basket made in Getting Ready
- small wrapped candies and/or small toys

For Getting Ready
- all materials listed for the Procedure, Part A

For the Procedure

Part A, per group

The class will make a total of 12 baskets, four for each of the three glue recipes. You may choose to divide the class into three large groups or six smaller groups. However, in the list below, the materials affected by group size are the number of balloons and the amount of flour, water, and newspapers.

- white flour
- water
- measuring cup
- bowl
- large spoon
- 2 or 4 large, round balloons
- newspaper cut into 1-inch-wide strips
- large pan
- pin
- 2 or 3 kinds of paint (watercolor, acrylic, etc.)
- hole punch
- knife
- scissors
- (optional) aprons or smocks

Part B, per group
- hole-punching instrument chosen by students in Part A
- strong string or wire
- tissue paper of various colors
- glue
- paint chosen by students in Part A
- small wrapped candies and/or toys

For the Extension for Further Science Inquiry
- all materials listed for the Procedure, Parts A and B
- extra newspaper

Safety and Disposal

No special safety procedures are required. The flour-water slurries can be flushed down the toilet or down a drain with lots of running water.

Getting Ready

1. Cut or tear the newspaper into strips about 1 inch wide.

2. Make a papier-mâché basket using Recipe 2 (equal volumes of flour and water) according to the Procedure, Part A, steps 2–4.

Procedure

Part A: Papier-Mâché Formulations

1. Tell students the goal of this experiment is for them to determine the best formula for the paste to be used in making a papier-mâché basket like the one you showed them in Bridging to the Science Activity. Tell them they will test three recipes. Discuss the criteria to be used to judge which is best. Also discuss the importance of making the test baskets in the same way so that the variable being tested will be the type of paste and not the construction of the basket itself.

2. Divide the class into enough groups to make four baskets using each of the glue recipes, for a total of 12 baskets for the class. You may choose to have three large groups (one for each recipe) or six smaller groups (two for each recipe). Assign each group a specific glue mixture as follows:
   - Recipe 1: Mix 2 cups flour with 1 cup water.
   - Recipe 2: Mix 1 cup flour with 1 cup water.
   - Recipe 3: Mix 1 cup flour with 2 cups water.

3. Have all of the groups inflate their balloons to approximately the same size. (About 6–8 inches in diameter works well.) When all of the groups agree on a size, they should tie off their balloons.

4. Have each group make two or four papier-mâché baskets by coating the 1-inch-wide newspaper strips with the glue mixture and wrapping the strips around each balloon with the edges of each strip slightly overlapping the edges of other strips. Students should apply approximately one layer of papier-mâché. Once the baskets have been made, allow them to dry for 4–6 days.

   The gluing process is messy, so students should hold the balloons over a pan as they apply the strips. It may be difficult for students to determine what constitutes "one layer" of papier-mâché. A good way to keep track of layers is to start near the top of the balloon (leaving an opening for the basket) and wrap strips around the balloon, working toward the bottom. At the bottom, short strips can be glued across the bottom perpendicular to the previously glued rings until all gaps have been covered.

5. When the papier-mâché baskets are dry, have students pop the balloons with a pin and remove the scraps of rubber. (Students may want to observe the balloons as they deflate.) Remind students to look at and handle their baskets carefully to avoid inadvertently breaking them.

6. As a class, discuss ideas for testing the following qualities (or other qualities students propose to test):
   - which glue recipe would make the most suitable piñata (keeping in mind that breaking a piñata should be a fun challenge but not impossible for a group of children);
   - which method produced the basket with the most pleasing appearance (without decoration);

- what method is best for making holes for the hanger (for example, a hole punch, scissors, or a knife); and
- what kind of paint works best on papier-mâché.

Students should keep in mind the number of baskets available, the importance of multiple trials, whether one test makes a basket unusable for other tests, and whether the proposed experiments simulate actual conditions of use.

7. Have students conduct their proposed experiments. We suggest the following general order of testing:
   - appearance
   - painting
   - hole-punching method
   - breakability test 1
   - breakability test 2

If the class is divided into six groups, have the groups with the same recipes work together, pooling their baskets. Groups could do two different breakability tests, using two baskets for each test. For example, one test might involve dropping two baskets from predetermined heights and comparing how many drops it takes to break the baskets. The second test might involve having one or more students actually hit the baskets with a stick and count how many blows it takes to break the baskets. (In this case, students should carefully consider how to control the strength of the blows to make them consistent class-wide. One method might be to have one student strike all the blows. Another method might be to have several students of different strengths take turns hitting the baskets.)

8. When all groups have finished testing, have them pool results on a class chart such as the one in Figure 1. Have students evaluate the results and choose which recipe and methods they think would make the best piñata.

Recipe	Test				
	Appearance	Hole-Punching Method	Painting	Breakability Test 1	Breakability Test 2
1					
2					
3					

Figure 1: This chart shows one way to organize test results, according to the suggested plan.

Part B: Making a Papier-Mâché Piñata

1. Instruct groups to make their own papier-mâché piñatas using a large balloon and the glue recipe the class chose in Part A, step 8. Remind them to leave a hole at the top so treats can be added.

2. After the balloons have been covered and allowed to dry for 4–6 days, have groups pop the balloons, paint and decorate the papier-mâché (using the chosen methods) to form piñatas, and allow the paint and glue to dry.

   The piñatas can be as simple or as fancy as desired. The book The Piñata Maker *(see the Featured Fiction Book) contains two examples of decorative piñatas students may want to try to make.*

3. Have each group punch holes in its piñata (using the chosen method) and thread wire or string through the piñata so it can be hung.

4. Have students play the piñata game with their piñatas. They may either break all of the piñatas themselves and observe which ones perform best, or they may give some piñatas to younger classes to play the game with.

Extension for Further Science Inquiry

Determine the effect of the number of layers of glued newsprint on the strength and design of the papier-mâché balloon. Test balloons covered with one, four, and eight layers of glued newsprint.

Science Explanation

 The following explanation is intended for the teacher's information. Modify the explanation for students as required.

Papier-mâché is a French term meaning pulped or chewed paper. Paste is a mixture of flour, water, and sometimes other ingredients that is used as an adhesive. The papier-mâché balloon sculpture is made from newspaper strips and a paste made of whole wheat flour and water.

The starch in the flour is a polysaccharide, a natural carbohydrate containing many glucose sugar units. Gluten is a mixture of protein in wheat flour and is a tough, sticky, somewhat elastic substance. It is grayish yellow and has almost no taste. When the flour is mixed with water and stirred, the gluten is separated from the flour. Gluten gives the paste adhesiveness or stickiness, allowing the newspapers to stick together and adhere to the balloons.

Starch is a white powdery substance found in green plants and thus present in the wheat flour. It thickens the flour mixture, causing the mixture to become pasty or jelly-like. It does not dissolve in water.

Part 3: Integrating with Language Arts

Featured Nonfiction Book: *The Piñata Maker (El Piñatero)*

Author: George Ancona
Publisher: Harcourt Brace   ISBN: 0-15-200060-7
Summary: The bilingual text describes how Don Ricardo, a craftsman from southern Mexico, makes piñatas for all the village birthday parties and other fiestas.

Observe the steps Don Ricardo follows to make his piñatas. Discuss how his piñatas are different from the ones the class made and how they are similar. What other materials does he use? Talk about how Don Ricardo began making piñatas and improved his technique through trial and error, just as the students do in the activity. Talk about the kind of person Don Ricardo must be and how he and the townspeople feel about each other. What clues does the story provide? Ask students whether they know any people like Don Ricardo.

Writing Extensions

- Have students use their science journals to write a summary of the experiment they designed and the results they found.
- Have students work in groups to brainstorm ideas about a special surprise that could be hidden in a piñata. Have them write clues about their surprise object(s) and take turns presenting their clues to the class. The class should try to guess what that group's surprise is. Alternatively, groups could write stories about piñatas that contain surprises and incorporate their clues into the story. One group member can read the story to the class, stopping after each clue to allow input from the class and then finishing the story.
- Have the students write creative stories entitled, "The Piñata for My Birthday Is…" The stories could describe what shape students would like for their piñatas, how the piñatas would be decorated, and what they might contain.
- Have students write to pen pals in Mexico to learn about each other's culture. Use the Internet to find schools willing to correspond.
- Have students make a travel brochure for Mexico highlighting various historical sites, foods, and climate.

Additional Books

Fiction

Title: *Cinco de Mayo (Circle the Year with Holidays)*
Author: Janet Riehecky   Illustrator: Krystyna Stasiak
Publisher: Children's Press   ISBN: 0516006819
Summary: Although Maria is not too successful helping her family prepare for Cinco de Mayo, she wins an art contest at the library and gets to break the piñata back home. Includes instructions for making tacos and three crafts.

Nonfiction

Title: *Fiesta!*
Author: Ginger Foglesong Guy   Illustrator: Rene King Moreno
Publisher: William Morrow   ISBN: 0-688-14331-8
Summary: The bilingual text describes a student's party and provides practice counting in English and Spanish.

Title: *Fiesta! Cinco De Mayo*
Author: June Behrens
Publisher: Children's Press   ISBN: 0-516-48815-5
Summary: Describes the commemoration of the victory of the Mexican army over the French army on May 5, 1862.

Part 4: Other Lesson Extensions

Art and Music

- Connect balloons to make animal shapes to use as forms. Cover these forms with papier-mâché.
- Have students make string-mâché ornaments using the 1/1 flour-water mixture, thin cotton cord (the kind used to tie packages or fly kites), glitter, and partially inflated balloons. Students can make designs on their ornaments by coating lengths of string with paste and draping it against the balloon in loops, curves, and other designs. The balloon should not be completely covered, but the lengths of string should touch enough other pieces of string so that the ornament does not collapse when the balloon is deflated. After students have pasted on the desired amount of string, they can shake glitter over the still-wet ornaments while holding them over a trash can, gently shake off the excess glitter, and hang up the ornaments to dry for 2–3 days. When the ornaments are dry, students should poke a pin into the balloons and very carefully extract them through one of the gaps in the string pattern.
- Have students make maracas out of papier-mâché and play them.

Mathematics

- Have students calculate and compare the cost of homemade piñatas versus purchased ones.
- As a class project, have students make piñatas to sell at a school fair or parent-teacher organization event. Have them determine costs, prices, and profits.
- Have students create a Spanish counting book with addition and subtraction problems in Spanish. Students can learn Spanish names of objects they use to illustrate the problems.

Social Studies

- Research the use of piñatas in Hispanic celebrations.
- Provide information on the use and construction of papier-mâché masks in various cultures. Show samples and pictures if available.
- Learn about Mexican culture and have a Mexican fiesta with authentic foods. Have this fiesta on or about May 5.
- Discuss how Mexico has impacted U.S. culture with regard to vocabulary, foods, and architecture. Have students brainstorm various Spanish words that have been incorporated into English.

Part 5: National Science Education Standards

Science as Inquiry Standards:

Abilities Necessary to Do Scientific Inquiry

Students question which paste works best for a papier-mâché piñata.

Students make papier-mâché baskets with different pastes and compare their properties to determine which paste makes the best piñatas.

Students pool their data and conclusions on a class chart and use it as a basis for discussion.

Physical Science Standards:

Properties of Objects and Materials

Objects, such as the papier-mâché baskets, are made from combinations of materials and can be described in terms of these materials.

Materials can exist in different states. The flour paste solidifies as the water in the paste evaporates.

Science and Technology Standards:

Abilities of Technological Design

Students question the best way to make a papier-mâché basket for use in a piñata.

Students propose testing different variables, such as paste formulations and number of layers of paper, to make the best piñata.

Students implement their proposals by making a variety of baskets and testing them.

Students evaluate their test results and those of other students and modify their designs accordingly.

Students share their test results and conclusions with the class.

History and Nature of Science Standards:

Science as a Human Endeavor

Piñatas were originally made from earthenware jars. People in various cultures have refined piñata-making by testing different methods, just as the students did with their papier-mâché baskets.

Mother's Day

Second Sunday in May
Culture: United States and others (different dates)

Mothers have been celebrated throughout history. The ancient Greeks and other early European cultures honored mothers during spring celebrations. In the 1600s, the English celebrated "Mothering Sunday" on the fourth Sunday in Lent. Servants who lived in the houses of their employers had the day off and were encouraged to spend the day with their mothers. Often, a special "mothering cake" was made for the celebration. As Christianity spread throughout Europe, the holiday was changed for a time to a celebration of the "Mother Church," but eventually the custom of honoring individual mothers returned and was blended with the church celebration. It wasn't until 1872, however, that a day for mothers was considered in America.

In 1872, Julia Ward Howe, the author of *The Battle Hymn of the Republic*, suggested having a Mother's Day. Little national attention was paid to her idea, but a Mother's Day committee met every year in Boston, Massachusetts. Later in the 19th century another woman, Anna Reeves Jarvis, also developed the idea of a national day to honor mothers. She shared her dream with her daughter, Anna Jarvis, who carried on the campaign after her mother's death. The younger Anna Jarvis finally succeeded in fulfilling her mother's dream; the first Mother's Day ceremonies were held in 1908 in Grafton, West Virginia, and in Philadelphia on the second Sunday in May, the anniversary of Anna Reeves Jarvis' death.

In 1910, the governor of West Virginia issued the first official Mother's Day proclamation. Mother's Day services were held in every state the following year. President Woodrow Wilson, in response to a joint resolution of Congress, set aside the second Sunday in May as Mother's Day in 1914, and the holiday has been observed ever since.

In America, special church services are held to recognize mothers on their special day. Often, the family will take the mother out to dinner or prepare a meal of her favorite foods, and give her gifts. Many countries, including Australia, Belgium, Denmark, Finland, Italy, and Turkey, celebrate Mother's Day on the second Sunday in May, as in the United States, but others observe the holiday on different days. Each country that celebrates Mother's Day, however, has different traditions and customs. For example, in the former

Mother's Day
Second Sunday in May
Culture: United States and others (different dates)

Yugoslavia, Mother's Day takes place the second Sunday before Christmas. Children good-naturedly tie their mother to a chair and release her only after she promises them candy and other treats. The Sunday before this, the parents good-naturedly tie their children to chairs, releasing them only after they promise to be good in the coming year.

References

Hatch, J.M. *The American Book of Days,* 3rd ed.; H.W. Wilson: New York, 1978; pp 439–440.

Holidays on the Net. Mother's Day on the Net—The Story. http://www.holidays.net/mother/story.htm (accessed 17 Feb 1998).

Spicer, D.G. *The Book of Festivals;* Women's Press: New York, 1937; p 344.

Mother's Day
Film Canister Sachets

• •

Mother's Day, celebrated on the second Sunday in May, is a day set aside to honor mothers.

In many cultures, children make their mothers special gifts, and the family takes Mom out to dinner or

prepares a dinner of her favorite foods. In this lesson, students will make

Film Canister Sachets as special presents for their mothers.

• •

Key Science Topics

- evaporation
- phase changes
- sense of smell
- volatility

Ingredients for a film canister sachet

Time Required

Setup   5 minutes
Performance   45–60 minutes plus about
                            5 minutes daily for
                            2 weeks for observations
Cleanup   5 minutes

Part 1: Building Bridges

Building Student Knowledge and Motivation

Set up a learning center including pictures of family members, including students' mothers. Have children draw pictures of their mothers or describe them and discuss feelings students have about mothers. (Be tactful in discussion to prevent hurting the feelings of students with painful family situations.) Give students the option of interviewing mothers or other family members and asking about their mothers. Discuss the history of Mother's Day and how it is celebrated in different parts of the world.

Bridging to the Science Activity

Set up a learning center with several different kinds of pleasantly scented objects, such as room deodorizers, sachets, air fresheners, fragrant candles, and soaps. Take care to avoid odors you or your students may be allergic to. Provide students with record sheets and allow them to visit the center in groups to observe the smelly items. They should describe what the item is, what they think its intended use is, and what it smells like.

After all of the students have had a chance to visit the center, discuss the answers to these questions. Use the responses to introduce the concept of how we smell and why different students might have different ideas about the smells.

Part 2: Science Activity

Materials

For the Procedure

Part A, per group of three students

- 3, 35-mm film canisters with lids

  These canisters can often be obtained at no charge from camera stores or photo-processing stores.

- 1 or 2 large cotton balls
- large marshmallow
- dropper
- 1 of the following:
  ○ fragrant oil
  ○ fragrant extract

  We recommend a different fragrance for each group. Be sure to include both oils and extracts. If possible, include herbal and floral fragrances such as lavender and rose, which will make pleasing sachets in Part C.

Part B, per group of three students

- all materials listed for Part A

    The numbers of materials listed are the minimum needed. Depending on the students' experimental design, you may need more.

Part C, per student
- 35-mm film canister with lid
- 1 of the following (determined by students based on Part A):
    ◦ large marshmallow
    ◦ 1 or 2 large cotton balls

Part C, per class
- fragrant oils and/or extracts suitable for sachets
- decorative items, such as the following:
    ◦ sequins, small beads, stickers, or similar items
    ◦ lace
    ◦ rubber bands
    ◦ narrow ribbon
- glue

For the Extension for Further Science Inquiry
- all materials listed for Part A

Safety and Disposal

Some people are allergic to certain fragrances and oils. Avoid using ones you know to be problematic. Also read and follow any safety labels on oil packages; some may be irritating to skin and eyes. No special disposal procedures are required.

Procedure

Part A: The Experiment

1. Divide the class into groups of three. If you have not already discussed the different sachets they observed in the center, do so. Tell students they will want to consider their observations as they design their own sachets made from film canisters. (A sachet is a small packet of perfumed substance often used in drawers or closets to scent clothes.)

2. Tell students they are going to test two variables, fragrance source and absorbent material, in designing their sachets. Ask them to consider the following questions:
    - Does the source of the fragrance matter? For example, do oils work better than extracts, or vice versa?
    - Is it desirable to place the fragrance on an absorbent material, such as a cotton ball or marshmallow? If so, which of the two works better?

3. Have students experiment to determine the answers to these questions as follows:

   a. Give each group a different oil or extract. This will enable the class to observe several different fragrances of each type.

   b. Have students test absorbent materials by putting a cotton ball in the bottom of one canister, putting a marshmallow in the bottom of a second canister, and putting no absorbent material in the third canister. Have them put 5 drops of fragrance in each canister.

   c. Have the groups leave their canisters open for at least two weeks. Have each student in the class record daily his or her ability to smell the scent in each canister. The broad sampling will be valuable because different people have different sensitivities to different odors.

4. Have the students discuss the results. Ask students which fragrances lasted the longest. Were they oils or extracts? Which type of absorbent material held scent the longest?

Part B: Student-Designed Experiment

1. Divide the class into groups of three. Tell the class that they are going to design an experiment to explore two more variables that could affect their film canister sachets. Remind them that all variables besides those being tested must remain constant in order for the experiment to be valid. Ask them to consider the following questions in designing their experiments:
   - Does it make a difference whether the lid is left on or off the canister between smellings?
   - Does it make a difference if the canister is stored in a cold or warm place between smellings?

2. Tell students to discuss their experimental designs and conduct their experiments in their groups. The groups should then share their ideas with the class.

3. Have students conduct their experiments and discuss the results.

Part C: Make the Film Canister Sachet

1. Have students apply what they learned in Part A to make their own film canister sachets to give as gifts to their mothers or other adult female relatives or friends.

   If necessary, encourage students to use fragrances suitable for sachets, such as lavender, rose, or a pleasing fruit smell. While scents like anise are very strong, they do not make pleasant sachets.

2. Have students decorate the canisters using such items as wrapping paper, cloth, and stickers. Sequins, small beads, or other items can be glued on using "tacky" (thick white) glue. A circle of lace about 3 inches in diameter or a square 3 inches x 3 inches can be used to cover the canister. Put the lace over

the opening of the decorated film canister and use a rubber band to hold it in place. A piece of ribbon can be tied over the rubber band to cover it if desired.

Extension for Further Science Inquiry

Investigate other variables, such as the minimum number of drops needed for the smell to last one week in an open canister at room temperature.

Science Explanation

 The following explanation is intended for the teacher's information. Modify the explanation for students as required.

The Science of Smell

All matter is made up of tiny particles. They are so small that you cannot see them; but in some cases you can detect their presence by smell. The fragrant oils and extracts used in this activity contain particles (called molecules) which have certain characteristic odors. Extracts are usually a mixture of several components that have been extracted from a seed, flower, or plant with alcohol or water and then concentrated. The molecules that are responsible for the characteristic odor of the extract are usually fairly volatile, which means they easily vaporize from the liquid state to the gaseous state. The fragrant oils are also mixtures. The molecules responsible for the smells of the oils are not as volatile as those in extracts, and thus the oils keep their odors much longer. Placing an absorbent material in the canister slows the evaporation of the fragrance.

The particles in the extracts and oils typically reach the nose by first evaporating (changing from a liquid to a gas). Once in the gaseous state, the particles travel through the air until they reach the nose. When these smelly particles reach special receptors inside our noses, a series of complex chemical reactions begins that ultimately results in the perception that we smell a particular substance.

Marshmallows seem to hold scent longer than cotton; this could be because of the chemical composition or the physical structure of marshmallows and cotton balls.

The History of Fragrances

Fragrances have been used for at least 6,000 years. Records from ancient Egypt contain many references to the use of scented products. Originally, fragrances were used only in religious rituals. Incense, aromatic oils, and scented unguents were prepared by priests and used in the temples. Egyptian priests were the first to create compound fragrances.

The use of perfumes gradually spread to other cultures and religions, including Hinduism, Buddhism, Shintoism, Islam, Judaism, and Christianity. Despite efforts by priests of all religions to restrict the use of perfumes to worship services, merchants soon started selling fragrances to royalty and nobility, and eventually even common people indulged, if only in cheaper fragrances.

Cleopatra was inventive and extravagant in the use of perfumes; for her first meeting with Mark Antony, she ordered the purple sails of her barge to be drenched with lily oil. Also, she had the floors of her apartments covered 18 inches deep with rose petals. The Roman emperors were also known for their lavish use of scented materials. Saffron, one of the world's most expensive spices, was often strewn in Roman and Greek halls, courts, theaters, and baths. Flowers rained from the ceiling in Nero's state dining room, and silver pipes in the walls sprayed perfume.

During Europe's Middle Ages, herbs were often strewn on floors to release scent when stepped on, and people often carried small bundles of fragrant herbs, since bathing and laundering were uncommon practices. During the 10th century the process of distillation to extract essences was perfected in Arabia. This knowledge was carried back to Europe by the Crusaders between the 11th and 14th centuries. Trade in spices and fragrances with India, China, Japan, Arabia, Egypt, Israel, Persia, Assyria, Greece, and Rome was brisk. In 1370 the first modern perfume, made from rosemary distilled in alcohol, was made for Queen Elizabeth of Hungary. This concoction became known throughout Europe as "Hungary Water."

By the 16th century, techniques for distilling toilet waters and essences from fresh materials were well known in Europe. Essences were extracted from plants by pressing or, in the case of delicate flowers, steeping in oil or wine to release their scents. Many women planted their own herb gardens and dried the materials to use in sachets and potpourri. Sachets were often used to scent clothing and linens and repel insects. Scent in various forms acted as soap, deodorant, detergent, and insect repellent. Pomanders consisting of fragrant materials enclosed in a perforated bag or box were at first carried to protect against disease and infection. Later, they were simply enjoyed for their fragrance and gradually became decorations for the home instead of personal accessories.

References for the Science Activity

Dig Magazine Web Site. Herb Crafting. Potpourri: Makes Scents to Me! http://www.digmagazine.com/94/12-94/scents.htm (accessed 20 Feb 1998).

Frontier Cooperative Herbs Web Site. Herbs. Potpourri—History and Lore. http://www.frontierherb.com/herbs/potpourri/history.html (accessed 20 Feb 1998).

Hériteau, J. *Potpourris and Other Fragrant Delights;* Simon & Schuster: New York, 1973; pp 97–99.

Plummer, B. *Fragrance: How to Make Natural Soaps, Scents, and Sundries;* Atheneum: New York, 1975; pp 28–29.

Sarquis, M. "Identifying Substances by Smell"; *Exploring Matter with TOYS: Using and Understanding the Senses;* McGraw-Hill: New York, 1997; p 135.

The Weaver. Issue No. 6, July 1995. Perfume. http://www.hyperlink.com/weaver/95/25_6/ healing/aromathe/perfume.htm (accessed 23 Feb 1998).

Part 3: Integrating with Language Arts

Featured Fiction Book: *The Mother's Day Mice*

Author: Eve Bunting   Illustrator: Jan Brett
Publisher: Houghton Mifflin   ISBN: 0-8919-387-0
Summary: Three little mouse brothers go into the meadow to find a present for their mother, but the smallest mouse comes up with the most unusual gift of all.

This story contains references to all of the senses. As you read, discuss each reference when you come to it. (For example, after awakening, the mice see one star in the dawn sky; as they cross the meadow, Little Mouse is comforted by the feel of Middle Mouse's tail; the mice can hear piano music coming from the cottage; and the honeysuckle smells wonderful. After the story is finished, discuss the gifts that the mice bring to their mother. What senses do the gifts appeal to? Why did Little Mouse originally want to give his mother honeysuckle? As a class, brainstorm sweet-smelling items that can be given as gifts, such as sachets, perfume, soaps, flowers, and candles.

Writing Extension

- Have students use their science journals to write a summary of the experiment they designed and the results they found.

Additional Books

Fiction

Title: *Happy Mother's Day*
Author: Steven Kroll   Illustrator: Marilyn Hafner
Publisher: Holiday House   ISBN: 0-8234-0504-4
Summary: One day when Mom returns home she is greeted by surprise after surprise from each of her six children and her husband.

Title: *I Love You*
Author: Iris Hiskey Arno   Illustrator: Joan Holub
Publisher: WhistleStop   ISBN: 0-8167-4440-8
Summary: This book describes, in a poetic style, the different jobs a mom can have, from being a stay-at-home mom to being an opera singer.

Title: *I Love You the Purplest*
Author: Barbara M. Joosse   Illustrator: Mary Whyte
Publisher: Chronicle   ISBN: 0-8118-0718-5
Summary: Two boys discover that their mother loves them equally but in
    different ways. While spending the day fishing, they continually seek her
    attention. She expresses that she loves one boy the "reddest," she loves the
    other boy the "bluest," and together she loves them the "purplest."

Title: *Mama, Do You Love Me?*
Author: Barbara M. Joosse   Illustrator: Barbara Lavallee
Publisher: Chronicle   ISBN: 0-87701-759-X
Summary: In an Arctic setting filled with animals, a child learns that a mother's
    love is unconditional. An informative section at the back of the book describes
    the Inuit culture and arctic animals.

Title: *Mucky Moose*
Author: Jonathan Allen
Publisher: Aladdin   ISBN: 0689806515
Summary: Mucky, the muckiest, smelliest moose in the forest, proves that
    smelling bad has its advantages when trying to outwit a fierce wolf.

Nonfiction

Title: *Bizarre and Beautiful Noses*
Author: Santa Fe Writers Group
Publisher: John Muir   ISBN: 1562611240
Summary: Describes the noses and sense of smell of such diverse animals as the
    lemur, turkey vulture, and salmon.

Part 4: Other Lesson Extensions

Art and Music

- Have students make pop-up cards for Mother's Day with pictures of their faces inside the cards. Their "noses" will be the pop-up part. (See Figure 1 below for instructions for cutting the pop-up part of the card.) After the pop-up part of the card is cut out, glue the sheet to a folded piece of paper the same size, being careful not to put glue anywhere on the pop-up nose. The nose should pop up when the card is opened. Use scents from the experiment to scent the card.

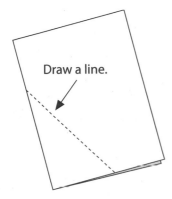

Step 1: Draw a diagonal line from the folded side of a sheet of paper to the bottom of the sheet.

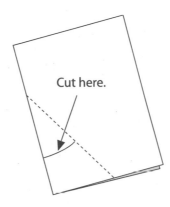

Step 2: Cut a curved line from the folded side to the line drawn in step 1.

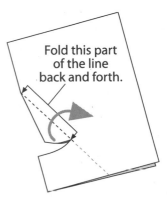

Step 3: Fold the paper back and forth along the line between the fold and the end of the cut.

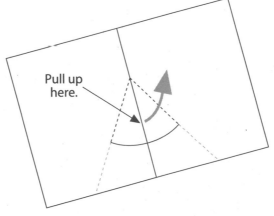

Step 4: Open the card and pull the cut middle pop-up piece toward you. Firmly crease the fold line so the pop-up piece points toward you.

Figure 1: Construct a pop-up nose for a Mother's Day card.

- Have students create a different type of sachet. Have them cut out square or circular pieces of lace about 8–10 inches across and pull up the sides to make a pouch. They can then fill the pouch with potpourri and secure it with a ribbon.

Mathematics

- Count the number of family members in *Happy Mother's Day* (see Part 3, Additional Books) and the number of things each did for the other. Express this data in terms of addition, multiplication, or division, or as a ratio.

Social Studies

- Find out how to say "I love you!" in different languages. Have students make a book entitled, "You Mean the World to Me!" On each page, have the students write a different way to say "I love you!" Students may include maps or names of countries where the languages are spoken.
- Have students share states and countries of origin for their mothers, grandmothers, and great-grandmothers. Mark these locations on a map using sticker dots or Post-it® Notes with the names of the students and their relatives.
- Discuss how distributors of natural gas add a smelly gas to the natural gas (which is odorless) for safety. Discuss what children should and should not do if they smell a natural gas leak. If possible, obtain natural gas smell and sniff cards from a local distributor to help students recognize the smell.

Just for Fun

- Lead students on a "smelling walk" around the school (indoors and outdoors), identifying the different smells they detect.

Part 5: National Science Education Standards

Science as Inquiry Standards:

Abilities Necessary to Do Scientific Inquiry

Students question what combination of fragrances and absorbent materials would hold scent the longest.

Students test different combinations of materials and use their senses to observe the results.

Students use their observations to draw conclusions about which fragrances and absorbent materials work best.

Students discuss their results and conclusions as a class.

Physical Science Standards:

Properties of Objects and Materials

Substances have observable properties, including, in the case of the oils and extracts, smell.

Substances can exist in different states. The oils and extracts gradually change from the liquid to the gas state.

Science and Technology Standards:

Abilities of Technological Design

Students question how to make the best film canister sachet.

Students design ways to test variables such as the number of drops of oil or extract needed.

Students work in small groups to test their designs.

Students evaluate their test results and those of other students and modify their designs as appropriate.

Students share their results and conclusions with the class.

History and Nature of Science Standards:

Science as a Human Endeavor

Technologies for making things smell good have existed for thousands of years.

Father's Day

Third Sunday in June
Culture: United States and others (different dates)

In Spokane, Washington, in 1909, a woman named Sonora Smart Dodd was listening to a Mother's Day sermon in her church, but her thoughts were on her father. Her mother had died when Sonora was very young, and William Smart had raised his six children on his own. Sonora felt that fathers should have a special day of recognition like mothers had, and she spoke with her minister. Together, they contacted other ministers in Spokane, and in 1910 the first Father's Day was observed on the third Sunday in June, the month of William Smart's birth. William Jennings Bryan, noted orator and politician, was one of the earliest supporters of Father's Day, saying, "too much emphasis cannot be placed upon the relations between parent and child."

Father's Day observances spread slowly throughout the country, and many cities honored fathers without realizing Sonora Smart Dodd had started the tradition. President Woodrow Wilson officially approved Father's Day in 1916, but two years later the day took on a special meaning. November 24, 1918 was "Father's Day," a day when fathers wrote letters to their sons in the fields of World War I France, and soldiers wrote to their fathers. Special arrangements were made to ensure the speedy delivery of these letters.

The National Father's Day Committee (now called the Father's Day Council, Inc.) was established in 1936 to coordinate activities for Father's Day, including a banquet held annually in New York City. At the banquet, the Council announces its Father of the Year award winner and honors the achievements of other fathers who have made special contributions to their children. In 1956, a Joint Resolution of Congress recognized Father's Day, but it wasn't until 1972 that the permanent observance of the holiday was established. President Richard Nixon signed the proclamation stating that the third Sunday in June, the day of the first Father's Day in 1910, was reserved for Father's Day in the United States.

More than 20 countries around the world celebrate Father's Day, although not necessarily on the same day as we do in the United States. For example, some Yugoslavians celebrate Ochichi, or Father's Day, on the last Sunday before Christmas. Children tie their father to his bed or a chair and do not release him until he has bought his way out of bondage by promising substantial gifts for Christmas. Fathers, however, also get their chance to play this game two Sundays before Ochichi on Dechiyi Dan, or Children's Day. Both parents tie their children up and do not release them until they promise to be good in the coming year. A corresponding holiday for mothers is held two Sundays before Christmas. Mothers buy their freedom by promising candy and small treats, while the next week the fathers must promise bigger gifts.

References

Hatch, J.M. *The American Book of Days,* 3rd ed.; H.W. Wilson: New York, 1978; pp 574–575.

http://www.zia.com/holidays/father/history (accessed May 1997).

Spicer, D.G. *The Book of Festivals;* Women's Press: New York, 1937; p 344.

Father's Day Thaumatropes

Father's Day is a time to celebrate the many contributions fathers make to their families. Cards and gifts are appropriate symbols of appreciation. In this activity, students make thaumatropes (spinning persistence-of-vision toys) and design their own thaumatrope greeting cards, which double as gifts.

Key Science Topic

- persistence of vision

Time Required

Setup	30	minutes
Performance	30–45	minutes
Cleanup	10	minutes

A Bird in a Cage thaumatrope

Part 1: Building Bridges

Building Student Knowledge and Motivation

Create a reading center containing flip books and resource books on movie making and animation. Include a log sheet in the center for students to list one or more interesting facts they found in the resource books and the names of their favorite movies and animated cartoons. Ask the students if they go to movies with their fathers. Have them ask their fathers if they like cartoons, and if so, which cartoons are their favorite. If desired, give students an opportunity to view an animated cartoon made in the 1920s or 1930s. From about 1913 into the 1920s the "Mutt and Jeff" series of silent cartoons was very popular. One of the best-known cartoons from this period is Disney's "Steamboat Willie," the first cartoon with sound. You may find other titles at a library or video store, or you could search an online catalog such as the Internet Movie Database (http://us.imdb.com/).

Bridging to the Science Activity

Ask students how many of them enjoy movies and animated cartoons. See if anyone knows approximately when movies and animated cartoons were first offered to the public for entertainment. Have them figure out whether movies and cartoons were around when their parents were young. How about grandparents and great-grandparents? Explain that before movies and cartoons were available, children enjoyed entertainments that were similar in some ways to movies and animated cartoons. Ask, "Did you see anything on the center table that was similar to movies and cartoons?" *Flip books.* Explain to the students that they will be making toys called thaumatropes, which are related to flip books, and using them as special Father's Day cards.

Part 2: Science Activity

Materials

For Getting Ready

You will make one Bird in a Cage thaumatrope to show the class and prepare materials for students to assemble their own in Part A of the Procedure.

Per class and per group
- Thaumatrope Pattern (provided at the end of this lesson)
- tagboard or manila folder larger than the Thaumatrope Pattern
- Bird in a Cage Pattern (provided at the end of this lesson)
- scissors
- glue or tape
- single-hole punch
- 4 self-adhesive hole reinforcers
- 2 narrow rubber bands

For the Procedure

Part A, per class
- completed Bird in a Cage thaumatrope (prepared in Getting Ready)

Part A, per group
- half-completed Bird in a Cage thaumatrope (prepared in Getting Ready)
- cut-out bird art (prepared in Getting Ready)
- tape

Part B, per student
- tagboard or manila folder big enough to trace the Thaumatrope Pattern onto
- pencil
- 4 self-adhesive hole reinforcers
- scrap paper
- 2 narrow rubber bands

Part B, per group
- Thaumatrope Pattern (provided at the end of this lesson)
- scissors
- markers and/or crayons
- single-hole punch
- tape

For the Extensions for Further Science Inquiry

 For the items below, see Part 4, Resources, for a list of books and suppliers.

❶ Per class
- flip book
- examples or pictures of other persistence-of-vision toys, such as zoetropes and phenakistascopes

❷ Per class
- pictures of segments of animated cartoon film

❸ Per class
- computer software for making flip books

Safety and Disposal

No special safety or disposal procedures are required.

Getting Ready

1. Make and practice using one Bird in a Cage thaumatrope as follows:

   a. Cut out the Thaumatrope Pattern. Trace it onto tagboard or a manila folder and cut it out.

b. Cut out the Bird in a Cage Pattern (birdcage art for the front and bird art for the back). Be sure to cut out the complete circle, because you will need to line up the small holes.

c. Glue the birdcage art to one side of the tagboard circle. Use the hole punch to make holes in the tagboard as indicated by the birdcage art. Make holes in the paper circle containing the bird art.

d. Lay the tagboard circle with the birdcage art face down. Lay the paper circle with the bird art on back of the tagboard circle and orient the punched holes to match. Make sure the bird will be right-side-up in the cage when flipped. Glue the bird art in place.

e. Apply self-adhesive hole reinforcers to the punched holes on both sides of the thaumatrope.

f. Push a narrow rubber band through each pre-punched hole in the circle. Pass one end of each rubber band through the loop in the other end and pull until the knot is firm against the edge of the circle. Don't pull so hard that the circle is bent.

The rubber bands are used for convenience only. Do not stretch the rubber bands, just rotate them as described in step g.

g. Grasp the rubber bands between the thumb and forefinger of each hand, about ¼ inch away from the edge of the circle. Roll the rubber bands back and forth quickly. The bird will appear to be inside the cage.

2. Prepare Bird in a Cage thaumatropes for Part A of the Procedure.

a. Use the thaumatrope pattern to cut one tagboard circle for each group of three or four students.

b. Cut out the birdcage art for the front, being sure to cut out the complete circle. Glue or tape the birdcage art to one side of the tagboard circle. Use the hole punch to make holes in the tagboard as indicated.

c. Push a narrow rubber band through each pre-punched hole in the circle. Pass one end of each rubber band through the loop in the other end and pull until the knot is firm against the edge of the circle. Don't pull so hard that the circle is bent.

d. Cut out the bird art so that the circle is about three inches in diameter and excludes the marks indicating the hole punches.

By doing this, you are removing clues that would provide an easy solution to the challenge in Part A of the procedure.

Procedure

Part A: Observing the Thaumatrope

1. Show students the cage side of the completed Bird in a Cage thaumatrope you made in Getting Ready. Ask them to name the object they see. *Birdcage.*

2. Demonstrate what happens when you rapidly spin the thaumatrope back and forth. Make sure all students have a chance to see the thaumatrope in action, but do not let them closely examine the side with the bird. Ask students to describe what they saw when the thaumatrope was turning. *A bird appeared in the cage.*

3. Ask students where they think the bird came from. Through a facilitated discussion, bring out the idea that the picture of the bird was on the back of the thaumatrope, but do not let students closely examine it.

4. Tell students that each group will get a circle with a birdcage on the front and rubber bands attached, and a picture of a bird. Explain that the challenge is for each group to get the bird to appear right-side-up and inside the cage when the thaumatrope is turned, just as yours did. Point out that it might be helpful for them to tape the bird lightly in the test position until their designs have been tested and the correct location found.

➤ *The bird will be easy to reposition if students use very little tape and press it down very lightly. A data sheet like the one shown in Figure 1 will help students keep track of trials and outcomes.*

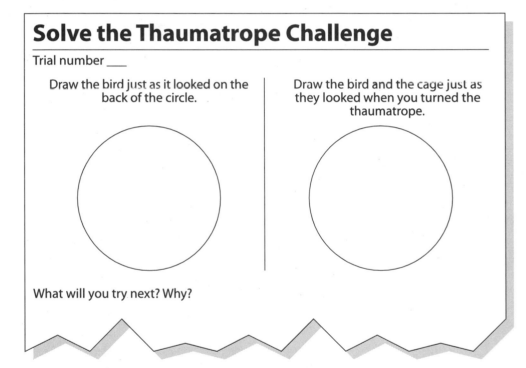

Figure 1: Make student data sheets for students to track trials and outcomes.

5. Allow the groups to test their designs until all have solved the problem.

6. Have each group briefly share what they did to find the solution to the problem.

7. Ask, "Why do you think we see both pictures when the thaumatrope turns?" Have students brainstorm ideas about how the thaumatrope might work and record these ideas on a science chart or chalkboard, but do not provide any explanations at this time.

Part B: Designing a Thaumatrope Father's Day Card

1. Tell students that they will use what they discovered about making thaumatropes to design a special Father's Day card. Part of the card will show on the front of the circle, and part of the card will appear when the circle is quickly turned.

2. Have students begin by tracing the Thaumatrope Pattern on a piece of scrap paper. Instruct students to make a simple sketch of how they want the thaumatrope card to look *while it is spinning*. Emphasize that this is only a planning sketch. Have them use one color for the parts they plan to draw on the front of the thaumatrope and another color for the parts they plan to draw on the back.

    You may want to provide a sample sketch and finished card to illustrate the process. One of the patterns provided already contains some text. This pattern may be more convenient for young children. The second pattern is completely blank to allow for more creative freedom. Although students should have creative freedom in designing their cards, they will find their cards much easier to complete if the items they plan to draw on the back of the thaumatrope are fairly simple and concentrated in one area. (See Figure 2.)

Figure 2: Have students sketch out their thaumatrope designs. In the examples above, the pictures would appear on one side and the text on the other.

3. Review the designs to help students avoid any serious problems with their thaumatropes.

4. Have each student use the Thaumatrope Pattern to make a 4-inch circle from tagboard or a manila folder. Then have students punch holes in the circles. Explain that the position of the holes is very important and that they should use the pattern as a guide for punching them. Instruct students to reinforce the holes with the self-adhesive reinforcers.

5. Have students draw and color the fronts of their thaumatropes, using their sketches as a guide.

6. Have students cut out pieces of paper just large enough to contain the drawings or words they planned for the backs of their thaumatropes. Have students draw and color these small pieces of paper, *not the backs of the cardboard circles*.

7. Show the students how to loop the rubber bands through the punched holes.

8. Have students lightly tape the drawings from step 6 on the backs of their thaumatropes and test them by spinning the thaumatropes. Instruct them to adjust the position of the drawings until they are satisfied with the result and then tape them permanently in place. The cards are now complete.

9. Give students a chance to look at other students' cards. Come back to the brainstormed list of ideas about how thaumatropes work. As a class, discuss how these ideas could be tested scientifically. Tell students that if they could conduct scientific tests, they would find out that the thaumatrope works like this: Our brains cause us to see an image of an object a fraction of a second after the object is gone. This is called persistence of vision. When objects are moving rapidly, such as the pictures on the turning thaumatrope, we may experience the illusion of seeing more than one object at a time. Explain that movies and animated cartoons depend on persistence of vision too.

Extensions for Further Science Inquiry

- Point out that for persistence of vision to be observed, two or more objects must be moving quickly in front of your eyes. Ask, "When we used the thaumatrope, how did that happen?" *We twirled it back and forth with the rubber bands.* Demonstrate a flip book. "How do the pictures move in front of our eyes with a flip book?" *You thumb through the pages and they flip along quickly.* If possible, demonstrate or show students pictures of other old-fashioned persistence of vision toys such as zoetropes and phenakistoscopes. (See Part 4, Resources, for suppliers of these items.) Discuss how each device enables the pictures to move past the eye quickly.
- Show students pictures of a segment of animated cartoon film. (See Part 4, Resources, for a list of books that contain examples.) Discuss how this film is similar and/or different from flip books. Discuss how animated cartoon pictures move quickly in front of our eyes. If possible, show a videotape of the making of an animated feature.
- Have students make their own flip books using special computer software. One program, called FlipBook™, is available for Macintosh from S.H. Pierce & Co., Suite 323, Building 600, One Kendall Square, Cambridge, MA 02139; 617/338-2222 (voice), 617/338-2223 (fax).

Science Explanation

 The following explanation is intended for the teacher's information. Modify the explanation for students as required.

The illusion of the bird appearing inside the cage (as well as the illusion of motion in movies, animated cartoons, and flip books) is caused by a phenomenon called persistence of vision. Your retina contains millions of molecules of retinal, a molecule that can exist in two different forms. One of the forms (cis-retinal) exists when no light is present, and the other (trans-retinal) is created when light is present.

In the activity, the light reflected from the cage side of the thaumatrope disk hits cis-retinal molecules in an area of your retina, quickly converting them to trans-retinal and triggering your brain to form an image of the cage. The trans-retinal form lingers briefly, causing the image of the cage to remain even after the disk turns to the bird side. This lingering is responsible for the persistence of vision we experience. After a few seconds, the trans-retinal is converted back to cis-retinal. However, in the interim, additional light is reflected from the bird side of the disk and hits a different part of your retina, and the transformation of cis-retinal to trans-retinal occurs. The process continues over and over as long as light is reflected off the turning thaumatrope. The persistence of one image (the cage) while another appears (the bird) creates the illusion (of the bird in the cage) that is seen when the thaumatrope is turned.

Reference for the Science Activity

Sarquis, M. "Bird in a Cage"; *Science Is Fun: A Handbook for Challenging Students of All Grades with Hands-on Science;* Terrific Science Press: Middletown, OH, 1990.

Part 3: Integrating with Language Arts

Featured Fiction Book: *A Perfect Father's Day*

Author: Eve Bunting   Illustrator: Susan Meddaugh
Publisher: Clarion   ISBN: 0-395-66416-0
Summary: When four-year-old Susie treats her father to a series of special activities for Father's Day, they just happen to be all of her own favorite things.

Before reading the story, have students list things they like to do with their father or father-figure. Read the story and compare activities from the story with the activities that the students listed. Discuss and list the characteristics of the father in the story. Have students list characteristics that describe their own fathers or father-figures. Use a Venn diagram to compare and contrast the characteristics of the two lists.

Writing Extensions

- Have students write a note to go with the Father's Day card, explaining how they made it and how to use it.
- Have students brainstorm things they would like to do like their fathers (or another man they know personally and admire). Read and discuss *Just Like My Dad* (see Additional Books). Have students create a book that parallels the story.

- Read and discuss *My Dad Is Awesome* (see Additional Books). Have students create their own books about why their dads are awesome. Students may give the books to their fathers as a gift.

Additional Books

Fiction

Title: *Come Home Soon, Baba*
Author: Janie Hampton
Illustrator: Jenny Bent
Publisher: Peter Bedrick
ISBN: 0-87226-511-0
Summary: Set in a small village in Zimbabwe, this wonderful story depicts rural African life and the love of a young boy for his father.

Title: *Daddy Calls Me Man*
Author: Angela Johnson
Illustrator: Rhonda Mitchell
Publisher: Orchard
ISBN: 0531300420
Summary: Four short verses about the happy home life of a young African-American boy. Family love and the shared stories and symbols that connect the generations are pervasive themes.

Title: *Daddy Played Music for the Cows*
Author: Maryann Weidt
Illustrator: Henri Sorensen
Publisher: Lothrop, Lee and Shepard
ISBN: 0-688-10057-0
Summary: A young girl grows up on a farm to the sound of music that her father plays from the barn. This book shows the special love and bond between a country child and her father.

Title: *Just Like My Dad*
Author: Tricia Gardella
Illustrator: Margot Apple
Publisher: HarperCollins
ISBN: 0-06-443463-X
Summary: A young child glories in the sights, sounds, smells, and activities of a day spent working on a cattle ranch as a cowhand, just like Dad.

Title: *Just My Dad and Me*
Author: Laura Geringer
Illustrator: Jeffrey Greene
Publisher: HarperCollins
ISBN: 0-06-024573-5
Summary: When other family members infringe on what she had hoped would be a special day with her father, a young girl imagines herself alone with fish that look like her family members. Glad at first to escape them all, she finds it is lonely and returns to the surface of the water and into her father's arms.

Title: *My Dad Is Awesome*
Author: Nick Butterworth
Publisher: Candlewick
ISBN: 1-56402-033-9
Summary: A young boy describes what makes his father awesome.

Title: *My Father*
Author: Judy Collins   Illustrator: Jane Dyer
Publisher: Little, Brown   ISBN: 0-316-15238-2
Summary: A shared dream carries family members out of their drab lives into a
    finer world of music and travel, a dream later fulfilled by the youngest
    daughter when she becomes a parent herself.

Nonfiction

Title: *Animal Dads*
Author: Sneed B. Collard, III   Illustrator: Steve Jenkins
Publisher: Houghton Mifflin   ISBN: 0395836212
Summary: Explores the various roles of fathers in the animal kingdom, from the
    emperor penguin that watches over eggs to a wolf that leads his pack hunting
    to the male seahorse that incubates his eggs inside a special belly pouch.

Part 4: Other Lesson Extensions

Art and Music

- Research the history of the thaumatrope and animated cartoons.
- As a class, discuss and list the hobbies of various fathers. Have students make
  another thaumatrope depicting a scene of their father's favorite hobby (for
  example, for an avid fisherman, the thaumatrope could show a fish on one
  side and a pond on the other). Alternatively, students could create a flip book
  showing their father's favorite pastime (for example, a golf swing).
- Have students learn the song "My Father," found in the book *My Father* (see
  Part 3, Additional Books).
- Show students the cover of *Daddy Played Music for the Cows* (see Part 3,
  Additional Books). Discuss why the book has this title. Read the story and
  compare results to predictions. In the story, the girl has a corn rattle that she
  plays along with her dad. Have students make birdseed rattles of their own to
  play as they sing a Father's Day song of their own composition.

Mathematics

- Review the concept of persistence of vision and how flip books utilize the
  phenomenon. Introduce the mathematics concept of transformations,
  including translations (slides), reflections (flips), and rotations (turns). Focus on
  the concept of translations in flip books. Demonstrate on grid paper how
  transformations can be created with various geometric figures. Have students
  create their own transformations using grid paper.

Social Studies

- Discuss how the term "father" is used in different instances, such as "the Father of our Country" and "Father Time." Have students research "fathers" of various inventions and discoveries and present their findings.
- Generate a list of the states and countries of origin of the fathers, grandfathers, and great-grandfathers of all students in the class. Mark a map with sticker dots or Post-it® Notes with the names of students and their relatives.

Resources

If you would like to investigate optical toys and illusions further, many resources are available to help you. Below are listed some resource books and mail-order suppliers of optical toys and kits.

Books

Title: *Disney's Animation Magic: A Behind-the-Scenes Look at How an Animated Film is Made*
Author: Don Hahn
Publisher: Hyperion   ISBN: 0786830727
Summary: This book describes the creative process behind Disney's animated classics, including story development and animation, and it contains hundreds of illustrations from the Disney archives.

Title: *How to Make Optical Illusion Tricks and Toys*
Author: Richard Churchill
Publisher: Sterling   ISBN: 0806968699
Summary: Presents more than 60 optical illusions that include tricks, drawings, and toys that can be assembled.

Suppliers

Optical Toys
RR5, Box 387
Brattleboro, VT 05346
Tel/Fax 802/254-6115
Or e-mail the owner, Andy Voda, at avoda@together.net

S.H. Pierce & Co. (This company produces the FlipBook software.)
Suite 323, Building 600
One Kendall Square
Cambridge, MA 02139
617/338-2222 (voice)
617/338-2223 (fax)

Part 5: National Science Education Standards

Science as Inquiry Standards:

Abilities Necessary to Do Scientific Inquiry

Students question why they see both pictures superimposed when the thaumatrope turns and how to position the two pictures so that this is possible.

Students plan how to position the two pictures, test their positions, and refine them as necessary.

Students manipulate the thaumatrope, cutting, connecting, punching, tying, and turning the components.

Students propose an explanation of how the thaumatrope works based on observations of their test model.

Students share their thaumatrope designs and results with the class.

Physical Science Standards:

Position and Motion of Objects

The motion of the two sides of the thaumatrope can be described by observing the thaumatrope over time.

Pushing on the rubber bands causes the thaumatrope to spin.

Science and Technology Standards:

Abilities of Technological Design

Students question how to draw two pictures that will superimpose well for their Father's Day thaumatrope.

Students design pictures that will produce an attractive combined image.

Students use their designs to produce thaumatropes.

Students evaluate their products as well as those of other students and modify their designs accordingly.

Students share their designs and products and relate them to the way a thaumatrope works.

History and Nature of Science Standards:

Science as a Human Endeavor

Thaumatropes and other similar optical-illusion motion toys have been around since the early 1800s and led to the development of cinematography and animation.

Bird in a Cage Pattern

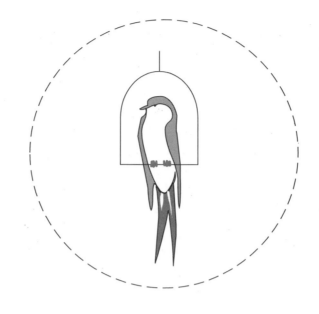

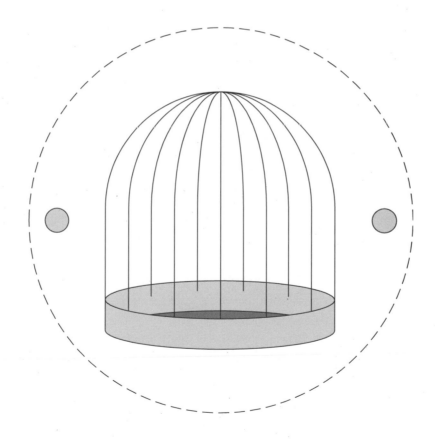

Thaumatrope Pattern

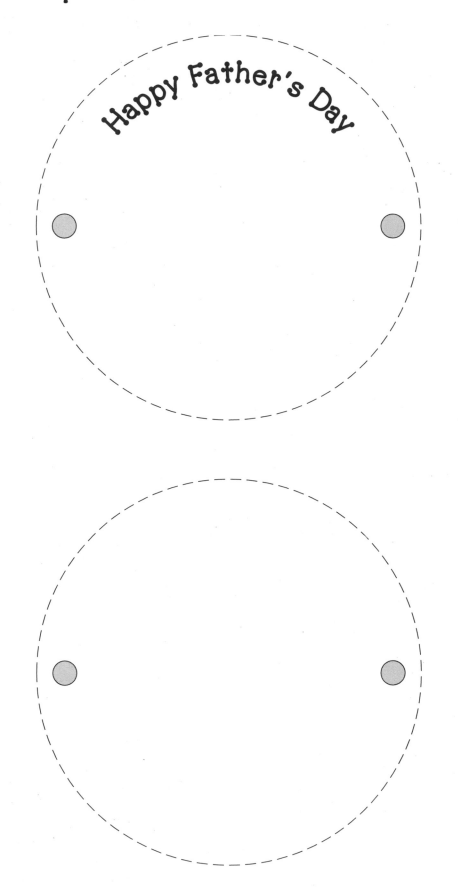

Happy Father's Day

Summer

For millions of school children across America, summer begins when the last school bell rings, heralding the start of the warmest season of the year. Astronomically, summer begins when the sun reaches its maximum and minimum declinations of ±23°27′. The "declination" of the sun is the latitude line on the earth where the sun appears to be directly overhead at noon. Latitude is measured from the equator and runs from 0° (the Equator) to 90° (the North Pole) in the northern hemisphere, and from 0° to -90° (the South Pole) in the southern hemisphere. On June 21, the sun is directly over the latitude line at 23°27′—the Tropic of Cancer—and summer begins for the northern hemisphere. Six months later, on December 22, the sun is directly over the latitude line at -23°27′—the Tropic of Capricorn—and summer begins for the southern hemisphere.

Depending on your location on the Earth, the sun appears in different places in the sky. For most people in the United States, the sun appears high in the sky (but not directly overhead) because most of the United States is near the Tropic of Cancer, which lies just south of Florida. Hawaii lies on or near the Tropic of Cancer, so the sun there is directly overhead during the summer. Alaska is much farther north, and the sun does not appear as high in the sky. During winter in the United States, the sun appears lower in the sky, because the Tropic of Capricorn is below the equator, farther away from the United States. Thus, in Alaska, the sun is much lower, sometimes rising only a little higher than the horizon.

The summer solstice for the northern hemisphere occurs about June 22, halfway between the vernal and autumnal equinoxes. At the solstice, the changes in the times of sunrise and sunset are almost imperceptible, and the sun is said to "stand still" for the next few days. (The term "solstice" is derived from the Latin words "sol," meaning "sun," and "sistere," meaning "to stand still.") This is because the Earth is at its aphelion—its farthest point from the sun—and travels more slowly at this point in its orbit. At the summer solstice in the northern hemisphere, the hours of daylight are the longest of the year. After the summer solstice, the days begin to grow shorter until the winter solstice (about December 22), when the hours of daylight are the shortest of the year. At the vernal and autumnal equinoxes, halfway between the solstices, day and night are the same length.

During the summer season of each hemisphere, that hemisphere's pole is tilted toward the sun, and the sun's rays hit the hemisphere directly—almost perpendicular to the surface. More solar radiation is absorbed by that hemisphere, and temperatures rise. Warmer temperatures coupled with longer periods of daylight make summer the prime growing season. Thus, ancient cultures often personified summer as a woman carrying sheaves of grain or other crops, symbolic of the abundant growth associated with the season. Ancient agricultural societies held festivals to celebrate the warmth and growth of summertime, and people would also take time to relax after the long planting season and before the strenuous harvests of the fall. Although summer festivals are no longer observed in most parts of the world, summer is still reserved for rest, relaxation, and enjoyment of the warm weather.

In the northern hemisphere, the hottest weather usually occurs in late July and August, the "dog days of summer." These days were named for Sirius, the "dog star." Sirius is the "eye" of the constellation Canus Major (the "Large Dog"), which rises high in the sky during the late summer months. As fall approaches, temperatures decrease, but sometimes they rise again in September or October, reaching summer-like highs. In the United States, this time is called "Indian Summer," because the early European settlers observed the Native Americans gathering more winter stores during these heat waves. The Native Americans would act as if it were summer and take advantage of the warm weather. In England, this autumn warming is called "All Hallown Summer," because it occurs during the season of All Hallow's Eve, or Halloween.

References

Hatch, J.M. *The American Book of Days,* 3rd ed.; H.W. Wilson: New York, 1978.

"Indian Summer" *Britannica Online.* http://www.eb.com:180/cgi-bin/g?DocF=micro/289/62.html (accessed 25 Sept 1997).

"Summer" *Britannica Online.* http://www.eb.com:180/cgi-bin/g?DocF=micro/572/77.html (accessed 25 Sept 1997).

Hot Summer Days and Those Cool Shades

The sunshine of summer is one of the most enjoyable things about the season. However, besides visible light, sunshine also contains other kinds of radiation, such as ultraviolet (UV) radiation, that can be harmful to humans. To protect ourselves, we often include sunglasses and sunscreen as part of our summertime equipment. In this activity, students observe the effect of UV radiation on UV-sensitive beads and light-sensitive paper and discover that sunglasses can block the sun's rays.

Key Science Topics

- chemical changes
- light

Time Required

Setup	5–10	minutes
Performance	20–40	minutes
Cleanup	5	minutes

Sunglasses, sun-sensitive paper, and
UV-detecting beads

Part 1: Building Bridges

Building Student Knowledge and Motivation

Since students are typically on vacation from school during summer, you may want to introduce this celebration of warm, sunny days before summer break or when school starts up for the year in late summer. If this is done, the lesson could incorporate student stories about their summer holidays.

Prior to the lesson, create a learning center containing items that are characteristic of summer. Be sure to include sunglasses in the display. Let students bring in any items they may have to add to the collection. Tell the students that when they visit the center they should look for recurring symbols associated with summer.

Bridging to the Science Activity

Ask students if they have sunglasses at home. If possible, suggest that students bring in old sunglasses from home, after getting permission to do so. (Tag all samples to facilitate returning them to their rightful owners.) Explore reasons why people wear sunglasses. Make a chart of who wears sunglasses, when they wear them, where they wear them, and what different colors sunglasses come in. Ask students in what season people are most likely to wear sunglasses.

While many types of sunglasses simply use dark lenses to reduce the amount of visible light that can reach the eyes, some types of sunglasses are treated with special chemicals that absorb the harmful ultraviolet (UV) wavelengths. UV-absorbing glasses provide more protection than lenses that are merely dark. Tell students that in the science activity they will determine whether the sunglasses the class has collected are UV blockers or not.

Part 2: Science Activity

Materials

For Getting Ready

- 5 ultraviolet- (UV-) detecting beads of assorted colors

  Ultraviolet-detecting beads (#UV-ast) are available from Educational Innovations, Inc. 151 River Road, Cos Cob, CT 06807; 203/629-6049, Fax 203/629-2739. Colors in the 240-bead assortment include red, yellow, orange, blue, and purple.

- 8-inch piece of pipe cleaner

For the Procedure

Parts A and B, per group
- 1 of each of the following:
  - UV-absorbing sunglasses
  - non-UV-absorbing sunglasses
  - (optional) variety of other sunglasses (UV-absorbing or not) of another type, such as gradient, mirror, polarized, or prescription

    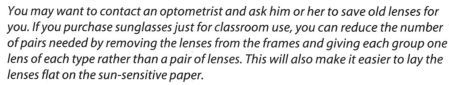

    You may want to contact an optometrist and ask him or her to save old lenses for you. If you purchase sunglasses just for classroom use, you can reduce the number of pairs needed by removing the lenses from the frames and giving each group one lens of each type rather than a pair of lenses. This will also make it easier to lay the lenses flat on the sun-sensitive paper.

Part A, per group
- access to incandescent or fluorescent lights

Part A, per student
- UV-detecting bead bracelet prepared in Getting Ready
- (optional) book or other opaque object to cover UV beads

Part B, per student or group
- 3–4 pieces of sun-sensitive paper

    Sun-sensitive paper is available in toy stores and nature stores or from Solargraphics, P.O. Box 7091, Berkeley, CA 94707; 800/327-9869 or 415/525-1776.

- small opaque objects such as keys, coins, pencils, and leaves
- stopwatch or wristwatch with a second hand
- wide, shallow container (such as a pie plate, small tub, or large bowl)
- water

For the Extensions for Further Science Inquiry
1. all materials listed for Part A or Part B
2. all materials listed for Part B
3. all materials listed for Part B plus the following:
   - plastic and glass prescription sunglasses
   - regular prescription glasses

Safety and Disposal

Instruct students not to lay the sunglasses on concrete or other rough surfaces with the lenses down. Remind students never to look directly at the sun, as it can cause permanent eye damage. No special disposal procedures are required.

Getting Ready

For Part A

String five ultraviolet-detecting beads (one of each color) on each 8-inch piece of pipe cleaner. Twist the ends of the pipe cleaner together to make a loose bracelet.

For Part B

Fill a wide, shallow pan with water. If the sunglasses are a cheap pair for classroom use only (not belonging to anyone), you may want to remove one or both lenses from the frame; this will reduce the number of pairs of glasses needed and make it easier to lay the lenses flat on the sun-sensitive paper. To save money, you may also wish to cut the sun-sensitive paper in half.

Procedure

Part A: Using Ultraviolet-Detecting Beads

1. Before going outside, distribute UV-detecting bead bracelets to all students. Have them observe the beads and record their observations. *Inside, the beads should appear to be plain white or possibly very pale in color.*

2. Take the class outside and have students observe the beads on their bracelets as they walk. (Do not walk far from the door.) Students should observe that the beads changed colors quickly—in fact, the beads probably changed within seconds after the students walked outside. Lead the students back inside the building and have them observe their beads as they walk. Discuss what happened to the beads after they were removed from the UV light source. *The color faded when the beads were removed from UV light.* Have students record their observations.

3. Ask students what they think might have caused these color changes. Accept all suggestions but do not give the answer yet.

4. Ask students if they can think of any other examples of objects that change color outside. Lead students to remember that, in some cases, people's skin can change color if they are outdoors for a long time during the day. Ask students if they have ever heard of someone getting a suntan indoors. If they say no, ask them if they have ever seen or heard of tanning lamps. Ask them how these lamps are different from regular lights such as the ones in your school building. Discuss the idea that tanning lights give off a special kind of light called ultraviolet light, which is also contained in sunlight. The standard lights used in schools or at home do not produce UV light—they are probably either incandescent or fluorescent lights. Ask students if they observed the beads changing color under incandescent or fluorescent lights.

5. Challenge the students to design an experiment to answer the question of whether the beads change color in incandescent and fluorescent light. Listen to their ideas and then have them try the best ideas. Be sure you and they

follow proper safety precautions. (You may want to direct them or help them by suggesting that they cover their bracelets with one hand, a book, or another opaque object for 10–15 seconds. On your signal, have them uncover their bracelets and observe the beads again.)

6. Have students develop an experiment using the beads to identify which of a set of two lenses is a UV blocker and which is not. One idea is to have each student hold one lens across his or her bracelet so that all light reaching the beads passes through the lens. Have students walk outside, continuing to hold their lenses over the beads. After about 10–15 seconds, have students carefully raise their lenses and quickly observe the beads. Discuss results.

> *Students may have some trouble at first positioning the lens so that all light striking the beads passes through the lens. If any sunlight strikes the beads directly, the results will not be valid. Have students practice this step several times to perfect their technique so that they can achieve consistent results.*

7. Have students repeat step 6 with another type of lens and compare the results.

Part B: Using Light-Sensitive Paper

Divide the class into groups, give each group one sunglass lens, and have students make sun prints according to the following procedure:

1. Remove a piece of sun-sensitive paper from the package. Keeping the colored side up, quickly place one or more small, opaque objects on the paper. Place the paper in direct sunlight for 2–5 minutes, until the paper fades to a very pale color—almost white. Time the exposure using a stopwatch or wristwatch with a second hand and record the time.

> *Objects must be placed very quickly on the paper, so plan ahead what objects you will use and where you will put them.*

2. Remove the objects from the paper and immediately rinse the paper in a pan of water in the shade for 1–2 minutes. Set the paper aside to dry in the shade. If necessary, set a small weight on the paper to keep it from blowing away.

3. Remove another piece of sun-sensitive paper from the package. Keeping the colored side up, quickly place a regular (non-UV-absorbing) sunglass lens on the paper. Place the paper in direct sunlight for exactly the same length of time as you did the first piece. Then rinse the paper as described in step 2.

4. Remove a third piece of sun-sensitive paper from the package. Keeping the colored side up, quickly place a UV-absorbing sunglass lens on the paper. Place the paper in direct sunlight for exactly the same length of time as you did the first piece. Then rinse the paper as described in step 2.

5. (optional) To show that other external conditions (such as temperature and wind) are not the controlling factor, the following trial can be used as a blank. Remove a fourth piece of sun-sensitive paper from the package. This time keep the paper colored side down and quickly place it in direct sunlight for exactly the same length of time as you did the first piece. Then rinse the paper as described in step 2.

6. After the prints have dried, compare them. Are the prints made using UV-absorbing sunglasses different from the prints made with non-UV-absorbing sunglasses? How do the prints of the sunglass lenses compare to the prints made using the opaque objects? If you did step 5, how do the first three trials compare with the last one? Discuss reasons for differences or similarities.

Part C: Tying It Together

Have students work in groups to evaluate the results of both the UV-bead and sun-sensitive paper tests. Have them make recommendations on the best type of sunglasses to purchase.

Extensions for Further Science Inquiry

- Do a time study, allowing the object being tested to cover the UV-detecting beads or sunprint paper for different periods of time. Compare results to determine whether a pattern exists. Test the same covering object for 30 seconds, 60 seconds, 90 seconds, and so on.
- Try using the sun-sensitive paper in different places and conditions, such as in the classroom, in the shade, on a cloudy day, and on a window sill. Compare the results.
- Does it make any difference whether the sunglass lenses are plastic or glass? What about regular prescription glasses? Do they block out sunlight as sunglasses do? Have students design experiments to answer these questions.
- Have students investigate health problems associated with sunburns.

Science Explanation

The following explanation is intended for the teacher's information. Modify the explanation for students as required.

Ultraviolet light is part of the electromagnetic spectrum. The electromagnetic spectrum includes all types of light energy—visible light, radio waves, infrared radiation, etc. The UV region of this spectrum includes light energy with wavelengths that are just longer than the x-ray region, to about 380 nanometers, just shorter than the violet radiation in the visible spectrum. (A nanometer is 10^{-9} m; one trillionth of a meter.)

UV radiation is present in sunlight but can also be produced artificially in arc lamps; "black lights" produce long-wavelength UV radiation (about 365 nanometers). While most of the UV component of sunlight is absorbed by the ozone layer of the atmosphere, some still reaches the Earth's surface. UV radiation is often classified into two kinds: UV-B radiation (280–320 nanometers) and UV-A radiation (320–400 nanometers). UV-B is the component identified to cause sunburns; it has also been linked to skin cancer.

The UV-detecting beads contain pigments that change color when exposed to ultraviolet light from the sun or other UV source. The beads become purple, red, orange, yellow, or blue depending on their original pigmentation. The beads are not affected by visible light and thus remain white indoors or when shielded from UV light. When the exposed (colored) beads are removed from UV light, they will lose their color and again turn white. The beads are capable of cycling back and forth (white to colored to white) more than 50,000 times. The purple beads are the most sensitive both in reacting to the UV light and in returning to the original white. The beads labeled "red" produce a color that is better described as dark orange. Commercial fluorescent and incandescent lights may activate some of the beads if the beads are exposed very close to these bulbs.

When sun-sensitive paper is exposed to UV radiation, the pigment in the paper undergoes a chemical reaction that causes it to change color permanently. The original (pale blue) pigment is water-soluble, but the product of the reaction (dark blue) is insoluble. Thus, when a piece of exposed sun-sensitive paper is rinsed in water, any remaining original pigment that was protected from UV radiation is washed away, while the insoluble product (dark blue) remains on the paper. This rinsing leaves a light silhouette of protected areas against the dark blue background. The intensity of the background color depends upon the nature and intensity of the light source and on the exposure time. The longer the exposure time and the greater the intensity of the light, the darker the color.

This activity shows that UV-absorbing sunglass lenses do block the color change associated with the UV beads or the sunprint paper exposure to the sun. The sun is a strong source of UV rays, even stronger than a typical commercial UV lamp. The sun's UV rays are blocked somewhat by clear glass and regular lenses, but not as much as those treated with a UV blocker. Commercial fluorescent and incandescent lights may activate some of the beads if they are exposed very close to these bulbs.

The National Weather Service's daily UV index forecasts the expected relative level of UV radiation at noon; depending on the region, it ranges from a low of 1 to a high of 10. It is thought that the ozone layer around the Earth is being depleted, allowing increasing amounts of ultraviolet radiation to reach the Earth's surface. Eyes are very sensitive, and they need protection from damaging UV rays. Research from Antarctica indicates that the Earth's UV-absorbing ozone layer in that area of the world is severely depleted. Grazing cows and sheep are going blind at a much higher rate than in the past.

References for the Science Activity

Levy, E. "Jill Wants Sunglasses," *Special Happenings;* Holt, Rinehart, and Winston: New York, 1973.

McNulty, K. "Shades of Summer," *Science World. 49* (14), May 7, 1993.

Sarquis, J.L.; Sarquis, M.; Williams, J.P. "Experimenting with Light-Sensitive Paper"; *Teaching Chemistry with TOYS: Activities for Grades K–9;* McGraw-Hill: New York, 1995; p. 275.

Part 3: Integrating with Language Arts

Featured Fiction Book: *The Lizard and the Sun*

Author: Alma Flor Ada   Illustrator: Felipe Davalos
Publisher: Bantam   ISBN: 038532121X
Summary: A traditional Mexican folk tale in which a faithful lizard finds the sun
and restores light and warmth to the world.

As you read the story, examine the pictures, particularly the colors used. How do
the colors help tell the story? After the story is finished, discuss the animals' hunt
for the sun. Where do they look for it? Why is everyone so anxious to get it back?
Discuss this story as an example of a myth—a story that explains a practice,
belief, or natural phenomenon. What practice and natural phenomenon are
explained in this story?

Writing Extensions

- Have students use their science journals to write a summary of the
  experiment they designed and the results they found.
- Have students write about what things look like through sunglasses.
- Have students look for other myths involving the sun.

Additional Books

Fiction

Title: *Sunshine*
Author: Jan Ormerod
Publisher: William Morrow   ISBN: 0688093531
Summary: In this wordless story, when the sun creeps in the window, the family's
day begins—breakfast together, brushing teeth, getting dressed, and leaving
the house on time.

Nonfiction

Title: *The Sun*
Author: Seymour Simon
Publisher: William Morrow   ISBN: 0688058574
Summary: This book describes the nature of the sun and its origin, source of
energy, layers, atmosphere, sunspots, and activity.

Part 4: Other Lesson Extensions

Art and Music

- Read *The Lizard and the Sun* (see the Featured Fiction Book) and have students compose lively songs and dances to help the sun wake up. Have them perform these dances for a sleepy "sun" (student volunteer or a large picture).
- Have students make finger puppets and scenery and present the story *The Lizard and the Sun* to a younger class.
- Have students use sun-sensitive paper and weeds, leaves, or flowers to make attractive "solar art."
- Have students draw a picture of a sunrise and a picture of a sunset. Have them draw a picture of an object seen through sunglasses and then the same object seen without sunglasses. Chalk and water color may be useful media.
- Have students design posters about sun exposure and health.

Mathematics

- Explore the concepts of seconds, minutes, and an hour as related to the sun.

Social Studies

- Divide the students into cooperative groups to make an advertisement for an imaginary brand of sunglasses or sunscreen that the group will market. Have them develop advertisements for different parts of the world. When would the imaginary products sell best in different countries?
- Research the history of sunglasses and sunscreens.
- Visit the office of an optician, optometrist, ophthalmologist, or dermatologist, or invite one to speak to the class.
- Invite a meteorologist to speak to the class about forecasting of UV levels.

Just for Fun

- Make orange and yellow lollipops in the shape of a sun. You will need the following ingredients:
  - access to an oven
  - orange or yellow hard candies (about 1 ounce per student)
  - heavy plastic bag
  - towel
  - meat mallet or small hammer
  - baking sheet
  - aluminum foil
  - several sun-shaped metal cookie cutters
  - tablespoon measure
  - oven mitt

- ∘ tongs
- ∘ lollipop sticks (1 per student)
- ∘ (optional) small decorative candies such as gumdrops or small nonpareils

Preheat an oven to 350°. Unwrap the hard candies and put them in a heavy plastic bag. Put the bag on top of a folded towel and crush the candies into small chunks with a meat mallet or small hammer. Line a baking sheet with foil and set three or four sun-shaped cookie cutters on the foil at least 2 inches apart. Pour about 1½ to 2 tablespoons crushed candy into each cookie cutter. Bake the candy for 6 to 8 minutes or until the candy is completely melted. Remove the tray from the oven and cool for 30 seconds. Remove the cookie cutters with tongs, allowing the melted candy to spread slightly. Quickly set a lollipop stick on the base of each sun shape, twisting the stick to cover it with melted candy. (To make fancier lollipops, carefully set small decorative candies, such as gumdrops and small nonpareils, on the lollipops after the sticks are inserted.) Allow the lollipops to cool completely, and then peel the foil from the lollipops. (Source; Hopkins, N.W. "Homemade with Love." *Better Homes and Gardens.* February 1998, p 172.)

Part 5: National Science Education Standards

Science as Inquiry Standards:

Abilities Necessary to Do Scientific Inquiry

Students question the cause of color changes in the ultraviolet-detecting beads.

Students design experiments to test the UV-detecting beads under different kinds of light and with UV-absorbing and non-UV-absorbing lenses.

Students use different light sources and lenses to test their UV-detecting beads. They use timers to clock the exposure of sun-sensitive paper to sunlight.

Students identify and control variables when testing their UV-detecting beads.

Students develop an explanation of the conditions necessary for the UV-detecting beads to change color.

Students share their experimental results and conclusions with the class through facilitated discussion.

Physical Science Standards:

Properties of Objects and Materials

Objects have many observable properties. In the case of UV-detecting beads and sun-sensitive paper, these properties include changes caused by exposure to UV light.

Light, Heat, Electricity, and Magnetism
The UV-detecting beads and sun-sensitive paper absorb UV light rather than reflecting or refracting it.

Science and Technology Standards:

Abilities of Technological Design
Students question the differences between UV-absorbing sunglasses, non-UV-absorbing sunglasses, and opaque objects.

Students propose a method for testing the ability of UV-absorbing sunglasses, non-UV-absorbing sunglasses, and opaque objects to block UV light.

Students use sun-sensitive paper to test the ability of sunglasses and opaque objects to block UV light.

Students evaluate their test results and make recommendations on what type of sunglasses to purchase.

Students discuss their test results and conclusions as a class.

Index of Science Topics

National Science Education Standards Matrix

This matrix shows how the activities in this book relate to the National Science Education Standards for grades K–4 and 5–8. The standards are taken from *National Science Education Standards;* National Research Council; National Academy: Washington, D.C., 1996.

	Activities			
	Birthday Water Globes	Suminagashi Greeting Cards for Grandparent's Day	Chromatography of Autumn Colors	A Columbus Day Challenge
Science as Inquiry Standards				
K–4: Abilities Necessary to Do Scientific Inquiry				
Ask a question about objects, organisms, and events in the environment.	✔	✔	✔	✔
Plan and conduct a simple investigation.	✔	✔	✔	
Employ simple equipment and tools to gather data and extend the senses.			✔	✔
Use data to construct a reasonable explanation.			✔	✔
Communicate investigations and explanations.	✔	✔	✔	✔
5–8: Abilities Necessary to Do Scientific Inquiry				
Identify questions that can be answered through scientific investigations.	✔	✔	✔	✔
Design and conduct a scientific investigation.		✔	✔	
Use appropriate tools and techniques to gather, analyze, and interpret data.			✔	✔
Develop descriptions, explanations, predictions, and models using evidence.			✔	✔
Think critically and logically to make the relationships between evidence and explanations.				
Recognize and analyze alternative explanations and predictions.		✔	✔	✔
Communicate scientific procedures and explanations.	✔	✔	✔	✔

	Spooky Spiders and Webs	Give Thanks for Corn!	Brrr! Winter Can Be Freezing!	My Hanukkah Dreidel	Christmas-Tree Light Toys	Candle-Making for Kwanzaa	Chinese New Year's Poppers	Groundhog Day Shadows	Secret Valentine Messages	St. Patrick's Day Spuds	Spring into Capillary Action	Recycling Paper for Earth Day	Easter Egg Geodes	Tricky April Fool's Day Toys	Magic Trees for Arbor Day	Piñata-Making for Cinco de Mayo	Mother's Day Film Canister Sachets	Father's Day Thaumatropes	Hot Summer Days and Those Cool Shades
Activities																			
	✔	✔	✔	✔	✔	✔	✔	✔	✔		✔	✔	✔	✔	✔	✔	✔	✔	✔
	✔	✔	✔	✔	✔		✔		✔	✔			✔	✔	✔			✔	✔
	✔	✔			✔	✔		✔	✔		✔	✔	✔		✔				✔
	✔	✔	✔	✔		✔	✔	✔	✔		✔		✔	✔	✔		✔	✔	✔
	✔	✔	✔	✔	✔	✔	✔	✔	✔	✔	✔	✔	✔	✔	✔	✔	✔	✔	✔
	✔	✔		✔	✔	✔	✔	✔	✔		✔		✔	✔	✔	✔	✔	✔	✔
	✔	✔			✔		✔	✔				✔	✔	✔	✔		✔	✔	✔
	✔	✔		✔	✔	✔		✔	✔		✔		✔		✔				✔
	✔	✔	✔	✔	✔	✔	✔	✔	✔	✔			✔	✔	✔		✔	✔	✔
											✔							✔	
	✔	✔	✔	✔		✔	✔	✔	✔				✔			✔	✔		✔
	✔	✔	✔	✔	✔	✔	✔	✔	✔	✔	✔	✔	✔	✔	✔	✔	✔	✔	✔

Physical Science Standards

K–4: Properties of Objects and Materials

	Birthday Water Globes	Suminagashi Greeting Cards for Grandparent's Day	Chromatography of Autumn Colors	A Columbus Day Challenge
Objects have many observable properties, including size, weight, shape, color, temperature, and the ability to react with other substances. Those properties can be measured using tools, such as rulers, balances, and thermometers.	✔		✔	✔
Objects are made of one or more materials, such as paper, wood, and metal. Objects can be described by the properties of the materials from which they are made, and those properties can be used to separate or sort a group of objects or materials.	✔	✔		
Materials can exist in different states—solid, liquid, and gas. Some common materials, such as water, can be changed from one state to another by heating or cooling.	✔			

5–8: Properties and Changes of Properties in Matter

	Birthday Water Globes	Suminagashi Greeting Cards for Grandparent's Day	Chromatography of Autumn Colors	A Columbus Day Challenge
A substance has characteristic properties, such as density, a boiling point, and solubility, all of which are independent of the amount of the sample. A mixture of substances often can be separated into the original substances using one or more of the characteristic properties.				✔
Substances react chemically in characteristic ways with other substances to form new substances (compounds) with different characteristic properties. In chemical reactions, the total mass is conserved. Substances often are placed in categories or groups if they react in similar ways; metals is an example of such a group.				

K–4: Position and Motion of Objects

	Birthday Water Globes	Suminagashi Greeting Cards for Grandparent's Day	Chromatography of Autumn Colors	A Columbus Day Challenge
The position of an object can be described by locating it relative to another object or the background.				✔
An object's motion can be described by tracing and measuring its position over time.				
The position and motion of objects can be changed by pushing or pulling. The size of the change is related to the strength of the push or pull.				
Sound is produced by vibrating objects. The pitch of the sound can be varied by changing the rate of vibration.				

5–8: Motions and Forces

	Birthday Water Globes	Suminagashi Greeting Cards for Grandparent's Day	Chromatography of Autumn Colors	A Columbus Day Challenge
The motion of an object can be described by its position, direction of motion, and speed. That motion can be measured and represented on a graph.				
An object that is not being subjected to a force will continue to move at a constant speed and in a straight line.				
If more than one force acts on an object along a straight line, then the forces will reinforce or cancel one another, depending on their direction and magnitude. Unbalanced forces will cause changes in the speed or direction of an object's motion.				

	Spooky Spiders and Webs	Give Thanks for Corn!	Brrr! Winter Can Be Freezing!	My Hanukkah Dreidel	Christmas-Tree Light Toys	Candle-Making for Kwanzaa	Chinese New Year's Poppers	Groundhog Day Shadows	Secret Valentine Messages	St. Patrick's Day Spuds	Spring into Capillary Action	Recycling Paper for Earth Day	Easter Egg Geodes	Tricky April Fool's Day Toys	Magic Trees for Arbor Day	Piñata-Making for Cinco de Mayo	Mother's Day Film Canister Sachets	Father's Day Thaumatropes	Hot Summer Days and Those Cool Shades
	✔	✔	✔		✔	✔	✔	✔	✔	✔	✔	✔	✔	✔	✔		✔		✔
					✔	✔				✔		✔	✔			✔			
		✔	✔		✔						✔				✔	✔	✔		
			✔		✔	✔				✔					✔				
							✔												
								✔											
	✔																	✔	
	✔			✔						✔					✔			✔	
	✔																		
	✔																		

	Activities			
	Birthday Water Globes	Suminagashi Greeting Cards for Grandparent's Day	Chromatography of Autumn Colors	A Columbus Day Challenge

Physical Science Standards

K–4: Light, Heat, Electricity, and Magnetism

Light travels in a straight line until it strikes an object. Light can be reflected by a mirror, refracted by a lens, or absorbed by the object.				
Electricity in circuits can produce light, heat, sound, and magnetic effects. Electrical circuits require a complete loop through which an electrical current can pass.				

5–8: Transfer of Energy

Light interacts with matter by transmission (including refraction), absorption, or scattering (including reflection). To see an object, light from that object—emitted by or scattered from it—must enter the eye.				
Electrical circuits provide a means of transferring electrical energy when heat, light, sound, and chemical changes are produced.				
The sun is a major source of energy for changes on the Earth's surface. The sun loses energy by emitting light. A tiny fraction of that light reaches the Earth, transferring energy from the sun to the Earth. The sun's energy arrives as light with a range of wavelengths, consisting of visible light, infrared, and ultraviolet radiation.				

			Activities															
Spooky Spiders and Webs	Give Thanks for Corn!	Brrr! Winter Can Be Freezing!	My Hanukkah Dreidel	Christmas-Tree Light Toys	Candle-Making for Kwanzaa	Chinese New Year's Poppers	Groundhog Day Shadows	Secret Valentine Messages	St. Patrick's Day Spuds	Spring into Capillary Action	Recycling Paper for Earth Day	Easter Egg Geodes	Tricky April Fool's Day Toys	Magic Trees for Arbor Day	Piñata-Making for Cinco de Mayo	Mother's Day Film Canister Sachets	Father's Day Thaumatropes	Hot Summer Days and Those Cool Shades
							✔						✔					✔
				✔														
							✔						✔					✔
				✔														

	Activities			
Science and Technology Standards	Birthday Water Globes	Suminagashi Greeting Cards for Grandparent's Day	Chromatography of Autumn Colors	A Columbus Day Challenge
K–4: Abilities of Technological Design				
Identify a simple problem.	✔		✔	✔
Propose a solution.	✔	✔	✔	✔
Implement proposed solutions.	✔	✔	✔	✔
Evaluate a product or design.	✔	✔	✔	✔
Communicate a problem, design, and solution.	✔	✔		✔
5–8: Abilities of Technological Design				
Identify appropriate problems for technological design.				✔
Design a solution or product.				
Implement a proposed design.				
Evaluate completed technological designs or products.				✔
Communicate the process of technological design.				✔